Born Together—Reared Apart

BORN TOGETHER—
REARED APART

The Landmark Minnesota Twin Study

NANCY L. SEGAL

Harvard University Press

Cambridge, Massachusetts, and London, England   2012

In memory of my parents, Al and Esther Segal,
   and
To twins—reared apart, reared together,
   and yet to meet.

Library of Congress Cataloging-in-Publication Data

Segal, Nancy L., 1951–
    Born together—reared apart : the landmark Minnesota twin study /
Nancy L. Segal.
        p.   cm.
    Includes bibliographical references and index.
    ISBN 978-0-674-05546-9 (alk. paper)
    1. Twins—Psychology—Research.   2. Nature and nurture—Research.   I. Title.
    BF723.T9S436   2012
    306.875—dc23   2011041636

Contents

Introduction

Genes and glands are obviously important, but social learning
also has a dramatic role. Imagine the enormous differences that
would be found in the personalities of twins with identical
genetic endowments if they were raised apart in two different
families—or, even more striking, in two totally different cultures.

    —Walter Mischel

COLUMBIA UNIVERSITY professor Walter Mischel has been a
prominent figure in personality assessment and the study of emotional control. He is also the 2011 recipient of the prestigious
Grawemeyer Award for contributions to psychology. The passage quoted
above, from his well-known undergraduate textbook, largely reflected
1970s' and early 1980s' views on factors affecting behavioral development, but it would not appear in textbooks today.[1] It has been replaced
by statements such as, "Currently, most kinship findings support a moderate role for heredity. . . . Heritability research also reveals that genetic factors are important in personality."[2] This shift in perspective, from general
neglect or even contempt to increased acceptance of genetic contributions
to behavior, was not caused by the Minnesota Study of Twins Reared
Apart (MISTRA), but many claim that the study was instrumental in its
progression.

·The classic twin method is a simple and elegant natural experiment for
examining genetic and environmental influences on behavior. The idea
of using twins to study factors affecting human behavioral variation was
first described by the British scholar Sir Frances Galton in 1875. Galton
recognized the usefulness of comparing twins who were "closely alike [in
childhood]" with those who were "exceedingly unlike." He asserted that
"their history affords means of distinguishing between the effects of tendencies received at birth, and of those that were imposed by the circumstances of their after lives; in other words, between the effects of nature
and nurture."[3] If what we now call monozygotic (MZ or identical) twins
show greater trait resemblance than dizygotic (DZ or nonidentical) twins,

then genetic influence is likely. The biological bases of twinning had not been established in Galton's time, but he correctly surmised that "look-alike" twins shared 100% of their genes and "less-alike" twins shared fewer.

Richard Rende and his colleagues do not credit Galton with being "Father of the Twin Method" because "he did not propose the comparison between identical and fraternal twin resemblance which is the essence of the twin method."[4] They give this distinction to Curtis Merriman and Hermann Siemens, whose 1924 writings described a more specific twin-based approach with more familiar scientific terms. Director of the Minnesota Study of Twins Reared Apart, Thomas J. Bouchard Jr., and human geneticist, Peter Propping, called Rende's assertion a "disingenuous argument" based on ranking quantitative arguments above conceptual ones. I would agree.[5]

The scientific study of twins did not become truly useful until the fundamental distinction between twin types and the methods for distinguishing between them were established.[6] These accomplishments were made by a series of investigators between 1919 and 1925. In 1922, Leslie Brainerd Arey proposed the labels "MZ" and "DZ" for "one egg" and "two egg" twins, respectively.[7] MZ twins share all their genes, having split from a single fertilized egg (zygote) within the first two weeks after conception. DZ twins share half their genes on average, by descent, having originated from two separately fertilized eggs. In 1924, Siemens introduced a similarity method for assigning pairs as one-egg or two-egg twins, based on co-twin (twin pair member) comparison of hereditary traits.[8] This method was widely used and is not unlike currently administered physical resemblance questionnaires.

In 1956, geneticist Gordon Allen proposed changing the terms to "monozygous" and "dizygous" because they capture the term "zygosis" that refers to zygote formation. He also argued that these terms had one less syllable, making them easier to write and say.[9]

Variations on the two types of twinning include MZ female twins who sometimes differ in the expression of X-linked genetic conditions (due to random inactivation of one X chromosome in each cell early in gestation), and DZ twins who can be conceived by different fathers (when double-ovulating women have multiple sexual partners close in time).[10] These twin pairs can help identify factors underlying co-twin differences in behavior and physique.

The classic twin method is a powerful investigatory tool. Despite some differences in the early development of twins and nontwins, Danish researchers established that after the age of six years disease incidence and mortality are comparable for twins and singletons (nontwins), a finding confirmed for most behavioral and physical traits. Thus, most twin research findings apply to the general population.[11]

The twin method rests on the *equal environments assumption*, the premise that the environmental factors affecting similarity in a given trait, such as sociability, are the same for MZ and DZ twin pairs. Although MZ twins generally share more activities than do DZ twins, this difference is problematic only if (1) MZ twins are required to share school activities to a greater degree than DZ twins, and (2) sharing activities affects sociability in a meaningful way. If sharing activities increases sociability, then the environments of the two types of twins would not be equivalent with respect to this behavior. The equal environments assumption would have been compromised in this hypothetical example. Here, the environmental effect (the requirement that MZ twins share their activities more often than DZ twins) is assumed to be an established school policy, unrelated to the twins' genetic proclivities.

Some critics have questioned the usefulness of twin studies, arguing that MZ twins' more similar rearing environments underlie their more similar behaviors relative to DZ twins. However, these challenges and others related to the equal environments assumption have been tested empirically and have been refuted in most cases—similar treatment of twins by others is not associated with similar behavioral outcomes. In their landmark study of twins taking the National Merit Scholarship Qualifying Test, John Loehlin and Robert Nichols showed that whether co-twins were dressed alike, slept in the same room, or had the same teachers was unrelated to their behavioral resemblance,[12] a finding replicated by others.[13] In addition, more physically similar MZ twins (as rated by parents) have not been perceived as being more alike in personality than less physically similar twins.[14] The lack of any biological connection between physical appearance and psychological traits argues against the former causally influencing the latter.[15] However, twin studies of handedness may violate the equal environments assumption because non-genetic factors affecting handedness differ for MZ and DZ twins, as discussed in Chapter 13.

Studying reared-apart MZ twins (MZA) and DZ twins (DZA) circumvents these challenges because the twins are raised in separate environments, often unaware of each other's existence. The first scientific treatment of MZA twins was a 1922 case study by psychologist Paul Popenoe of twins Bessie and Jessie.[16] The timing of this report is interesting because the idea of studying twins raised apart had been brought to Galton's attention forty-seven years earlier. In a letter to Galton (circa 1874–75, the same period Galton published his classic paper on twins), M. Townsend described his identical twin great-uncles who were "separated through life" and who "rejoined one another at about 50."[17] Whether Galton tried to study these twins or other separated twin pairs is unknown; they were never mentioned in his writings.

Several case reports and studies of separated twins appeared in the years that followed, such as Hermann J. Muller's 1925 detailed analysis of Popenoe's twins.[18] The last major reared-apart twin investigation was conducted by Danish Professor Juel-Nielsen of Denmark in 1965[19]—until the MISTRA came into being.

The Climate of the Times

The MISTRA, initiated in March 1979, arrived at a critical juncture in the history of psychology. Understanding the prevailing psychological winds at that time is requisite to understanding why a reared-apart twin study was so compelling yet controversial, why it attracted worldwide attention, and why 1979 was an ideal time for it to start.

An environmentalist view, promulgated by the behaviorist James Watson, dominated psychological theory and research from the 1930s through the 1970s. Other than being born with a general capacity to learn, human behavior was explained almost exclusively by forces outside the individual. Several important events were also instrumental in making the late 1960s and 1970s a time of heightened sensitivity to the origins of individual and group differences. The 1964 Civil Rights Act outlawed discrimination and segregation on the basis of color or race. The women's rights movement gained momentum in the 1960s, focusing on sex discrimination in the classroom and workplace. Hovering above the scene was the legacy of the Nazi regime (1933 to 1945) that promoted the genetic superiority of some populations over others and racial purification by eliminating individuals considered biologically inferior.[20] It was in that social climate that Arthur Jensen published the 1969 article "How Much Can We Boost IQ and Scholastic Achievement?" which included a section on possible genetically based race differences in intelligence test scores (IQ).[21] His discussion provoked angry outbursts from many academics, educators, and others.[22]

The credibility of reared-apart twin research, published between 1943 and 1966 by British psychologist Sir Cyril Burt, was challenged by then Princeton University Psychology Professor Leon Kamin and others in the early 1970s, casting doubt over previous and subsequent twin studies.[23] Kamin called attention to the implausibility of Burt's .771 IQ correlations, reported for three successive IQ analyses with samples of twenty-one (1955), "over 30" (1958), and fifty-three (1966) MZA twin pairs.[24] It was also the case that no one had seen pictures of Burt with his twin subjects or staff, although their absence is not proof of fraud. In fact, none of the books by three early MZA twin investigators includes photographs of the researchers with their twin participants, although photographs of every pair appear in the American study headed by Horatio Newman and a few pairs appear in the British study directed by James Shields.[25] The Danish investigator Juel-Nielsen altered the names of the MZA twins for whom he presented detailed case histories, so it is understandable that he did not include any available pictures. In light of the Burt situation, Bouchard would make it a practice to appear in pictures with every twin pair we studied and every staff member we hired.

Charges that Burt fabricated both his data and his assistants have been debated for years. The attention his case received is explained by Burt's leadership position in the psychological field (he was the first British psychologist to be knighted) and his subject matter, about which scientists cared greatly.[26]

Science historians Robert B. Joynson in 1989 and Ronald Fletcher in 1991 concluded their inquiries into the Burt affair by attributing the suspicious correlations to clerical errors and questionable aspects of his twin sample to insufficient information about the participants and test conditions.[27] A 1995 study presented the views of five leading scholars in the field, four of whom dismissed the charges but one of whom did not.[28] The study's editor concluded that there was suspicion of fraud but no conclusive evidence of guilt. The concerns over Burt's twin research raised as recently as 2007 are the same as those that were raised by James Shields in 1978. Shields, who published a reared-apart twin study in England in 1962, noted the unlikely ease with which Burt recruited so many early separated twins over a brief time period. Shields suggested (half seriously) that Burt's increasing MZA twin sample reflected a competitive "one-upmanship" with Shields's research.[29]

The Burt affair is unresolved at present; his data are no longer cited in the psychological literature, but their omission has no effect on conclusions over genetic influence on mental ability. The MISTRA, the Swedish Adoption and Twin Study of Aging, the three early MZA twin studies, and countless reared-together twin and adoption studies tell the same story.

Attention to a discredited study headed by New York psychoanalyst Peter Neubauer of intentionally separated infant twins has occasionally surfaced and accentuated the dim view of reared-apart twin studies.[30] Beginning in the 1960s, Neubauer gathered longitudinal data on the members of five MZA twin pairs and one MZA triplet set whose families were purposefully not told they were adopting children of multiple births. The controversial aspects of his data collection procedures attracted considerable media attention in the early 1980s and still does. Recent attempts by scientists and filmmakers to gain access to the original data have been fruitless—prior to his death in 2008, Neubauer bequeathed the material to Yale University's Child Study Center with the stipulation that the file remain closed until 2066.[31] Psychiatrist Viola Bernard, consultant for the Louise Wise Adoption Agency that placed the twins, favored their separation. Bernard donated her twin-related documents to Columbia University, denying public access to the material until 2021.[32]

Most psychology and psychiatry textbooks in the 1960s, 1970s, and early 1980s reflected environmentalist views. Others in the medical community also subscribed to a largely environmentalist paradigm in those years. In an extraordinary case involving an accidentally castrated MZ male twin infant during circumcision, the sex researcher, John Money, argued that a child's gender identity could be altered if surgical and psychological interventions were introduced by eighteen months of age.[33] His findings went unchallenged publicly until 1997.[34] Child psychiatrist Leo Kanner blamed the apparently cold, conflicted practices of so-called refrigerator mothers for the onset of autism and other behavioral disorders in young children.[35] This belief persisted until the early 1970s.

In short, anyone suggesting that genes affected human behavior took a huge academic risk. Harvard biologist Edward O. Wilson, famous for his seminal work *Sociobiology* (1979), was doused with a bucket of water as he approached the podium at the 1978 American Association for the Advancement of Science (AAAS) convention in Washington, D.C.[36] The tensions of those times are well captured in a review of essays on race, social class, and IQ,[37] and a book on the subject.[38]

At the same time, there were growing signs of discontent with the prevailing environmentalist perspective. The roots of this dissatisfaction came from a variety of sources. Research conducted in the 1950s and 1960s showed that pairings of some stimuli did not always produce predicted responses. An example is the Garcia Effect, in which rats learned to avoid food associated with nausea but could not learn to avoid loud noises or flashes of light when paired with the nausea.[39] Thus, there appeared to be biological constraints on behavior that stimulus-response paradigms could not explain. The Garcia Effect was not fully appreciated by psychologists until the late 1960s and 1970s.[40]

Continuing advances in human genetics strengthened the idea of gene-behavior relationships. In 1959, investigators discovered that an extra chromosome 21 was responsible for the behavioral and physical attributes of Down syndrome (trisomy 21).[41] In 1982, the detection of a link between mental deficiency associated with phenylketonuria (PKU) and lack of the enzyme phenylalanine hydroxylase further demonstrated a genetic underpinning to behavior.[42]

Cognitive psychology, the branch of psychology concerned with how people acquire, process, and store information, was also gaining ground in the 1950s, 1960s, and 1970s.[43] A biological view of language development was introduced, claiming that language was too complex to be taught as the behaviorists believed. Instead, the theory asserted that children were born with the capacity to learn language and to master its rules almost automatically.[44] Computer models of information processing drew attention to how the mind might work to solve problems.[45]

Research summarized in an individual differences textbook by the late Lee Willerman, published in 1979 (the year the MISTRA began), shows the gradual but steady infusion of a genetic perspective into thinking about behavior.[46] Some of these studies predated those of many of the behaviorists. As early as the 1920s, Edward Tolman showed that rats could be bred to be "maze-bright" or "maze-dull." In the 1920s and 1930s, Barbara Burks's and Alice Leahy's twin and adoption studies demonstrated a genetic component to intelligence. In 1963, Nicki Erlenmeyer-Kimling and Lissy Jarvik showed that IQ similarity varied positively with degree of genetic relatedness. Several now classic twin and adoption studies by David Rosenthal, Len Heston, and Irving Gottesman and James Shields indicated a genetic basis for schizophrenia.[47] The notion that a person's behavioral problems or learning disabilities were mostly learned from, and reinforced by, his or her parents was weakening. The Behavior Genetics Association came into being in 1970 in response to these trends, holding its first annual meeting in Storrs, Connecticut, in 1971.[48]

By the late 1970s, the accumulating evidence against the behaviorist perspective was becoming difficult to refute. Many individuals were primed for a vision of human development that allowed for hereditary as well as environmental effects. There was "just enough" doubt about the primacy of the environment.[49] It was this fluid academic climate of the late 1970s and one investigator's seizing of an opportunity to study a rare separated twin pair that enabled the MISTRA to come into existence when it did. The investigator was University of Minnesota Professor Thomas J. Bouchard Jr.

The MISTRA

The MISTRA came into being in 1979 and lasted for twenty years. It conducted comprehensive psychological and medical assessments of eighty-one MZA and fifty-six DZA twin pairs, with each assessment lasting for an entire week. The study's goal was to identify associations between differences in the twins' life histories and the twins' behavioral differences. The MISTRA was not originally conceived from a developmental or longitudinal perspective, but was exploratory in nature. Nevertheless, developmental data provided by the different pairs were revealing and relevant to the ongoing longitudinal twin[50] and adoption studies[51] that were finding genetic influences on behavioral and physical changes. Hypotheses were not specified at the outset, except in a few instances.

Like Shields who had studied separated twins in the 1960s, the MISTRA investigators took the view that the MZA twin design was a unique and valuable research tool.[52] It could generate ideas and predictions, and provide results that could be used alongside results from other twin and adoption studies. Findings of greater MZA than DZA twin similarity would be consistent with, but not proof of, genetic effects on the traits under study.[53]

I was associated with the MISTRA from 1982 to 1991, for three years as a postdoctoral fellow and six years as Assistant Director of the Minnesota Center for Twin and Adoption Research. I scheduled twins' assessments, gathered psychological data on 86 of the 137 separated pairs, and contributed to scientific reports. I revisited the University of Minnesota in October 2009, April 2010, and October 2010, thirty years after the MISTRA assessed the first reared-apart pair. The purpose of these visits was to gather critical perspectives and personal reflections from the principal MISTRA investigators. How did they view the study from a 2009–2010 vantage point? How had the study impacted their area of expertise in particular, and the psychological and medical fields in general?

Jay Samuels, professor of education at the University of Minnesota, who developed the spelling and reading tests given to our separated twins, concluded, "The timing was right. [The MISTRA] came about when behaviorism was losing popularity and cognitive psychology was gaining rapidly. I would argue that in addition to [Noam] Chomsky's attack on language acquisition [by modeling and reinforcement], Bouchard's work had a major influence in bringing in a new paradigm." Samuels's views were echoed by the over fifty collaborators and former students with whom I spoke. Many also emphasized that the psychology department's academic networks made the University of Minnesota especially well suited for a study of twins reared apart. Many of the collaborators had professional connections to one another early in their careers.

Thomas J. Bouchard Jr. joined the University of Minnesota in 1969. He was an industrial organizational psychologist who had earned his PhD degree with Donald MacKinnon and Harrison Gough at the University of California–Berkeley Institute for Personality Assessment and Research. Irving I. Gottesman joined Minnesota's faculty in 1966 after completing his degree in that department in 1960. Gottesman had a rich history of twin research involving studies of adolescent twins in Minnesota and schizophrenic twins in the United Kingdom with James Shields that pre-dated David Lykken's twin research.[54] Gottesman takes credit for "chang-ing Bouchard's career" from industrial organizational psychologist to behavioral geneticist, and Bouchard agrees: "He put stuff in my mailbox— I never took a course in behavioral genetics in my life."[55]

Bouchard had considered starting a reared-together twin study before the start of the MISTRA, but he did not want to encroach on his col-league David Lykken's area of research. Gottesman, however, suggested to Bouchard that he launch a study of twins reared apart. Gottesman pointed out that no one had done such investigations since Newman, Freeman, and Holzinger's 1937 study in Chicago, Shields's 1962 study in England, and Juel-Nielsen's 1965 study in Denmark. Gottesman was familiar with the Danish study and had authored the introduction to Juel-Nielsen's 1980 follow-up study of the twelve MZA twin pairs who comprised the original 1965 sample. Gottesman wrote, "Identical twins brought up apart are scarce, indeed, and their potential for stimulating research ideas about the origins of normal and abnormal characteristics is great."[56]

Following discussions at the university's faculty club with Gottesman, Lykken, and psychologist Auke Tellegen, Bouchard had eventually given up on the idea of a reared-apart twin study in Minnesota because there was no obvious or systematic way to locate these rare separated sets. Juel-Nielsen had obtained most of his twins through Denmark's popula-tion registry, but the United States did not have a comparable resource. Finding separated twins through radio or television broadcasts, as New-man and Shields had done, seemed impractical. Then Bouchard read about the Jim twins in a newspaper article on February 20, 1979. His crumbling maroon leather-bound calendar bears the following inscription for that date: "Heard About Twins." Consequently, the individual differences text-book Bouchard was writing was never completed, and his work with Gottesman on a book of readings, intended to update James Jenkins and Donald Paterson's 1961 individual differences volume,[57] was discontinued.

Instead, studying reared-apart twins became Bouchard's first priority. As Gottesman said, "We both got too busy."

The Study in Context

Jim Lewis and Jim Springer are the separated twins whose February 1979 reunion was ultimately responsible for the launch of the MISTRA. The press reported that both Ohio twins smoked Salems, chewed their fingernails, suffered from tension headaches, vacationed on the same Florida beach, and had twice married women with the same first name (Linda and Betty)—without ever having met.[58] The only difference seemed to be that Springer combed his hair down over his forehead while Lewis slicked his back. This difference should have made it possible to tell them apart, but it did not. Their angular features, unhurried speech, and laid-back manner made differentiation nearly impossible for everyone outside their families.

Twin researchers are accustomed to the matched personality and appearance of identical twins; however, the Jim twins' similarities were especially striking because they were "MZAs"—monozygotic twins reared apart—for thirty-nine years. Just by being themselves they could offer unique insights into factors affecting variation in human traits. But until the Jims could be observed and studied, the research team viewed some of the similarities reported in the press with "healthy skepticism."[59]

Not all MISTRA co-twins would be as similar as the Jims across all the traits that we measured, but this fact does not discount genetic explanations of behavioral and physical traits. Instead, it shows that common genotypes can interact with different prenatal and postnatal environmental features to produce different outcomes. The MZA twins in some of our pairs differed in IQ, religiosity, or body size, but the MZA twins as a whole showed greater within-pair resemblance than the DZA twins, indicating genetic effects.

Research Focus

Twin research operates at two levels. The first level includes studies directed at the unique physical and behavioral aspects of twinship, such as the effects of prenatal competition for nutrition and the experience of growing up with a same-age sibling. Research has, for example, considered the effects of low birth weight on twins' language development[60] and the advisability of placing twins in the same or separate classrooms.[61] The second level includes studies using twins as tools for estimating genetic and environmental influences on physical and behavioral trait variation. This is accomplished by comparing resemblance between MZ and DZ twin pairs, reared together and/or reared apart. Such studies provide knowledge and insight for everyone, not just for twins and their families. The MISTRA operated mostly at the second level, but some of our analyses, such as our study of the twins' social relationships discussed in Chapter 12, operated partly at the first.

The MISTRA has had substantial impact on our understanding of individual differences in intelligence, personality, values, interests, religiosity, sexual orientation, mate choice, job satisfaction, sociality, and health. It accomplished this in two ways: (1) by identifying a unique subject group (MZA and DZA twins who were mostly adoptees) and (2) by administering an extraordinarily comprehensive assessment battery to its participants. There is no other study of ordinary twins (or nontwins) for whom such a wide range of psychological and medical findings is available.

Nearly every MISTRA personality paper was a "first" because a particular inventory or questionnaire had never been administered to twins reared apart. This was important with respect to replicating prior findings based on other kinships, but there were other forces driving our assessment. More important was that researchers acquiring rare samples want to study every behavioral and medical trait possible because great opportunities do not repeat themselves. We also had to stay current with developments in the field, such as assessing social attitudes and religiosity when reared-together twin studies in those domains began appearing. Despite our best efforts, some traits were never measured—Bouchard always regretted that he didn't record the twins' favorite colors, or their shoe, hat, and glove sizes.

Some results from the study were surprising—for example, the degree of personality similarity was the same for MZA twins and MZ twins reared together (MZTs). Furthermore, many of the findings showing genetic influence on intelligence, special mental abilities, height, and weight were comparable with and consistent with those from extant research on twins reared together. How, then, is it possible to explain the constant public and professional attention that the MISTRA attracted? First, the findings were more compelling because the twins had grown up apart, often without knowledge of the other's existence. Second, the twins' life histories and surprise reunions appealed to the general public as well as to academics and members of the press. People cared about these twins, possibly because growing up apart runs counter to the general sense that twins belong together. The parallels in the twins' lives were fascinating, even to those who clung to social views of human behavior.

The consistently greater resemblance between the MZA than DZA twins showed that genes affect virtually every measured trait. Reared-apart twins also showed that environments matter, but not in the ways most people thought they did. People are not passive recipients of experience but rather are active seekers and shapers of opportunities and events that are compatible with their genes, assuming a normal range of human environments. Some MZA twins, like Bridget and Dorothy from Great Britain, ended up being very much alike despite being raised in very different environments.[62] One twin enjoyed rich educational opportunities in her home while her sister did not—still, their IQ scores were quite close, and both twins were avid readers of historical novels: Dorothy read works by Catherine Cookson, whereas Bridget read works by Caroline Marchant, Cookson's pen name. Apparently, the less educationally advantaged twin actively sought new learning experiences, creating her own environment from the sources available to her; for example, she often visited the public library. Purposefully seeking activities and events that are enjoyable is something that we all do. Thus, MZA co-twins' family environments can vary considerably without masking their genetically influenced tendencies.[63]

Reared-Apart Twin Research

The MISTRA was not the first investigation of reared-apart twins. A 1937 Chicago study by Horatio Newman (biologist), Frank Freeman (educational psychologist), and Karl Holzinger (statistician) examined nineteen MZA sets. Their work was followed by a 1962 study in Great Britain by James Shields (psychologist) that included forty-four MZA sets and a 1965 study by Niels Juel-Nielsen (psychiatrist) in Odense, Denmark, that examined twelve. Several additional case reports followed the Minnesota study.[64] Other investigations have since been launched in Sweden,[65] Finland,[66] and Japan,[67] but none are as comprehensive as the MISTRA in terms of the behaviors that were studied. And none of the other still ongoing studies are as judicious in gathering the separated sets—some of their twins, identified through registries, lived together until late childhood, whereas the MISTRA twins were separated much sooner.

The MISTRA was also the first study of its kind to include both MZA *and* DZA twin pairs.[68] Bouchard's decision to use DZA twins as controls was made in a very early memo to the "Twin Research Team."[69] This was an important methodological improvement over past projects. Some early investigators recruited only identical twins, so they may have unintentionally excluded the less-alike MZA sets. That is, prescreening of participants may have led researchers to believe that MZA pairs with physical and/or behavioral differences were DZA, so such pairs may have been overlooked. In contrast, twins were accepted into the Minnesota study without reference to their twin type, ensuring that the MZA pairs represented a broader range of within-pair differences. In fact, twin type was not confirmed by laboratory testing until the end of the assessment week or after the twins had left Minnesota.

Compelling and Controversial

The MISTRA drew supporters and converts, but also critics. Gordon Allen, then National Institute of Mental Health (NIMH) scientist and president of the International Society of Twin Studies, told the *New York Times* (December 9, 1979), "Such studies provide a lot of clues, if not definitive answers, about all human beings." In 1990, the late Daniel E. Koshland Jr., a specialist in enzyme kinetics and former editor of the prestigious journal *Science,* invited Bouchard to submit a paper reporting the IQ findings from the study. Interesting sidelines to this story are reported in Chapter 5.

At the same time, the idea of genetic influence on seemingly environmentally driven traits such as intelligence, religious commitment, traditionalism, and work values rattled the status quo within the psychological field. Critics outnumbered admirers, at least in terms of those publicly venting their views. Frequent objections were that the twins' matched behaviors were explainable by similarities in their prenatal environments, rearing homes, degree of contact prior to assessment, and/or physical attractiveness rather than by their shared genes. Critics also charged that the social contact between the twins while they were in Minnesota increased the resemblance of their responses. Some believed that we focused mainly on behavioral similarities at the expense of differences.[70]

Another source of contention was the partial funding of the study by the Pioneer Fund, an organization based in New York that has given grants for research on race differences in intelligence. I will return to these criticisms and to the study's relationship with the Pioneer Fund in the final chapter.

Others faultfinders decided that a large enough sample of reared-apart twins would never be found. Some even accused the twins of going public for financial advantage. In 1989, a talk show guest (and medical geneticist) disparaged the MISTRA for publishing findings in the popular press rather than in peer-reviewed journals. However, in 1989, ten years after the study began, the MISTRA had published approximately twenty papers and book chapters, ten in the peer-reviewed scientific literature. Because of the study's comprehensiveness, the material was published in a wide variety of medical and psychological journals, possibly giving the appearance of no publications. The misperception that the MISTRA findings were available only in the press or not at all has continued, which is one reason why I decided to write this book.

The MISTRA continued until data were gathered on 137 reared-apart pairs. The project has produced more than 150 scientific papers and book chapters; a complete listing is provided on the Web site designed for this book (www.DrNancySegalTwins.org). Most importantly, the MISTRA stimulated dialogues among behavioral and medical science investigators, forcing everyone to reconsider their methods and interpretations. Everyone's understanding of behavioral phenomena benefited from this process.

A Closer Look at the MISTRA

As I indicated, reports from the MISTRA are published in a variety of psychological and medical journals. This fact attests to the comprehensiveness of the project. However, in pre-Internet days, and for individuals who do not often conduct literature searches outside their fields, there have been complaints regarding the lack of publication and impact.

A comprehensive overview of the scientific findings is needed to explain how the study got started, who was involved, how the twins were identified, and how the study functioned. These are the goals of this book. Some of the reared-apart twin pairs will also be introduced to illustrate certain concepts and findings. Examining their life histories alongside the scientific findings will make the data come alive for readers as it did for me during the many weeks I spent with the twins.

Now that the data have been gathered, the papers published, and the director retired—and the controversies quieted (somewhat)—it is time to take a closer look at this important project. The material is presented chronologically to capture events as they unfolded during the course of the study, and to track repeated analyses as the sample size grew. This form of presentation was also chosen to convey the excitement and concerns that many of these events brought with them. However, this approach made choosing chapter titles tricky because unrelated topics are sometimes grouped together. Surveying unrelated topics in the same chapter may seem strange and somewhat disorganized, but it actually makes perfect sense because the MISTRA gathered all kinds of data simultaneously. We took the twins for stress tests on the same day that they completed IQ tests, and we had them complete eye exams on the same day that they filled in interest inventories. The various data were analyzed when each investigator was ready and able to do so.

I joined the MISTRA in August 1982 as a postdoctoral fellow and stayed for nine years. Working on the MISTRA and writing this book came naturally to me because of my background in twin research. I had completed my doctoral thesis at the University of Chicago in 1982, "Cooperation, Competition, and Altruism within Twin Sets: A Reappraisal," and the MISTRA offered opportunities to reexamine some of the ideas and findings generated by that work, using twins reared apart. I am also a fraternal twin.

I have been given access to all files and documents associated with the MISTRA. I have also interviewed nearly every investigator, many research assistants, and some reared-apart twins who were part of this project. Some twins' names have been changed to preserve their identity.

The Twins

Many twins used their time in the Twin Cities to capture the fun they had missed by not growing up together. For example, MZA twins Mark and Jerry (both volunteer firefighters, hence their nickname "fireman twins") dunked their vitalogs (the activity monitors that continuously measure heart rate and motion) in Coca-Cola after we had recorded their data. The DZA twins Dewayne and Paul celebrated their first birthday together in our laboratory at age seventy with party hats and favors.

Casual observations sometimes guided components of the assessment schedule. Flirtatious exchanges between reunited opposite-sex co-twins prompted us to add questions about sexual attraction to one's co-twin. Some reunited adult siblings as well as parents and their adult children have experienced sexual feelings for one another, associated with having been apart during children's early years.[71] I will return to this topic in the discussion of the sexual life history study.

The more immediate rapport we observed among the MZA than the DZA twins led to our development of a twin relationship survey. Associations between genetic overlap and social relatedness were timely topics within the growing field of evolutionary psychology, and still are. Moreover, meeting one's twin for the first time is an extraordinary life-changing event. Many twins were overwhelmed with introductions to new in-laws, nieces, nephews, and even parents. Their letters to Bouchard still move me:

> I must tell you that it has been the most wonderful experience of my life to be re-united with my sister and that when we met it was like a coming home. (DZA female twins, met at age 56)

You can imagine how amazed I was to learn [that I was a twin] 36 years later . . . We have now had eleven happy months of getting to know each other—and what happy months! (MZA female twins, met at age 36)

The reared-apart twins also learned a lot about their early circumstances and medical life histories. They could finally understand that their mechanical aptitude or seasonal allergy had a partial genetic basis, which was satisfying knowledge to adoptees without access to their biological past. Most twins enjoyed each other's company and stayed in touch, but even those who did not felt gratified to have met their twin at last.

CHAPTER ONE

The Jim Twins (February–March 1979)

O N FEBRUARY 19, 1979, the *Lima News* in Ohio reported the reunion of thirty-nine-year-old identical twins Jim Lewis and Jim Springer, separated at four weeks of age (Figure 1-1). The twins, born to an unwed mother, had been placed in the Knoop Children's Home in Troy, Ohio, and had been adopted separately by two local families. They grew up forty miles apart, Lewis in Lima and Springer in Piqua.[1]

The couples who adopted the twins were Jess and Sarah Springer, and Ernest and Lucille Lewis. Both families had been told that their child was a twin whose brother had died. The source of this misinformation and the reasons for it have never been determined. The Springers, who adopted two weeks ahead of the Lewises, would have taken both twins had they known both twins survived. In fact, several years later the Lewises adopted identical twin boys, Larry and Gary, even though court officials suggested that they take just one.[2] Perhaps the court reasoned that raising one child would be easier for parents than raising two. By then, Lucille Lewis knew that her son's twin was alive, and she refused to separate another set.

When Lewis was a toddler, his mother visited the Miami City, Ohio, court regarding some adoption matters. A court officer blurted out that the other family had also named their son Jim. Shocked by this information, Lucille waited until her son Jim turned five to tell him he had a twin. Over the years she encouraged him to find his brother, but he hesitated. Then, shortly before his thirty-ninth birthday and for no apparent reason "the time was right." Lewis asked the Piqua court to contact his twin.

Springer learned that he had a twin when he was eight, but he had accepted the story that his brother had died. Then, at Jim Lewis's urging, the Piqua court told Jim Springer that his brother was alive and how to contact him. Springer called Lewis and left a message with his call-back telephone number. Lewis returned the call, and the twins met for the first time.

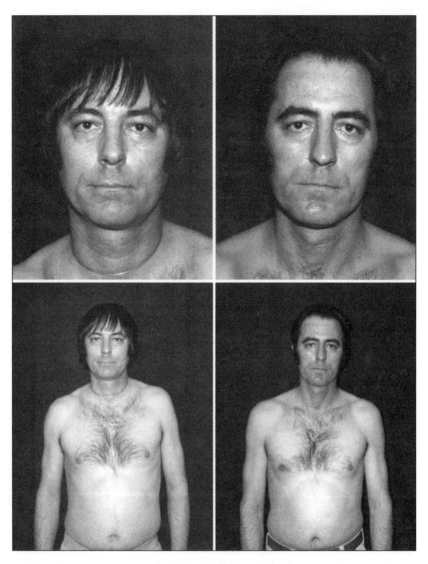

Figure 1-1. The Jim twins: Jim Springer (left) and Jim Lewis. (Photo courtesy Thomas J. Bouchard Jr. Unposed photographs taken in David Lykken's laboratory.)

Three weeks after they met, Springer served as best man in the cere-mony for his twin brother's third marriage. Newspapers chronicled the twins' striking similarities, including their first names (Jim), their favorite school subject (math), their dreaded school subject (spelling), their pre-ferred vacation spot (Pas Grille Beach in Florida), their past occupations (law enforcement), their hobbies (carpentry), and their sons' first names (James Alan and James Allan). The article about them was reprinted in newspapers around the country, including the *Minneapolis Star Tribune*.

Jim and Jim were not the first separated twins to surface in the United States since the publication of a series of case studies in 1949 by Barbara Burks and Anne Roe.[3] MZA twins Tony Milasi and Roger Brooks were reunited in 1962, at age twenty-four, after Roger was mistaken for Tony by a busboy in a Miami, Florida pancake house. Their reunion was cov-ered in the press, and a book describing their lives appeared in 1969.[4] When the book appeared, Bouchard had just joined the University of Minnesota faculty and Lykken had not begun to study twins.

On February 20, 1979, the day that the *Star Tribune* article appeared, University of Minnesota psychology graduate student Meg Keyes showed the story to her professor, Thomas J. Bouchard Jr. She had taken Boucha-rd's course in individual differences in behavior, a class that included read-ings about separated twins. A second copy of the *Star Tribune* article was left in Bouchard's mailbox by psychology professor Gail Peterson. Peter-son appended a note saying, "I thought you would get a kick out of this."

Meg, now Dr. Keyes of the Minnesota Twin Family Study, remembers that Bouchard was "excited from the get-go—he moved fast getting funds, staff, and tests together." "I had to find the twins—I thought someone else would go for the Jims, but no one did," said Bouchard.

Every once in a while, a scientist encounters an unusually fascinating research problem, issue, or situation that is irresistible. Such projects usu-ally involve some degree of risk in terms of time, funding, and reputation, but the process is exhilarating if the topic is right. Few people had the opportunity to compare, firsthand, the behaviors of identical twins reared apart from birth. Bouchard admitted that he had formed a "big plan" in a few hours, but with no money.[5]

Bouchard telephoned the Associated Press in Cincinnati, Ohio, in an attempt to locate the twins. He told the person on the other end that he was prepared to "beg, borrow and steal" to support this case study. On February 25, 1979, the *New York Times* ran the front-page story, "Iden-tical Twins Seen as Offering New Clues in a Psychology Study; Searched for Brother." Bouchard was quoted as saying, "I'm going to beg, borrow and steal and even use some of my own money if I have to. It is important to study them immediately because now that they have gotten together they are, in a sense, contaminating one another." The *New York Times* apparently had obtained the story over the Associated Press wire; Bouchard recalls hearing typing on the other end as he spoke, explaining why his words were repeated.

Bouchard's original letter of invitation sent to Jim Lewis and Jim Springer introduced the investigators and provided an overview of activities the twins would complete. The letter also explained that the project covered airfare, food, lodging, some lost wages, and a modest honorarium to offset miscellaneous expenses. Bouchard also invited each pair to dinner one evening.

The Core Research Team

Bouchard established a core research team consisting of psychologists David T. Lykken (now deceased), Irving I. Gottesman, Auke Tellegen, and psychiatrist Leonard L. Heston (Figures 1-2 and 1-3). Each had heard about the Jim twins directly from Bouchard. At first, Lykken wondered if studying just one pair was worth the trouble, but Bouchard told him,

Figure 1-2.   Left to right: Leonard L. Heston, David T. Lykken, Niels Juel-Nielsen, Elke D. Eckert, and Thomas J. Bouchard Jr. (Photo courtesy Thomas J. Bouchard Jr. Photograph taken in May 1981 by a waiter in a Minneapolis restaurant. The occasion was the visit by Dr. Niels Juel-Nielsen, who had studied reared-apart twins in Denmark.)

"You are my friend—humor me."[6] Lykken did and became intrigued. Gottesman was immediately interested and suddenly confident that additional pairs could be found.

Heston felt that the Jim twins would make an "interesting case that was worth doing," but he doubted that the work would progress beyond the single-study stage. His views changed once the group had assessed seven or eight pairs, making him aware that the study had "real potential." Heston was also responsible for inviting University of Minnesota psychiatrist Elke D. Eckert to become part of the core team. Tellegen spoke for both Lykken and himself when he said that both thought studying the Jim twins would be a "one-time opportunity" and that it required sophisticated idiographic methodology—standard psychological procedures were not appropriate for research on just one set. Initially, he and Lykken tried to develop statistical techniques that would replace multiple subjects with multiple observations, but when the sample size grew this proved unnecessary.

The University of Minnesota's psychology department had a long history of individual differences research, much of it with a behavioral-genetic bent. Therefore, studying development by way of twins reared apart was natural for that time and place. Following Gottesman's 1957 twin study dissertation, conventional identical-fraternal twin comparisons had been ongoing since 1970 under the direction of David Lykken, who developed the Minnesota Twin Registry between 1983 and 1990. The

Figure 1-3. Left to right: Irving I. Gottesman, Auke Tellegen, and MZA twin Jim Lewis. (Photo courtesy Thomas J. Bouchard Jr. Photograph taken by a media center staff member, March 1979.)

Minnesota Twin Registry includes information on 901 twin pairs born between 1904 and 1936, 4,307 twin pairs born between 1936 and 1955, and 391 male twin pairs born between 1961 and 1964; see *Twin Research* 2002. Bouchard called his department's atmosphere "fabulous—you cannot create it, it must exist."

Lykken became Bouchard's most frequent coauthor—according to Bouchard, "We never really disagreed." Gottesman was famous for his 1960s twin studies of schizophrenia conducted with James Shields (who conducted the 1962 British reared-apart twin study), and for having administered the Minnesota Multiphasic Personality Inventory (MMPI) to adolescent twins. Heston had published a seminal 1966 adoption study of schizophrenia and was the father of identical twin daughters, Barbara and Ardis. Heston and Gottesman had become acquainted in the mid-1960s when Heston joined the Medical Research Council (MRC) Unit in Psychiatric Genetics in London. Gottesman was already there and had encouraged Heston to come.[7] Eckert, a specialist in eating disorders, found the idea of reared-apart twins fascinating: "It was a chance to look at genetic and environmental influences on behavior, something I hadn't studied much."

Tellegen had recently developed the Differential Personality Questionnaire (now the Multidimensional Personality Questionnaire).[8] The Multidimensional Personality Questionnaire is an eleven-scale form for assessing individual variation in personality. Tellegen had worked collaboratively with Lykken on psychophysiological twin studies involving more than five hundred pairs. Tellegen also credited a supportive department chair, John (Jack) Darley Sr. for facilitating study of the Jim twins.[9] Matt McGue, now Regents Professor in the psychology department at Minnesota, was a graduate student at the time, in charge of setting up the twins' information processing tasks. "When I came back it was very exciting here. The MISTRA put us on the map."

Another factor favorable to the study's success was that the university's psychology department and medical school were located on the same campus, facilitating assessment of behavioral and health-related traits. For the first time, reared-apart twins were undergoing cardiac, pulmonary, dental, periodontal, ophthalmologic, and endocrinological testing, as well as psychological assessment. Some medical tests, such as the electrocardiogram (ECG), were administered from the beginning; others, such as the periodontal examination, were added later.

The Assessment

Every colleague acknowledged that Bouchard's extraordinary ability to generate enthusiasm was key to starting the study and keeping it going.

When the study began, Bouchard was investigating factors affecting general intelligence and special mental abilities. His 1970s publications included studies of spatial ability, problem-solving strategies, and intelligence testing. He quickly put together a comprehensive assessment schedule that required four days for the twins to complete. The Jim twins and the pairs who followed became the first separated sets to complete psychological, psychophysiological, psychomotor, life stress, and sexual life history protocols; previous reared-apart twin studies focused on general intelligence and personality traits.

The research program could not be completed in four days, so the Jim twins returned to Minnesota five months later. The assessment schedule eventually expanded to fill five full work days, plus one evening and two half-days.

An important activity of the first assessment day was a series of unposed photographs of the twins taken alone, then together. The MZA twins' typically similar body postures and the DZA twins' typically dissimilar ones were unexpected findings, suggesting that there is genetic influence on these behaviors. We would also see genetic effects on body movement and gestures suggested by the MZA twins during separate videotaped interviews held later in the week. Bouchard recalls a pair of British women who continually twirled a strand of pearls around their necks as they spoke. Details of all the tests and inventories that were administered are provided in subsequent chapters and in this book's Web site.

The medical tests began on the first full study day and continued over the next three days. Dr. Naip Tuna, then Director of Electrocardiography and Non-Invasive Cardiology, first learned about the Jim twins from Bouchard. Tuna was "very interested" but uncertain as to the importance of heredity in adult cardiac functioning. "I thought genetics played a greater role in children's heart disorders," he admitted. Nevertheless, Tuna was intrigued and assumed the role of primary physician and cardiologist for the study. Eckert and Heston administered the twins' psychiatric interviews and medical life histories until clinical psychologist Will Grove replaced Heston, who joined the University of Washington in 1990.

Other physicians saw the reared-apart twins as a unique opportunity to conduct research in their own fields. Dr. Michael Till, a pediatric dentist, read about the project in the university's newspaper, the *Minnesota Daily*. Till brought the study to the attention of his colleagues in adult dentistry, but there was little interest. He attributes their cool response to patient overloads, heavy teaching responsibilities, and emphasis on restorative dental procedures. But Till was captivated. He contacted Bouchard, whom he did not know at that time, and the addition of a dental component to the project was decided over coffee. Till's only concern was that the walls of his examining room were decorated for children and the examination chairs were on the small side.

Thanks to my own periodontal problems, a periodontal evaluation was added to the project in 1986. While having my gums probed at the university's clinic, Dr. Mark Herzberg asked me about my twin research. It was hard to talk, but I managed to describe what we were doing and finding. He immediately recognized the research possibilities for his own specialty and put us in touch with his colleagues Bruce Pihlstrom and Bryan Michalowicz. During my 2009 visit to Minneapolis, Michalowicz (like McGue) told me that the MISTRA had put the University of Minnesota's periodontal department "on the map" in terms of defining genetic risk for periodontitis.

Informal clinical interviews were offered to the first twenty-three twin pairs as either a respite from the rigorous assessment schedule and/or an opportunity to discuss personal life history issues. These interviews were administered by Lloyd Sines, then professor in the university's psychiatry department and a colleague of Heston and Eckert, who brought him into the study. I have never met Sines, but I have seen his name on our early files. Over the course of a long telephone conversation in May 2011, I heard a different take on what the reared-apart twins might tell us.

"I had no mission," Sines told me. "I only had to talk to [the twins] in a friendly, professional manner." But there was more. "I did not share the highly biological perspective of the others. I may have expressed misgivings to them. Part of my motivation, in addition to the intrigue and importance of the endeavor, was to do something different with the twins—to approach them with a more clinical, subjective point of view." Sines recalled the well-known MZA twins Oskar and Jack, raised Catholic in Nazi Germany and Jewish in Trinidad, respectively, and speculated about the effects of their rearing situations on their personalities and politics. "[Oskar's opinion on World War II] vindicated my involvement in the study—I knew I had found something that the biological approach had missed." I will return to our findings on Oskar and Jack in later chapters of this book. Sines's interviews were discontinued (as were some other tests and activities) once the assessment schedule grew longer, but Bouchard has always said that the twins appreciated them.

The University of Minnesota is situated in a large city that offers access to many types of specialists. The Minneapolis War Memorial Blood Bank, directed by Dr. Herbert F. Polesky, was just downtown.[10] Polesky analyzed the twins' blood group profiles, classifying them as MZA or DZA. (I will say more about this process in Chapter 2.) In 1985, we discovered Tourette syndrome in all three members of an MZA/DZA triplet set. Dr. Maurice W. Dysken, a psychiatrist at the Minneapolis Veteran's Administration Hospital, immediately arranged a sleep study for one of the triplets. This interesting case is described in Chapter 7.

Ultimately, Bouchard did not have to beg, borrow, or steal to bring the Jim twins to Minnesota. He was serving on the university's graduate school research advisory committee when the Jim twins were found, and he knew that this body dispensed faculty research grants, sometimes on an emergency basis. He secured $6,500 within a couple of days, bringing the Jim twins to Minnesota on March 11, 1979, just three weeks after they were found. The funds were not intended to cover spouses, but the Jims insisted on coming to Minnesota with their wives. This posed a financial burden, but it also enabled comparative normative data to be gathered on nontwins (and nonadoptees) by having spouses complete some of the same tests as the twins. Analyses of spouse similarity (assortative mating) could be performed on various traits of interest. As the study progressed, it became clear that having spouses, children, or friends travel with the twins provided an added incentive for the twins to participate. According to Bouchard, a family member's presence may have yielded a more representative sample; otherwise, only the more adventuresome twins might have participated.

In the wake of the publicity surrounding the Jim twins, Bouchard's department chair, John Darley, told him, "You will find more twins, so you will need more grants." Darley telephoned the Spencer Foundation in Chicago, an organization that supports research on educational issues and values. The next meeting of the awards committee was ten days away, but Bouchard submitted a grant and received $32,000. "By then we had a few more pairs, and things rolled." Bouchard recalls his encounter with his chair as one of several unplanned events that moved the study along. "Jack Darley was paying attention to what was happening in the department. His actions became a model for me when I was chair." At about this time, Bouchard had also secured a $10,000 grant from the publishing house Harcourt Brace Jovanovich. Both the Spencer and Harcourt funds covered the research period from spring 1979 to summer 1980. The funds covered the twins' travel costs, some medical tests, the assistants' salaries, and other research-related expenses.

The Jim Twins

Excitement peaked in the psychology department when the Jim twins first visited the university. Everyone involved in the research had undergone hours of preparation for what he or she thought would be a one-time case study. Graduate students, Meg Keyes and Susan Resnick were responsible for most of the psychological data collection. Francie Gabbay (now a research professor at the Uniformed Services University in Bethesda, Maryland) was a visiting graduate student in David Lykken's psychophysiological laboratory. Bruce Hanson (now an internist at the Minneapolis Veteran's Administration Hospital) was a premedical student at the time; he did not gather information directly from the twins but helped process allergy data in a laboratory run by Dr. Malcolm Blumenthal. Blumenthal was a key figure in the twins' allergy testing protocol. Hanson participated later in analyses of the twins' ECG data.

Meg Keyes was struck by the Jims' similar personalities. "They were both so patient and kind, and also very serious." Susan Resnick was in the observation booth during the videotaped interviews: "Their gestures, the way they crossed their legs, were remarkably alike. This was all new to us at the time." When the twins returned to Minnesota in August, Lewis's younger identical twin brothers (Gary and Larry) and their wives, and Springer's younger brother (also Larry) and his wife completed an abbreviated version of the test battery. Gathering data from the twins' unrelated siblings (with whom they had shared environments but not genes) was another way to assess the relative effects of genetic and environmental influences on behavior. In fact, as the study progressed, a number of the twins' unrelated brothers and sisters were recruited for participation.

Keyes recalls that the Jims, who were raised apart, seemed as much alike as Gary and Larry who had been raised together. Furthermore, the Jims resembled each other both physically and behaviorally more than they resembled their adoptive siblings. As the data accumulated, these casual observations were confirmed; empirical quantitative analyses showed very modest shared environmental effects on many traits. Behavioral similarity appeared to be explained more by common genes than by common environments.

Most of the MISTRA data were gathered by the six primary investigators, University of Minnesota physicians, and graduate student assistants. The exception was the Wechsler Adult Intelligence Scale (WAIS) that was administered to twins at the same time by separate examiners hired through the university's neuropsychological clinic. (The rationale for this procedure is explained in Chapter 5.)

Virtually every colleague found studying the Jims and the other reared-apart twins to be "fun" and even "exhilarating." Nevertheless, it was recognized that the twins' value lay not in providing definitive answers but in raising new ideas about the origins of human behavior. For example, both of the thirty-nine-year-old Jims had gained ten pounds at the same time for no apparent reason. Heston found this remarkable because, while weight gain often occurs between the ages of thirty-four and forty, the Jims' weight change had occurred simultaneously. He suggested that what appeared to be an "improbable coincidence" might reflect genetic influence on physical changes associated with aging.[11] Heston was also captivated by the Jims' similar mixed headache syndrome (a tension headache that turns into a migraine), which first affected both twins in their teens. Lots of people have headaches, but in separate interviews the Jim twins used the same words and concepts to describe their disability and pain. Springer said, "It feels like somebody's hitting you in the back of the neck with a two-by-four," and Lewis noted that "It's centered in the back of the neck, and it damn near knocks me out sometimes."[12]

The Jim twins' striking resemblance created intense interest among the media, colleagues, and, of course, the Minnesota investigators. Members of the research team said many times that they did not expect the twins to be as similar as they were. Relying on statistical findings, Bouchard discovered that on most of the twenty-three vocational test categories, the Jims were as alike as the same person taking the same test twice.[13] And their California Psychological Inventory scale scores were so alike that one twin's profile could be superimposed upon the other's. The twins' performance (nonverbal) IQ scores were just one point apart, although their full scale scores differed by nine points. Bouchard himself told the *New York Times* that "If someone else brought the material to me and said, 'This is what I've got,' I'd say I didn't believe it."[14]

The twins' physical measures and other medical characteristics were also highly matched. Lewis weighed 154.90 pounds and was 70.90 inches tall, while Springer weighed 154.59 pounds and was 71.40 inches tall. Springer had had two heart attacks, and Lewis had been hospitalized for a suspected heart problem. The average male age for having a heart attack is sixty-six, so the thirty-nine-year-old twins' heart problems were unusual.[15] Their biological family's health history may have placed them at higher risk, but this information was unknown. The twins' smoking habits and visual acuity were also alike.

There is something to be said for being present in order to appreciate and absorb what was taking place during the reared-apart twin assessments. Bouchard once explained that the MISTRA actually took place on two levels, *statistical* and *anecdotal*. The statistical level involved comparing the magnitude of correlations and concordance measures between the MZA and DZA twin pairs. Such data are gathered objectively, systematically, and uniformly across sets. The anecdotal level involved examiner observations and participant reflections specific to given pairs. Observation-based information was revealed in a casual way over the course of each study week, often during lunches and coffee breaks. James Shields, author of the 1962 reared-apart twin study, also acknowledged these two approaches, calling them *biometrical* and *case history*, respectively.[16]

Biographical sketches, appended to the three reared-apart twin studies that preceded the MISTRA, included descriptive data on the twins' rearing circumstances, personality traits, and social relations.[17] This information was a useful complement to the quantitative outcomes. Anecdotal findings, so striking to those who observe them directly, are rarely welcome in professional journals, but they can offer fresh ideas about behavioral phenomena. We saw beer cans held with pinky fingers underneath for support, heard about hand washing before and after using the toilet, and observed quarter pieces of toast left uneaten on two plates. No one suggests that specific genes are responsible for these behaviors, but genetic effects might underlie positioning of the bones, tendencies toward tidiness, and feelings of satiety or restraint.

Juel-Nielsen, investigator of the Danish reared-apart twin study, visited the University of Minnesota in 1981. Bouchard specifically asked him if he had observed unusual habits or quirks in his MZA twin pairs. He said that he had, but he had not published the information because it might have detracted from his quantitative findings. He also worried that no one would believe it.

Before the Jim twins arrived, Bouchard had wondered as well if the newspapers had exaggerated the twins' similarities. Once they left, he concluded that they had not.

Jim Twins: The Aftermath

The original plan was to conduct a single clinical case study of the Jim twins. However, the stream of news reports and television shows kept the Jim twins in the public imagination. For many, reared-apart identical twins who end up alike despite their different backgrounds pose a great challenge to explanations of behavior. The Jim twins' stories of separation and reunion were also poignant and moving—they both spoke of emptiness in their lives that disappeared after meeting one another. Both twins agreed that finding each other was the best thing that had ever happened to him. Eight years later, both twins characterized their relationship as "closer than best friends."

Bouchard began receiving letters and calls from reared-apart twins across the country and around the world, due almost exclusively to the media's response to the Jim twins. Bouchard relished the publicity because he might have spent millions of dollars on recruiting new separated sets with little yield, but the press was far-reaching. Many people, not just academics, knew about the study. McGue agreed: "Bouchard used the anecdotes as a way to find twins. IQ correlations just do not captivate people."

The single case study plan was revised to allow for the study of several separated twin sets. The sample grew to fifteen by February 1980, and the MISTRA formally came into being. By early 1983, the MISTRA had examined more than fifty pairs. According to Bouchard, "By then I was convinced that I had something. The genetic effects were sufficiently strong, showing that developmental studies reporting correlations between parents and children in support of environmental effects were misleading." Parents and children share both their genes and their environments, so correlations between them do not necessarily imply environmental influence on behavior. Sports-minded parents may offer swimming and tennis lessons to children, but children may also inherit genetic predispositions for good athletic performance.

The MISTRA lasted for twenty years, but it might have lasted longer.[18] Just as some events favored its inception and early progress, continuing controversies and a few disappointing—even absurd—grant reviews worked against it. For example, one grant reviewer suggested that the investigators "spend their money hiring private detectives" to verify the backgrounds of twins Dorothy and Bridget, who arrived in Minneapolis wearing "seven rings on seven fingers." Both twins, in fact, were wearing seven rings, three bracelets, and a watch when Bouchard met them at the airport. Their long slender finders and hands, plus the ability to afford such adornments, may partly explain their attraction to jewelry (Figure 1-4).[19] (Dorothy and Bridget also were the twins who enjoyed books by the same author.) Another grant reviewer proposed a "feasibility study" to secure a sample of 150 MZA and 150 DZA twin pairs. Reared-apart twins are rare—in 1981, about twenty pairs had been studied, and Bouchard's grant proposal called for assessing seven additional sets.

There were also laudatory reviews—"The topic of this proposal is certainly one of the most important issues in psychology," and "[the twin sample] provides the strongest methodological basis for estimating the form and extent of environmental influence on given dependent variables." The clash among reviewers hurt the study's federal funding prospects, causing the research team to rely on private sources.

Looking back over the history of reared-apart twin studies, it is clear that Bouchard's decision to include DZA twin pairs was correct. (Shields's 1962 study had included limited data on eleven DZA twin pairs.) Not one DZA twin set rivaled the Jims as the most alike pair, although there were strong candidates among the MZAs. But even if an exceptional DZA set had shown the Jims' extraordinary resemblance, it would not have altered the study's conclusions. The gene-environment balance is best gauged by comparing as many MZA and DZA twin pairs as possible—only then can "informed weights" be assigned to the various sources of influence.[20] Single sets cannot provide definitive answers, not even the Jims.

The Jim twins triggered a chain of events, including newspaper coverage, televised interviews, an invitation to Bouchard to address the American Adoption Congress and, consequently, the identification of new reared-apart twin pairs. Bouchard's daughter Elizabeth recalled that "that first summer was heady, with all the talk of possibilities of where this research might go." Bouchard claims "no responsibility" for this, seeing the process as serendipity.[21]

If the Jim twins had not been as alike as they were, the MISTRA may have gone in a different direction—or in no direction at all. Not all MZA

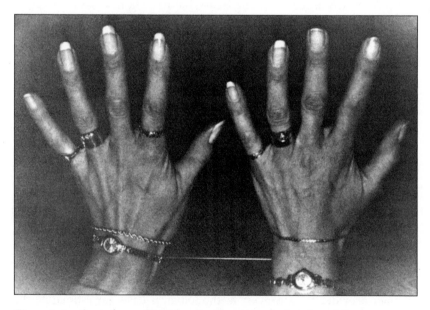

Figure 1-4.   Reared-apart British twins' long, slender hands and fingers, showing their shared taste for jewelry. (Photo courtesy Thomas J. Bouchard Jr. Photograph taken in David Lykken's laboratory.)

twin pairs were as alike as the Jims—if one of these pairs had reunited first, there might have been less media attention, and fewer separated sets would have surfaced. It was fortunate that the Jims were as similar as they were. Without them, science and society might have been deprived of the wealth of data gathered from the 137 reunited sets and the over 150 publications that resulted. Others are still being written.

CHAPTER TWO

15,000 Questions × 137 Pairs

THE MISTRA EVOLVED rapidly following the Jim twins' 1979 assessment, especially with respect to methodology—how we found the twins, what we asked them to do, and where we had them do it. This chapter provides detailed descriptions of the participants, test schedule, genetic terms, and statistical concepts needed to understand the inner workings and quantitative findings of the project.

From the start, each twin completed protocols such as a life history interview (covering their separation, reunion, contact, residential history, and rearing family composition), personality and interest questionnaires, and the Wechsler IQ test. We added tests and questionnaires (such as the Woodcock-Johnson Reading Mastery Test and the Neuroticism-Extraversion-Openness Inventory) and eliminated some procedures in the interest of time. The changes were often prompted by new twin-based findings in the scientific literature. We added the Public Opinion Inventory and the Wilson-Patterson Conservatism Scale in 1986 when Nick Martin and his team published a provocative reared-together twin study showing genetic effects on radicalism, tough-mindedness, and conservatism, behaviors measured by those instruments.[1] Thinking at that time was that social attitudes were mostly due to family influences, so these new findings could completely revise our understanding of the origins of people's opinions. It was important for us to study attitudes and opinions in reared-apart twins to see if we would also find genetic influence using a different twin method.

We estimated that the twins completed 15,000 questions during the study week. This many questions completed by a modest size sample raises the possibility of obtaining significant results by chance alone. An important methodological feature of the study was including more than one test of many of the traits we studied. This enabled within-study replications of our analyses to see if the results were consistent. Furthermore, by using questionnaires and inventories administered previously to reared-together twins we could compare our findings with those from other studies, and we found very consistent patterns with some exceptions.

Participant Identification

Identifying participants for the MISTRA was almost as exciting as the study itself. We mostly learned about reunited twin pairs from newspapers, but we also received tips from colleagues, family members, and acquaintances. We studied DZA as well as MZA pairs to avoid the criticism of possibly attracting the most similar sets. We studied DZA opposite-sex as well as same-sex pairs to determine if male-female pairs were less alike on some traits than their same-sex counterparts.

It was more exciting to find twins by oneself than from our other sources. On December 6, 1979, when I was a graduate student, I summarized my dissertation research on twins for the Children's Home and Aid Society of Illinois and mentioned the MISTRA. A social worker confessed to me that her agency had separated female twins, Barbara and Judy, thirty-one years earlier, yet neither twin knew they were part of a set. The social workers believed that separating the twins was advisable because Barbara (the fussy twin) might not receive the attention she needed if placed with Judy (the engaging twin). I pushed for information about the twins, but the society suggested that I have Bouchard contact the Executive Director, Edwin Millard. Bouchard did, and nine months later, in September 1980, Barbara and Judy were reunited in Minneapolis at age thirty-two. However, the process of finding these twins was complex.

When I spoke with the society's former research director, Joan DiLeonardi, in April 2010, she recalled the case immediately. "If my student and I had decided not to do it, it would never have happened. The 1940s were the 'heydays of secrecy in adoption,' but by the 1980s things had changed." Fortunately, DiLeonardi's field student, Ellen Smith, was fascinated by the possibility of bringing twins together, and searched hundreds of Chicago-area records. When the twins were finally located, DiLeonardi placed several calls to each one, first inquiring about their respective adoption experiences. In her second call to Barbara, DiLeonardi told her, "You have a special sibling." "Oh?" "You have an identical twin."

Barbara screamed with excitement. It was no different for Judy, who said, "I will call her right now!"

For a while, Barbara and Judy held the status of "best MISTRA pair" because they had had no contact prior to assessment and were previously unaware of having been born a twin. Bouchard, who witnessed the twins' reunion, was captivated by them—"It was as if they had known one other all their lives." Bouchard recalled that "not a nanosecond went by between the time that one twin spoke and the other twin answered— I've been married thirty years and I don't do this with my wife!" DiLeonardi was also at the airport, having flown to Minneapolis to witness the twins' reunion. She recalled that Bouchard immediately examined the shapes of their ears, which typically match in MZ twins, and believed they were identical. She also said that by the time they arrived at the hotel the twins were finishing each other's sentences. "I have identical twin cousins who did this, and I thought it was because they had grown up together."

Another wonderful moment concerned opposite-sex twins, Iris Johns and Aro Campbell, New Zealanders who met at age seventy-five (Figure 2-1).

Figure 2-1.   Aro Campbell (left) and Iris Johns. The twins, separated at six weeks of age, met for the first time at age seventy-five. (Photo credit Nancy L. Segal.)

I learned about them accidentally in April 1991 when I checked the *Guinness Book of World Records* to see if one of our DZA pairs, De-wayne and Paul, who were reunited at sixty-nine, were recognized as the longest separated pair in the world. But Dewayne and Paul were the longest separated "American pair," whereas Iris and Aro set the world's record. Bouchard did not think we would find the twins, but after two phone calls made within five minutes I proved him wrong.

Iris and Aro were delighted to come to Minnesota. Each had grown up believing that the other twin had died, but Iris had harbored doubts. She appeared on *Missing*, a TVNZ television program for people searching for family members. Someone who knew Aro and had seen the show was responsible for bringing the twins together. "We had to wipe away so many tears that night," Iris said.[2]

Introducing the Twins to the MISTRA

Once we located twins, our next step was to call them on the telephone to invite them to campus. I loved making these calls because the twins often provided interesting information that the press hadn't reported. Ann Blandin and Barbara Parker were such a pair. Three of us found them simultaneously—I called Bouchard from New York when I saw the story in a New York newspaper during a visit home; Bill Fine, a friend of Bouchard's, had seen the story in a San Francisco newspaper; and jour-nalist Lew Cope from the *Minneapolis Star Tribune* had also sent word. Barbara and Ann each described herself as a "picky bedspread picker-outer"—so when Ann peeked into Barbara's bedroom for the first time she was astonished to see that they had chosen the same unusual bed-spreads. Perhaps it was the color, the texture, or the price of the spread that both twins found appealing.

Ideally, researchers would want to find separated twin sets in national population registries that record all occurrences of multiple births and rearing circumstances. Such resources are available in the Scandinavian countries, which allowed Juel-Nielsen to assess the complete population of reared-apart Danish twins that met his criteria.[3] Population-based twin registries are also available in large regions of China[4] and in other nations, but a national twin registry does not exist in the United States. However, localized registries, such as the Minnesota Twin Registry at the University of Minnesota and the Mid-Atlantic Twin Registry at Virginia Commonwealth University have been created by investigators to facili-tate their research. Other more specialized rosters include the Vietnam Era Twin Registry, the Chronic Fatigue Twin Registry, and the Interna-tional Registry of HIV-Exposed Twins.

Lacking a national registry, the MISTRA studied a collection of cases because our reared-apart twins surfaced in many ways and at any time (Table 2-1). The twins themselves and the people who heard about them contacted us because they knew about the MISTRA largely through the media attention the study had attracted. Our professional colleagues also knew about the study because of publications, presentations, and the usual academic word of mouth. We also identified twins through adoption registries, social service agencies, and search groups. The majority of pairs were identified by self-referral, but most of the twins learned about the study through media reports.

We studied 137 reared-apart twin pairs between March 1979 and April 1999. Close to seven new pairs, on average, were studied each year that the study was ongoing, and forty-four pairs returned for follow-up study beginning in 1987. Table 2-2 shows that the number of new twin pairs was highest during the first four years of the study, then tapered off somewhat as the study progressed. Most twins accepted our invitation to participate. The fewer numbers of reared-apart pairs studied after 1994 may have reflected the dwindling of such pairs as well as our limited funding. However, after the MISTRA ended in 1999 several new twin pairs, separated mostly because their families could not care for one or both of them, were identified. It is likely that better search options, many available on the Internet, allowed these twins to meet. The actual numbers of reared-apart twins may not have declined as much as we had thought.

That twin registries were unavailable does not mean that the group of twins we studied was unrepresentative of twins generally—in fact, the reared-apart twins resembled ordinary reared-together twins in many ways. Table 4 in our 1990 *Science* paper, discussed in Chapter 5, shows

Table 2-1.   Sources of Reared-Apart Twins from the MISTRA

Source	Number of Pairs (N = 137)	Percentage of Total
Media reports	11	8.0
Adoption services/Search groups	26	19.0
Referrals from colleagues	26	19.0
Self-referrals	50	36.5
Previous twin participants	16	11.7
Other	8	5.8

Note: These values reflect the most direct source of information. The majority of self-referrals and referrals from colleagues and previous participants were in response to media coverage of the study. Other sources included the twins' attorney, the *Guinness Book of World Records,* and the interested public.

Table 2-2. **Reared Apart Twin Pairs Studied Each Year**

Month/Year	Pairs (N = 137)
3/1979–2/1980	14
3/1980–2/1981	12
3/1981–2/1982	15
3/1982–2/1983	10
3/1983–2/1984	3
3/1984–2/1985	10
3/1985–2/1986	8
3/1986–2/1987	13
3/1987–2/1988	4
3/1988–2/1989	9
3/1989–2/1990	4
3/1990–2/1991	6
3/1991–2/1992	7
3/1992–2/1993	4
3/1993–2/1994	6
3/1994–2/1995	3
3/1995–2/1996	1
3/1996–2/1997	2
3/1997–2/1998	4
3/1998–4/1999	2

that MZA and MZT twins display about the same degree of resemblance on most measured physiological and psychological traits. For convenience, however, I will refer to our twins as a sample (a representative subset of the members of a population).

Separation and Contact

In order to participate in the MISTRA, twins had to have been separated by four years of age and have spent their formative years apart. Several pairs met as children, but most met as adults, and several met for the first time in Minneapolis. Some contact did not disqualify twins from participating; in fact, the variable amounts of contact between co-twins provided opportunities to evaluate associations between degree of contact and similarity in intelligence, personality, and other behaviors. It turned out that contact was *not* associated with resemblance between the twins across virtually all the behaviors that we studied. For example, time spent apart until the first reunion correlated only 0.08 with the within-pair (co-twin) difference in IQ, showing that twins who met at earlier ages were not more alike in intelligence than were twins who met at later ages.

The twins' mean age at separation was 218.21 days (standard deviation = 343.59) and ranged from 0.00 to 1,644 days. Expressed in years, the mean age at separation was 0.60 years (standard deviation = 0.94) and ranged from 0.00 to 4.50 years.

Determining Twin Type

Determining the zygosity (twin type) of most pairs was accomplished by the comparative study of blood group systems. Blood samples were drawn from each twin during the middle of the study week and forwarded to the Minneapolis War Memorial Blood Bank. A standard protocol involved testing for the following blood group systems: ABO, Rh (rhesus), MNSs, Kell; Lewis, Duffy, Kidd, P; serum proteins: Gc (group specific factor), Tf (transferrin), Hp (haptoglobin), AK (adenylate deaminase), and 6-PGD (6-phosphogluconate dehydrogenase); and red cell enzymes: Cp (ceruloplasmin), PGM1 (phosphoglucomutase), AcP (acid phosphatase), EsD (esterase-D), and GLO (glyoxalase I). Based on their identity across these factors, twins were classified as MZ with over 99 percent certainty, and discordance in any of these blood factors indicated that the twins were DZ.

The specific blood groups, proteins, and enzymes that were assayed changed over the years. Current twin studies decide zygosity based on within-pair concordance or discordance across 13–15 DNA short tandem repeat (STR) markers or DNA segments. Each individual inherits one copy of an STR from each parent. The number of repeats in each marker shows considerable variation among people, making these markers useful for establishing the twins' zygosity. The chance that two nonidentical twins would match for 13 STRs is one in one billion.

In later years, testing of standard DNA markers was used to classify the MISTRA twins. Three DNA markers (probe MS43, locus D12S11; probe V1, locus D17S79; and probe SLi989, locus D7S467) were added to the analysis in 1994, and new ones were added by the time the study was completed.[5] The reliability of this procedure is high, and the current expense is low (approximately $150/pair). DNA can be derived from buccal smears, obtained by gently swabbing the inner cheek, a procedure that is less invasive than drawing blood.

The blood group data, together with fingerprint resemblance (Slater's Z score, a measure of co-twins' similarities and differences in total ridge-count or number of lines across each fingertip), ponderal index (body height/cube root of body weight), and cephalic index (head breadth/head length) yielded a probability of misdiagnosis of less than 0.001.[6] Thus, the possibility of misclassifying twin pairs was extremely small. Opposite-sex pairs were assigned as DZ based on their sex difference, although their blood groups were analyzed in the interest of completeness. The zygosity of one MZA twin pair was determined by their concordance for six red blood cell markers and similarities in fingerprint and anthropometric traits. The zygosity of one DZA twin pair was determined by their discordance for highly heritable physical features such as hair color. These latter pairs did not visit Minnesota but were assessed in England by Bouchard and assistant Dr. Alison MacDonald from the Institute of Psychiatry in London.[7]

Zygosity determinations were not available until the end of each study week or until after the twins left Minneapolis. Nevertheless, our global impressions of the twins and our inspection of their highly heritable characteristics, such as hair color, eye color, and ear shape, were informative visual clues to twin type. Race and Sanger, who collaborated with James Shields on his twin studies, noted that "the blood groups practically never contradict the opinion of such a skilled observer of twins."[8] I confirmed this observation in a 1984 study by showing that my immediate impressions of twin type, based upon the twins' similarity in appearance, showed 96 percent agreement with blood type determinations.[9]

We were generally correct in our informal zygosity assessments, but in one exceptional case we were wrong. The DZA twins Kerrie and Amy looked enough alike to be MZA twins—after all, it was mistaken identity that had reunited them—but they looked just different enough to make us wonder (Figure 2-2). By the end of the study week, we were convinced that Kerrie and Amy were "similar-looking DZAs" rather than "dissimilar-looking MZAs," and the blood-typing laboratory work proved that our later impressions were right.

The physical similarity of this pair was enhanced by their concordance for brittle hair and sparse hair growth. The twins were examined by a University of Minnesota dermatologist who confirmed the limited hair growth in one twin and ectodermal dysplasia in the other twin. Ectodermal dysplasia refers to a group of conditions involving abnormalities of the skin, hair, nails, teeth, and sweat glands. The twins had apparently inherited this trait from their biological father, but to different degrees—when their biological mother saw their reunion picture in the newspaper, she called them to say, "Girls, you have your father's hair." One twin had transmitted the condition to two of her three children.[10]

Kerrie and Amy were adopted as infants by families in different parts of Vermont. When Kerrie was eighteen, she moved to a larger city in another part of the state. Suddenly people started calling her Amy. When

Kerrie turned twenty-five, she met a man at a party who said he'd bet a million dollars that she and someone named "Amy" were twin sisters.[11] After a series of telephone calls, the twins met and were struck by their resemblance. Their adoption agency eventually confirmed what they already knew. Kerrie is angry that she and Amy missed their growing-up years together. "They didn't realize what [separation] can do to somebody," she said.

Kerrie and Amy were our only DZA twins to be reunited because one twin was confused for the other. Their experience underlines the wide variability among DZ (and DZA) twins and full siblings with respect to similarities in appearance and behavior.

The question of biased data collection based on visual impressions of twin type is a concern in every twin study. We handled this issue in various ways, based on the different tests and activities we administered, but general rules were followed to maintain impartiality. For example, the IQ tests were administered by different examiners who were not part of the research team, the twins were kept apart while they completed questionnaires, and each twin received the same protocols at the same time as his or her co-twin (or one immediately after the other) to avoid exchange of information. We also requested that the twins refrain from discussing the tests until both had completed them. There were exceptions to these rules. Bouchard, for instance, noted that twins given the special mental ability

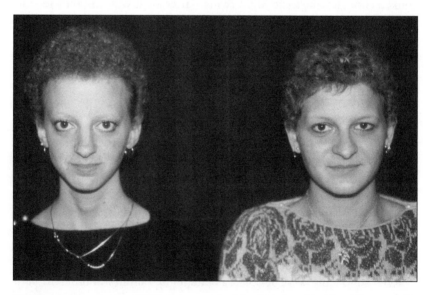

Figure 2-2.   Look-alike DZA twins reunited by mistaken identity. (Photo credit Thomas J. Bouchard Jr.)

battery by different examiners showed larger score differences than twins who were tested together. Subtle differences in examiner explanations and/or rapport were the likely causes. Thus, the decision was made to test the twins together, seating them on opposite sides of the room facing away from one another. There were some other exceptions to our rules, and their possible effects on the data will be considered.

The Final Reared-Apart Twin Sample

There were two final reared-apart twin samples. The individual sample (N = 262 individual twins or triplets) counted each participant just once and was used for descriptive and correlational analyses. For example, the individual file was used to examine correlations between different measures such as parental education and twins' IQ score.

The paired sample (n = 137 pairs) was reserved for quantitative data analyses, such as calculating IQ intraclass correlations (measures of twin resemblance) and estimates of personality heritability (degree to which personality traits were influenced by genetic factors). The paired file was also created to accommodate two MZA male triplet sets and two MZA/DZA triplet sets; the MZA/DZA triplet sets were each composed of two MZA females and a DZA male co-triplet. Depending on the measure, the two MZ triplet sets were variously entered as one MZ set composed of two triplets chosen randomly (triplets 1–2 or triplets 1–3), as three pairs each (triplets 1–2, triplets 2–3, and triplets 1–3), or as one group of three (triplets 1–2–3). In my analysis of the twins' social relationships I entered the MZA triplets as three separate twin pairs because the relationship qualities among the different pairings could differ. The two MZA/DZA triplet sets were usually entered as one MZ female twin pair and two DZ opposite-sex twin pairs, although the two male-female sets were sometimes eliminated to avoid data duplication.

Three MZA pairs (two male and one female) who were under eighteen years of age were, with some exceptions, routinely omitted from the data analyses because we wanted to report findings on adult twins. An additional MZA female pair that was discordant for severe cardiac difficulties and other physical complications, presumably due to fetal transfusion syndrome (shared prenatal blood circulation), was also generally excluded. The data from these pairs have, however, been included in the descriptive tables presented in this chapter in the interest of completion. The zygosity and sex composition of the two complete samples are displayed in Table 2-3.

The twins' mean (average) age at assessment and contact measures are presented in Table 2-4. Contact measures refer to how much time the twins spent together before and after their separation. The variability

Table 2-3. Zygosity and Sex Composition of the Individual and Paired Reared-Apart Twin Samples

Zygosity	Individual Sample (individuals)	Paired Sample (pairs)
MZA	156	81
Male	58	32
Female	98	49
DZA (same sex)	76	38
Male	24	12
Female	52	26
DZA (opposite sex)	30	18
Male	16	—
Female	14	—
Total	262	137

Note: The paired sample in the table includes all possible pairings of the members of each of the four triplet sets. The MZA female twins with a male co-triplet (two sets) are entered in the MZA female individual sample, explaining why the number of individual female opposite-sex twin individuals is lower than the number of males.

(standard deviation [SD]) and range (minimum and maximum values) of each measure are also provided.

The MZA twin pairs were younger at assessment than the DZA twin pairs, a difference associated with their younger age at reunion ($r = 0.72$, $P<.001$). These differences are a likely reflection of the greater ease with which MZA co-twins find each other, due to their similar appearance; consequently, the period of time between separation and first contact was shorter for MZA twins than for DZA twins. Note that the MZA twins were separated at an earlier age than the DZA twins, so they had less early contact. However, the length of time from reunion to assessment was longer for MZA than DZA twins, a finding that explains their greater contact before coming to Minneapolis. This makes sense because MZA twins met sooner than DZA twins, giving them more opportunity to interact. Still, the percentage of lifetime living apart was nearly identical for the MZA and DZA twin pairs (95 percent and 97 percent, respectively).

Critics have focused on MZA-DZA differences in (1) time between reunion and assessment and (2) contact prior to assessment to explain the greater behavioral resemblance of the MZA than DZA twin pairs. Clinical psychologist Jay Joseph, a harsh critic of behavior genetics,[12] has also argued that length of contact may be less critical than the age at which the contact occurs.[13] He claims that contact between twins in infancy or childhood cannot be equated with contact in adulthood, which he says would have a greater impact on behavior. Joseph's objection fails because

Table 2-4. **Age at Assessment and Contact Measures for MZA and DZA Twins**

	MZA	DZA	Total
Age at assessment (years)[a]			
N (individuals)	156	106	262
Mean	39.75	45.71	42.16
(SD)	(13.48)	(13.45)	(13.76)
Range	11–68	22–77	11–77
Time together before separation (days)[b]			
N (pairs)	81	56	137
Mean	146.10	322.52	218.21
(SD)	(246.7)	(429.69)	(343.59)
Range	0–1,461	3–1,644	0–1,644
Age at reunion (years)[c]			
N (pairs)	78	55	133
Mean	31.45	42.35	35.95
(SD)	(15.46)	(13.71)	(15.67)
Range	0.33–65.11	20.92–75.11	0.33–75.11
Separation to first contact (years)[d]			
N (pairs)	78	55	133
Mean	31.29	41.71	35.60
(SD)	(15.63)	(13.71)	(15.68)
Range	0.50–75.17	17.00–75.17	0.50–75.17
Reunion to assessment (years)[e]			
N (pairs)	78	55	133
Mean	8.01	3.12	5.99
(SD)	(13.15)	(6.88)	(11.23)
Range	0–47.25	(0–30.00)	0–47.25
Length of contact (years)[f]			
N (pairs)	80	56	136
Mean	1.65	0.96	1.37
(SD)	(3.46)	(1.16)	(2.77)
Range	0.02–23.67	0.02–4.52	0.02–23.67
Lifetime apart (percentage)			
N (pairs)	80	56	136
Mean	95.62	97.57	96.42
(SD)	(7.52)	(2.52)	(6.05)
Range	52–99	86–99	52–99

Note: Contact means either telephone or personal contact, not contact by letter. A few complex cases were omitted from some measures. SD: standard deviation.

a. MZA<DZA [$t(260)=-3.51, P<.001$].

b. MZA<DZA [$F=18.18, P<.001, t(80.07)=-2.77, P<.01$].

c. MZA<DZA [$t(131)=-4.19, P<.001$].

d. MZA<DZA[$t(131)=-3.98, P<.001$].

e. MZA>DZA [$F=18.29, P<.001, t(122.18)=2.79, P<.01$].

f. MZA>DZA [$F=6.61, P<.01$; the mean values do not differ significantly].

most contact measures had little influence on the twins' behavioral outcomes and some associations were in a counterintuitive direction. For example, in my analysis of the twins' social relationship, I discovered a slight but significant correlation ($r = 0.16$) between days before separation and feelings of familiarity at the time of assessment. This implied that the twins who were together longer felt less familiar with one another than those who were separated sooner! This counterintuitive association was possibly a chance finding.

The MISTRA sample also included the twins' spouses, children, parents, siblings, and siblings' spouses, for a total of 214 nontwin individuals. These nontwins completed a shorter version of the assessment battery that included IQ tests, life history interviews, and inventories. Their data were often included in the age- and sex-correction procedures we performed prior to data analysis.

Age- and sex-correction procedures remove the effects that shared age and sex might have on trait similarity. For example, two women aged fifty-six years who were born in the 1950s would most likely have been childhood readers of the Bobbsey Twins, teenage fans of the Beatles, and adult users of calcium supplements to offset bone loss—more so than two people of differing age and sex. If reading preferences, favorite songs, and medical treatments are associated with age and sex, then it is important to control for them. We did this according to the statistical procedures described by McGue and Bouchard.[14] Data from the nontwins also allowed us to see if the different measures were affected by assortative mating. The age and sex of the nontwins are shown in Table 2-5.

Country of origin, summarized in Table 2-6, was considered the place where twins resided at the time of the study. Most twins came from the United States (45.4 percent) and England (32.4 percent). The study was generally limited to twins from English-speaking countries, although several twins originally from Germany, China, and the Netherlands participated with the assistance of interpreters and/or protocols translated into their native languages. Several twins were unable to travel to Minneapolis, so they completed an abbreviated portion of the study in their hometowns. In such cases, the protocols were administered by the study staff and by other trained individuals, as in the case of the British twins described earlier.

A small subgroup of pairs included twins raised in different countries— Germany and Canada, China and the United States, and England and Australia, to name a few. But the twins with the most exotic rearing differences were Jack Yufe and Oskar Stohr (Figure 2-3), who were mentioned briefly in Chapter 1.

Table 2-5. Age and Sex of Nontwin Participants

Relationship	Number	Age (SD) Range	Percentage Female
Spouse of twin/triplet	144	45.76 (11.91) 21–79	43.1
Child of twin/triplet	4	28.75 (14.15) 15–45	50.0
Adoptive parent	8	46.50 (5.01) 39–53	87.5
Sibling of twin	28	38.96 (14.58) 20–68	67.9
Spouse of sibling	8	37.75 (13.92) 23–65	75.0
Other	22	43.91 (14.67) 17–72	72.7
Total	214	44.09 (12.84) 15–79	52.3

Table 2-6. Country of Residence for Reared-Apart Twins

Country	Percentage	Number (individuals)
Australia	5.3	14
Canada	1.9	5
England	32.4	85
Germany	1.9	5
Israel	0.4	1
Netherlands	0.8	2
New Zealand	0.8	2
South Africa	0.4	1
Sweden	1.1	3
United States	45.4	119
Mixed/Uncertain	10.0	26
Total	100.0	262

Jack and Oskar were born in 1933 to a Romanian Jewish father (Josef) and a German Catholic mother (Liesel) who had met on a ship headed to Trinidad. The couple separated when the twins were six months old— Josef kept Jack in Trinidad and raised him Jewish, while Liesel took Oskar to Germany and raised him Catholic. Jack grew up fearful of his German roots in British-controlled Trinidad, while Oskar concealed his Jewish ones in Nazi Germany. Both twins dealt with these fears in complementary ways—Jack by becoming "very British" and Oskar by becoming "very German." The twins met briefly in Germany in 1954 at age twenty-one. It wasn't a friendly reunion because, aside from their language barrier, they regarded each other with suspicion. They didn't meet again until 1980 after Jack's wife read about the MISTRA in *People* magazine. When the twins met at the Minneapolis International airport, both were wearing light-blue shirts with epaulettes on the shoulders and wire-rimmed glasses.

There was a lot of public fascination surrounding this pair. The reunion of "Nazi and Jew" appeared in newspaper headlines, but this was an exaggeration because Oskar was only twelve years old when World War II ended. Like other boys his age, he had been required to join the Hitler Youth League, an activity he enjoyed mostly for its sports opportunities.

The twins' different rearing circumstances extended beyond their extraordinary cultural divide. Jack was raised by a father, and Oskar by

Figure 2-3.   MZA twins Jack (left) and Oskar. (Photo courtesy Thomas J. Bouchard Jr. Photograph taken in David Lykken's laboratory.)

a grandmother (his mother was often absent). Jack joined the Israeli navy and worked on a kibbutz; Oskar worked in the coal mines in the Ruhr. But their Minnesota Multiphasic Personality Inventory (MMPI) personality profiles matched almost completely, and they displayed a number of unusual similarities—washing their hands before and after using the toilet, collecting rubber bands around their wrists, and intentionally sneezing loudly in crowded elevators. Oskar savored Jack's spicy Caribbean cuisine, so different from his German diet of bread and bratwurst. These twins are a great example of how common genes can lead to shared behaviors even when environments diverge dramatically. Oskar and Jack were fascinated by their shared habits and tastes, but repelled by their contrasting political and religious beliefs. They engaged in a love-hate relationship until Oskar's death in 1997, a very sad event for Jack.[15]

The substantial percentage of British twins is due to interest taken in the MISTRA by the late John Stroud, former Assistant Director of Social Services for Hertfordshire, about ten miles outside London. Tall, heavy-set, and imposing with a bushy beard, twinkling eyes, and dry sense of humor, Stroud took great pleasure in reuniting families, especially twins, and he developed a national reputation for doing so. Stroud's death in 1989 was a personal and professional blow to everyone who knew him and to twins still hoping to meet some day.[16]

Passage of the Children Act in 1975 gave adopted British children the right to know their biological parents. This act, and the fact that time of birth (for twins only) is recorded on birth certificates in England and Wales, facilitated Stroud's efforts.[17] However, twins in one British DZA female pair did not benefit from this practice because they were born in different months—one on October 31, the other on November 1—a situation that delayed their reunion for some time. In another case, a clerk reviewing a record for a twin searching for biological kin inadvertently placed her thumb over the time of birth while inspecting the birth certificate, hiding the fact that the person in the search was a twin.

Stroud commented, "The aspects I enjoy are the detective work which goes into these cases . . . and the sheer happiness that comes when such separated twins meet each other. I think every twin I have helped has used the same phrase, 'I am over the moon.' "[18] During our life history and twin relationship interviews, some participants told me they discovered their twinship while searching for their biological parents. They admitted that, once this was known, finding their twin became more important than finding their mothers and fathers.

Why Twins Were Separated

The MISTRA twins were separated because of parental divorce (7.3 percent), parental death (6.6 percent), illegitimate birth (44.5 percent), physical incapacity of parents to provide child care (3.7 percent), financial limitations (13.1 percent), and miscellaneous causes (13.9 percent). The reasons for separation were unknown in 10.9 percent of the cases. Several unusual separation circumstances are of particular interest. A set of MZA

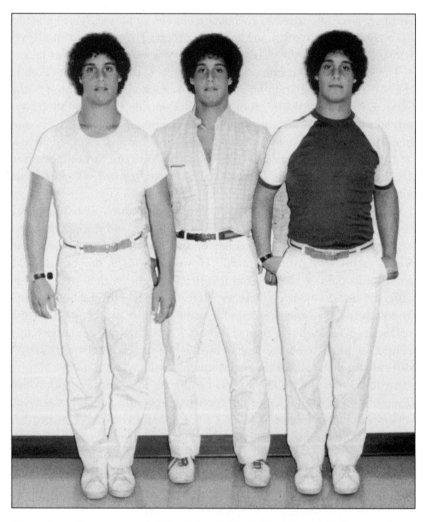

Figure 2-4. Reared-apart MZA triplets Eddy Galland, David Kellman, and Robert Shafran (left to right) who participated in the MISTRA at age nineteen. (Photo credit Thomas J. Bouchard Jr.)

male triplets from New York City, Eddy, Dave, and Bob (Figure 2-4), were placed in different adoptive homes at the advice of Columbia University psychiatrist Viola Bernard. Bernard believed that separate rearing benefited multiple birth children because they would enjoy undivided parental attention and a special place in their families. These triplets (and five MZA twin pairs who were not in the MISTRA) were part of the discredited 1960s study of separated twins by Neubauer that resulted from these placements, as mentioned in the Introduction.[19]

Other unusual circumstances kept some twins apart. Canadian MZA twins Brent and George were inadvertently switched with a nontwin infant, Marcus, while being moved to a second foster home. Members of MZA male set Bill and Bruce were separated because their parents already had a daughter and had planned on having only two children in total—the ideal American family—so they gave Bruce away. Professor William Tucker, in questioning the size and characteristics of Cyril Burt's MZA twin sample, found it "a tad preposterous that a middle class couple, unexpectedly finding themselves the parents of twins, pick one infant to send to an orphanage so as not to put a crimp in their life style."[20] Nevertheless, we had such a situation in our study.

When I asked Bouchard to name the most memorable reared-apart pair we studied, he didn't hesitate. Jim and Jim were "the most spectacular"—so were Oskar and Jack as well as Bridget and Dorothy, the twins who each wore seven rings, three bracelets, and a watch. Mark and Jerry (both volunteer firemen) were "pretty interesting." But Bill and Bruce were "the greatest pair on earth." One evening, Bouchard invited the eighteen-year-old twins and their two families to his former home on Lake Minnetonka in Wayzata, Minnesota. While he was entertaining their parents, he noticed that the twins had walked to the dock holding hands—"they wanted to talk," he said.

I remember being in the testing room, watching Bill's parents watching Bruce. They seemed greatly in awe and very uncomfortable seeing a replica of their son, the twin they had given away.

Twins are, presumably, separated less often today than in the past because adoption agencies have been sensitized to the importance of twin and sibling relationships. Most jointly placed brothers and sisters do as well as, or better than, singly placed children or siblings, though a few do worse.[21] Current research recommends placing siblings together, while evaluating each situation on a case-by-case basis in the event of exploitation or bullying of one sibling by another.[22] The MISTRA twins' life stories and reunions, as well as research documenting the significance of the twin relationship, have been used to support common placement in cases involving twins' custody.[23]

Joan DiLeonardi, who helped reunite twins Barbara and Judy, recalled that a former executive at Illinois's Children's Home and Aid Society felt that separating twins was an acceptable practice. Years later, when she met the former executive at a reception, he said that he was puzzled over efforts to bring twins together, implying that there was nothing special about twin children. The social stigma attached to illegitimate birth has lessened in many societies, allowing unwed mothers to raise their infants comfortably. However, twins continue to be reared apart for other reasons. Assisted reproductive technology often results in multiple births, a situation some families are emotionally or financially unable to manage. An estimated tens of thousands of female infants were abandoned under China's One-Child Policy, indirectly resulting in an unknown number of separated twins sets, some of which I am studying.[24] Several switched at birth twin cases have also been identified over the years.[25] Given inadequate procedures for linking mothers and newborns in some hospitals, it is likely that other cases exist but may never be detected.[26]

Rearing with a Parent or Family Member

A large proportion of the MISTRA twins (70.2 percent) were reared by an unrelated family. The remainder were raised in other circumstances, including biological or nonbiological caretakers or multiple placements with relatives or nonrelatives. Individuals who had multiple early place-

Table 2-7. **Reared-Apart Twins' Rearing Circumstances**

Rearing Circumstance	Percentage	Number (individuals)
Unrelated family	70.2	184
Biological mother	3.8	10
Biological father	1.5	4
Grandparents	0.8	2
Uncle/aunt	3.1	8
Multiple families (relatives)	1.5	4
Multiple families (nonrelatives)	5.3	14
Biological mother and father	2.7	7
Unrelated, stable by age 5	1.5	4
Multiple relatives, stable by age 5	.8	2
Multiple nonrelatives, stable by age 5	1.5	4
Complex case	7.3	19
Total	100.0	262

Note: Individuals in four triplet sets are each counted once.

Table 2-8.   Rearing Circumstances of Reared-Apart Twin Pairs Organized by Zygosity (Pair Data)

Rearing Circumstance	MZA		DZA	
	%	n (pairs)	%	n (pairs)
		81		56
Unrelated-unrelated	70.4	57	62.5	35
Related-related	7.4	6	5.4	3
Unrelated-related	14.8	12	12.5	7
Complex case–other	7.4	6	19.6	11

Note: Rearing categories in this table were collapsed across the specific biological and nonbiological rearing circumstances listed in Table 2-7.

ments with both relatives and nonrelatives or who had no primary care-takers were assigned as "complex" cases. These data are summarized in Table 2-7.

Some critics have claimed that the reared-apart twins' behavioral similarities are enhanced when co-twins are reared by biological relatives. However, those conducting the analyses have a different perspective on this question. In 1958, Shields, who was in the early stages of his own investigation, emphasized the advantages of having twins variously raised by related and unrelated families "because of the possibility for making internal comparisons."[27] (This issue is examined again in the next chapter.) The co-twins in most of our pairs were both reared by unrelated individuals (67.2 percent). The next most frequent arrangement was one in which one co-twin was reared by biological relatives and the other was reared by nonrelatives (13.9 percent), as shown in Table 2-8.

Family and Environmental Measures

The twins' family and environmental measures were gathered as part of the life history battery. Specific measures included the mean rearing parents' years of education, the highest occupational status attained by mothers and fathers, the twins' number of residences, and the presence of forty-one different physical facilities (e.g., a world atlas and a pet dog or cat) in the rearing home. The parents' highest occupational status was coded with the Duncan SEI system using the methods of Charles W. Mueller and Toby L. Parcel.[28] The largest percentage of fathers for whom information was available were managers, officials, proprietors/craft, and the largest percentage of mothers were homemakers. The occupational data are presented in Table 2-9 for the full sample of individual twins, organized by zygosity.

Another common criticism of the study was that similarities in the rearing home might largely explain the MZA twins' behavioral similarities.

Table 2-9. **Rearing Parents' Best Occupation (Duncan SEI) for MZA and DZA Twin Individuals**

| | Rearing Father | | | |
| | MZA | | DZA | |
Occupation	n	%	n	%
Professional/technical	29	20.1	9	9.2
Managers/officials/ proprietors	36	25.0	28	28.6
Clerical	8	5.6	7	7.1
Sales	5	3.4	4	4.1
Craft	35	24.3	28	28.6
Operatives	17	11.8	10	10.2
Service	7	4.9	1	1.0
Nonfarm labor	4	2.8	6	6.1
Farmer/farm manager	3	2.1	4	4.1
Farm laborer	—	—	1	1.0

| | Rearing Mother | | | |
| | MZA | | DZA | |
Occupation	n	%	n	%
Professional/technical	20	14.4	10	11.0
Managers/officials/ proprietors	8	5.8	10	11.0
Clerical	30	21.6	16	17.6
Sales	11	7.9	4	4.4
Craft	3	2.2	3	3.3
Operatives	18	12.9	11	12.1
Service	23	16.5	9	9.8
Nonfarm labor	1	0.7	—	—
Farmer/farm manager	1	0.7	—	—
Homemaker	24	17.3	28	30.8

Note: MZA females in two MZA/DZA triplet sets are entered as individuals in the MZA sample only. Data were incomplete for rearing parents in some cases.

We found that the percentages of pairs in which the co-twins' rearing parents held similar jobs were comparable for the MZA (rearing father: 20 percent, rearing mother: 24 percent) and DZA twins (rearing father: 17 percent, rearing mother: 20 percent). Therefore, if the parents' occupation did affect their children's intellect, the effect would be the same for both types of twins. Most importantly, however, for this criticism to be meaningful, it is first necessary to demonstrate that a specific home feature is trait-relevant. That is, a causal link between the parental occupation and the children's behavioral outcome (such as children reared by law-yers excel in verbal skills) must be demonstrated if the argument is to be taken seriously.

The Reared-Apart Twins' Reunion Circumstances

Information on how twins found each other was available for all but five pairs (four MZA and one DZA). Most twins (n = 99, 75.0 percent) lo-cated each other after one or both contacted adoption agencies, placed notices in the media, called names in telephone books, or visited old neighborhoods. Other events responsible for the twins' reunions in-cluded mistaken identity (n = 18, 13.6 percent) and family knowledge of the other twin (n = 13, 9.9 percent). The remainder (n = 2, 1.5 per-cent) met due to various other circumstances. For example, MZA twins Caroline and Margaret Shand met when they recognized each other at a church.

The Shands grew up just twenty miles apart in Scotland. Each knew that she had a twin, but each had been told not to ask questions about their birth. They were interested in one another, but they never searched. Then, at age sixty-four, Caroline was working in a church, and one day she heard a knock at the door. When she finally answered, the two visitors had walked to a nearby gravesite. Caroline approached them and saw herself in one of them. "Are you my sister?" she asked Margaret. They "hugged, laughed and, of course, cried."[29]

Shields, author of the 1962 British MZA twin study, assessed twins who had met under somewhat similar circumstances. MZA twin girls Jessie and Winifred were drawn to one another at age two, but their meetings were not encouraged by Jessie's family. The twins lived within a few hun-dred yards of one another, and when they became school friends at age five, Jessie's mother enrolled her daughter in a different school. At this juncture, the girls were told they were twins. When they turned eight, they ended up at the same school for administrative reasons, becoming Shields's youngest separated pair. Shields wondered if there might be a biological basis to MZA twins' attraction, "based on likeness . . . not just a matter of cultural attitudes to twins."[30]

Comment on Recruitment

Several recruitment examples are worth describing because they show that the more similar MZA twin pairs did not always participate in the MISTRA. One case concerned MZA female twins who were both extremely fearful of flying to Minneapolis from the East Coast. The twins declined Bouchard's offer to be driven to Minnesota by staff members or to have testers visit their homes. According to Bouchard, they looked "strikingly alike" and displayed the same "high stress reaction." A second example concerns an MZA male twin nearing retirement who initially declined our invitation. Bouchard visited the twin while traveling and learned that this individual had a heart problem that in his state was considered work-related and would earn him a higher retirement pension. If, however, the problem was found during the study and proved to be genetically linked, then his higher pension would be denied. We solved this situation by delaying the assessment until the twin's retirement was final, an option that had not been raised in previous communications. Thus, both participation and lack of participation by individuals could be explained in many ways.

Bouchard maintained a file of twins who were searching for their co-twins. Approximately eight twins had not been reunited with their twin brothers and sisters when the study ended.

The Assessment in Full

Once twins were scheduled for the assessment, they received a packet of materials with information about the study and a list of items to bring, such as adoption documents and childhood photographs. All travel and hotel expenses were covered by the project. Twins were also given a modest honorarium for miscellaneous expenses ($75.00 to $275.00), although various other costs such as child care, pet sitting, and up to $200 in lost wages were reimbursed directly. The project also paid for one individual (usually a spouse) to accompany twins to Minneapolis and to complete a short form of the psychological assessment.

Twins traveling to Minneapolis from the United States or Canada arrived the day before the study began (Saturday); twins traveling from other countries arrived two days earlier (Friday) so that they could recover from jet lag. Twins departed on the final day of the study or remained in the United States at their own expense.

By February 1980, nearly one year after the study began, the standard assessment schedule ("twin week") included five full days and two half-days. The first half day was a Sunday, and the second half-day was the following Saturday. One evening was set aside for sexual life history interviews for twins only.

Bouchard usually drove the twins from their hotel to the university on Sunday afternoon and escorted them to a large room (the "twin room") on the fourth floor of the Psychology Department, located in Elliott Hall.

Two or three assistants (myself included) would already be present, having prepared the test materials, inventory booklets, and refreshments. It was exciting—actually thrilling—-to meet the twins and to discover what they were really like.   .

We first reviewed the week-long schedule with the twins as part of the informed consent procedure. We encouraged them to complete all the medical and psychological tests we administered, but we assured them that they were free to decline any activity they preferred not to do. We explained to the twins that we wanted to keep the data as free from bias as possible so we asked them to refrain from discussing any of the tests or procedures with one another until they both had completed them. We also assured them that all the data we gathered from them would be kept confidential and that we would not release findings to their twin, spouse, or anyone else without their written consent.

Beginning on Monday, Bouchard or a staff member picked up the twins at their hotel each weekday morning at 7:45 and brought them back between 5:00 and 6:00 each night. Each participant's progress was recorded on a checklist that was updated continually (Figure 2-5). The schedule worked well because responsibilities and assigned times were decided in advance and were consistent across pairs.

Figure 2-5.   Bouchard updating the twins' checklist, May 1985. A pair of MZA male twins from Great Britain and their wives were undergoing assessment at the time. (Photo credit Nancy L. Segal.)

We examined the twins in testing rooms located in Elliott Hall, the building that housed the Psychology Department, and in the University of Minnesota's hospital complex. Time was set aside for completion of scheduled inventories and questionnaires that we had prepared and bound into four (later five) spiral notebooks (Psychological Batteries I–V). Twins completed these forms in Elliott Hall and in hospital lounges while waiting for medical appointments. It is estimated that of the 15,000 questions answered by the twins, 4,000 came from the inventory booklets. This number may seem high, but most twins completed the full battery during their assigned week; occasionally, twins took remaining questionnaires home and returned them by mail.

Journalists, writers, and television producers were often interested in interviewing twins. We always asked the twins in advance if they would agree to media coverage and we arranged this only with their consent. Actual data collection sessions were never filmed.

A complete annotated list of the psychological, physical, and medical tests appears on the Web site. Information on administration, results, and conclusions are provided in subsequent chapters as this research story unfolds.

Genetic Terminology

The field of human genetics has many terms and concepts, but only some require definition for the purposes of this book. Some terms will be defined as they occur in the text, and others are further explained in the Glossary. Individuals familiar with the genetics field and/or with quantitative genetic analysis may wish to skip the next two sections of this chapter.

Genes are the hereditary units that occupy a specific location (locus) on one of our twenty-three pairs of chromosomes. *Chromosomes* are the structures in the nucleus of each of our cells that contain our genetic material, or DNA. *DNA* stands for *deoxyribonucleic acid* and is the double-helical molecule that carries genetic information. Different forms of a gene at a certain locus are called *alleles*.

Each parent transmits 50 percent of his or her genes to each child. The egg and sperm (sex cells or gametes) each contain one copy of each of the twenty-three pairs of chromosomes; thus, each child has a maternal allele and a paternal allele at each locus. Full siblings (and DZ twins) have a 50 percent chance, on average, of sharing the same gene at a given locus. Some siblings (and DZ twins) will share over 50 percent of the same genes, and some will share less. This may depend upon chance, but it may also depend upon whether mothers and fathers match on genetically influenced traits *(assortative mating)*. Assortative mating can lead to greater than expected trait similarity among siblings and DZ twins. However, assortative mating will not affect trait similarity between MZ twins because they share 100 percent of their genes.

The *genotype* of an individual refers either to all the genes he or she carries or to the genes that are relevant for a specific trait that he or she carries. The *phenotype* refers to a measurable or observable trait. For example, a person with type A blood (phenotype) may carry either two genes coding for type A, or one gene coding for type A and one gene coding for type O (genotype). This is because the gene for type A blood is *dominant,* meaning that it is expressed regardless of other genes with which it is paired. The gene for type O blood is *recessive* because it is not expressed if paired with a dominant gene; people with type O blood must have two type O (recessive) alleles.

Close correspondence of genotypes and phenotypes does not always occur as it does in the blood type example given above. Some phenotypes may change depending upon the environment. A person who is allergic to penicillin will not show an adverse reaction unless he or she receives the medication. A person with a tendency toward weight gain may add or lose pounds depending upon his or her diet and exercise.

Discrete traits are those that are affected by genes at one location, or locus, on a chromosome. Discrete traits include the major blood groups (A, B, or O), phenylketonuria (an inborn error of metabolism), and Huntington disease (a lethal condition linked to a specific gene on chromosome 4). Such traits have been called "either-or" traits because either you have them or you do not. In contrast, *continuous traits* (also called *polygenic* or *biometrical traits*) are those associated with many genes on different chromosomes. Examples include verbal ability, running speed, and body weight. These traits differ from either-or traits because everyone (within the normal range of human development) has verbal ability, can run, and has weight. The different values of these traits, representing fluency, quickness, and size, form a population distribution along which each individual is located.

Some traits (continuous or discrete) are affected by *epistasis* or interaction between several genes at different loci (chromosomal locations). An example in humans is the Bombay phenotype in which individuals lack a protein called the H antigen. Such individuals will show the type O blood phenotype even if they carry type A genes.[31] Epistasis is likely to reduce full sibling and DZ twin resemblance because the odds that a second sibling (or DZ twin) will inherit the same multiple gene combination as his or her co-sibling (or co-twin) is slim (25 percent for the same maternal allele *and* the same paternal allele at a given locus, but less for multiple alleles at different loci). This also explains why MZ twin resemblance for complex polygenic traits (those involving many different genes) should be high, and full sibling and DZ twin resemblance should be relatively low. MZ twins inherit 100 percent of the same genes and, consequently, all their unusual gene combinations, whereas DZ twins inherit 50 percent of the same genes, on average, by descent.

Lykken introduced the term *emergenesis* to describe complex traits that show large resemblance differences between MZ and DZ twin pairs (i.e., when the DZ twin correlation is less than half the MZ twin correlation). Emergenesis can be considered a grand version of epistasis; it is discussed further in Chapter 9. Epistasis and emergenesis are likely to reduce parent-child resemblance in some traits because the gene combinations underlying these traits in the parental generation become disentangled in the children's generation.

Quantitative Analyses

The MISTRA and other twin studies use *intraclass correlations* and *biometrical modeling* to assess genetic and environmental contributions to trait variation (individual differences). These terms are used throughout the book in conjunction with the specific analyses. Additional details about the different procedures are available in behavioral genetics textbooks[32] and twin methods manuals.[33]

Correlations express the extent to which two measures vary or change with one another. Correlations vary from −1.0 to +1.0, with 1.0 indicating a perfect positive relationship, −1.0 indicating a perfect negative relationship, and 0.0 indicating no relationship at all. For example, traditionally the number of candles on our birthday cakes go up by one for every year that we age. The correlation between candles and age would be positive (and 1.0) since they both change in the same direction and by constant amounts. In another example, the weight of one's clothing is likely to go down as the outside temperature increases. The correlation between clothing weight and temperature would, therefore, be negative because these measures are changing in opposite directions. The correlation for these two measures might conceivably be −0.80. The relationship between them might not yield a perfect correlation because some people wear protective hats and scarves in the sun, thereby adding weight, and because changes in the two probably do not occur at a constant rate.

Some measures show no relationship—that is, both may increase or decrease in ways that are unrelated to each other. For example, it is unlikely that height and hair color are related in a meaningful way. Tall and short people are probably equally likely to have dark or light hair.

Ordinary correlations that express the relationships between two measures, as in the examples, are not ideal for assessing twin similarity. For one thing, twin (and sibling) similarity is concerned with the agreement in the same test or inventory given to two different people. In addition, twin researchers are interested in finding the amount of trait variation that is shared between co-twins. This can be accomplished by using a special type of correlation called the intraclass correlation. *Intraclass correlations* (r_i) express the ratio of the between-pair variation (differences among twin pairs) to the total variation (differences among twin pairs plus differences within twin pairs). These types of correlations are calculated separately for MZA and DZA twin pairs and compared. Relatively greater differences between pairs yield higher intraclass correlations, reflecting greater resemblance within pairs. Relatively lower differences between pairs yield lower intraclass correlations, reflecting reduced resemblance within pairs.

Suppose that the members of twin pair A in one group obtained IQ scores of 100 and 105, and the members of twin pair B obtained scores of 125 and 120. Next, suppose that the members of twin pairs C and D in a second group obtained IQ scores of 100 and 105, and 102 and 107, respectively. In both groups, the average within-pair difference is 5. However, in the first group the co-twins in each pair score closer to each other than they do to the members of the other pair. Here, the between-pair differences would be high relative to the within-pair differences, yielding a high intraclass correlation. However, in the second group, the co-twins score closer to the members of the other pair than they do to their own co-twin. Here, the between-pair differences would be low relative to the within-pair differences, yielding a lower intraclass correlation than found for the first group. Of course, researchers would calculate intraclass correlations using much larger samples!

Genetic effects on a trait are demonstrated when MZ (or MZA) intraclass correlations exceed DZ (or DZA) intraclass correlations.[34] Emergenic effects would be suggested when the DZ (or DZA) intraclass correlation is less than half the size of the MZ (or MZA) intraclass correlation.

Two other concepts—genotype by environment interaction and genotype-environment correlation—are important to think about with reference to twins reared apart. *Genotype × environment interaction* (G × E) means that how the environment affects a phenotype depends on the genotype. For example, strenuous activity (environment) may strengthen the body (phenotype), but the resulting strength will vary with individuals' general body build (genotype). And if one basically fit MZA twin was reared in a home emphasizing a healthy diet and his or her co-twin was reared in a family that feasted on junk food, both twins might still end up with similar health histories because the twin with the poorer diet may have been resistant to the effects of the diet and other adverse environmental conditions—up to a point.

Genotype-environment correlation (G-E) refers to associations between individuals' genes and environments, of which there are three types. *Passive G-E* involves parental transmission of both genes and environments to children. Musically gifted parents might transmit both genes and environments conducive to musical talent to their children. *Reactive (evocative) G-E* involves reactions to individuals based on their expressed behaviors. The teachers of bright MZA twins might be likely to provide them with intellectually stimulating activities. *Active G-E* involves individuals' seeking out opportunities that support their interests and talents. Sports-minded MZA twins might independently seek opportunities to practice their skills. Passive G-E would apply to MZT twins but not to MZA twins who are reared apart. However, teachers might react the same way to two bright MZA twins despite their separate rearing. And two musically talented MZA co-twins might both seek opportunities to perform even in very different environments.

The reared-apart twin study by Newman, Freeman, and Holzinger illustrates another important interpretive issue regarding differences within and between pairs. The MZA r_{is} for the Binet IQ score was 0.67, indicating substantial genetic influence.[35] Thus, the MZA co-twins were more like their co-twins in IQ than they were like the members of the other pairs. At the same time, the ordinary correlation expressing the relationship (within pairs) of the co-twins' IQ differences and their educational differences was 0.79. This meant either that (1) the higher scoring twin had had more schooling or better schooling than his or her co-twin, or (2) the higher scoring twin had sought out more educational experiences. Some people have interpreted the second result as discounting genetic effects on IQ, but this is a mistake because the co-twins in each pair were generally more similar to one another than they were to the members of the other pairs.

People differ across traits due to the genetic and environmental differences among them. *Heritability* is the proportion of population differences in intelligence, height, or running speed that is associated with genetic differences among the members of a population. To say that running speed has a 33 percent heritability in ten-year-old females means that about one-third of the population differences in that trait are explained by the genetic differences among the young female members.[36] It does not mean that one-third of a particular young girl's running speed is associated with her genes. Heritability does not refer to individuals for whom genes and environments are inextricably intertwined.

Heritability tends to go up when people's trait-relevant environments are more uniform: when environments are alike, the differences between people are more closely tied to their genetic differences. Conversely, heritability tends to go down when people's trait-relevant environments are more variable: when environments differ, the differences between people can reflect these effects. (This is what makes MZA twins' similarities striking.) Furthermore, heritability estimates characterize only a particular population at a particular point in time, so they cannot be generalized to other populations. The heritability of a trait can also change depending upon the environment, although some traits are more resistant to change than others. A healthier, more uniform diet can increase the average height of a population—in doing so it could also increase the heritability of height because individuals' height differences would more closely reflect the genetic differences among them. The extent to which individual differences in a trait are explained by genetic and environmental factors can be estimated using the biometrical techniques described later in this section.

There are two types of heritability: narrow and broad. *Narrow heritability* is associated with genes that work in an additive fashion. *Additive genetic variation* refers to the independent effects of genes adding up to produce a given trait. In other words, the genetic effect is a simple summation—one gene does not affect the expression of other genes. If the effect of one allele is "1" and the effect of the other allele is "1," the total effect is "2." Additive genes are responsible for most of the genetic resemblance between family members. *Nonadditive genes* are those that interact with one another and may involve two genes (dominance), several genes (epistasis), or many genes (emergenesis). In other words, they do not add up. MZ twins share their nonadditive genes; recall that DZ twins and siblings have a 25 percent chance of inheriting the same paternal and maternal alleles (at a given locus) as their co-twin or co-sibling, but less chance of sharing alleles across many loci.

Broad heritability is associated with all sources of genetic effects (additive and nonadditive). The MZA intraclass correlation directly estimates broad heritability because MZA twins share all their genes but do not share their rearing environment.[37] In other words, MZA co-twins have only their genes in common, so their observed similarities reflect their shared genes. The DZA intraclass correlation directly estimates half the heritability because DZA twins share 50 percent of their genes, on average;

therefore, doubling the DZA correlation also estimates broad heritability. This calculation assumes that there is no assortative mating—if there were, the DZ twins' increased resemblance would reduce heritability because their degree of similarity would be closer to that of MZ twins.

Narrow heritability refers only to additive genetic effects. It can be indirectly estimated by calculating the difference between the MZT r_i and the DZT r_i and doubling the difference ($2[\text{MZT } r_i - \text{DZT } r_i]$), known as Falconer's formula.[38] Based on a survey of many studies, the overall MZT r_i for IQ is 0.86, and the DZ r_i is 0.60.[39] The IQ heritability would then be equal to $2(0.86 - 0.60)$ or 0.52. Falconer's formula may overestimate narrow heritability in the presence of nonadditive genetic variance.

Intraclass correlations can be interpreted as causal because twins are experiments of nature (individuals who share 100 percent of their genes or share 50 percent of their genes, on average) and experiments of society (rearing together in the biological family or rearing apart in a nonbiological family).[40] For example, both MZT and DZT twins share their rearing environment, but DZT twins share half as many genes, on average. Thus, higher MZ than DZ intraclass correlations demonstrate genetic influence on a trait. MZA and MZT twins both share 100 percent of their genes, but only MZT twins share their rearing environment. IF MZA and MZT twins show the same degree of resemblance for a trait, this shows that sharing a family environment does not make family members alike.

Age- and sex-corrections, statistical procedures for removing the effects of age and sex on a trait, have been applied in virtually all the MISTRA's data analyses. MZ twins and approximately two-thirds of DZ co-twins are the same age and sex, factors that can inflate trait similarity between them just as it would between two unrelated people who are both twenty and both female. The age- and sex-adjustment procedures used in the MISTRA have been described by McGue and Bouchard.[41] Briefly, test scores are corrected for the effects of age, sex, age^2, $age \times sex$, and $age^2 \times sex$, and analyses are performed on the residuals (the values remaining after the various age and sex effects are removed).

Most of the MISTRA's heritability analyses used biometrical modeling techniques as well as intraclass correlations. The simple comparison of the MZ (or MZA) and DZ (or DZA) intraclass correlations is an important first step in behavioral-genetic analysis because this demonstrates whether or not there is genetic influence on the trait. *Biometrical modeling,* developed since the 1970s, is a more informative approach to understanding the origins of a trait because it allows genetic and environmental factors affecting traits to be estimated simultaneously. The genetic component can be subdivided into additive variance and nonadditive genetic variance, as we saw earlier, whereas the environmental component can be subdivided into shared and nonshared environmental effects. *Shared environmental effects* are the common events or experiences that lead to similarities between family members. For example, siblings in a family share meals, so they might develop similar tastes in food. *Nonshared environmental factors* are events or experiences that affect only one person in a family, making that person different from his or her relatives. If one sibling took piano lessons and the other sibling took acting lessons, their musical and theatrical abilities might diverge.

Biometrical methods can test how well a model fits a given set of data. *Model fit* refers to the discrepancy between the actual data (observed values) and the results implied by the model (expected values). The simplest such models assume that shared genes underlie similarity between relatives, mating occurs at random (is not assortative), genetic effects are additive, genetic and environmental effects are independent from each other, and genetic and environmental effects combine additively.

Additive genetic effects, nonadditive genetic effects, and shared environmental effects cannot be estimated simultaneously with only MZT and DZT twin pairs.[42] Fortunately, multiple kinships such as reared-apart and reared-together twins, or twin families consisting of twins, their parents, and/or their children can be incorporated into the same biometrical model, leading to improved estimates of genetic and environmental effects. Investigators can compare the fit of several models and decide, for example, if a model that includes genetic and nonshared environmental components fits the data better than a model that also includes a shared environmental component. Random error measurement is often considered as a nonshared environmental effect, but with appropriate data can be modeled separately as well.

The early researchers of reared-apart twins did not have the benefit of the latest sophisticated analytical techniques that were developed over the last several decades. These methodological tools are among the most important contributions made by behavioral geneticists to the fields of psychology and medicine.

Beyond the Laboratories

The human interest of the reunited twins extended beyond their similarities and differences. An especially satisfying part of each assessment week was watching the twins' social relationships evolve. Many lives changed for the better once the twins met and became better acquainted. Sixty-four-year-old Scottish twins Margaret and Caroline Shand, both unmarried, became friends and housemates. Thirty-nine-year-old British twins Elaine Alin and Mary Holmes became close companions and confidantes, especially when Elaine developed breast cancer. Thirty-two-year-old bachelors and firefighters Mark Newman and Jerry Levey swapped firehouse stories over Budweiser beers, each placing a pinky finger underneath the can. And Tony and Roger enjoyed an all-you-can-eat pizza entrée for the price of one—these tall, dark-haired, food- and fun-loving twins pretended to be the same person until a waitress baffled by the number of "seconds" requested by her patron refused to bring more.

CHAPTER THREE

Early Findings (1979–1983)

Almost any experiment that one might think of doing with
human subjects will be more interesting and yield more valuable
results if one does it with twins.

    —David Lykken

Our First Findings

The third International Congress on Twin Studies, held in Jerusalem,
Israel, in 1980, was an opportunity to present preliminary findings from
the MISTRA and to introduce the study to twin research colleagues from
around the world. The first two presentations in Jerusalem were largely
qualitative in nature, quite different from the quantitative treatment of
the data as the sample grew. These early cases suggested that possible
life-history factors were associated with the co-twins' differences in selected behaviors. For example, twins in one MZA pair did not share their
fear of snakes, a difference traceable to one twin having been bitten as a
child. Periods of heavy drinking were reported by just one twin in several
pairs, an apparent response to major situational stress. Both behavioral
similarities and differences were of interest, and helped to identify topics
for future study.

A paper co-authored by Bouchard and colleagues described the impe-
tus for the project (the discovery of the Jim twins) and outlined a sample
assessment schedule with descriptions of inventories and interviews.[1]
Some developmental findings and other life-history data were captured
in several illustrative cases. These observations, as they were reported
during the project's earliest stages in 1980, follow. I have presented two
of these cases to illustrate how data were compiled when the project
began, before it transitioned from a small series of reared-apart pairs to
the MISTRA. This change will become clearer as the story of the study
is told.

Case 1. MZA males, age 23, separated at age 5 days, and reunited at
   age 22 years.[2]
- Both twins were overweight until junior high school, then
  became quite thin.
- Both twins were openly and actively homosexual prior to
  meeting.
- Both twins had speech problems for which they, respectively,
  received therapy in kindergarten and grade school.
- Both twins were diagnosed with hyperactivity in kindergarten or
  first grade.

Case 2. MZA females, age 57, separated at age 6 weeks, and reunited
   at age 10 years.[3]
- Both twins had experienced enuresis (bed-wetting) until age 12 to
  13 years.
- Both twins had nightmares beginning in their teens, lasting for 10
  to 12 years. The dream content included doorknobs and fish-
  hooks in their mouths and feelings of being smothered.
- The twins had similar marital and educational backgrounds.

The twins' similarities in complex behaviors, such as temperamental
traits, sexual orientation, speech problems, and nightmares, were not expected by Bouchard and the others. "Having been familiar with the literature on the heritability of temperament, we were not ready for what we
found."[4] The lack of methods for capturing these observations quantitatively and objectively placed a limit on evaluating these early findings.
Therefore, one of our future goals was to try to explain these behaviors
with reference to specific features of each twin's rearing circumstances,
such as their parental relationships, educational opportunities, and home
atmosphere.

In the absence of clear rules or guidelines, deciding what constitutes
co-twin concordance (resemblance) versus discordance (nonresemblance)
for some traits can be difficult and somewhat subjective. We observed
differences between MZA co-twins, but they appeared mostly as "variations on a theme," suggesting quantitative rather than qualitative discrepancies. One twin might appear less extraverted, fearful, or fastidious
than his or her co-twin but still display some level of that trait. Designa-
tions of the MZA co-twins as extraverted-introverted, fearful-fearless, or
fastidious-untidy were, therefore, less likely. This dilemma, which occasionally confronts all twin investigators, was revisited by Len Heston in
November 2009 during my interview with him at his home in Palm Springs,
California.

Heston coauthored our controversial 1986 paper on the reared-apart twins' sexual orientation, which included six twin sets. One MZA male pair was especially vexing to categorize. One twin was very open about being gay—he had had two brief heterosexual encounters in his late teens before becoming exclusively homosexual at age nineteen. He went on to have sexual contact with seven men, one for a prolonged period of time. In contrast, his co-twin regarded himself as exclusively heterosexual. He was married and had four children, but he had had an affair with an older man between the ages of fifteen and eighteen before having his first heterosexual experience with his future wife at age twenty.

Heston speculated that the twins' rearing circumstances might have affected their sexual identities and behaviors. The first twin was raised in a large city where opportunities for sexual diversity were available and relatively acceptable. The second twin grew up in a small farming community in which homosexuality was probably highly stigmatized, making him more sexually restrained. "I still don't know how to count this [pair]," Heston admitted. Classifying individuals as gay or straight, autistic or nonautistic, or schizophrenic or nonschizophrenic depends on the diagnostic criteria (strict, intermediate, or broad) that the individual in question must meet. Knowing that someone has an affected identical twin can potentially bias this process. Therefore, professional judgments of behavior are ideally made by several individuals who are blind to the twin status of the person in question. One of the famous Genain quadruplets, studied at the National Institute of Mental Health in the early 1960s, might not have been diagnosed as schizophrenic if not for her more severely affected sisters.[5] A firm decision about the sexual classification of the reared-apart male twin pair previously described was never made. I will say more about our sexual behavior studies later.

The second MISTRA paper presented in Jerusalem described preliminary findings of psychiatric traits among the first fifteen MZA twin pairs (seven female and eight male).[6] The twins ranged in age from sixteen to fifty-seven years. Each twin was interviewed separately, one on Monday afternoon and the other on Tuesday afternoon, by psychiatrists Heston and Eckert in sessions lasting from one and a half to three hours. The interview followed a semistructured format, but Heston and Eckert posed additional questions about specific issues that the twins described. This procedure changed to a structured format in 1982 following our decision to administer the Diagnostic Interview Schedule to each co-twin by different psychiatrists.

Our early analysis revealed similarities in psychiatric traits among some pairs, but it was not uncommon for one twin to be more severely affected than his or her co-twin. Sample findings based on three pairs are presented in Table 3-1 as they appeared in the original publication. Collectively, we observed that MZA co-twin differences in psychiatric traits often show quantitative versus qualitative variation. Statistical analyses of the psychiatric data did not occur until 1990 when the reared-apart twin sample was larger.

The MISTRA participants were not clinical referrals. Years later, Eckert recalled that "there was not much that was striking in the medical or psychiatric interviews—these were ordinary people who probably represented the larger general population [with respect to psychiatric symptoms]." None of the twins showed eating disorders (anorexia or bulimia), Eckert's area of expertise. A similar view was also voiced by periodontist Bryan Michalowicz, who detected little advanced gum disease in the twins.

Most of the MISTRA twins were adoptees, for whom many studies suggest a higher rate of behavioral problems relative to nonadoptees.[7] However, recent work is revising this view. Several studies have reported that adoptees may be at only slightly greater risk for behavioral disorders than nonadoptees, and may even score more favorably in some problem areas (such as social difficulties).[8] Regardless, the extent to which the reared-apart twins represented the greater population was important to consider if the results were to be generalized. This topic will be addressed further in coming chapters.

Bouchard presented a third, solely authored paper at the Jerusalem twin conference.[9] It was not about the MISTRA specifically, but some of his points were relevant to the project. Bouchard argued that general intelligence is *the* major mental ability underlying a variety of mental ability tests, although he recognized the presence of special mental skills such as perceptual speed and spatial visualization. As such, he favored using the Wechsler Adult Intelligence Scale (WAIS) over the Raven Progressive Matrices as a general ability measure. (The WAIS consists of six verbal and five nonverbal or performance subtests, whereas the Raven is a nonverbal test of problem-solving ability and thus is less comprehensive.)

Bouchard also supported using multiple measures of general and special skills in behavioral genetic studies, especially the MISTRA. He decided to have the reared-apart twins complete two general intelligence measures (WAIS and Raven/Mill-Hill composite) plus two special mental ability batteries (Hawaii Ability Battery and Comprehensive Ability Battery). This approach would allow assessment of the stability or consistency of participant behavior, thereby increasing confidence in the findings.

The climate surrounding genetic studies of IQ in general, and reared-apart twin studies in particular, was highly contentious. Throughout the 1970s, university faculty members who presented such topics in their

Table 3-1. Preliminary Summary of Psychiatric Traits in Three MZA Twin Pairs

Pair	Twin	Age	Sex	Alcohol, Drug Abuse	Fears, Phobias	Speech Problem	Enuresis (bed-wetting)	Other Psychiatric Traits
5	A	35	F		+		+	Adjustment reaction with anxious mood
	B				+		++	Same as above
10	A	16	M			+	+	Emotionally stable
	B					+	++	Moody, nervous, sociopathic traits, hyperactive
13	A	24	M		+			Emotionally stable
	B				+			Emotionally stable

+ = Abnormality present; ++ = Abnormality more pronounced.

Source: Adapted from Elke D. Eckert et al. (1981), "MZ Twins Reared Apart: Preliminary Findings of Psychiatric Disturbances and Traits," in *Twin Research 3: Part B. Intelligence, Personality and Development*, ed. Luigi Gedda, Paolo Parisi, and Walter Nance, 179–188 (New York: Alan R. Liss, Inc., 1981).

classes were subject to ridicule, even harassment. "Fire Bouchard" had been painted on the outside of a building close to Elliott Hall.[10] The campus newspaper referenced the attack on Bouchard from the Students for a Democratic Society in an editorial defending freedom of speech on campus.[11] Bouchard persisted in teaching and in researching these topics, as did many of his colleagues.[12]

The 1974 Behavior Genetics Association meeting in Minneapolis organized an impromptu session in which four members (including Bouchard) discussed their experiences teaching behavioral genetics concepts and findings as they applied to IQ. Once behavioral genetics entered the mainstream of psychology in the 1980s, there was less need for such events, although evidence of genetic influence on intelligence was still challenged.[13] However, a planned 1992 conference on genetics and criminality was forced to reschedule in 1995 due to protests over possible misuse of the findings.[14]

Constructive Replication: Challenges to Reared-Apart Twin Research

The MISTRA's inclusion of multiple measures of general intelligence allowed attempts at *constructive replication*, a concept developed by Lykken.[15] Constructive replications are efforts to confirm findings when one or more conditions of the original experiment or analysis differ, such as the specific test or the participant sample. Such replications may be conducted by the original researcher or by an independent investigator.

In 1980, Princeton University sociologist Howard Taylor published *The IQ Game*, in which he reanalyzed IQ data from the three previous reared-apart twin studies.[16] Taylor was interested in whether MZA co-twins were more alike in intelligence if they were separated after 6 months, reunited prior to testing, reared by biological relatives, and/or raised in similar environments. Based on his analysis of the reared-apart twin data from the three early studies, Taylor concluded that genes contributed little to individual differences in measured general intelligence.[17]

Taylor's conclusion was stunning, coming as it did in the midst of the IQ debate over whether, and to what extent, genes affect mental ability. It turned out that the studies by Newman and colleagues and Juel-Nielsen had included a second major general intelligence measure. In 1983, Bouchard applied Taylor's criteria for partitioning the early reared-apart pairs according to separation, rearing, reunion, and contact, but with reference to the alternative general intelligence measure. Bouchard was unable to replicate Taylor's findings—time of separation, age at reunion, relatedness of rearing relatives, and environmental similarities were unrelated to IQ.[18]

In 1981, clinical psychologist Susan L. Farber continued Taylor's thesis that increased contact should lead to increased MZA IQ resemblance.[19] Her book was both highly acclaimed and solidly rejected by many in the field, a good reflection of the intense divisiveness on questions concerning the genetic basis of ability and the soundness of twin methodology.[20] As was true of Taylor, Farber's views are still embraced by critics of twin methodology, despite the available data that challenge those views.[21] However, her book remains a useful compendium of reared-apart twin data organized into chapters covering intelligence, personality, psychopathology, and physical complaints.

As recently as 2007, statistics professor Jack Kaplan, in a 2007 letter to the *New York Review of Books,* raised many of the same objections as Taylor.[22] Author and science historian Frank Sulloway responded, "[Kaplan] seems unaware that these issues have all been addressed empirically during the last two decades and are no longer regarded as 'highly questionable.' "[23] A more recent challenge to twin studies of IQ heritability appeared in a 2009 book by University of Michigan psychology professor Richard Nisbett.[24] Nisbett claimed, "The direct estimate of heritability based on the correlation between the IQs of identical twins reared apart makes a tacit assumption that is surely false—namely, that the twins were placed in environments at random."[25] Nisbett's other objection, that MZ twins' shared intrauterine environment enhances their behavioral similarity, is also raised frequently.[26] In fact, adversities posed by MZ twins' common prenatal environment more often have the opposite effect.[27] That is, MZ twins experiencing shared blood supply, fetal crowding, or other unfavorable circumstances are likely to differ in size and health.[28]

The finding that some reared-apart twins may have had similar rearing environments does *not* negate the notion of random placement. In fact, the expectation is that some co-twins *would* be reared in similar environments if placement were truly random. The MISTRA twins did not meet strict requirements for complete randomization of placement, but their environments were far less alike than those of twins reared together. Our analyses showed mostly negligible placement effects on the different traits and on co-twin resemblance in these traits.

Furthermore, many twin and adoption studies show that common rearing contributes only modestly to intellectual development and only during childhood. I found that forty-three virtual twin pairs (same-age unrelated children, raised together since infancy who mimic twinship but without any genetic link) showed an IQ correlation of 0.30 at age 5.1 years, and a correlation of 0.11 at age 10.7 years.[29] Other research has shown that the IQ correlation for different-aged adoptive siblings approaches 0.00 when they reach adolescence.[30]

The MISTRA at Age Two

In the year 1981, data had been gathered on fourteen reared-apart twin pairs and two reared-apart triplet sets. The first quantitative analysis of MZA twin data was presented at the eleventh annual meeting of the Behavior Genetics Association, held at the State University of New York in Purchase. That paper described the twins' information processing battery, discussed the twins' similarities in these measures, and contrasted them with similarities on a comparable psychometric battery.[31] (An expanded version of this paper, published in 1984, is discussed in the next chapter.) Twenty-four MZA twin pairs had been assessed when the conference took place, so, with only one interesting exception in 1990, the case studies from the MISTRA were replaced by statistical presentations of grouped data.

The year 1982 continued the transition from case descriptions to quantitative summaries of early findings, mostly embedded in empirical papers, review articles, and book chapters as the number of reared-apart twin pairs increased. Early findings on IQ and on the clinical and content scales of the Minnesota Multiphasic Personality Inventory (MMPI) were presented at the 1982 Behavior Genetics Association meeting in Ft. Collins, Colorado. These results relied on small samples, but they started a trend that evolved into a more stable pattern of genetic effects.[32] Many of our early findings also came from Lykken's psychophysiological laboratory.

Lykken's Laboratory

David Lykken's 1981 presidential address to the Society for Psychophysiological Research was a comprehensive overview of reared-together twin studies that included preliminary findings from the MISTRA.[33] Putting these different sources of data in the same tables provided hints as to how much genes and shared environments affected behavioral variation. Lykken began by summarizing age, age at separation, and age at reunion for the three previous twin studies and the MISTRA, as shown in Table 3-2. By 1982, our MZA sample was second in size only to Shields's. Twins in the MISTRA were separated earlier and reunited later, on average, than those in the other three studies.

The MZA and MZT correlations for fingerprint ridge count and for height, shown in Table 3-3, were quite similar, and both were much higher than the corresponding DZT correlations. These data conformed to predictions based on a model in which the genetic effects reflect the adding

Table 3-2.   The Four Major Studies of MZA Twins Reared Apart

Study	Age When Studied	Age at Separation	Age at Reunion
Newman et al. (1937), n=19	26.1	1.6	12.5
Shields (1962), n = 44	38.8	1.4	11.0
Juel-Nielsen (1965), n = 12	51.4	1.5	15.9
MISTRA, n = 30	36.1	0.3	23.9

Source: Adapted from Lykken, "Research with Twins: The Concept of Emergenesis," *Psychophysiology* 19 (1981): 361–373.

Table 3-3.   Intraclass Correlations for Three Anthropometric Variables (1982)

Variables	DZT (n = 146)	MZT (n = 274)	MZA (n = 30)
Fingerprint ridge count	0.46	0.96	0.98
Height	0.50	0.93	0.94
Weight	0.43	0.83	0.51

Note: The reared-apart twins' height, weight, and fingerprint data were gathered in David Lykken's laboratory. Height, weight, and fingerprints were also gathered in Thomas Bouchard's laboratory; and height and weight were additionally measured during the general physical examination. The handprints that were also obtained in Lykken's laboratory are not presented here.

Source: Adapted from Lykken, "Research with Twins: The Concept of Emergenesis," *Psychophysiology* 19 (1981): 361–373.

up of many genes. In contrast, the .51 heritability estimate for weight, based on the MZA twins' weight correlation (a direct estimate of heritability), was considerably lower than the 0.80 heritability estimate resulting from doubling the difference between the MZT and DZT intraclass correlations. This finding suggested possible violation of the equal environments assumption,[34] but, as I have indicated, the equal environments assumption has been upheld in most twin studies.[35] The discrepancy between the MZA and MZT correlations suggested that weight is affected by shared environmental factors.

The most important feature of our early findings was that they were generally similar to those from reared-together twin studies. We found this to be very encouraging because our twins were not gathered systematically as were most twins in the reared-together studies. Bouchard pointed out that because the MISTRA participants were chosen as they were it was "crucial" to show that they were not aberrant on any measures, relative to twins from other studies.[36] We were also able to show that the MZA and MZT twins were comparable for the electroencephalogram (EEG) parameters (brain wave spectra) that we measured.

Each twin spent three to four hours in Lykken's psychophysiology laboratory. Both twins arrived at Lykken's laboratory on a Monday afternoon for individual and joint photographs. Lykken liked taking his own pictures because he enjoyed studying the twins' physical features in detail, and anyone who visited Lykken's laboratory will recall the rows of matched faces, eyes, and ears that decorated his walls, appearing on the wall opposite his photographs of the reared-apart pairs. (This compelling display is reproduced in Figure 3-1.) However, only one twin was assessed on Monday afternoon; the second twin, who was studied the following day, was escorted to the University of Minnesota hospital complex for medical and psychiatric interviews. Findings did not differ between twins as a function of their order of assessment.

A significant component of Lykken's assessment was the EEG readings.[37] Some earlier work, including a 1974 study by Lykken, showed a genetic influence on EEG spectra, but little data were available on twins in general and very little on separated pairs.[38] Twins in just one of Shields's sets had been tested, and both showed the same spike and wave patterns, despite their discordance for epilepsy. Nine of Juel-Nielsen's pairs had been tested and showed "complete concordance."[39]

Lykken used a six-channel polygraph to record the EEG data from each twin. Five channels were dedicated to brain wave recording from the occipital lobes and at the temporal lobes. The sixth channel was used to remove eyeblink artifacts from the EEG recordings.[40] Participants sat alone in a shielded booth. A resting EEG was taken for the first five minutes while the twin sat quietly with eyes closed. Next, twins listened to five minutes of jazz music, followed by a Shafer auditory event-related

Figure 3-1. Reared-apart twins' eyes and ears. (Photographs by David Lykken.)

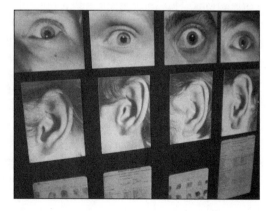

potential[41] and a visual event-related potential. (Event-related potentials are brain activities during cognitive processing.) A five-minute resting EEG was recorded again at the end of the session.

The data were examined for four parameters characterizing the EEG spectrum. The four parameters were defined by the mean activity within each of the classic EEG frequency bands: delta, theta, alpha, and beta. A fifth parameter, known as phi, is the median frequency of alpha activity. These measures were obtained at the start and at the end of each session.

The EEG data for the first four measures generally suggested a simple additive model because the DZT correlations (0.30–0.50, n = 53) were approximately half the size of the MZT (0.72–0.86, n = 89) and MZA (0.61–0.93, n = 25) correlations. The mean correlations for the four classic parameters were .40, .81, and .81 for the DZT, MZT, and MZA twin pairs, respectively. The exception was phi, which Lykken explained by emergenesis (the effects of multiple genes on complex traits), due to the marked correlational difference between the DZT twins (0.13) and both the MZT (0.81) and MZA (0.89) twins. The MZA EEG data mimicked the MZT EEG data, showing that the two groups were comparable on this measure.

Bill Iacono, University of Minnesota Regents Professor of Psychology and Lykken's former colleague, believes that Lykken's 1982 published address had a real impact on the way psychophysiologists thought about their measures at that time. That is because his findings drew attention to a heritable component that was difficult to ignore. Iacono was less enthusiastic about the lasting influence of the actual EEG findings because the methods used today are quite different—today one would apply multivariate imaging techniques.

Lykken's psychophysiological assessment also included studies of electrodermal response (skin conductance after exposure to a series of auditory stimuli). He presented only brief descriptive MZA findings in his 1982 paper—we are told that of the twenty-seven MZA twin pairs who were tested, only four pairs showed discordant electrodermal habituation curves. A more comprehensive analysis of these data, based on a larger twin sample, was completed by Lykken in 1988 and is discussed in Chapter 6.[42]

Another component of Lykken's test battery (that allowed constructive replication within the project) was the Raven Progressive Matrices and Mill-Hill. Both tests were administered by a PDP-12 computer as untimed ("power") tests.[43] Their sum yielded a separate IQ estimate, based on norms from over 130 twin pairs (Table 3-4).

Table 3-4.   Intraclass Correlations for the Raven and Mill-Hill Intelligence Tests for Reared-Apart and
Reared-Together Twin Pairs

Intelligence Measures	MZA (n = 29)	MZT (n = 71)	DZT (n = 42)
Raven	0.58	0.66	0.19
Mill-Hill	0.78	0.74	0.37
IQ (R + M)	0.71	0.78	0.14
Raven/Time	0.64	0.72	0.39
Mill-Hill/Time	0.71	0.76	0.49
IQ(R/T + M/T)	0.71	0.80	0.39

Source: Adapted from Lykken, "Research with Twins: The Concept of Emergenesis,"
Psychophysiology 19 (1981): 361–373.

The MZA correlations did not differ substantially from the MZT
correlations, and both exceeded the DZT correlations. The composite IQ
(R + M), like the Raven, produced DZT correlations that were much less
than half the MZA and MZT correlations, suggesting emergenic effects.[44]
The Raven and composite IQ scores, when converted to "rate-of-processing"
scores by dividing each twin's score by their average response time, produced correlations consistent with an additive genetic model.

These data showed that the MZA twins were not atypical in general
mental ability compared with the MZT twins. The MZA twin sample was
small at this stage in the study, but the 0.71 composite IQ correlation
would remain stable as we tested new pairs and replicated findings from
the three early reared-apart twin studies.

Auke Tellegen, one of the primary MISTRA investigators, had spent
twelve years, from 1970 to 1982, devising the Differential Personality
Questionnaire. This form (now the Multidimensional Personality Questionnaire) yielded scores for eleven personality traits. A full analysis will
be presented later, but an early look at selected scales suggested that social potency (forceful and persuasive versus letting others take charge)
and positive affect (well-being and achievement versus depression and
nonpleasurable engagement) were emergenic traits (Table 3.5). It was also
striking that the MZA twins (0.74, n = 28) were more alike in Conservatism than the MZT twins (0.58, n = 247), a finding we did not obtain for
the other traits. There was no immediate explanation for this result, but
it was intriguing in 1982 because of the following relevant findings in the
literature.

In 1964, Gerrit J. S. Wilde reported that MZT twins living apart for
five years were more alike in psychosomatic complaints than twins living

Table 3-5. Intraclass Correlations for Four Differential Personality Questionnaire Measures for
Reared-Apart and Reared-Together Twin Pairs

DPQ Measure	MZA (n = 28)	MZT (n = 247)	DZT (n = 122)
Social potency	0.67	0.65	0.07
Conservatism	0.74	0.58	0.44
Positive affect	0.57	0.63	0.02
Negative affect	0.65	0.67	0.43

Source: Adapted from Lykken, "Research with Twins: The Concept of Emergenesis,"
Psychophysiology 19 (1981): 361–373.

together, with the reverse found for extraversion.[45] Ten years later, Scottish psychologist Gordon Claridge reported that MZT twins living apart for five years were more alike in extraversion and divergent thinking than MZT twins living together.[46] Shields had found that his MZA twins were more alike in extraversion and neuroticism than his MZT twins. Shields and Claridge suggested that because twins living apart do not need to differentiate from their co-twin, they could express their genetically based potentials more freely than those living together. Whether this effect was trait-specific and whether it would appear in later MISTRA data analyses were of interest. However, with larger samples in 2003 and 2004 no difference in conservatism between the MZA and MZT twins was found, making it likely that the high MZA correlation in 1982 reflected small sample fluctuation.

Lykken devised a Recreational Interests Survey that yielded eight different interest factors, four of which he discussed in his presidential address (Table 3-6). The MZA twins (0.65–0.80, n = 28) were more alike than the MZT twins (0.46–0.55, n = 140) on three of the four measures (blood sports: hunting and trapping; intellectual: reading and self-educating; and husbandry: making and fixing things; but not Sierra Club: camping and wilderness trips), a finding Lykken attributed to sampling bias. But as Shields suggested, perhaps twins living apart did not feel pressured to differentiate from their co-twin. Both the MZA and MZT twins were more alike than the DZT twins, with the exception of the Blood Sports measure, for which the DZT twins (0.68, n = 70) were somewhat more alike than the MZT twins (0.54). Mutual influence may have affected the DZT twins on this measure. Organizing the twins by sex would have been of interest with reference to Blood Sports, but the sample size was too modest at this stage. These data were analyzed again in 1993.

Table 3-6.   Intraclass Correlations for Four Recreational Interests for Reared-Apart and Reared-Together Twin Pairs

Interest	MZA (n = 28)	MZT (n = 140)	DZT (n = 70)
Blood sports	0.80	0.54	0.68
Sierra Club	0.49	0.57	0.28
Intellectual	0.69	0.46	0.42
Husbandry	0.65	0.55	−0.07

Source: Adapted from Lykken, "Research with Twins: The Concept of Emergenesis," *Psychophysiology* 19 (1981): 361–373.

Pulmonary Studies

Concern over the physical consequences of smoking cigarettes was a major concern in 1982, and it still is. The MISTRA enabled the first pulmonary function study of twins reared apart in an attempt to address the genetic factors.[47]

The twins underwent thirteen pulmonary tests administered by the same technician. They blew into a spirometer, a device measuring the volume of air that is inhaled and exhaled, and completed a respiratory symptom questionnaire. Six twin pairs were concordant for nonsmoking, three pairs and the triplet set were concordant for smoking, and six pairs were discordant for respiratory problems (five pairs for smoking and one pair for asthma).

Only two of the thirteen respiratory tests—activity in the lower airways[48] and change in lung volume over time[49]—separated the smokers from the nonsmokers. However, a third test measuring the volume of air expelled during the first second of forced exhalation[50] provided the most sensitive measure of difference between smoking and nonsmoking twins within a pair. Genetic factors affecting this third test were indicated by small pulmonary differences within the smoking-concordant and non-smoking concordant twin pairs, in contrast with the marked differences between twins in the smoking-discordant pairs.

Our findings and those of others demonstrated that genetic factors affect some measures of susceptibility to airway obstruction from cigarette smoke.[51] However, it was puzzling that the groups of smoking concordant and discordant pairs did not differ on the other pulmonary measures. Given the vast research linking respiratory problems to smoking, it would be wrong to conclude from just one study that cigarettes did not interfere with respiratory functioning.

Visit from Niels Juel-Nielsen

There is a videotape that could become a classic in the history of psychology, but probably no one watched it until I converted the clunky three-quarter inch tape to DVD in November 2011. In May 1981 Bouchard had invited Dr. Niels Juel-Nielsen, the Danish reared-apart twin investigator, to visit the MISTRA, at which time a discussion between the two was recorded. Like Bouchard's, Juel-Nielsen's sudden discovery of a set of reared apart co-twins captivated his interest in studying their behavioral similarities and differences. And as happened in Minnesota, the media's attention to this first case attracted several others, although Juel-Nielsen drew most of his pairs from the Danish Twin Registry. Finally, like Bouchard, Juel-Nielsen was "impressed" by the twins' unexpected similarities and struggled with defining their differences in a practical sense.

Bouchard was rarely in the position of interviewer as he was in this particular setting. Still, he explained that his reading of Newman et al.'s study convinced him of the beauty of the twin research design—"cutting and definitive"—although "the neatness of the design is overwhelmed by the complexity of the twins' lives." By then, Bouchard had studied twenty-one MZA twin pairs and "had not settled down and absorbed" the indication that MZAs were about as similar in many ways as MZTs, challenging current views of shared environmental effects on behavior. "How long will it take me?" he asked.

New Twin Pairs and the New Minnesota Center for Twin and Adoption Research

Even while we were all paying more attention to the statistical findings, we remained fascinated by the compelling stories of the newly identified twin pairs. A lasting contribution to the new reared-apart twin "culture" had occurred in the early years with the 1981 publication of a Charles Addams cartoon. Undoubtedly inspired by MISTRA findings reported in the press, the cartoon depicts the now famous, fictional Mallifert twins, who were identical in every way (Figure 3-2). None of our pairs were as alike as the Malliferts across all measured traits, but the individual elements of this scene were accurate. For example, Lucky and Dianne, red-headed and vivacious, shared a love for dogs: one showed dogs professionally, and the other taught obedience classes. Barbara and Daphne had the same naturally crooked pinky fingers and distaste for politics. Several DZA twins also displayed striking similarities—male twins Bouchard discovered in 1984 had both decorated their bodies with sixteen tattoos—but such observations were seen less frequently among the DZA twins.

When Kimerly (Kim) Wilcox and I arrived in 1982 as MISTRA post-doctoral fellows, we both felt extremely lucky to be at exactly the right place at the right time. The data we worked with was fresh and new, and people cared about it.

When I had been in Minnesota for about a year, some faculty and staff organized a birthday party for Bouchard. Kim and I designed a t-shirt for him with the number ".771." This number was the critical MZA IQ correlation that had been repeated in several of Sir Cyril Burt's updated analyses, which was still regarded with suspicion. Very early on and for a brief time, the MISTRA IQ correlation was 0.771 as well. Our presentation of Bouchard's t-shirt was a success, although some eyes rolled. That figure is worth mentioning because it comes up again.

Figure 3-2. "Separated at birth, the Mallifert twins meet accidentally." (© Charles Addams, with permission from the Tee and Charles Addams Foundation.)

In 1983, Bouchard established the Minnesota Center for Twin and Adoption Research, a named unit within the Department of Psychology. Its goals were to provide information about twins and adoption, assist separated twins in search of their co-twins, provide administrative support to twin-based projects, and encourage understanding of the biological and social aspects of twinship. Most importantly, the center gave separated twins the resource they needed to find one another.

CHAPTER FOUR

Sexual Orientation, Cognition, and Medical Traits (1984–1987)

In 1984, I had been working on the MISTRA for two years. Every pair I studied provided a unique take on nature-nurture questions. MZA twins Bill and Tim showed the same side-to-side sway as they walked. MZA twins Stan and Mitch were both homosexual despite being reared apart their entire lives. Greater insight into the twins' behavioral and physical similarities and differences began to emerge from the analyses we conducted between 1984 and 1987. Many of our findings continued to be reported in the press.

The MISTRA had matured greatly since my arrival in 1982. The number of empirical papers in scientific journals, relative to descriptive accounts in book chapters and review papers, was growing. By the start of 1984, we had studied fifty-four reared-apart twin pairs (thirty-eight MZA and sixteen DZA). Interesting trends were emerging in information processing, cardiac functioning, immunology, ophthalmology, and sexual preference, all of which we reported in psychological or medical journals. Chapters and reviews now included tables with preliminary statistical findings on physical characteristics (height, weight, and fingerprint ridge count) and psychological traits (general intelligence, special abilities, personality, and interests). Previous studies of twins reared apart and together offered a backdrop against which to appraise these early results.

The Minnesota Center for Twin and Adoption Research, established in 1983, was in its first full year of operation. By the end of 1984, we had added seven new twin pairs and one new triplet set to the study. The sample now included sixty-four separated sets (forty-four MZA and twenty DZA), the largest number of twin pairs studied by any research team.

Five papers and three book chapters were published between 1984 and 1987, including one of the first on information processing.

Information Processing

Studies in the early 1980s had found relationships between the rate of performing tasks involving memory scanning and psychometric cognitive ability measures, although the reasons were uncertain.[1] Genetic effects on information processing parameters and on cognitive measures were also of interest, but had never been examined using twins reared apart. The MISTRA had the data to address both these issues.[2]

The twins completed three information processing measures: Posner Letter Identification,[3] Sternberg Memory Search,[4] and Shepard-Metzler Cube Rotation.[5] The Posner measure presents two letters—in a physical identity condition (e.g., A, A) or in a name identity condition (e.g., A, a)—that participants must identify. Name identity minus Physical identity is the difference in time between presentation of the problem and response in the two conditions. The Sternberg measure asks participants to memorize one, three, or five digits from 0 to 9. Participants then indicate if a number that appears on the screen several seconds later is part of that series.[6] The Shepard-Metzler measure presents pairs of three-dimensional cubed figures on a two-dimensional screen. The two figures may be the same but shown from different angles, or they may be different figures. Participants decide if the pairs are the same or different.[7]

Each twin was tested separately, usually by the same examiner. Given the straightforward instructions, push-button response procedure, and correct/incorrect response format, meaningful tester bias was unlikely. The order in which the tasks were presented was the same across participants: (1) Posner, (2) Sternberg, and (3) Shepard-Metzler. Testing usually took place over two days, with most items administered on the first day (approximately 90 minutes) and the second set of Shepard-Metzler items administered on the second day (approximately 30 minutes). Testing never began until the twins were comfortable with the concepts and procedures.

Graduate students Dan Moloney and Mary Moster administered the Shepard-Metzler Rotations to many of the twins between 1984 and 1990. Dan liked doing this because he was good at these problems and solved them silently as the twins worked. When I spoke with him by telephone in April 2010, he said that he regretted not tape-recording the twins during these sessions. "I sat quietly behind them," he said. "The strategies were so different between twin pairs, but within the MZA pairs they were so similar. Both twins vocalized or turned around or stared at the screen or solved the problems quickly. It was amazing. I smiled to myself when I saw these things, thinking no one would believe me. When the twins were successful or frustrated they both reacted a certain way and maybe there is a genetic component to such behavior."

In addition to the information processing tests, the twins completed the Wechsler Adult Intelligence Scale (WAIS), and selected subtests from the Hawaii Study of Cognition and Kit of Factor-Referenced Cognitive Tests. The availability of these mental ability data let us analyze the twins' information processing abilities as a two-part study. Part 1 examined relationships between the information processing measures and the special ability and general intelligence measures. Part 2 looked at the relative contributions of genetic and environmental factors to individual differences in information processing skills. These analyses included twenty-eight to thirty-one MZA twin pairs and eleven to thirteen DZA twin pairs. Many detailed results were presented in the information processing paper, so only a selective sampling is provided here.

The information processing data were organized into three components: overall speed of response (29.8 percent), speed of information processing (20.8 percent), and speed of spatial processing (16.7 percent); the percentages reflect the proportion of variation in information processing explained by these components. Overall speed of response correlated significantly with the general cognitive ability measures ($r=-0.31$), verbal reasoning ($r=-0.18$), and perceptual speed and accuracy ($r=-0.20$). The negative correlations mean that faster responding was associated with higher test scores. Speed was associated with both general and specific mental abilities, supporting the view that processing speed is a major part of intelligence. Speed of information (memory) processing correlated significantly with general cognitive ability ($r=-0.32$) and with verbal reasoning ($r=-0.27$). Speed of spatial processing correlated mostly with spatial processing measures ($r=-0.32$).

Significant MZA twin resemblance for information processing measures tapping general speed of response was found ($r_i s=0.37$ to 0.60). The MZA correlations were also significant for the percentage correct on the Sternberg ($r_i=0.79$) and Shepard-Metzler tasks ($r_i=0.62$). In contrast, genetic influence was not indicated for measures reflecting the speed of specific cognitive processing.[8] The DZA twin sample was too small to allow reliable conclusions regarding genetic effects.

The reared-apart twin data enabled many information processing analyses beyond the MZA-DZA comparisons. For example, the presence of a verbal-spatial distinction for the information processing measures, similar to that found for the ability measures, was supported. Thus, the reared-apart twins contributed to the debate over the nature of information processing components and their relationship with general intelligence and special mental skills. The significant MZA intraclass correlations for speed of response measures were exciting to see, supporting the idea that processing speed contributes importantly to general intelligence.

Cardiac Functioning

Franz Halberg is founder and director of the Chronobiology Laboratory at the University of Minnesota. Chronobiology is the study of cyclical phenomena and their adaptation to lunar- and solar-related rhythms. Halberg had heard about the MISTRA from psychiatrist Elke Eckert and was immediately interested in studying the twins. When we began working with Halberg, the cyclical features of the human heart had been well documented, but less had been done regarding genetic factors.

Longitudinal measurements of the human heart have established the presence of several components, such as ultradian rhythms (having a frequency of greater than one cycle in twenty hours), infradian rhythms (having a frequency of less than one cycle in twenty-eight hours), and circadian rhythms (having a frequency of one cycle in approximately twenty-four hours). Even when people are in social isolation the heart maintains its circadian rhythmicity, consistent with genetic origins. Only one very small twin study of circadian rhythms, showing that pulse was genetically influenced, was available when the MISTRA began.[9] Thus, the reared-apart twins presented "a new challenge" to our colleagues in the departments of laboratory medicine (Bruce Hanson), chronobiology (Franz Halberg), and cardiology (Naip Tuna).[10]

Every Wednesday morning, twins visited the University of Minnesota's Variety Club Heart Hospital to be hooked up to a twenty-four-hour Holter monitor that records heart activity continuously.[11] The device hangs by a strap over the shoulder, much like a travel bag. Twins were also given booklets for recording their meal times and significant changes in physical activity, such as walking up stairs. Showering was forbidden during this period. Each twin of a pair was monitored during the same week, and usually on the same day.

We compared the twins' resemblance in the mesor (rhythm-adjusted mean), amplitude (the extent of rhythmic change), and acrophase (timing of rhythm in relation to a reference point).[12] The sample included eighteen MZA twin pairs (eleven male and seven female) and four DZA twin pairs (two male and two female); three MZA male pairs were generated from a set of triplets.

The MZA intraclass correlations for the three cardiac parameters ranged from 0.61 to 0.68, showing that genetic factors explained about 60 to 65 percent of the variance in these measures. (The small DZA twin sample could not provide reliable results.) When we organized the data by sex, the mesor and amplitude correlations stayed significant for males, but the mesor correlation dropped to near zero for females. The possibility that genetic effects on cardiac measures work differently for men and women was raised by these data, but needed to be confirmed with larger samples. Age was eliminated as a factor affecting twin similarity because the correlations between unrelated same-age twins created from the sample were negligible.

Thus, the previously indirect indication of genetic influence on circadian rhythms among individuals in isolation was confirmed directly. Hanson and colleagues concluded that the detection of genetic effects in "a variable as noisy as heart rate,"[13] studied over a brief period and with a small sample, is methodologically meaningful. When I spoke to Hanson in 2009, he wondered whether the MZA twin data were driven by the twins' similar activities during their study week. Of course, the DZA twins' activities were also synchronized, but the small DZA sample prevented this comparison. We did establish that rhythm parameters did not differ between twins studied on the same versus different days.

Halberg continued studying genetic effects on the circadian amplitude of the human heart rate with a larger number of reared-apart twin pairs (thirty-five MZA and twenty-two DZA). In a 2003 study on circadian findings, he included a graph showing a significant heritable effect (MZA $r_i = 0.55$).[14] In contrast, the DZA correlation was negligible, suggesting an emergenic effect. Halberg was also interested in blood pressure and regretted that we had recorded the twins' measurements only over one night rather than the full week. However, extended blood pressure recordings would have been difficult with the large and noisy machines of the time (recordings can be made less intrusively today). In fact, Halberg insists that people should wear blood pressure monitors every day of their lives—"womb to tomb" is what he said, and I believed he was serious. I am certain that he would have liked monitoring the twins' heart activities for the entire week as well.

One DZA female twin (not included in the present analysis) decided to have sex on the night that she wore her Holter monitor. Her twin sister did not, even though her spouse was also present. To the extent that our heart rates are affected by sexual activities, these DZA twins would have shown differing numbers during the nighttime hours, partly associated with their different choices that night.[15] I wish I had taken a closer look at the printouts they handed to us the next morning, but we were rushing to get the twins to breakfast and to the allergy laboratory.

Immunology

Only a handful of conventional twin studies examining immunological regulation were available when the Jim twins were found. Genetic factors in total levels of immunoglobulin or antibodies had been reported, but these measures had never been studied in reared-apart twins prior to the MISTRA.[16] Total immunoglobulin refers to the basic protein structure of the immune system and is expected to be similar in MZ twins. Antibody titers reflect different challenges to the immune system.[17] If one co-twin had hepatitis and the other co-twin did not, then their different antibody titers should reflect this difference.

The immunological information often took weeks to process—a portion of the blood sample used in the immunological studies was processed in Denver where our collaborator, Peter Kohler, had his laboratory. The five classes of immunoglobulins (IgG, IgM, IgA, IgD, and IgE) provide resistance by the release of antibodies. The immunoglobulin (Ig) measures included total IgM, IgG, and IgA levels. Twin similarity in specific antibodies to tetanus toxoid and to polyvalent (several antibodies that counteract specific antigens) and other substances was also assessed.[18] Sera (blood with clotting factors removed) from twenty-six MZA twin pairs and ten DZA twin pairs were used in the first paper from this laboratory.

The results from our twin analysis were compelling: "In spite of different environmental exposures to antigens, the predominant factor(s) determining total immunoglobulin and isotypic antibody levels in these twins was genetic rather than environmental."[19] Occasional differences within selected MZA twin pairs were linked to marked variation in tetanus toxoid immunizations and exposure to *Streptococcus pneumococci*, as expected.

There is a bigger story here: the MZA twins' greater similarity in total concentration (Ig: MZA 0.80 to 0.82, DZA −0.40 to 0.35) than antibody titers (IgA: MZA 0.25, DZA 0.17; and IgM: MZA 0.59, DZA 0.54), and their reduced similarity in response to specific antibodies suggested that genetic regulation plays a greater role in the former. Based on this work, future research would probably show a stronger genetic effect from antibody responses to immunization with defined antigens. If MZA co-twins had both been vaccinated for smallpox or hepatitis B then their reaction to specific antibodies should be similar. Knowing that genetic factors can affect the body's response to toxic substances may improve disease prevention and treatment, especially for people whose relatives show resistance to certain vaccines or sensitivity to specific antigens.

Ophthalmology

The MISTRA twins' visual characteristics were studied by the late Dr. William H. Knobloch, from the University of Minnesota's Department of Ophthalmology. Eye examinations were scheduled for 1:00 P.M. on Wednesday afternoons and took several hours to complete. The twins' eyes were dilated during the course of this visit, which made them unable to read and complete the questionnaires. They left the hospital wearing protective eyeglasses and were taken by Bouchard on a tour of the Twin Cities' lovely lakes. How much scenery they actually saw has never been determined.

The twins' eyes were examined at the same time by separate ophthalmologic technicians. Each twin completed a brief eye history, including questions about their visual health during childhood. Next, assessments were made of their visual acuity (clearness of vision), refraction (ability of the eye to bend light so an image is focused on the retina), intraocular pressure (fluid pressure inside the eye), and muscle balance (ability of the eyes to work together). Dilation of the eyes enabled inspection of the anterior segment (front third of the eye) and fundus (interior surface opposite the lens), procedures completed by an ophthalmologist. Stereo photographs of the optic nerve (nerve connecting the eye to the brain), macula (small part of the retina providing the best vision), and standard fields (area that is seen at a given moment) were also made; the twins' identities were masked prior to evaluation of these photographs. A 1985 article reported the findings for eighteen MZA and eight same-sex DZA twin pairs.[20]

- *Refractive error.* Concordance rates for refractive error were 75 percent for the MZA twin pairs and 50 percent for the DZA twin pairs. These values, which agree with both past and current studies, demonstrate genetic effects on visual acuity.
- *Motility.* Concordance for esotropia (a condition in which the visual axes are nonparallel such that the eyes appear to be looking in different directions) was observed in both members of three MZA twin pairs and in one member of one DZA twin pair. Most striking to Knobloch was the "biologic clock" demonstrated by the three concordant MZA pairs: twins in pair A began wearing glasses at ages seven and eight; twins in pair B developed estropia at an early age and wore eyeglasses during their preschool years; and

twins in pair C had had strabismus surgery (to correct the inward turning of the eyes), one twin at eighteen and the other at nineteen.
- *Optic nerve and stereo photographs.* The fundus refers to the eye's interior surface and includes the retina, optic disc (eye region where the optic nerve emerges from the eyeball), macula, fovea (center of the macula and responsible for sharp vision), and posterior pole (back of the eye). Similarity of the fundus was measured by the cup to disc ratio (area in the center of the optic disc), based on measurements from the stereo photographs. Concordance was 90 percent for the MZA twins and 50 percent for the DZA twins, indicating a genetic influence. Marked discordance in one MZA twin pair was noted.

The most striking eye findings were the genetic effects on refractive error and estropia. The coordinated appearance and treatment of eye conditions in selected pairs suggested the presence of genetically mediated timelines underlying these conditions. This phenomenon was well illustrated by fifty-eight-year-old MZA male triplets (not included in our 1985 paper) in which one member showed macular degeneration (breakdown of the visual structure surrounding light-sensitive cells), while his two brothers showed only early signs. A final insight from the ophthalmology study (communicated informally by Knobloch at a later date) was that he could predict twin type almost perfectly from the similarity of the fine structures on the retina, a bit of information that has never been reported in a scientific journal.[21]

Little knowledge of the twins' birth histories was available. This is unfortunate because administering oxygen to premature infants can impair the visual apparatus and twins are at increased risk for early birth.[22] Thus, it is possible that concordance among some MZA (and DZA) pairs reflected this early treatment, reducing the contribution from genetic factors.

Twins continued to visit the eye clinic until 1995, yielding a sample of approximately 125 pairs. Unfortunately, Knobloch passed away in 2005, and the full data set has never been analyzed.

Sexual Life History

The MISTRA was the first study to systematically gather comprehensive data on the separated twins' sexual life histories in general, and on female twins in particular. The MISTRA's 1986 article describing sexual orientation findings for six MZA twin pairs suggested that "male homosexuality may be associated with a complex interaction, in which genes play some part."[23] That article was not the first to suggest that sexual orientation has a genetic basis. In 1968, Heston and Shields had published a twin and family study of homosexuality that suggested genetic influence,[24] and a handful of other twin studies, published between 1953 and 1971, reached the same conclusion. Heston, acknowledging that his 1986 conference paper on this topic "could not support a sweeping conclusion" due to the small number of pairs, decided to "describe the findings and let people draw their own conclusions." His presentation of these data at an international congress generated considerable discussion, not all positive.

The genetic and environmental origins of sexual preference continue to be debated. Twin studies conducted in the early 1990s, using self-selected and targeted samples, yielded higher concordance values than those conducted more recently. A summary of studies published between 1952 and 1993 show median concordance rates of 52 percent for MZ twins and 17 percent for DZ twins. In contrast, median concordance values for twin registry and population-based studies conducted since 2000 yield concordance values of 24 percent for MZ twins and 13 percent for DZ twins.[25] A 2000 study, using a large anonymous Australian sample and applying strict criteria for sexual orientation, found concordance figures of 20 percent for MZ male pairs, 24 percent for MZ female pairs, 0 for DZ male pairs, and 10.5 percent for DZ female pairs.[26] The different recruitment methods used in the older and newer studies most likely explain the different findings.

Evidence from a growing number of twin and adoption studies (including additional separated pairs in the MISTRA) support moderate genetic influence on male sexual orientation, and little or none in females. The Australian study reported heritabilities of 0.45 for males and 0.08 for females. A 2010 population-based study of nearly 4,000 Swedish twin pairs reported somewhat comparable figures of 0.34–0.39 and 0.18–0.19 for male and female sexual preference, respectively.[27]

Homosexuality has also been examined with reference to prenatal effects on behavior. Hormonal explanations suggest that the level of prenatal androgen exposure may influence the development of brain structures relevant to sexual orientation. Higher birth order in males with older brothers has been linked to homosexuality, possibly reflecting maternal immune reactions to testosterone. Pregnancy stress has also been linked to homosexuality in some but not all studies. Psychosocial theories in which later-born male children develop feelings of inadequacy or are raised by overprotective mothers, leading to homosexuality, have been proposed but not substantiated. It is possible that parents may react in specific ways to children who display gender nonconformity, although it is less likely that they create it.[28] These sources of influence could be associated with MZ twin concordance or discordance for sexual orientation.

Previous reared-apart twin researchers did not investigate sexuality, perhaps because they worried that such a personal topic would make some twins uncomfortable. Nevertheless, homosexual experiences were noted in two male reared-apart pairs studied by Juel-Nielsen, and in one female pair studied by Shields. However, the information is sparse, making these pairs difficult to classify in terms of concordance or discordance for sexual preference.[29]

The MISTRA's Sexual Life History assessment took place one evening after dinner, mostly in psychology department facilities. Co-twins completed these interviews at the same time, but in different locations and with different examiners. Spouses and other individuals who accompanied the twins to Minneapolis did not participate in this phase of the study—we wanted twins to answer freely and honestly, so it was important that their companions be unaware of the questions that we posed.

The Sexual Life History battery consisted of a Sexual Meaning Survey, Sexual Life History Timeline, Sexual Behavior Questionnaire, and Semi-Structured Interview. The different components were developed by Drs. Joseph Bohlen and Margaret Sanderson from the University of Minnesota. The Sexual Meaning Survey was presented as a semantic differential in which twins indicated the extent to which words in fifty-one pairs (e.g., strong-weak; exciting-boring) were meaningful to them in a sexual sense. Two questions concerning the personal importance of sex and the importance of sex in their current relationship were also included. The Sexual History Timeline listed various events (e.g., kissing, intercourse) for which twins indicated if such events had happened in their lives and, if so, at what age. The Sexual Behavior Questionnaire asked about the frequency of sexual activities (e.g., sexual dreams, sexual fantasies). The Semi-Structured Interview allowed twins to expand upon sexual behaviors and themes that were relevant to them.

The estimated percentage of Americans who identify as gay is 1.7 percent.[30] Therefore, the number of pairs in which one or both twins were homosexual was understandably small—the sample included only six pairs (two male and four female) out of the 55 pairs that had been studied when the paper appeared in 1986.[31] But sexual behaviors in these unique pairs were of interest.

The data posed some curious dilemmas while also presenting new ideas. Twins in one male pair were clearly concordant for homosexuality. They were reunited after one twin was mistaken for his brother when he visited a gay bar in another town. Both twins had been active homosexuals since age thirteen, although one twin had had several heterosexual encounters. Most reared-together homosexual twins deny sexual interest in one another; however, as indicated in the MISTRA's 1986 report, these twins became sexual partners following their reunion.[32] Shortly thereafter, due to our observations of flirtatious behavior between DZA opposite-sex twins, we began asking all the twins if they had sexual interest in one another. We were especially interested in the answers from the opposite-sex pairs—as indicated earlier, it was conceivable that in their case their separate rearing prevented development of the Westermarck Effect.[33]

Genetic sexual attraction is the counterpart to the Westermarck Effect, and may develop in its absence. It refers to the strong sexual connection experienced by some biological mothers and sons, fathers and daughters, and brothers and sisters who were separated since birth and reunited as adults.[34] The Westermarck Effect cannot occur in such cases because it requires early cohabitation, thereby allowing possible sexual feelings to flourish. Consistent with this view, mate selection studies show that people are generally attracted to others with whom they are similar in some physical and behavioral features such as height, intelligence, or values.[35] Interestingly, experimental evidence shows that females prefer the odors of males with whom they share intermediate numbers of paternally transmitted histocompatibility genes (genes controlling the immune system) compared with males with whom they share few.[36] These findings suggest an optimal balance between inbreeding and outbreeding. The few reported cases of attraction and marriage between reared-apart opposite-sex twins are comprehensible in light of these effects.[37]

Sexual feelings between reunited MZA twins shows that genetic sexual attraction can occur between reared-apart same-sex as well as opposite-sex siblings. Homosexual MZA twin pairs are rare, yet mutual sexual attraction was demonstrated in one of our male sets, and sexual attraction by one co-twin toward his brother was indicated in a second set. One member of a male pair studied by Juel-Nielsen accused his twin brother of making sexual advances toward him.[38]

Twins in our second male set posed the classification conundrum that I described in Chapter 3: one of the twins considered himself homosexual, and felt sexually attracted to his brother when they met at age thirty-five. However, his co-twin considered himself heterosexual—at the time of assessment he was married with children. He engaged in intercourse infrequently, yet seemed satisfied with his sexual life. But he had had an affair between the ages of fifteen and eighteen years with an older man.

The concordance or discordance of this pair was never settled in the minds of the investigators. The same uncertainty presented itself in the case of one of our four female pairs, but was eventually resolved.

The female pair in question concerned forty-eight-year-old MZA twins, one of whom was exclusively heterosexual, while the other had had a homosexual affair that was "intense and prolonged."[39] However, she regarded herself as heterosexual since her marriage at age twenty-nine, but felt attracted to both males and females nonetheless. She was classified as bisexual by Eckert and Heston. The other three female pairs were discordant for homosexuality. A review of their life histories revealed nothing remarkable in their rearing circumstances that could explain the difference. However, some common threads seemed worth pursuing. The homosexual member of each of the three discordant female pairs had (1) a higher body weight and height at the time of the study, (2) a "larger" body size throughout their lifetime, (3) a later age at menarche, (4) a relative delay in the development of secondary sexual characteristics such as breast development, and (5) a relative delay in the onset of sexual experiences.

Genetic influence on male homosexuality was suggested by our early data, consistent with reared-together twin studies. In contrast, environmental effects on female homosexuality seemed more important. The twins' medical histories did not reveal illnesses or other events that were specific to the homosexual twins.

The study concluded that "the findings are descriptive only, and should be regarded as clues upon which to base hypotheses."[40] Eckert and Heston called for further investigation of the female findings. Subsequent research on large reared-together twin samples has supported a larger genetic origin of homosexuality in males, but less than was previously reported. Genetic effects on homosexuality in females have also been found, albeit to a lesser degree. Social and environmental explanations of female sexuality are still prevalent.[41]

Our goal in the sexual orientation study was to demonstrate possibilities. That was one of the beauties of the reared-apart twin study design.

Physical and Psychological Traits: Early Findings

Bouchard's 1984 chapter in Sidney W. Fox's edited volume provides an informative capsule of the MISTRA.[42] Referring to that chapter twenty-five years later, Bouchard recalled, "I was pretty persuaded that we really had our hands on something significant." In 1986, he published another overview of the project that included findings on anthropometric measures, special mental abilities, and vocational interests.[43]

The correlations were quite similar to those from previous studies of twins reared apart and reared together. The data continued to show genetic effects on fingerprint ridge count (0.97 for both MZA males, n = 17, and MZA females, n = 21) and height (0.92 for MZA males, n = 17; 0.81 for MZA females, n = 23). We also found that the MZA female twins were less alike in weight (0.49, n = 23) than the MZA male twins (0.91, n = 17), a difference also found by Shields (0.87 for MZA males, n = 15; 0.37 for MZA females, n = 29).

Cousins are not frequent subjects in behavioral genetic research, perhaps because they are harder to locate or are less enthusiastic than twins about participation. It was reasoned that first-cousins' rearing situations approximate the maximum possible degree of placement similarity of separated twins. Cousins' home environments might be similar to the extent that their related parents are both intelligent or athletic and provide their children with books or basketballs. Cousin correlations would also be affected by their average 12.5 percent genetic overlap.

A great deal of special mental ability data had been gathered in the Hawaii Family Study of Cognition, and by administering these tests we had access to a wealth of comparative data.[44] The MZA (0.41–0.66, n = 29) correlations consistently exceeded the cousin (0.11–0.30, n = 246) correlations, with the largest difference occurring for spatial ability (0.66 and 0.11, respectively). These data demonstrated genetic influence on special mental skills, while weakening contributions from rearing factors.

Vocational interests had not been a major focus of behavioral geneticists, one reason why the Strong-Campbell Interest Inventory was included in the MISTRA test battery. Data from a large 1974 twin study using scales from the Holland Vocational Preference Inventory were available for comparison with the MISTRA data.[45]

The overall pattern suggested by the findings was one of genetic influence. The correlations ranged from 0.20 to 0.51 for the MZA twins (n = 39), 0.43 to 0.55 for the MZT twins (n = 979), −0.14 to 0.35 for the DZA twins (n = 17), and 0.20 to 0.31 for the DZT twins (n = 607). These results were consistent with an adoption study of the Holland interest styles that reported average correlations of 0.09 and 0.11 for unrelated opposite-sex siblings (n = 60) and unrelated same-sex siblings (n = 23), respectively.[46] More comprehensive treatments of the MISTRA's vocational interest data would eventually appear in 1991, 1994, and 1997 articles.

1984 to 1987

The MISTRA years between 1984 and 1987 were productive in many ways. A symposium, "The Minnesota Study of Twins Reared Apart," was held as part of the fourteenth annual Behavior Genetics Association meeting, in Bloomington, Indiana, May 1984. The presentations included early findings on IQ, personality, fears, physical attractiveness, and the Minnesota Multiphasic Personality Inventory (MMPI).

The year 1986 was the second busiest (after 1981) in terms of studying new twin pairs—we saw a total of ten new separated twin sets plus one set of triplets. The six principal investigators and two postdoctoral fellows presented findings at many conferences across the United States and abroad, including the Behavior Genetics Association and the International Society for Twin Studies.

In 1985, Bouchard became chair of the Department of Psychology, at which time he appointed me assistant director of the Minnesota Center for Twin and Adoption Research. I was now more directly involved in scheduling twins and managing the assessments. Despite his administrative responsibilities, Bouchard stayed involved in every twin assessment.

Figure 4-1. The 1987 reunion of British reared-apart twins, held at the Priest House in Derby, located in the East Midlands of England. Bouchard is in the center, standing behind John Stroud, who is seated in the wheelchair. (Photo courtesy Thomas J. Bouchard Jr. Unpublished newspaper photograph.)

Matt McGue joined the psychology department faculty in 1985, lending his behavioral genetic expertise to many reports from the MISTRA. Kimerly Wilcox, the postdoctoral fellow who joined the study in 1982 when I did, remained on campus working on epilepsy studies at the Dight Institute for Human Genetics. In 1986, we added a periodontal component to the assessment schedule, conducted by Drs. Pihlstrom, Michalowicz, Herzberg, and Wolff. Every fall new graduate students began working on the project, turning their efforts into doctoral dissertations and publications. In March 1987, our dental collaborator, Dr. JoAnn Boraas, presented the first paper on the twins' dental findings at the Annual Meeting of the International Association for Dental Research.[47] In September 1987, we began follow-up assessments of our earliest reared-apart pairs.

Several new University of Minnesota faculty members became increasingly involved with the MISTRA during these years. Stephen Rich joined the university in 1980 as a genetic epidemiologist, working on studies of epilepsy and type 1 diabetes at the Dight Institute. He eventually developed working relationships with Bouchard, Lykken, Tellegen, and others. Over the next several years, Rich would play a key role in analyses of our personality and heart-rate data. Rich remained at the University of Minnesota until 1994 when he joined Wake Forest University's School of Medicine in Winston-Salem, North Carolina.[48]

A 1987 British twins' reunion, held in Derby in honor of John Stroud, was the last one Stroud attended before his death in 1989. Looking at a photo of this event (Figure 4-1), Bouchard remarked, "[It] reminds me of how many twin pairs we had from England. Quite amazing when you think about it."

In 1984, Barbara Unell, a writer and mother of opposite-sex twins, launched and edited *Twins Magazine*. *Twins Magazine* was (and remains) a monthly publication devoted entirely to twin development and parenting issues, now under the editorship of Christa D. Reed. I held the position of research editor from 1984 to 1998. In my first article, "The Nature vs. Nurture Laboratory," I described our work with separated twins. I would phrase the title differently today, either as Nature-Nurture or Nature and Nurture, because it is now widely appreciated that the two effects work together and are separable only in a statistical sense. Thinking about developmental processes has clearly changed.

CHAPTER FIVE

Pivotal Papers: Personality and IQ (1988 and 1990)

The Personality Paper

The genetic makeup of a child is a stronger influence on personality than childrearing according to the first study to examine identical twins reared in different families. The findings shatter a widespread belief among experts and laymen alike in the primacy of family influence and are sure to engender fierce debate.[1]

Daniel Goleman of the *New York Times* published the conclusion to our first major analysis of the personality data before it appeared in a scientific journal. In fact, he used our conclusion as his opening lines. The University of Minnesota's public affairs office provided Goleman with a draft of the study approximately eighteen months before its 1988 publication in the *Journal of Personality and Social Psychology.*[2] Bouchard had told the university's public relations representative that the paper would be published, but he did not give it to her. He explained to her that rules prohibited the release of scientific findings in the popular press prior to their publication in the scientific literature. "But she finagled the paper from Lykken—he didn't know her intentions. When the research appeared in the *New York Times* she thought she had done a great thing. It really pissed me off."

The findings attracted considerable media attention. The paper and the article were controversial for the way they were released as well as for their content. A 1990 article in *Science Writer* by Lisa Lynch addressed the media attention, albeit in an uninformed way: "Three years ago, by prepublishing the results of their study, the Minnesota group made it impossible for other scientists to answer their claims."[3] Neither Lynch (nor Goleman) really knew how our paper was released. And by the end of our twenty-year study fifty-six DZA twin pairs had been assessed, barely half of the nearly one hundred DZA sets Lynch had alleged.

Our finding that shared environments had little effect on most personality traits engendered new debate. Parents' contributions to their children's developmental outcomes were defended in the psychological literature and questioned in the popular press.[4] In fact, our paper raised the possibility that family interaction norms might explain our social closeness findings, a personality measure that did show significant familial effects.

Evidence of genetic components to personality was still controversial even though other investigators had produced similar results. The investigators of the three previous reared-apart twin studies had each included personality assessments in their programs. Their methods differed from ours, but all three found that genetic factors explained about 50 percent of the variation in personality. Moreover, all three described marked personality differences within some early pairs that they associated with the twins' differences in physical factors, rearing practices, and social influences.

Newman et al. and Shields also had access to MZT and DZT twin pairs, so they made additional comparisons. Newman's group suggested that the nature of personality and the unreliability of the Woodworth-Matthews Questionnaire his team administered prevented the emergence of a discernible trend in their data.[5] However, their MZA ($r_i = 0.58$) and MZT ($r_i = 0.56$) correlations were nearly identical and were higher than the corresponding DZT correlation ($r_i = 0.37$), challenging explanations of personality based mostly—or wholly—on shared environments.[6] The Downey Will-Temperament Test, despite its "detailed character and the many opportunities for variation," yielded five pairs with nearly identical scores, ten pairs with considerably similar scores, and only four pairs with widely different scores.[7] Newman and colleagues suggested that this test assesses relatively stable personality dimensions.

Shields found higher extraversion and neuroticism correlations for his MZA (0.61 and 0.53, respectively) than MZT pairs (0.42 and 0.38, respectively).[8] He explained his findings with reference to the MZT twins' intrapair dynamics—that is, differentiation due to the twin relationship, a process that would not affect MZA twins. Still, both the MZA and MZT twins in Shields's study were more alike in extraversion and neuroticism than the DZT twins (−0.17 and 0.11, respectively), which was consistent with genetic influence. Shields's own rating system indicated greater personality differences between the MZA than between the MZT twins, although his most similar pairs were found in both groups. In the years that followed, many reared-together twin studies produced corroborating evidence of genetic influence on personality traits.[9]

Except for Shields,[10] none of the early investigators had access to DZA twins, or to the sophisticated biometrical modeling techniques that partition genetic and environmental effects on behavior that have been developed since the 1970s. Therefore, the first significant analysis of our data was unique in that it was the first study to (1) include all four twin groups, organized by zygosity and rearing status (MZA, DZA, MZT, and DZT) and (2) apply biometrical modeling techniques to the data. The reared-together twins were identified through the Minnesota Twin Registry that Lykken had been developing since 1983.[11]

Access to the four twin groups allowed us to estimate the relative contributions of additive genetic effects, nonadditive genetic effects, shared environmental effects, and nonshared environmental effects on the variance in personality traits. It was of interest to see if any of the traits showed greater MZA than MZT resemblance, as did extraversion and neuroticism in Shields's study. Our early findings on conservatism (summarized in Chapter 3) showed greater similarity between MZA than MZT twins, a difference that was tracked in later analyses.

The data for our first personality study came from Tellegen's Multidimensional Personality Questionnaire,[12] which consists of 300 items presented in a true-false format. Sample items include (1) "Basically I am a happy person" and (2) "I suffer from nervousness." The items yield eleven primary personality scales and three higher order factors, listed in Table 5-1 (descriptions of each are provided on the Web site). The primary scales were developed to be relatively independent, to show no overlap among one another.

The twins' four (later five) questionnaire booklets were presented in the order of their importance. The Multidimensional Personality Questionnaire was the first item in Booklet 1, closely followed by a second major personality questionnaire, the Minnesota Multiphasic Personality Inventory, which I discuss later. The personality assessment forms, variously distributed across the questionnaire booklets, also included the 16 Personality Factor Questionnaire, and the California Psychological Inventory, among others.[13]

Our first personality study included 44 MZA pairs, 27 DZA pairs, 217 MZT pairs, and 114 DZT pairs. The results, as seen in Table 5-1, were straightforward: the MZ twins were more alike than the DZ twins, regardless of rearing status. The median correlations were 0.49 (MZA), 0.52 (MZT), 0.21 (DZA), and 0.23 (DZT), a pattern demonstrating substantial

Table 5-1.   Intraclass Correlations for Scales from the Multidimensional Personality Questionnaire for Twins
Reared Apart and Together

Scale	MZA (n = 44 pairs)	DZA (n = 27 pairs)	MZT (n = 217 pairs)	DZT (n = 114 pairs)
Primary scale				
Well-being	0.48	0.18	0.58	0.23
Social potency	0.56	0.27	0.65	0.08
Achievement	0.36	0.07	0.51	0.13
Social closeness	0.29	0.30	0.57	0.24
Stress reaction	0.61	0.27	0.52	0.24
Alienation	0.48	0.18	0.55	0.38
Aggression	0.46	0.06	0.43	0.14
Control	0.50	0.03	0.41	−0.06
Harm avoidance	0.49	0.24	0.55	0.17
Traditionalism	0.53	0.39	0.50	0.47
Absorption	0.61	0.21	0.49	0.41
Higher order factors				
Positive emotionality	0.34	−0.07	0.63	0.18
Negative emotionality	0.61	0.29	0.54	0.41
Constraint	0.57	0.04	0.58	0.25

Source: Adapted from Tellegen et al., "Personality Similarity in Twins Reared Apart and
Together," *Journal of Personality and Social Psychology* 54 (1988): 1031–1039.

genetic influence. Interestingly, the correlations for traditionalism suggested that common rearing enhances the similarity of that trait for DZT
twins more than for MZT twins who are genetically the same—the MZA
(0.53) and MZT (0.50) correlations hardly differed, but the DZT correlation (0.47) was larger than the DZA correlation (0.39). Testing this
idea would require a closer look at the social-dynamics within the different twinships.

Most revealing, *the MZA twins were about as similar as the MZT twins
across the eleven different personality scales.* These results would challenge
psychologists to rethink the role of parental practices and home environments in child development. The impact of this finding was profound,
no doubt the reason why Goleman opened his article with the study's
conclusion.

Reactions to our key result—that shared family environments have
little effect on individual personality differences—ranged from acceptance to dismissal. Psychologist Robert Plomin called it "the single most
important finding in behavioral genetics in the last decade."[14] Psychiatric
geneticist Elliot Gershon, referring to our study in particular and to the
behavioral genetics field in general said, "The more familiar you are with

the evidence the more persuasive it becomes."[15] In contrast, psychology professor Leon Kamin claimed, "These are very ambiguous data that can be interpreted any way you want. I'm not saying anyone is falsifying facts or anything, just that we know very, very little."[16] Kamin, who raised the possibility of fraud in Burt's MZA twin studies, was a severe critic of the MISTRA, continually demanding the original data to conduct the analyses himself. Psychology professor Jerome Kagan questioned our heritability estimates, arguing that personality inventories may not capture how people act in everyday life.[17]

Some behavioral geneticists were also skeptical. Indiana University psychology professor Richard J. Rose, one of Lykken's most distinguished former graduate students, had recently reported that greater social contact between twins he studied in Finland led to their greater similarity in neuroticism.[18] However, as Lykken and colleagues argued in response, more similar twins probably sought each other out more often than less similar twins.[19] The Lykken-Rose debate continued.[20] Of course, arguments favoring causal links between degree of social contact and personality similarity must be reconciled with research from separated twins, something Rose and colleagues tried to do. They argued that some traits may be more or less sensitive to contact than others, and that understanding the effects of contact will help to explain behavioral variation. I wonder if the nature of contact experienced by twins growing up together differs from that experienced by twins who meet occasionally but have never lived together. For example, twins reared together have shared life histories and may take one another for granted as companions. In contrast, twins reared apart may continually provide details of their lives to one another and may view each meeting as a special occasion. Whether these distinctions are real or relevant to twins' personality similarity is unknown, but MZA and MZT twins' relations with one another are worth investigating in this regard. Nevertheless, the MZT twins were not more alike in personality than the MZA twins, challenging the Rose et al. study's conclusions.

The foregoing exchange masks the high esteem with which Rose and Lykken regarded each other.[21] According to Rose:

> When David and I engaged in this friendly but public dispute, it was like a continuation of our student-mentor interactions. Several years after our exchange of articles, he confided that he had enjoyed this repartee, for I "had mounted a good defense," although my argument and data were not compelling. In retrospect, our argument, like so many in the behavioral sciences, rested on shaky data. I had asked whether shared experience enhanced sibling similarity, and sought answers in the relative similarities of twin siblings

who differed in the duration of their cohabitation. More incisive evidence of common environmental influences—it now seems obvious to me—comes from genetic strangers (adoptive siblings) reared together.[22]

The Minnesota personality findings were misinterpreted by many. We did not say that parenting does not matter—parents can help shy children feel at ease or help rambunctious kids calm down, as Kagan had shown.[23] One implication of our work was that parents should pay close attention to each child's unique character traits and nurture each child's individual interests. Paradoxically, parental fairness seems more likely to come from treating children differently in accordance with their individual behaviors than from treating them alike.[24] Of course, this assumes that family environments are within the normal range (i.e., free of abuse and deprivation).

The bottom line from our data was that growing up together does not make family members alike. Instead, our findings showed that personality similarity between relatives seems to come mostly from their shared genes. Furthermore, environmental effects that are most important in personality development appear to be those that are experienced apart from the family—the nonshared environmental factors; their contributions to the different personality traits were often close to those from genetic factors. A final point is that the Multidimensional Personality Questionnaire was *not* designed to assess personality heritability; rather, it was designed to assess personality variation. This feature of the instrument increased our confidence in the genetic effects that emerged.

Our biometrical analyses of the personality data, shown in Table 5-2, shed additional light on the genetic structure of personality. Estimates of genetic influence (heritabilities) for the eleven personality scales ranged from 0.39 to 0.58. The model included additive genetic, shared familial, and nonshared familial components. The genetic, shared familial, and nonshared familial components sum to 1.0. The model also included a C parameter indicating the extent to which the genetic component was additive (closer to 0.5) or nonadditive (closer to 0.0).

Nonadditivity was indicated for two personality scales (social potency and control) and one higher order factor (positive emotionality).[25] Thus, some personality traits seemed to be shaped by many interactive genes, reflecting the emergenic quality described in Chapter 3. Simple additive models of personality, endorsed by many personality psychologists at that time, were challenged by our data.

We had some surprises. One unexpected finding was the lack of a systematic shared environmental effect for traditionalism (endorsement of

Table 5-2. **Genetic and Environmental Components Estimates for the Multidimensional Personality Questionnaire's Primary Scales and Higher Order Factors**

	Genetic	C	Shared Environment	Nonshared Environment
Primary scale				
Well-being	0.48[a] (0.08)	0.29 (0.16)	0.13 (0.09)	0.40[a] (0.04)
Social potency	0.54[a] (0.07)	0.05[a] (0.21)	0.10 (0.08)	0.36[a] (0.04)
Achievement	0.39[a] (0.10)	0.13 (0.27)	0.11 (0.11)	0.51[a] (0.05)
Social closeness	0.40[a] (0.08)	0.19 (0.22)	0.19[a] (0.09)	0.41[a] (0.05)
Stress reaction	0.53[a] (0.04)	0.49 (0.17)	0.00[b]	0.47[a] (0.04)
Alienation	0.45[a] (0.13)	0.50[b]	0.11 (0.12)	0.44[a] (0.04)
Aggression	0.44[a] (0.05)	0.27 (0.19)	0.00[b]	0.56[a] (0.05)
Control	0.44[a] (0.05)	0.00[a,b]	0.00[b]	0.56[a] (0.05)
Harm avoidance	0.55[a] (0.04)	0.31 (0.15)	0.00[b]	0.45[a] (0.04)
Traditionalism	0.45[a] (0.10)	0.50[b]	0.12 (0.10)	0.43[a] (0.04)
Absorption	0.50[a] (0.10)	0.50[b]	0.03 (0.10)	0.47[a] (0.04)
Higher order factor				
Positive emotionality	0.40[a] (0.08)	0.00[a,b]	0.22[a] (0.07)	0.38[a] (0.04)
Negative emotionality	0.55[a] (0.11)	0.50[b]	0.02 (0.11)	0.43[a] (0.04)
Constraint	0.58[a] (0.04)	0.40 (0.14)	0.00[b]	0.43[a] (0.04)

Note: Standard error in parentheses. C: additivity-epistatic component; NSE: nonshared environmental component; SE: shared environmental component.

a. Differs significantly from the null value at $P<.05$.

b. Boundary solution, so no standard error computed.

Source: Adapted from Tellegen et al., "Personality Similarity in Twins Reared Apart and Together," *Journal of Personality and Social Psychology* 54 (1988): 1031–1039.

conventional family and moral values). However, in 1986, Australian twin researchers found genetic influence but little common environmental influence on the transmission of social attitudes such as right-wing authoritarianism. The Australian paper appeared the same year that we submitted our personality paper for publication. Likewise, a 1970s study showed little adoptive parent–child resemblance in authoritarianism, relative to biological parent–child pairs. Thus, our findings were consistent with those of others.

We also noted that Social Closeness (sociability; warmth and affection toward others) was the only primary scale to show significant within-family effects. We speculated that because people within families generally respond to affiliative or nonaffiliative behaviors in kind, a shared family effect on social closeness was not unexpected.[26] Thus, the data showed that some personality traits differed in heritability from others, although a number of traits showed similar heritabilities. Bouchard would revisit the Multidimensional Personality Questionnaire data in 2003 with an expanded reared-apart twin sample.

The 1989 ABC *Nightline* program on our personality findings was memorable. I regard it as one of the best media portrayals of our study because it let our participants speak for themselves. The show featured the then twenty-eight-year-old MZA triplets Robert (Bob) Shafran, David (Dave) Kellman, and Edward (Eddy) Galland, reunited when they were nineteen years old. Bob plainly stated one of the key findings in our paper: "We're very much alike—yet our parents are very different . . . we're alike in ways that had nothing to do with who our parents were."[27]

Bobby's views personify *active genotype-environment correlation*—the idea that people seek experiences consistent with their genetically based tendencies. Bouchard later captured this concept in his wonderful phrase "nature via nurture"—the idea that genetic factors are expressed "by influencing the character, selection, and impact of experiences during development."[28] Bouchard agreed with our critics that MZA twins probably do have more similar environments than DZA twins, *but they are environments of the twins' making.* Bouchard added that if people actively shape their environments, then individually tailored interventions for even highly heritable traits are possible.

The *Science* IQ Paper

The *Science* IQ paper was a significant moment in the history of the study. The MZA twin sample was large enough to present the long-awaited IQ data as well as findings from other physical and behavioral domains. A master table (Lykken's idea) compared the MZA data with available MZT data across twenty-two physical and behavioral traits, strengthening our findings and conclusions. Many people read this report, and we discovered new twin pairs as a result of the publication's reach. As Bouchard said, "The paper legitimated the study."

The *Science* paper was our first publication devoted almost exclusively to IQ, but it was the second submission on this topic. In the early 1980s, Bouchard had submitted an IQ report to *Science* based on twenty-nine MZA twin pairs and twelve DZA twin pairs, much fewer than the forty-eight MZA twin pairs in our 1990 paper. The decision to publish was based on pressure from one of our funding sources, which wanted to see how the scientific community responded to the findings. The article was rejected largely due to the small sample size, so Bouchard delayed publishing the IQ data until additional pairs were assessed. Note that the studies by Newman et al. and Juel-Nielsen included nineteen and twelve MZA twin pairs, respectively, and as early as 1981 the MISTRA had studied thirty.[29]

The genesis of the 1990 IQ article can be traced to a 1982 conference on the biological bases of individuality.[30] Bouchard recalled that his talk on the MISTRA was attacked "up one side and down the other" by a participant who believed that nurture was the primary influence on behavior. The following day, Bouchard was pulled aside by a biochemist from New York who asked him for a detailed description of the reared-apart twin design. It was Daniel E. Koshland Jr., the man who would become *Science*'s editor in chief in 1985. In a roundtable discussion after Bouchard's presentation, Koshland called the MISTRA "a terrific study."[31]

Several years later, Koshland called Bouchard to request a paper on the MISTRA for a special genome issue of the journal—and he needed it in six weeks. Bouchard, who had just become the department chair, wasn't sure he could deliver it in that amount of time. Koshland asked, "Do you know who you're talking to?" To which Bouchard replied, "Yes, the editor of *Science*, and we'll have a paper to you in six weeks."

We had studied more than one hundred reared-apart twin and triplet sets by the time our *Science* paper was in progress. The paper reported IQ analyses for forty-eight MZA twin pairs for whom we had processed data; the DZA twin sample was still modest (thirty pairs), and several recently assessed pairs were omitted. Given the significance of this paper in the history of the study, in Table 5-3 I have displayed the descriptive characteristics for the fifty-six MZA twin pairs we had assessed at that point in time. Both parents' educational levels (mean: two years of high school) were below those of volunteer adoptive parents, and their educational attainment and socioeconomic status were quite variable. The twins' average IQ score exceeded the population mean of 100, because the sample lacked twins in the lowest ranges (below 70).

Three general intelligence measures were available for the MISTRA twins: the Wechsler Adult Intelligence Scale (WAIS),[32] the Raven/Mill-Hill Composite,[33] and the first principal component (a variable subsuming a larger number of correlated variables) based on the special mental ability tests in the Hawaii and Comprehensive Ability Batteries. The WAIS is an individually administered test consisting of six verbal subtests (Information, Digit Span, Vocabulary, Arithmetic, Comprehension, and Similarities) and five nonverbal subtests (Picture Completion, Picture Arrangement, Block Design, Symbol, and Object Assembly). It was the first activity scheduled for Tuesday morning, so twins were well rested during its

Table 5-3. Age, Contact Measures, IQ Score, and Parental Education for 56 MZA Twin Pairs

Measure	Age (Years)	Time Together prior to Separation (months)	Time Apart to First Reunion (years)	Total Contact Time (weeks)	IQ Score (WAIS)	Father's Years of Education	Mother's Years of Education
Mean	41.0	5.1	30.0	112.5	108.1	10.7	10.3
SD	12.0	8.5	14.3	230.7	10.8	4.5	3.7
Range	19.0–68.0	0–48.7	.5–64.7	1–1,233	79–133	0–20	0–19

Note: SD: standard deviation; WAIS: Wechsler Adult Intelligence Scale.
Source: Adapted from Bouchard et al., "Sources of Human Psychological Differences: The Minnesota Study of Twins Reared Apart," *Science* 250 (1990): 223–228.

administration. Each twin was tested at exactly the same time by a different professional psychometrist, who had no affiliation with the study and who scored the protocol immediately upon completion.

The Raven is a nonverbal measure of problem-solving skill, and the Mill-Hill is a multiple-choice test of word knowledge. These two tests are often given together and were administered to the twins by computer as part of Lykken's laboratory assessment. There was no time limit for completing these tests. According to Lykken, allowing unlimited time shows how quickly an individual thinks and how long he or she persists at a task before giving up, factors that may work multiplicatively.[34] The special mental ability tests were administered to twins in several sessions during the week. The rationale for testing them together is discussed in Chapter 2.

The intraclass correlations for the general intelligence measures completed by the MISTRA twins and twins in the three previous reared-apart twin studies are shown in Table 5-4. The consistency of the findings across studies in the primary, secondary, and tertiary tests was striking, suggesting that 64 to 74 percent (separate tests) and 69 to 75 percent (mean of multiple tests) of the IQ variance is associated with genetic factors. Thus, replication both between and within studies was demonstrated. This range was higher than the 47 to 58 percent range indicated by other kinship studies. However, most twin and sibling studies used young samples, whereas our study and the previous reared-apart twin studies used

Table 5-4.   IQ Intraclass Correlations and Standard Deviations for the Four Reared-Apart Twin Studies

Study and Test (Primary/Secondary/Tertiary)	n (pairs)	Primary Test	Secondary Test	Tertiary Test	Mean
Newman et al.					
SB/Otis	19/19	0.68 ± 0.12	0.74 ± 0.10	—	0.71
Juel-Nielsen					
WB/Raven	12/12	0.64 ± 0.17	0.73 ± 0.13	—	0.69
Shields					
MH/Dominoes	38/37	0.74 ± 0.07	0.76 ± 0.07	—	0.75
Bouchard et al.					
WAIS/RMH/FPC	48/42/43	0.69 ± 0.07	0.78 ± 0.07	0.78 ± 0.07	0.75

Note: The original data from Newman et al. (SB: 0.670, Otis: 0.727) and Juel-Nielsen (WB: 0.62) were presented as correlations, not as intraclass correlations. Bouchard recalculated the data to compute intraclass correlations. Juel-Nielsen did not present the correlation for the Raven. FPC: First Principal Component; MH: Mill-Hill; RMH: Raven/Mill-Hill; SB: Stanford-Binet; WB: Wechsler-Bellevue.

Source: Adapted from Bouchard et al., "Sources of Human Psychological Differences: The Minnesota Study of Twins Reared Apart," *Science* 250 (1990): 223–228.

mostly adults. This was an important difference because IQ heritability has been shown to increase with age.[35]

We examined the IQ data with reference to (1) associations between the twins' environmental similarities and their IQ scores, (2) contributions of prereunion and postreunion contact to IQ resemblance, and (3) similarity of the MZA and MZT twins across other behavioral and physical measures. These efforts were undertaken partly in anticipation of critics' comments, although, as I will explain later, we did not predict one of the most common criticisms—our alleged incorrect reporting of how much IQ variance was due to genetic factors.

Answers to questions about the effects of correlated rearing environments on IQ came partly from the twins' responses to a "Physical Facilities in the Home" checklist. This inventory asked twins to indicate the presence of musical instruments, cars, foreign language books, and other items in their childhood homes. They were also asked to list household items that they recalled but were missing from our list. We obtained information about their parents' educations and occupations (socioeconomic indicators) as part of the Life History Interview. Each twin also completed the Moos Family Environment Scale, a form requesting information about their parents' treatment and rearing of them in childhood and adolescence. We calculated placement coefficients (indicating the degree of co-twin similarity for socioeconomic status indicators, home facilities, and rearing factors), correlations between IQ scores and these environmental measures, and estimates of the degree to which similarity in these measures contributed to the twins' WAIS IQ similarity. The placement coefficients and other results from these analyses are displayed in Table 5-5.

The maximum contribution to the MZA trait correlations from a single variable was 0.03 (Material Possessions). We did not detect significant effects on the twins' IQ scores or on their IQ resemblance from the environmental measures. Family influences have been shown to affect sibling similarity in cognition[36] and rate of skill acquisition in young children,[37] but these effects diminish in adolescence and adulthood.

Our findings did not suggest that environmental variables did not affect the twins' IQ scores in individual cases. Some reared-apart twins with more favorable educational backgrounds outperformed their less advantaged co-twins, but the effects were not systematic. Recall that the Newman et al. study found substantial correlations between educational advantage and IQ score (0.79 and 0.55), but also found intraclass correlations of 0.68 and 0.74 for their two IQ measures.[38] Despite some twins' more favorable educational upbringing, MZA co-twins reared apart were gen-

Table 5-5.   Placement Coefficients for the Environmental Variables, Correlations between IQ and the Placement Variables, and Contributions of Placement to the Twins' IQ Resemblance

Placement Variable	MZA Similarity (R_{ff})	Correlation: IQ-Placement Variable (r_{ft})	Contribution: Placement to MZA Correlation $(R_{ff} \times r^2_{ft})$
SES indicators			
Father's education	0.134	0.100	0.001
Mother's education	0.412	−0.001	0.000
Father's SES	0.267	0.174	0.008
Physical facilities			
Material possessions	0.402	0.279[a]	0.032
Scientific/technical	0.151	−0.090	0.001
Cultural	−0.085	−0.279[a]	−0.007
Mechanical	0.303	0.077	0.002
Relevant FES scales			
Achievement	0.110	−0.103	0.001
Intellectual orientation	0.270	0.106	0.003

Note: FES: family environment scale; SES: socioeconomic status.
a. Indicates correlation that is statistically significantly different from zero at $P<.01$.
Source: Adapted from Bouchard et al., "Sources of Human Psychological Differences: The Minnesota Study of Twins Reared Apart," *Science* 250 (1990): 223–228.

erally more similar to one another than they were to members of other twin pairs.

We found that the degree of social contact between co-twins was not associated with their IQ similarity. We also examined correlations between the absolute within-pair IQ difference and four contact measures to see if the twins who had spent more time together were more alike in IQ. However, these correlations were all small and not statistically significant.[39] Again, these findings do not mean that environmental variables do not affect some twins' IQ scores. Instead, they tell us that environmental variables work in ways that differ from how most psychologists believed they did. Specifically, shared genes, rather than social contact between family members, explained the twins' resemblance in measured intelligence.

Table 4 in the *Science* paper reported the MZA and MZT correlations and reliabilities (consistency or repeatability of a measure) for nine classes of variables. It is an informative compilation of data in that the MZA and MZT twins showed remarkable similarity across measures. This was evident for physical characteristics (e.g., systolic blood pressure, electroencephalogram [EEG] activity, and heart rate) and behavioral traits (e.g., personality, religiosity, and social attitudes). Again, these data show that shared environments have minimal effects on many traits once individuals reach young adulthood. An abbreviated version of that table is shown as Table 5-6.

We drew three key conclusions from our IQ analysis:

1. *Approximately 70 percent of the population variance in intelligence in middle-class, industrialized societies could be linked to genetic factors.* This finding would not apply to impoverished or underprivileged individuals for whom severe conditions may not support normal development.[40] None of our reared-apart twins came from such adverse backgrounds. This finding also did not imply that intelligence could not be enhanced by educational or remedial interventions.

2. *Modern Western societies' institutions and practices did not greatly constrain the development of individual variations in psychological traits.* The heritability of traits increases when individuals have access to similar, trait-relevant opportunities (e.g., baseball games

Table 5-6.   Intraclass Correlations (r_i) for MZA and MZT Twins across Selected Measures

Variables	MZA		MZT		
	r_i	n (pairs)	r_i	n (pairs)	Reliability
EEG					
8–12- HZ alpha activity	0.80	35	0.81	42	NA
Midfrequency alpha activity	0.80	35	0.82	42	NA
Physiologic					
Systolic blood pressure	0.64	56	0.70	34	0.70
IQ scores					
WAIS-Full scale	0.69	48	0.88	40	0.90
WAIS-Verbal	0.64	48	0.88	40	0.84
WAIS-Performance	0.71	48	0.79	40	0.86
Information processing					
Speed of response	0.56	40	0.73	50	NA
Psychological interests					
Career and leisure (mean of 23)	0.39	52	0.48	116	0.82
Occupational (mean of 17)	0.40	40	0.49	376	0.75

Note: EEG: electroencephalogram; NA: not applicable; WAIS: Wechsler Adult Intelligence Scale.

Source: Adapted from Bouchard et al., "Sources of Human Psychological Differences: The Minnesota Study of Twins Reared Apart," *Science* 250 (1990): 223–228.

are available for most boys, so baseball skills should be heritable). Similarly, heritability decreases when environments are variable (e.g., language characteristics are closely tied to national regions, so accents and idioms should reflect environmental effects). Members of Western societies display considerable variability in intelligence, personality, interests, and attitudes, all of which show relatively high heritabilities. In other words, individual differences in the behaviors we measured were allowed freedom of expression within the participants' environments. If we had measured the male twins' baseball skills, it is likely we would have found genetic effects. In fact, twin studies of athletic skill have found genetic influence on running speed, static strength, and oxygen uptake.[41] Had we compared the accents and idioms of our twins from Georgia and Michigan, or Kentucky and Connecticut, we would have probably found environmental effects.

3. *The MZA twins' striking behavioral resemblance was largely due to their shared genes, which increased the probability that their environments were alike.* The immediate causes of most psychological variations are probably environmental in nature. However, the environments of individuals are significantly fashioned by their genotypes that selectively guide them toward certain people, places, and experiences and away from others (i.e., active genotype-environment correlation). Children with sports interests will choose these activities at school and on weekends. According to Martin and colleagues, learning experiences "augment rather than eradicate the effects of the genotype on behavior."[42] We believe that though the twins grew up in different homes they had choices, and what they chose largely reflected their genetically influenced abilities and interests. That is, it may be that the twins' environments were similar in the sense that each took an active role in creating them and that this tendency continued to adulthood. The Jim twins had workbenches in their basements, and the fireman twins had social lives centered around their fire stations. We concluded that environmental interventions in the areas of intelligence, personality, and temperament would be more effective if tailored to the specific interests and needs of individuals.

We ended the *Science* paper with a consideration of the relevance of our findings to the then new discipline of evolutionary psychology. Evolutionary psychology is concerned with identifying behavioral mechanisms that evolved to meet the environmental challenges and demands faced by our ancestors. It attempts to understand how and why the human mind is designed the way it is, what the mind is designed to do, and how environmental events interact with the mind to eventuate in behavioral phenotypes. Two classes of explanation—ultimate and proximal—are recognized. Ultimate explanations emphasize behavioral and cognitive functions with reference to survival and reproduction. Proximal explanations consider the immediate events giving rise to different behaviors.[43]

Evolutionary psychology focuses on species-typical behaviors, whereas behavioral genetics focuses on individual differences. But both are concerned with identifying the origins and functions of behavior. We suggested that whatever the answer, behavioral variation is characteristic of modern society and cannot be ignored.

Results from the *Science* paper appeared in hundreds of newspapers, magazines, and broadcasts across the country and around the world. Psychology professor Robert Plomin applauded the study, emphasizing the rarity of explaining even 10 percent of the variation in complex traits. Psychology professor David Rowe, while not denying the importance of parenting, reiterated our view that parents may be less responsible for their children's behaviors than they thought.

In contrast, Dr. Norman Krasnegor of the National Institute of Child Health and Human Development said that if the 70 percent IQ heritability estimate was true "it shouldn't matter what you do or where you go to school." However, heritability does not deny the importance of learning and experience. Bouchard said it best in a passage repeated in several news sources: "We think of each pair of identical twins as one piece of music played by two different musicians. The music can be played fantastically or it may not run right. But you'll always be able to recognize the piece. That's because nature writes the score. Environment is responsible for the playing technique."[44]

More interesting than the media reports were the letters we received from *Science* readers. Harvard University biologist Edward O. Wilson wrote to Bouchard directly:

> The extraordinary effort and care you and your associates put into this landmark study should remind all of the fundamental interest and importance, and reasonableness, of genetic variation in human behavior, while silencing all but the diehard critics, who would go down fighting even if you laid out the full nucleotide sequences with mathematically perfect forms of reaction. (October 31, 1990)

There were more critical comments than congratulatory notes, but this did not mean that most readers rejected our findings. The three individuals who reviewed the manuscript upon submission were enthusiastic, but they all requested modifications—even though the paper had been invited by *Science*'s editor, it was not accepted unconditionally. One asserted that "Twins reared in different homes provide the clearest and most easily comprehended estimates of the degree to which genetic resemblance directly affects phenotypic resemblance." Another wrote that "[The paper] has great scientific merit, and it is also of wide general interest," and asked for clarification of the environmental interactions likely to affect IQ. The third reviewer was the most revealing with respect to his or her initial reservations and final opinion:

> I have read this manuscript as a hostile reader. I have looked to find the errors in your ways. In fact, I cannot lay my finger on any specific item that would invalidate the paper ... It is quite astounding to me that [general intelligence] data collected at different times [by three reared-apart twin studies], with different techniques, with different instruments, with different populations, all result in very similar numerical values. The results are too good to believe. Perhaps the evil influence of Burt [whose data proved questionable] has come into the picture ... I would hope you would show [your statistical colleagues] these results and see if they feel that they are a bit too good to believe. Such an analysis might make many of your readers happier.

The expected criticisms of our *Science* report were familiar, having been raised by Taylor in 1980. There were seventeen such comments in my files, but those by MIT mathematician Richard M. Dudley and Harvard University microbiologist Jonathan Beckwith were emblematic of readers' concerns. They focused on the effects of the co-twins' rearing and educational similarities on their IQ scores, the pressure on the twins to appear alike, and the inability of readers to examine the original material.[45]

We responded to these challenges in a letter to *Science*. Within-pair correlations between co-twins' IQ differences and educational differences do not weaken genetic explanations of individual differences in intelligence. "It is the correlation between a measured environmental feature and the variance in IQ *not accounted for by genetic factors*."[46] Some higher-IQ twins in our study and in the others had an educational advantage, but the direction of causation was unclear. It was also unlikely that "social pressure to appear to be similar" could explain the twins' similarities in our measures of mental abilities, psychophysiology, personality, and vocational interests because the twins had not seen these protocols until they arrived in Minnesota.[47] Lastly, the University of Minnesota's institutional review board (like all university review panels) requires confidentiality of participant data. This was stated in our protocol, and the twins signed a consent form acknowledging their understanding of this agreement.

The surprise was the eight letters voicing concern that our percentage of IQ variation associated with genetic factors was 0.49, not 0.70. In other words, these correspondences indicated that we should have squared 0.70 to arrive at 0.49. However, while ordinary (Pearson) correlations are squared to derive the proportion of variance in one measure explained by the variance in the other measure, intraclass correlations already express the proportion of variance shared by the twins.[48] Other explanations of the differences between the two types of correlations are available.[49]

As indicated earlier, many people have wondered whether MZ twins' shared prenatal environments contribute to their intellectual resemblance. Information on the reared-apart twins' prenatal and perinatal histories was largely unavailable. Twins, especially MZ twins, are more highly subject to adverse birth events (e.g., fetal transfusion syndrome or prematurity) than DZ twins and nontwins.[50] These events may result in IQ differences between co-twins when they are young, although their effects may lessen over time.[51] The late developmental psychologist Ronald Wilson suggested that developing organisms have "buffering mechanisms" that may protect them from early insults and that some individuals can withstand early trauma better than others.[52]

Our *Science* IQ paper findings have held up, having been confirmed by reared-apart twin studies conducted elsewhere. In 1992, the Swedish Adoption and Twin Study of Aging reported a 0.78 IQ intraclass correlation for forty-five MZA twin pairs.[53] These data, together with the findings from the three early studies and the MISTRA, yielded a weighted average correlation of 0.73, based on 162 MZA twin pairs.[54] This finding is extremely robust. The controversy over whether or not intelligence is genetically mediated seems to have dissipated somewhat as scientific interest and public attention have focused on factors affecting other phenotypes, such as sexual orientation and obesity. But that does not prevent our findings from being misused—the *Science* IQ article is posted on the Web site of former Louisiana Republican State Representative and Ku Klux Klan member David Duke under the tags, "Intelligence: Heredity Vs. Environment" and "Racial Differences."[55] Race differences in intelligence were never addressed in our article.

During the years of the personality and IQ papers and beyond, many articles were published on many topics. In late 1988, Lykken's Swiss colleague Hans H. Stassen reviewed the EEG findings from a somewhat larger sample of our reared-apart twins, twenty-eight MZA and twenty-one DZA.[56] Evidence of genetic effects on these measures continued—the MZA co-twins' EEGs were as similar to each other as the EEGs of a single individual measured over time. Other papers reported the first reared-apart twin analyses of job satisfaction and responses skin conductance. None of these publications drew the same attention as did the *Science* article, but some findings strongly challenged conventional theories within certain disciplines, industrial relations being one of them.

CHAPTER SIX

Job Satisfaction, Cardiac Characteristics, and More (1989–1990)

THE *SCIENCE* IQ PAPER was a key accomplishment during the years 1988–1990, but not the only one. Our study of job satisfaction was the first attempt by anyone to examine genetic influence on the workplace experience. During these years, we also reported analyses of the electrical conductance of the skin, heart rate, special mental abilities, information processing, psychopathology, religiosity, intelligence, and personality. The choice of behaviors to be analyzed, and when, were affected by the amount of accumulated data, significant twin findings reported by other laboratories, and personal time available to the investigators. Most of our analyses concerned intelligence and personality because there were comparable data from the earlier reared-apart twin studies and because these topics interested psychologists in general.

Job Satisfaction

Our collaborators on the job satisfaction paper were Dr. Richard D. Arvey from the University of Minnesota's Industrial Relations Center and his graduate student Lauren M. Abraham.[1] Both of them viewed studying reared-apart twins as a novel and exciting approach to understanding factors affecting job satisfaction.

As a Minnesota graduate student in the late 1960s, Arvey became acquainted with Bouchard over discussion of a possible dissertation topic. He returned to the University of Minnesota as a faculty member in industrial relations in 1983. The source of Arvey's inkling that genes might affect job-related attitudes is uncertain, but he had followed the progress of the MISTRA since it began. "I contacted Bouchard to ask if he was gathering job satisfaction measures on the twins and he said 'no—why?' We talked about the possibility that genes contributed to job satisfaction, then he said 'let's do it!' That was Tom. That was the start of our collaboration, and I am grateful to him for it." By 2010, an *Economist* essay describing twin studies in management science showed how far the field had progressed in the past twenty-five years.[2]

In the mid-1980s, individual differences in job satisfaction were well known to researchers in industrial relations. In 1986, investigators found that affective dispositions (the emotional state of the person, such as their initiation of humor or need for reassurance) that influenced job satisfaction were constant over time. But the investigators could not disentangle the genetic and environmental sources of these dispositions, possibly because their archival data on individuals from three longitudinal growth studies lacked genetically informative kinships, such as twins and adoptees.[3] It seemed to us that heredity *could* affect the ways in which people react to their work contexts, given that genetic factors had been shown to affect a wide variety of other behaviors.

The reared-apart twins completed a work history questionnaire as part of the standard life history assessment. The work history component included the short form of the Minnesota Job Satisfaction Questionnaire developed in 1967 by David Weiss and colleagues.[4] The questionnaire manual specifies an "intrinsic" satisfaction scale that measures workers' personal values and interests affecting job satisfaction. The manual also specifies an "extrinsic" scale that measures external working situations and standards that may affect job satisfaction. A general satisfaction scale is created by summing the scores from the intrinsic and extrinsic scales. We also administered a one-item question measuring overall job satisfaction and classified the twins' occupations according to complexity, motor skills, physical demands, and undesirable working conditions. Data were available for thirty-four MZA twin pairs—twenty-five female and nine male—who completed the questionnaire between 1983 and 1987.

The reared-apart twins showed significantly higher job satisfaction levels than the normative group on all three scales (intrinsic, extrinsic, and overall), but the differences were slight. Intraclass correlations for the twenty individual items ranged from 0.043 (working conditions) to 0.371 (be "somebody" in the community), and five were statistically significant. Intraclass correlations for the three satisfaction scales, the overall satisfaction item, and the four job-rating scales are displayed in Table 6-1.

The intraclass correlation for the general satisfaction scale was statistically significant ($r_i = 0.309$). Upon removing the thirteen twin pairs

Table 6-1.   MZA Intraclass Correlations for Job Satisfaction Measures

Variable	r_i
Four scales	
Intrinsic satisfaction	0.315[a]
Extrinsic satisfaction	0.109
General satisfaction	0.309[a]
Overall satisfaction	0.166
Job rating scales	
Complexity	0.443[a]
Motor skills	0.356[a]
Physical demands	0.338[a]
Unusual working conditions	—

a. $P<.05$. Intraclass correlations less than zero were not reported.

Source: Adapted from Arvey et al., "Job Satisfaction: Environmental and Genetic Components," *Journal of Applied Psychology* 74 (1989): 187–192.

that included housewives, the correlation remained virtually unchanged ($r_i=0.304$). Most interesting, the intrinsic satisfaction scale correlation was statistically significant (r_i 0.315), but the extrinsic satisfaction scale correlation was not (r_i 0.109). We had expected this result because intrinsic aspects of job satisfaction are probably tied more directly to individuals' work experiences, such as challenge and achievement. In addition, favorable or unfavorable working conditions, like long lunches or insufficient pay, are likely to make everyone happy or upset, whereas not everyone gains personal gratification from being creative or productive.

Intraclass correlations for three of the four job-rating scales (complexity, motor skills, and physical demands) showed that the MZA twins held jobs that were similar on these attributes, a finding exemplifying active genotype-environment correlation—people generally seek jobs that satisfy their interests. Little change in the job-satisfaction scales was seen upon controlling for the job scores, confirming that personal values are key to satisfaction on the job.

Job interests often coincide but may be expressed differently due to circumstances. An MZA female twin reared in the United States obtained an advanced science degree, while her twin sister reared in China received little education. Both twins were extremely talented in mathematics, and the China-raised twin used her quantitative skills as a cashier. When MZA male twins Jake and Keith met at age twenty-three, Jake was a pump mechanic, and Keith was a welder, jobs requiring manual dexterity and technical skill. At age fifty-five, both twins had become computer network information technology (IT) administrators.

Even though we found significant genetic effects (approximately 30 percent) underlying intrinsic and general job satisfaction, the remaining 70 percent might be linked to factors such as drive time to work or child care responsibilities. And, contrary to our expectation, the MZA intraclass correlation for intrinsic satisfaction, while indicating a genetic effect, was not significantly higher than the corresponding correlation for extrinsic satisfaction; a larger sample might have yielded a statistically significant difference between them. Lastly, our small sample was composed largely of women, limiting the generalizability of the findings; perhaps females are less vocal about unfavorable aspects of their professions. In later years, we would revisit the origins of job satisfaction with larger samples and learn that our initial findings did not change.

Industrial organizational psychologists Russell Cropanzano and Keith James challenged our findings.[5] They suggested that the twin's similarity in job satisfaction may have been inflated by their similar socioeconomic circumstances and that more sophisticated statistical methods should have been applied. However, we found little co-twin resemblance in the twins' relevant child-rearing accounts, so it seemed that they were raised in dissimilar environments. Furthermore, there were no available studies showing that early family environmental factors were substantially linked to later job satisfaction—although this did not mean that there were none. We agreed that job satisfaction studies would benefit from larger samples and quantitative modeling, but the methodological approach we took was straightforward and appropriate to the study as conducted.[6]

Arvey continued to collaborate with us on work-related papers until he left Minnesota in 2006. Until 1992, Lauren Abraham (later Lauren Keller) did as well, as a faculty member in the Department of Management and Finance at St. Cloud University in Minnesota. Arvey recalled being surprised by the 0.30 heritability of job satisfaction—he expected it to be higher, given that genetic effects on behavior are pervasive. He also said that our 1989 paper was considered "revolutionary" by several of his colleagues because it challenged the predominantly environmental views held by industrial relations researchers at that time.

Skin Conductance

Lykken's laboratory in Diehl Hall, located in the mass of hospital buildings on the south side of the campus, was fascinating to me. His quarters were remotely located at the end of a series of narrow hallways that were hard to navigate at first. Staff members, myself included, delivered and picked up one twin on Monday and the other twin on Tuesday afternoons.

(Twins arrived together on Monday afternoons for photographs, hand-prints, and fingerprints, after which one twin was escorted elsewhere for medical and psychiatric interviews.) While the twins were at these appointments, the research staff and I reviewed their inventory booklets and updated their progress on the participant checklist taped to the wall of our Elliott Hall headquarters.

Lykken's psychophysiological laboratory was packed with computers, wires, and a booth with a soundproof door for silence while twins were tested. His publications, such as a 1998 study of the heritability of skin conductance, revealed a great deal about the science that went on there.

There are many meaningless stimuli in our environments such as the sounds of washing machines cycling and the whistles of trains passing. If we could not habituate (stop responding) to these noises, it would be nearly impossible to focus on important tasks.

Skin conductance response refers to changes in specific electrical properties of the skin. These changes, associated with sweat gland activity, are elicited by stimuli causing arousal, orienting (immediate response to a change in the environment), and emotions such as fear and anger. Research in this area may offer insight into why some people are more distracted by leaking faucets than others, and why some people are more task-oriented than others.

Skin conductance response decreases in a negatively accelerating way when individuals are presented with what Lykken called "a punctate stimulus," a brief tone that is presented repeatedly. However, he pointed out that habituation (elimination of a response due to continuous exposure to the stimulus that triggered the response) may be confounded by how research subjects individually interpret the significance of such stimuli. For example, some individuals might start counting repeated sounds, assuming that acquiring this information was part of the experiment. Lykken and his colleague, William Iacono, resolved this problem in 1979 by instructing the participants to ignore any tones or other sounds they might hear, while encouraging them to focus on an engaging task they provided.[7] They repeated this approach with our twins.

Ours was not the first laboratory to consider a genetic influence on skin conductance response. A 1966 study of eleven MZT twin pairs and eleven DZT twin pairs found correlations of 0.75 and 0.13, respectively, for a measure of habituation.[8] However, not all early twin studies in this area produced consistent findings. Beginning in March 1979, the constant stream of reared-apart pairs through Minneapolis enabled new analyses of psychophysiological questions. Nine years later, in 1988, Lykken and other MISTRA investigators reported skin conductance findings based on the same four-group design used in our personality paper: MZA (n=43 pairs), MZT (n=36 pairs), DZA (n=25 pairs), and DZT (n=17 pairs).[9] The material that follows comes from the original publication that included numerous detailed findings, charts, and graphs.

The reared-apart twins were older (mean age: 40.8 years, standard deviation [SD]=12.7, range: 12–61 years) than the reared-together twins (mean age: 21.5 years, SD=4.8, range: 16–45 years). Three socioeconomic indices of the separated twins' adoptive homes were modestly but significantly correlated (0.21–0.30, P<.05), as were their fathers' and mothers' highest completed school grade (0.25 and 0.40, respectively). However, none of these variables related to the psychophysiological measures.

The measurement procedures were essentially the same for reared-apart and reared-together twins. The only exception was the use of a different method of eliciting an estimate of maximal skin conductance response for use in what is called range correction. A person's skin conductance varies over a particular range because of the nature of the skin and/or the electrode area, so these factors need to be controlled.[10]

Twins were seated in the experimental chamber for many of the tasks they completed in Lykken's laboratory. Several MZA twins expressed concern over being placed in a small, windowless space with the door shut, and their co-twins usually had the same response.

In order to estimate the maximum skin conductance response, twins used a sterile mouthpiece to blow up a small balloon suspended in a clear cube; a pin at the top of the cube punctured the balloon when it had filled with sufficient air. The maximum value for reared-together twins was the peak skin conductance during the task minus the tonic (muscle tension or contraction) skin conductance level before the task. An additional maximum estimate was obtained for reared-apart twins: the twins were told they would hear a loud blast of noise within the next minute following the balloon test. The maximum value was the amplitude of the skin conductance response detected within three seconds after the loud noise began.

There was also interest in how quickly the twins habituated to stimuli. Lykken told the twins he was interested in finding out how fast they could learn to ignore a series of loud tones. He instructed them to focus on a story that they would hear from a speaker on the opposite wall. Electrodes were attached to the index and third fingers of both twins' hands,[11] and data collection commenced three seconds after the onset of the stimulus. An explanation of the biometrical model used for data analysis is provided in the appendix of Lykken's paper.

The MZT (0.42 to 0.72) and MZA (0.16 to 0.61) twin correlations for the different skin conductance measures were generally substantial and exceeded the DZ (DZT and DZA combined) correlations (–0.05 to 0.35), indicating a genetic influence. The MZA twins were about as similar as the MZT twins on most measures, showing an absence of shared environmental effects. In addition, the majority of MZT and MZA correlations were larger than twice the DZ correlations, suggesting that skin conductance characteristics are complex emergenic traits.

Lykken also looked at the MZA data organized by sex. This time, the MZA males were the most alike on almost all the measures. This was not the only time that greater MZA male than MZA female twin similarity was found—the weight and sexual orientation studies also produced such findings. The observed sex difference in skin conductance could have a genetic basis in that MZ female twins differ in X-inactivation patterns, or the silencing of one X chromosome in each of their cells about six to eight days after conception.[12] In fact, genes on the X chromosome can cause one type of sweat gland anomaly.[13] Repeating the biometrical analysis with only the male twins increased the heritabilities and reduced the shared environmental estimates to zero. This showed that some factors, possibly genetic in origin, differentially affect male and female skin conductance response.

These findings confirmed the 1966 study showing much higher MZ than DZ twin resemblance in skin conductance response. In fact, about 40 percent of the total variance and most of the stable variance in the number of trials to habituation appeared to have genetic origins. Variation in physiological processes associated with sensitivity to insignificant environmental stimuli may underlie the individual differences Lykken found in this twin study and in the individual behavioral differences in the people around us.

These findings mattered because low electrodermal reactivity, although rare among healthy individuals, had been found among patients with major affective disorders such as bipolar disorder and depression. Nonresponding also occurs independently of symptoms shown by schizophrenic, unipolar, and bipolar patients. Based on Lykken's findings of genetic influence, skin conductance response might be a reliable index of predisposition to a psychiatric disorder among people with affected family members.

Note that the habituation stimuli (tones) consisted of alternate sounds presented to the twins as they exhaled or inhaled. This procedure balanced the possible effects of sinus arrhythmia (normal increase in heart rate when breathing in) on one of several cardiovascular measures that was recorded, but not analyzed in Lykken's 1988 paper.

Cardiac Characteristics

Cardiovascular characteristics were of great interest to the medical team headed by Dr. Naip Tuna, a Romanian-born Turkish cardiologist who charmed the twins even though he often made them wait. Genetic factors in heart functions were the subject of a 1989 paper by Drs. Bruce Hanson, Tuna, Bouchard, and others.[14]

When the MISTRA was underway, several reared-together twin studies had reported genetic contributions to variability in measures of the heart.[15] One problem with these studies was that the heritabilities of the cardiac measures were estimated using intraclass correlations alone. As indicated in Chapter 2, doubling the difference between the MZT and DZT intraclass correlations estimates a trait's narrow heritability (additive genetic effects), but modeling procedures allow further partitioning of genetic and environmental variance. This situation was rectified by using a model fitting approach that permitted the simultaneous analysis of the reared-apart twin data from the MISTRA and the reared-together twin data from studies conducted in Finland and the United States.[16]

I remember escorting twins to the University of Minnesota's Variety Club Heart Hospital for their electrocardiograms (ECGs), echocardiograms, and exercise stress test. An ECG traces the heart's electrical activity during a cardiac cycle (all cardiac events occurring between two consecutive heartbeats). An echocardiogram uses ultrasound to produce one- and two-dimensional images of the heart. Twins especially enjoyed the echocardiogram because they could see a visual picture of their heart's movement. An exercise stress test evaluates the exercise capacity and the electrocardiographic response (rate, rhythm, and changes in ECG waveforms) during maximal stress.

The twins were examined separately, in succession. As usual, they worked on their questionnaire booklets while waiting to be called, seated far apart.

The twins in the cardiac characteristics study included twenty-nine MZA female pairs, twenty MZA male pairs, one MZA male triplet set, seventeen female DZA pairs, and seven DZA male pairs. The twins' vectorcardiograms (graphic representation of the heart's electrical activity) were recorded for forty-three pairs, but only the ECG data were analyzed.

The ECG readings for the first twenty-four twin pairs were measured manually and read by a cardiologist according to the Minnesota Code methodology, developed in 1960 and updated in 1987. The subsequently studied twin pairs had their data read by a cardiologist who confirmed the computer-generated data and reports. Corroboration was critical, according to Hanson:

> It truly takes an experienced eye to confirm that an abnormality called by the computer is correct. It was also possible that a cardiologist might discover an abnormality that the computer had missed. Tuna would sit there with his ECG calipers and confirm measurements before signing off on ECGs from hospital patients. As I recall, Tuna looked at all the electrocardiograms, but he allowed his colleagues to officially read them as they were blind to the twin status of the subjects.

Hanson also emphasized to me that normal variations in cardiac characteristics are of medical interest. There was, however, very little variation among our twins, and few showed cardiac pathology. For example, British MZA twins Barbara and Daphne had slight heart murmurs of a nonserious nature.[17] Our only exceptions included two MZA male triplets who showed right bundle branch block (obstruction of conduction of cardiac electrical impulses along the right bundle branch of the heart's conduction system), and one MZA female twin who showed an atrioventricular block—a delay or interruption in conduction between the atria (the two upper chambers of the heart) and the ventricles (the two lower heart chambers). These sets were excluded from our analysis. Table 6-2 displays the intraclass correlations for the cardiac characteristics that were

Table 6-2. **MZA and DZA Intraclass Correlations for Cardiac Characteristics**

ECG Measure[a]	MZA Twins		DZA Twins	
	r_i	n (pairs)	r_i	n (pairs)
PR interval	0.78[b]	49	0.50[b]	24
QRS duration	0.45[b]	49	0.70[b]	24
QT interval	0.65[b]	49	0.22	24
QTc interval	0.48[b]	49	0.43[b]	24
Ventricular rate	0.49[b]	49	0.34	24
P duration	0.00	23	0.69[b]	16
ΣQRS (mV)[c]	0.73[b]	24	0.49[b]	18
ΣP (mV)[c]	0.60[b]	24	0.16	18
ΣT(mV)[c]	0.17	24	0.69[b]	18

a. Parameter definitions are provided in the book's Web site. ECG: electrocardiogram.

b. $P < .05$.

c. Measured from the X, Y, and Z leads of the vectorcardiogram. mV: voltage magnitude.

Source: Adapted from Hanson et al., "Genetic Factors in the Electrocardiogram and Heart Rate of Twins Reared Apart and Together," *American Journal of Cardiology* 63 (1989): 606–609.

measured. Descriptions of the measured cardiac characteristics are provided on the Web site.

Three cardiac variables showed statistically significant MZA, but not DZA, resemblance: the QT interval, the ventricular rate, and the EP (mV). The P duration correlation was high and statistically significant for DZA twins, but it was 0.00 for MZA twins, a finding for which there was no obvious explanation other than the small sample size and/or unreliability of the measure. The MZA and DZA correlations did not differ significantly for any of the nine measures, so biometrical modeling analyses were performed (to add statistical power), using the American and Finnish samples as controls. There was no support for shared environmental effects across the two analyses. We did find that heritability estimates were consistent across the two studies for the QT interval (US: 0.50, Finland: 0.50), while estimates for the other three measures differed to varying degrees (PR interval, US: 0.41, Finland: 0.60; QRS duration, US: 0.30, Finland: 0.51; and ventricular rate, US: 0.52, Finland: 0.46). It was possible that sample differences in these measures reflected relevant population-specific genetic factors.

Overall, genetic effects on cardiac characteristics were indicated by our analyses, but our sample was too small to detect nonadditive genetic variance. It is also possible that the measurement and recording procedures overlooked small differences in some measures that would only be detectable with larger samples.

Tuna said the cardiac paper was read with interest and elucidated an area that was not well known at that time. He did point out that our findings were indirect, consisting of observational data and statistical calculations—in contrast, studies conducted after 1989 were using more direct DNA analyses for evaluating the heritability of ECG measures. He noted to me, however, that a German study done as recently as 2009 has confirmed many of our findings (albeit by way of reared-together twins) through more modern techniques.

Special Mental Abilities

Unlike the closed-door activities that took place in Lykken's laboratory, I was very familiar with what happened across campus in Elliott Hall, the building that housed our psychology laboratory. Special mental ability testing was a major component of the MISTRA, and we designated a separate room for this purpose. Special mental ability testing included a wide variety of verbal, spatial, perceptual, and memory tasks, seventeen from the Hawaii Ability Battery and fourteen from the Comprehensive Ability Battery (a description of these tests is provided on the Web site).

Bouchard chose the Hawaii Battery because it had been used previously in a large family study of cognition, providing a great deal of comparable data. (Our MZA correlations are contrasted with the Hawaii Study's cousin correlations in Chapter 4.) The version we used also included three tests from the Kit of Factor-Referenced Cognitive Tests (Identical Pictures, Cubes, and Paper Folding). Two Hawaii Battery tests were omitted (Social Perception and Progressive Matrices) because they resembled tests already included in the assessment schedule. The Comprehensive Ability Battery includes twenty tests, although we omitted six (Aiming, Auditory Ability, Spontaneous Flexibility, Ideational Fluency, Originality, and Representative Drawing) because of time limitations and because some of these tests were less reliable and less valid than others. Looking back, Bouchard regretted not having data from the creativity tests (Spontaneous Flexibility and Originality), a decision discussed further in Chapter 11. The Comprehensive Ability Battery's Esthetic Judgment test was administered, but it is not a mental ability test and so is not discussed here.

The sample at this time included forty-nine MZA twin pairs (forty-seven twin sets and two triplet sets) and twenty-five DZA twin pairs, although occasional data were missing for some individuals.[18] We computed intraclass correlations for all special mental ability tests and tested the fit of two models to the data. (Additional details about these procedures are available in our 1989 publication, which is discussed later in conjunction with information processing.)[19]

The mean MZA special ability correlations (0.45, 0.48) exceeded the mean DZA correlations (0.34, 0.35) for tests from both test batteries. We also used a statistical procedure called factor analysis to reduce the separate tests to four factors (Verbal, Spatial, Perceptual Speed and Accuracy, and Visual Memory). The mean intraclass correlations and model fitting results are summarized in Table 6-3.

Genetic effects were generally highest for the Spatial Ability tests and lowest for the Visual Memory tests. This pattern repeated in our subsequent analyses, suggesting that memory is affected substantially by experience and training. Information that is best remembered may be either personally meaningful or important for survival, so individual differences are minimized. We also found significant genetic effects for some individual tests (e.g., Pedigrees, a test in which subjects answer questions about family relationships displayed schematically).

The final section of our article presented a meta-analysis or summary of all special mental ability twin correlations that had been reported up to the time of our study. It was Bouchard's idea to plot the previous twin

Table 6-3. Reared-Apart Twin Intraclass Correlations (Mean) and Genetic Model Analysis for the Special Mental Ability Tests

Test	MZA r_i	DZA r_i	h^2
Hawaii Ability Battery	0.45	0.34	0.47
Comprehensive Ability Battery	0.48	0.35	0.52

			Parameter Estimates			P values	
Factor	MZA r_i	DZA r_i	G	E	h^2	General Model	No Genetic Effect
Verbal	0.57	0.51	0.60	0.45	0.57	.33	.001
Spatial	0.71	0.40	0.74	0.30	0.71	.98	.001
Perceptual speed and accuracy	0.53	0.54	0.56	0.49	0.53	.18	.001
Visual memory	0.42	0.07	—	—	—	.006	—

Note: Parameter estimates are missing when the genetic model did not fit the mean squares. The mean battery correlations and heritabilities are from our 1990 paper and the factor correlations and genetic test data are from our 1989 chapter. E: environmental effect; G: genetic effect; h^2: heritability.

Source: Adapted from Bouchard et al., "Genetic and Environmental Influences on Special Mental Abilities in a Sample of Twins Reared Apart," *Acta Geneticae Medicae et Gemellologiae (Twin Research)* 39 (1990): 193–206.

data as four stem-and-leaf plots organized by the four ability factors (Verbal, Spatial, Perceptual Speed and Accuracy, and Memory) and four twin groups (MZA, MZT, DZA, and DZT). These plots allow the spread of correlations across studies to be seen easily. The diagrams (which are not reproduced here) let us compare our findings with findings from multiple studies. Here, we calculated the heritabilities for reared-together and reared-apart twins by doubling the difference between the MZ and DZ twin correlations. The heritabilities of the four ability factors yielded by the meta-analysis were very close to ours. However, except for Memory, the estimates were slightly higher for reared-together than reared-apart twins (Verbal 0.36, 0.28; Spatial 0.48, 0.44; Perceptual Speed and Accuracy 0.42, 0.16; and Memory 0.32, 0.40, respectively), suggesting that shared environmental factors can affect special mental skills. The relatively low 0.16 heritability for Perceptual Speed and Accuracy, based on the reared-apart twins, could have reflected the high DZA correlation for speed tests and/or sampling variation associated with the small number of tests.

When I left the University of Minnesota for California in 1991, I took copies of every MISTRA protocol with me. Looking through these materials years later reminded me of the mental ability instruction booklet we used exclusively with the twins. Completion times were marked in red, and important guidelines were underlined. We penciled in notes regarding particular twin pairs when called for (e.g., "12-Mar-85, Sally had me repeat the instructions, but got the concept," "4-Oct-1988, John coughed repeatedly through the Spelling test, but he finished it"). This booklet was an informative record of what actually occurred in the testing room, and we discussed such events at staff meetings held after each assessment.

Information Processing

Besides showing us that genetic and environmental factors variously affect the different special mental abilities, the data were informative in another way. McGue and Bouchard used the data to explore relationships between information processing and special mental abilities, as they had done in 1984. The MISTRA data also provided a look at the extent to which individual differences in cognition could be linked to specific features of the twins' rearing homes. For example, it was possible that twins from higher socioeconomic backgrounds outperformed twins from lower socioeconomic backgrounds, or that twins whose parents subscribed to books and magazines excelled on verbal tests relative to the twins whose parents provided little reading material.

This research would also help decide which of two hypotheses—innate neurological structure, or experience producing drive—best fit the genetic processes involved in cognition. These perspectives are not necessarily incompatible.

The Innate Neurological Structure Theory, so named by McGue and Bouchard, posits that structural and functional brain differences underlie individual differences in IQ.[20] Thus, genetic differences in cognition would be explained by genetic differences in neurological structures. In support of this theory, psychologist Tony Vernon at the University of Western Ontario in Canada showed that information processing tasks involving speed are associated with general intelligence test scores.[21] For example, the speed with which items are recalled or object similarities and differences are recognized shows a moderate but consistent relationship with general mental ability.

The Experience Producing Drive Theory proposes that intelligence consists of learned facts and skills, such as knowing the names of capital cities or the constellations of the northern hemisphere.[22] The theory claims that individuals seek experiences commensurate with their intellectual levels. Inherited intellectual potentials are the tendencies to engage in activities that facilitate learning, such as reading or observing. Thus, the inherited potentials are not the intellectual capacities themselves.

The Experience Producing Drive Theory encapsulated the concept that individuals actively select and create their own environments. When the theory was conceived in 1962, it referred to multiple drives and a single general learning capacity. In 1995, Bouchard reformulated this perspective as the Experience Producing Drive Theory–Revised, suggesting that specialized brain structures underlie specialized mechanisms that affect capacity and drive.[23] Simply put, Bouchard wrote, "genes drive behavior and . . . behavior determines the environments we experience."[24]

The theory could potentially tell us how and why our MZA twins were so behaviorally alike, despite their separate rearing. The MZA twins Brent Tremblay and George Holmes unnerved Brent's father with their focused discussion of sports statistics when he drove them home after dinner one evening. People with sharp mathematical minds and good memories might stay attuned to statistical tidbits about census changes or team sports, depending on their interests.

In support of Experience Producing Drive Theory–Revised, positive associations have been reported between children's cognitive abilities and the features of their homes, such as their parents' socioeconomic status. However, genes and environments cannot be separated when biological parents raise their biological children. Children from more advantaged families might show superior language skills relative to children from less advantaged families, but it would be wrong to interpret parental status as causally connected to children's behavior. Parents transmit both genes and environments to their children, and more socially advantaged parents are likely to provide their children with rich linguistic opportunities *and* the genetic potential for good language skills. The MISTRA disentangled the genetic and environmental effects by examining associations between the twins' abilities and the characteristics of their separate rearing homes.

The participants in the information processing study were the same forty-nine MZA and twenty-five DZA twin pairs included in our special mental ability study. The three information processing tasks were the Posner Letter Identification, the Sternberg Memory Search, and the Shepard-Metzler Cube Rotation (all described in Chapter 4), and the ability measures were those from the Hawaii and Comprehensive Ability Batteries. The four ability factors (Verbal Reasoning, Spatial Ability, Perceptual Speed and Accuracy, and Visual Memory) accounted for 55.1 percent of the variance in ability. These results generally agreed with those from the original 1976 Hawaii Family Study of Cognition.[25]

The twins' special abilities and information processing measures were correlated with their adoptive parents' years of education, the adoptive mother or fathers' highest occupational status, the twins' number of residences between ages one and nineteen years, and the availability of forty-one different physical facilities in the home. The forty-one home facilities were organized into four independent groups by factor analysis: Material Possessions (e.g., tape recorder, power tools), Scientific/Technical (e.g., stopwatch, telescope), Cultural (e.g., atlas, classical records), and Mechanical (e.g., fishing equipment, leather-working tools). The physical facilities checklist, mentioned in Chapter 5 in conjunction with the IQ data, is described more fully here.

The fifty-seven correlations computed between the special abilities and rearing-home characteristics (parental education, parental occupation, and number of residences) ranged between −0.19 and 0.16. Only four correlations were statistically significant, but three of the four appeared in a counterintuitive direction. For example, one of the three correlations suggested that lower cognitive ability was associated with a higher rearing social status. Several significant correlations between the cognitive ability and physical facilities measures also exhibited a counterintuitive direction. McGue and Bouchard suggested that "whatever the relevant environmental contributors to a child's cognitive development may be, these factors are unrelated to the educational and socioeconomic status of that child's parents."[26] In other words, environmental factors clearly affect cognitive skills, but they are not the parental factors people generally associate with child development. Psychologists need to look more widely for these influences, perhaps in children's peer groups, community centers, and extracurricular activities.

Significant twin resemblance was found for parental education, material possessions, and mechanical possessions, indicating that the twins' rearing homes were not chosen entirely at random. However, McGue and Bouchard did not attach considerable meaning to this finding because the environmental measures were only weakly linked with the cognitive measures, and because the degree of environmental similarity was the same for the MZA and DZA twins. Twin similarity in rearing factors did not appear to explain twin similarity in special mental abilities or information processing.

The three information processing components (Speed of Response, Acquisition Speed, and Speed of Spatial Processing) were the same as those we reported for the smaller 1984 and 1986 twin samples.[27] The relationships found between these components and the special abilities were also similar to those found earlier, showing overlap between these two types of measures.

The genetic analysis of the special ability data showed that, with two exceptions, the general model fit the data, and all genetic components were statistically significant. About 50 percent of the variance in Verbal Reasoning, Spatial Ability, and Perceptual Speed and Accuracy was associated with genetic factors. The two exceptions were the Hawaii Ability's Word Beginning and Endings test (generating words beginning and ending in specified letters) and the Immediate Visual Memory factor (memorizing an object list and immediately identifying those objects in a new list). The general model fit most of the information processing measures except for two Sternberg parameters (percentage correct, and secondary or long-term memory).

McGue and Bouchard noted (somewhat surprisingly) that the amount of time required for twins to decide whether two letters are the same or different correlated as highly with verbal abilities (mean: −0.39) as the verbal abilities correlated among themselves (mean: 0.43). The reasons behind such results are speculative. For example, the correlation between the speed factor and the specific abilities could be due to a general speed factor common to all the speed measures. Alternatively, several independent processes with specific associations to the cognitive skills, combined into the composite factor, could be the cause as well. The MISTRA data did not allow a decision as to which of these two alternatives was the better interpretation.

The component and composite speed measures differed in terms of the pattern and magnitude of genetic effects. McGue and Bouchard suggested that the composite measures might have reflected inherited features of neurological structure that are important to a wide range of tasks, consistent with the Innate Neurological Structure Theory. However, the component speed measures could have reflected acquired processes important to problem-solving in specific cognitive domains, consistent with Experience Producing Drive Theory.

The MZA twins' similar abilities and information processing skills may come from their having the same genetic blueprint that guides them toward interesting opportunities and the mastery of new skills. This can help us understand why Mark and Jerry became firefighters, why Barbara and Daphne found humor in most things (Figure 6-1), and why Oskar and Jack preferred reading books from back to front.

1989 to 1990

The genetic effects found for job satisfaction, heart rate, mental abilities, and information processing were generally what I expected. The striking

Figure 6-1. The "Giggle Twins," Daphne Goodship (left) and Barbara Herbert. The twins had been close friends for thirty years; Daphne's passing in 2011 in her early seventies was a great loss for her sister. (Photo credit Nancy L. Segal.)

finding from so many of our analyses was the negligible effect of the rearing-home environment on behavior. Recall, also, the finding that environmental effects outside the home were important, and often explained more of the variance than the genetic ones. For example, cardiac characteristics were affected by nonshared environments, but not by shared environments, and intrinsic job satisfaction was only 30 percent heritable. Both findings surprised people who subscribed to the more conventional view that families significantly influence individual differences in their children's behavior—especially people who had never worked with twins, adoptees, or children.

I have found that parents of dizygotic multiple birth children and parents of adopted children are very wise regarding behavioral origins. They know without being taught that their sons and daughters have distinctive cognitive skills, temperaments, and talents and—most significantly—that they differ considerably from their siblings no matter how much their parents try to raise them the same way. In February 2010, I had the rare opportunity to attend an awards reception at the White House where I met a celebrity mother of female dizygotic twin infants. "They are so different!" she told me. "Is that normal?" Similarly, the father of a virtual twin pair in one of my studies (same-age unrelated siblings who provide direct estimates of shared environmental influence on behavior)[28] had expected his daughters to be somewhat different, "but not like night and day."[29]

The reared-apart twins kept us occupied in many ways during 1989 and 1990. Bouchard and postdoctoral fellow Kimerly Wilcox published an encyclopedia article on new developments in behavior genetics.[30] Findings from the MISTRA were included in that article (and would also appear in the 1992 and 1997 updates). Bouchard and I published a commentary in response to a target article on sex differences in mathematical reasoning ability.[31] Bouchard also contributed to an adoption bibliography published by the American Adoption Congress, something he could not have done had it not been for the MISTRA.[32] Our *Science* IQ article was reprinted in *Le Journal International de Médecine*, an international European journal,[33] and Lykken published a full description of the Minnesota Twin Registry.[34]

A curious twist in the history of the MISTRA is that while federal funding was mostly denied, our study laid the groundwork for the success of the Minnesota Twin Family Study, which has been federally funded for more than twenty years since its launch in 1989. Lykken's Minnesota Twin Registry, started in 1983 and completed in 1990, also received federal funding.

The MISTRA team continued to share its findings with colleagues. Bouchard and I delivered twenty-five formal presentations, many at scientific meetings, and appeared on approximately twenty television or radio programs. In addition to studying six new sets of twins in 1989 and five in 1990, we studied four follow-up sets, two adoptive siblings of the reared-apart twins, and several of their biological siblings. Eighteen articles about the study appeared in newspapers, magazines, and other sources, including the *New York Times Magazine, Science News,* and the *1990 World Book Year Book.*

I didn't see all these articles when they first appeared, but Bouchard collected them in annual reports that he sent to the study's funding sources. It was worth reading them years later because they reminded me of why people appreciated the twins' stories so much. "Keith Quilter's happiness will be complete when the twin brother he grew up not knowing joins him for his wedding day," wrote British newspaper columnist Allison Kelly.[35] "When we first laid eyes on each other it was just a shock," said Jake Hellbach of his reared-apart twin, Keith Heitzmann. "And it seemed like right off, we had this bond, right from the second we met each other."[36] Mark Newman observed that meeting his reared-apart twin Jerry Levey

Figure 6-2. Professor Bouchard and his "identical twin." (Photo credit Rich Ryan Photography.)

was "like returning from a vacation"—when they were reunited, their rapport was instant, and they only had to fill in the details.

It is understandable that news of twins finding one another at any age elicits happiness from the twins, their families, and the public. The fact that twin reunions *are* news shows what people value. Bouchard was not a twin, but one photographer pretended that he was, as shown in Figure 6-2.

As we approached the 1990s, there was evidence that findings from the MISTRA were affecting the ways that some scientists thought about behavior and the value of behavioral genetic studies. According to anthropologist Melvin Konner, the substantial contribution of genetic effects and the negligible impact of shared environments were seen to "fly in the face of our modern beliefs about how we have come to be who we are." He added that "it is perhaps the crowning irony of current research that we need behavior genetics to help us find out."[37]

CHAPTER SEVEN

Psychopathology and Religiosity (1990)

Tourette Syndrome

I learned about Tourette syndrome when I was a graduate student assistant at the Illinois State Psychiatric Institute in Chicago between 1974 and 1982. I noticed someone there who showed continual grunting and clearing of the throat, and periodic twirling of a lock of hair with the forefinger of one hand. I asked one of my supervisors about these behaviors, and he said, "Tourette."

Tourette syndrome was first described in 1885 by the French neurologist Georges Gilles de la Tourette.[1] The symptoms are distinctive—they include involuntary motor and phonic tics that appear by age seven, but they can appear as late as age eighteen. Some patients also display coprolalia, the use of loud and obscene language. So, in 1985, when Bouchard and I were visited by one female member of an affected MZA female/DZA male Swedish triplet set, I knew what I was seeing.

This was my first meeting with Elsa, who had participated in the MISTRA in 1981 at age fifty, the year before I arrived. She took part in the study with her MZA twin sister Frida and co-triplet brother Erik, both of whom showed the signs and symptoms of Tourette. These siblings were separated at two months of age and reunited at forty-eight years. Elsa didn't know she was adopted until she was twelve, when she asked her mother for birth documents required by her school. When her mother brought the papers home she momentarily hid the word *adopted* with her hand before telling her daughter that she was an adopted triplet. When she finally revealed the truth, Elsa cried and insisted to her mother, "I am yours."

Growing up, Elsa felt different from her family, partly because she believed her parents were much smarter than she was, but also because of her tics. She told me she developed frequent eye blinking at age three, and in childhood began counting things obsessively and turning her body continuously in a clockwise direction as she walked down stairs. Some of her relatives who knew she was adopted believed that her adoption experience had provoked these symptoms.

Over the years, Elsa was both curious and worried that her biological triplet siblings would reject her. Then, when Elsa was in her forties, she became a headmistress at a daycare center in a Swedish community away from her home. One day, she was "drawn into a certain shop" to purchase some dress material. The shopkeeper greeted Elsa warmly, not realizing that she didn't really know her—when Elsa said that she had a twin, the shopkeeper explained that she had made a wedding dress for Frida and had confused the two. At this point, Elsa asked the woman to deliver a message to her sister. When Frida called her at work, Elsa replied, "I know your name." This was the first contact between these sisters in over forty years. They met their brother several weeks later after finding him in Sweden through hospital and church records.

The triplets presented a new medical case history. No one had formally diagnosed Tourette syndrome in reared-apart twins or triplets, although some characteristic behaviors had been described in two early cases.[2] Tourette-like symptoms were also noted in a pair of our thirty-five-year-old MZA female twins. Both twins were compulsive counters of just about anything, keeping track of the wheels on trucks and counting themselves to sleep. Such repetitive, ritualistic behaviors are part of the suite of symptoms characterizing Tourette, but they do not alone warrant a diagnosis of the syndrome.

Several studies of Tourette syndrome in twins reared together had been published by the time Elsa returned to Minneapolis in 1985. A study published that same year[3] and several subsequent clinical studies demonstrated genetic contributions to the disorder.[4] Thirty years later, in 2005, Yale University researchers would discover that chromosome 13 inversion (rearrangement of genetic material within a chromosome) was linked to some cases of Tourette, providing new evidence that this disorder has a genetic basis.[5]

In September 1983, psychiatrist Maurice W. Dysken, whom I had known at the Illinois State Psychiatric Institute, had relocated to the Minneapolis Veterans Administration Medical Center. Dysken arranged to have Elsa observed in an overnight sleep laboratory at the nearby Hennepin County Medical Center. We also reviewed all three triplets' medical records and interviewed Elsa more extensively about the nature and timing of her symptoms. We arranged for all three triplets to complete a survey, based on questionnaires created by Yale University psychologists David L. Pauls and Kenneth K. Kidd. These surveys were translated into Swedish and administered to the triplets in 1987 and 1988 by nursing staff at the Karolinska Institute in Stockholm. They included questions about each triplet's symptoms and those of any biological family members with whom they were familiar. The triplets had half-brothers and half-sisters on both sides of their biological family and had had meetings and telephone contact with some of them.

All three triplets met Diagnostic Statistical Manual (DSM)-III criteria for Tourette syndrome, demonstrating genetic influence.[6] We discovered that the triplets' biological father and uncle were both affected with the disorder.[7] The fact that the triplets were not raised with these relatives strengthened a genetic explanation of this disorder. Adding to this view was the fact that the son and daughter of Elsa's MZA female co-triplet had both been affected. Most importantly, all three triplets had been reared apart since early infancy, and each had developed his or her symptoms independently. The MZA female co-twins did not show identical symptom profiles, a finding that we linked to unknown environmental causes. This outcome had been reported before—the famous identical Genain quadruplets were concordant for schizophrenia, but varied markedly in the nature and severity of their symptoms.[8]

This Swedish triplet set with Tourette disorder was the only MISTRA case study we ever reported in the scientific literature; we preferred to publish statistical findings on as many separated pairs as possible. It was also important to honor our informed consent agreements with the twins by keeping their life history data confidential.[9]

Psychopathology

Our first quantitative analysis of psychiatric symptoms appeared in 1990 in the journal *Biological Psychiatry*.[10] The lead author on this effort was clinical psychologist Will Grove. Grove earned his doctoral degree from the University of Minnesota's clinical psychology program in 1983, working under Paul Meehl; he then spent a year in the University of Iowa's psychiatry department. He returned to the University of Minnesota as a faculty member in psychiatry in 1985, and also joined the psychology department in 1990. His research specialties include the etiological and behavioral genetic aspects of psychopathology. Grove, along with Elke Eckert, administered the Diagnostic Interview Schedule to many of our twins beginning in 1990.

The Diagnostic Interview Schedule is a structured protocol used with nonclinical populations (i.e., healthy individuals without psychiatric diagnoses). It covers a number of DSM-III diagnoses, but only three—alcohol abuse/dependence, drug abuse/dependence, and antisocial personality disorder—were examined with regard to our reared-apart twin sample.

Investigations in the 1960s and 1970s had shown that psychiatric disorders and symptoms in children and adults (e.g., alcoholism, drug abuse, and antisocial personality traits) run in families. Environmental explanations were often attached to these findings, although evidence of genetic effects was accumulating from twin and adoption studies. In fact, genetic effects on psychiatric disorders had been suggested in the previous MZA studies. Depending upon the criteria for separation, these cases included twelve or fourteen pairs with schizophrenia (seven or nine concordant).[11] Co-twins in one other pair were concordant for bipolar disorder, and several sets were concordant for depressive disorders. These early studies also indicated genetic effects on alcohol consumption. Seven sets were concordant for nondrinking, three sets were concordant for heavy drinking, and six sets were concordant for moderate or light drinking; three discordant sets included one light drinker and one nondrinker.[12]

Our first formal analysis included sixty-five members of thirty-two MZA twin and triplets sets who had participated in the study between 1979 and 1988. These twins had completed the psychiatric interview separately and with different examiners who were blinded to the twin's zygosity and other information about them. The Diagnostic Interview Schedule was not introduced into the MISTRA until 1982. Prior to that time, psychiatric interviews for the first forty-two pairs were unstructured in format and nonblind in administration. In order to increase the replicability of the findings and to control for possible examiner bias, all new pairs and all follow-up pairs studied in 1982 and later completed the interview under the new conditions.

The twins were normal volunteers, meaning that very few met the criteria for Diagnostic Statistical Manual-III Axis I psychiatric disorders or antisocial personality.[13] Grove, therefore, decided to use signs and symptoms that counted toward DSM-III, Research Diagnostic Criteria, or St. Louis group criteria diagnoses of alcohol abuse/dependence, drug abuse/dependence, childhood aspects of antisocial personality disorder, and adult aspects of antisocial personality disorder.[14] In other words, some individuals might show several symptoms of drug abuse (e.g., took drugs five times or more) or antisocial personality (e.g., was fired from two or more jobs), but not enough to warrant a diagnosis of these conditions. Four quasi-continuous scores were obtained for these symptom categories.

Twelve individual twins satisfied the criteria for alcohol abuse and/or dependence (18 percent), nine for drug abuse and/or dependence (14 percent), and seven for antisocial personality (11 percent). The proband-wise concordance rates (probability that a twin is affected if his or her co-twin has a given condition) for these conditions were 33 percent, 36 percent, and 29 percent, respectively.[15] These concordance rates were low, but they did not mean that genes were unimportant—rather, we suspected that using diagnoses was inappropriate because our twin sample was generally nonclinical. Grove explained that if two twins are heavy drinkers, one twin might fulfill the criteria for alcohol abuse, but his or her co-twin, while a heavy drinker as well, might miss the benchmark for abuse. Such twins would be discordant according to formal criteria for alcohol abuse, but they would both be alcohol abusers. He thus analyzed the data using symptom counts.

The heritabilities found for drug abuse/dependence (0.45), childhood antisocial personality (0.41), and adult antisocial personality (0.28) were significant at the 0.10 level. The heritability for alcoholism (0.11) was lower than the 0.67 probandwise concordance value that had recently been reported for reared-apart twins in Finland, although it was similar to the 0.14 intraclass correlation reported for reared-apart twins in Sweden. We also computed heritabilities, phenotypic correlations (extent of resemblance between two observed measures), and genetic correlations (extent to which two traits are affected by common genes).

We found a high genetic correlation between alcohol and drug abuse/dependence (0.78), suggesting that these disorders are affected by shared genetic factors. However, the phenotypic correlation between alcohol and drug abuse/dependence was low (0.26). When one trait shows low heritability (e.g., alcoholism) but shows a high genetic correlation with another trait (e.g., drug abuse), then there are probably only a few genes that modestly influence both traits. The genetic correlations for the other behaviors ranged from 0.53 to 0.87, suggesting genetic overlap among them.

There were several limitations to this study. First, the data were not gathered on more than one occasion to determine whether the twins' responses remained constant. Second, some younger twins may not have passed through the risk periods for symptom development, resulting in "pseudo discordance." Third, despite the power of the MZA twin design to separate genetic and environmental effects, the sample size was modest, running the risk of small sample fluctuation. Fourth, more complex genetic models, encompassing genotype × environment interactions and environmental effects, could not be applied because of the small sample.

Even while the twins were nonclinical volunteers, the rates of alcohol abuse/dependence, drug abuse/dependence, and antisocial personality slightly exceeded those reported in the general population: 11 percent, 5 percent, and 2 percent, respectively. Therefore, our sample was not "super-normal," as some of our colleagues had suspected. Of course, our 1990 analysis included only a subset of the reared apart twins (31 MZA pairs and one triplet set). It was possible that sampling variation due to the small sample size contributed to the high rate of antisocial personality.

In August 1990, I attended the World Psychiatric Association's Regional Meeting in Oslo, Norway. I presented a sampling of the findings from our studies of Tourette disorder, substance abuse and antisocial behavior, and personality. I also presented an updated analysis of our studies on sexual orientation that built upon our 1986 article.[16]

When the 1986 article appeared, we had studied fifty-five pairs and had observed concordance for homosexuality in one MZA male pair, questionable concordance in another MZA male pair, and discordance in four MZA female pairs. Four years later, we had studied ninety-five separated twin sets, sixty-two MZA and thirty-three DZA. We identified eight MZA twin pairs (three male and five female) and two DZA pairs (one male and one female) in which at least one member displayed homosexual or bisexual preferences. Twins in our most recently studied MZA male pair at that time were discordant for homosexuality. Twins in our more recently studied MZA female pair and DZA pairs were also discordant. As in our 1986 study, the homosexual female twins had experienced delayed puberty and a larger adult maximum body weight relative to their heterosexual co-twins.

It still seemed to us (at the time) that male homosexuality might involve a complex genotype × environment interaction, whereas female homosexuality was more closely tied to environmental influences because none of the MZA female pairs were concordant. The lack of concordance in our two DZA pairs was consistent with a genetic contribution to sexual orientation, although the small number of twins was limiting. This updated analysis was published in the 1990 proceedings from the conference in Norway.[17]

Religiosity

Behavioral Genetics is the most complete compendium of behavioral genetic research around.[18] This book gets larger with each reprinting, a change that reflects the accumulation of new methods, findings, and perspectives. Some sections undergo considerable revision, making it instructive to compare older and newer editions as a way of tracking progress in the field. It has been revised four times since its first publication in

1980.[19] The 1990 version included the following passage on religious beliefs and commitment:

> Although some attitudes and beliefs, such as conservatism, appear to be influenced by heredity, others are, as we might expect, due primarily to shared environmental influences. In Loehlin and Nichols's (1976) large study of high school twins, identical and fraternal twin correlations were, respectively, 0.56 and 0.67 for belief in God and 0.60 and 0.58 for involvement in religious affairs.[20]

That same year the MISTRA published a genetic analysis of religious interests, attitudes, and values.[21] Compelling evidence of genetic influence on religiosity was observed, a finding that was replicated by others over the next few years. This body of work explains the changes that were apparent in subsequent editions of *Behavioral Genetics*—the relevant section in the 2008 volume, most recent to the time of this writing, reads:

> A twin-family analysis confirmed heritabilities of about 50% for traditionalism as well as showing high heritabilities for sexual and religious attitudes . . . Religious attitudes were the focus of a special issue of the journal *Twin Research* . . . A recent study suggests that the heritability of religiousness increases from adolescence to adulthood.[22]

The wave of behavioral genetic analyses of attitudes in the 1990s was probably inspired by the 1986 Australian study showing genetic effects (50 percent) on conservatism and traditionalism.[23] People were variously excited by and skeptical of these findings. Two of the more excited individuals were University of Minnesota psychology graduate students, Niels Waller and Brian Kojetin. Waller and Kojetin asked Bouchard if they could analyze the MISTRA religious interest data, and he agreed.

The results were striking—about 50 percent of the observed variance in five measures of religiosity was tied to genetic factors. Waller wanted to turn this work into his doctoral dissertation, but Bouchard talked him out of it. Genetic influence on religious attitudes and values was controversial at that time, and Bouchard worried that Waller wouldn't get a job upon graduating. Waller and Kojetin still analyzed the religiosity data, publishing their article in 1990 in *Psychological Science*.[24] The study included five measures of religious interests, attitudes, and values that were embedded within the standard inventories we administered:

- The Religious Fundamentalism Scale. This scale included twelve items from the Minnesota Multiphasic Personality Inventory that assessed fundamental religious beliefs.[25]
- The Religious Occupational Interests Scale. This was a four-item scale that measured interest in religious occupations.[26]

- The Strong-Campbell Scale. This scale measured interest in religious occupations, school subjects, and activities. It was modified slightly from the Religious Activities Basic Interest Scale of the Strong-Campbell Interest Inventory.[27]
- The Religious Leisure Time Interests Scale. This was a five-item scale that measured interest in religious leisure time activities such as attending services.[28]
- The Allport-Vernon-Lindzey Religious Values Scale. This was one of six scales that assessed the salience of a religious values system.[29]

The reared-apart twin sample included fifty-three MZA twin pairs (twenty male and thirty-three female) and thirty-one DZA twin pairs (nine male and twenty-two female). The reared-together twin sample from Lykken's registry included 458 MZT twin pairs (156 male and 302 female) and 363 DZT twin pairs (123 male and 240 female). The reared-apart twins completed all five scales, while the reared-together twins completed the Religious Leisure Time Interests and Religious Occupational Interests Scales only. Intraclass correlations for the different scales are summarized in Table 7-1.

The MZA and MZT correlations were uniformly higher than the corresponding DZA and DZT correlations, consistent with genetic effects. We also noted that the Leisure Time scale correlations were higher for reared-together twins than for reared-apart twins, although the differences were not statistically significant because of the small reared-apart twin samples.

Table 7-1. Intraclass Correlations for Five Religious Interest Scales for Twins Reared Apart and Together

Scale	MZT (458 pairs)	DZT (363 pairs)
Leisure time	0.60	0.30
Occupational interests	0.41	0.19
	MZA (31–52 pairs)	DZA (21–31 pairs)
Leisure time	0.39	0.04
Occupational interests	0.59	0.20
Leisure time	0.55	−0.22
Occupational interests	0.49	0.15
Leisure time	0.55	−0.08

Source: Adapted from Waller et al., "Genetic and Environmental Influences on Religious Interests, Attitudes, and Values: A Study of Twins Reared Apart and Together," *Psychological Science* 1 (1990): 138–142.

Model fitting was performed twice, once using all four twin groups who had completed two scales, and once using the MZA and DZA twins who had also completed the other three scales. The genetic analyses let Waller and Kojetin partition the environment into shared and nonshared components. Neither a purely genetic nor purely environmental model could explain the data. Instead, genetic influence explained approximately 50 percent of the variance in all five measures, as did nonshared environmental factors.[30] The shared environment contributed little to the variance. The twins' Verbal, Performance, and Full-Scale IQ scores could not account for the genetic component underlying religiosity.[31]

The 50 percent genetic influence on religiosity and the negligible shared environmental effect were fairly new and controversial findings. These findings meant that parents had less influence than they thought over their children's religious activities and interests as they approached adolescence and adulthood. Instead, the study showed that religious pursuits were affected more by individuals' behavioral predispositions in conjunction with their unique experiences, such as attending a workshop, taking a class, or reading a book.

Bouchard considered the findings striking. Years later, he told *Time* magazine that the data "completely contradicted my expectations."[32] When Bouchard presented the religiosity results and others at the 1990 American Association for the Advancement of Science meeting, biologist Garland Allen objected: "Behavioral genetic studies, such as these, tend to lead the public to blame behavior, such as alcoholism and criminality, on genetics."[33] However, behavioral geneticists believed that the findings could help the public understand these behaviors and work more effectively toward their control.

Subsequent twin and family studies (including our own) continued to support the original results. Debate over the degree to which genes influence religious behaviors has continued, although most researchers agree that religious affiliation (e.g., Catholicism or Judaism) is decided by one's rearing family.

The MISTRA investigators believed that complex behaviors such as religious interest are probably influenced by many genes, each having a tiny effect on the outcome. It made sense that the pathways from genes at the molecular level to behavior at the observable level might operate through personality traits such as traditionalism, absorption (emotional responsivity to engaging sights and sounds), or harm avoidance (tendencies that might encourage individuals to seek religious activities or community support).

Several MZA twin pairs were memorable because of their religious attitudes and activities. Debbie Mehlman and Sharon Poset, who met at age forty-five, are the best example of twins whose affiliations differed but whose religious involvements were closely aligned. The twins were separated as infants and adopted by different New Jersey families—living just forty-five minutes apart. Debbie was raised Jewish, while Sharon was raised Catholic before becoming a Protestant.

Debbie learned at age forty-five that she had been adopted *and* that she had a twin. One weekend after Debbie's father had died, her mother decided that the time was right to tell her daughter about her true background; Debbie thought her mother's visit was for the "money talk"—to acquaint Debbie with the family's bank accounts "in case anything happened." "Boy, was I in for a surprise!" she recalled. Debbie hired a private investigator who located Sharon in Nicholasville, Kentucky, about 650 miles from Debbie's West Hartford, Connecticut, home. Sharon knew she had been adopted, but neither she nor her family knew she had a twin.[34] The private investigator first contacted Sharon's parents in New Jersey, and they decided to travel to Kentucky to tell Sharon the news. Sharon also assumed her parents were coming for the "money talk."

Prior to being found by her sister, Sharon had prayed that someone special would come into her life after her son had relocated to Colorado. She said Debbie was the answer to her prayers. The twins' televised reunion shows them falling into each other's arms at Bradley International Airport in Windsor Locks, Connecticut.[35] A photo taken a month later shows them wearing t-shirts imprinted with the words "I'm With My Twin Sister."[36]

After learning she was adopted, Debbie worried that she was not really Jewish because Jewish law states that Jewish children are born to Jewish mothers. Consequently, Debbie completed a conversion ritual along with her daughter, and remarried her husband of twenty-three years. Her rabbi advised Debbie to do this in order to have formal proof of her Judaism. It eventually turned out that the twins' biological father was Jewish, but their biological mother was Protestant.[37]

Sharon had stopped going to church on Sundays because her husband worked on those days and she did not want to go alone. But when her son was born she wanted to "be more grounded and know how to raise him religiously," so she returned to the Catholic Church. However, she was disillusioned to find that practices such as fasting had been "watered down." Sharon eventually chose a nondenominational Evangelical Christian Church that does not have the strict rules her Catholic church once had but does offer the "right blend of faith, morality, forgiveness, and grace." She feels she should have been pleased by the Catholic Church's more relaxed atmosphere, but she saw the change as possibly reflecting a lack of substance or meaning. Sharon wished that her life was as organized around her faith as Debbie's—both twins liked the rituals and formality of religious services and holidays. But Sharon was dissatisfied following "rules that made no sense," though she still missed "calendar things" and liked the idea of holidays that do not fall on the same day each year, as occurs in Judaism. Some aspects of Judaism were familiar to Sharon while she was growing up because of her father's Jewish clients.

Debbie and Sharon are both strong followers of their respective religions, something they acknowledge in themselves and each other. They discuss religious issues with each other more easily than with most of their adoptive siblings who do not have the same interest or involvement. Each twin participates in the other twin's religious activities when they visit. Their different religious worlds are mutually enriching.

Soon after meeting, the twins discussed how they would feel if one convinced the other to convert to the other's religion. But that never happened, and they say they have more respect for each other for staying with their respective faiths. Debbie and Sharon also exemplify the MISTRA's religiosity studies in their belief that each would have embraced their co-twin's religion had their rearing families been reversed. Sharon said, "I think I am programmed to be religious . . . whatever religion I was exposed to as a child would have been very important to me through my life."

The practices of other MZA twin pairs also agreed with our findings. Mark and Jerry, the volunteer firefighters who met by chance at age thirty-one, had been raised by adoptive Jewish families. Neither twin showed any interest in religion as an adult, but both consider themselves Jewish when asked.

Two of the more interesting religious life histories concerned British twins Elaine Alin and Mary Holmes. As Mary wrote in her 2008 book *Being You,* both twins were raised Catholic, but religion was a major presence in Mary's home and a moderate presence in her sister's. Over the years, Mary and Elaine have tried to reconcile their belief in genetic influence and their belief in God, but these conversations with each other end "ambiguously." Mary eventually turned away from her faith, wondering if this was because "it strangled my early years." Mary also asked, "Does Elaine's belief in a God stem from her freedom of choice?"[38] She may be right to associate their current religious differences with the religious differences in their rearing homes.

Mary and Elaine knew as children that their biological mother was Jewish, information that fascinated Mary but meant nothing to her twin at the time. In her book, Mary described a visit to Israel with her husband Tony whose idea it was to take that trip. When Mary stood at the top of Masada (Israel's historic site where, in A.D. 73, the Jewish people committed suicide rather than surrender to a Roman legion) and saw the landscape and surrounding Dead Sea, she believed she had been there before. Perhaps her knowledge of being half-Jewish made her feel connected to that historic site, reviving a sense of spirituality.

Mary and Elaine's different outlooks never interfered with how well they got along together, but not all twins' religious lives synchronized so well. Religious differences were a source of contention between MZA female twins Betty and Alice. Betty rejected most religious beliefs, while Alice was deeply involved in her spiritual life. These tendencies were not apparent during the twin's assessment in February 1983, soon after their 1982 reunion, but they developed years later. Over the years, Betty and Alice sought counseling to hold their relationship together and are still friendly. Their efforts along these lines underscore the significance of the twin relationship—it is fair to assume that most people would not tolerate companions with such opposing views but would tolerate their twin. This situation was also exemplified by MZA twins Jack and Oskar who were raised Jewish and Catholic, respectively (see Chapter 2). These twins alternately liked and angered each other until Oskar's death in 1997.[39]

Data on the twins' religious interests and behavior continued to be gathered, although another article on this topic was not published until 1999.[40]

Personality and Environment

By the late 1980s, behavioral geneticists and some personality researchers were satisfied with the evidence showing that genes affected personality. The new focus was no longer on whether or not genes affected personality traits, but instead on *how* genetic and environmental factors combined or interacted to produce personality differences among people. A 1987 review in *Behavioral and Brain Sciences* by behavioral geneticists Robert Plomin and Denise Daniels had summarized extant evidence showing the limited role of shared environmental factors in personality development.[41] Their two lines of evidence were (1) biological relatives reared apart and together do not differ in their degree of personality similarity, and (2) nonbiological relatives reared together show little personality resemblance, patterns researchers (including the MISTRA investigators) were finding in their data. But the idea that shared family environments affect personality persisted because most developmental psychologists studied intact biological families in which genes and environments cannot be disentangled. It seemed intuitively correct to explain parent-child and sibling similarities according to common upbringing and shared experience. But these conclusions did not fit the behavioral-genetic findings.

Some 1980s psychologists, such as Theodore Wachs, pointed out that twin and family studies had not paid enough attention to specific features of the environment, such as home facilities, parental involvement, and cultural factors that might influence personality development. Wachs studies the role of physical and social environmental influences on behavior and has interests in behavioral genetics.[42] He raised a legitimate concern with which Bouchard and McGue concurred. In particular, they noted that behavioral geneticists often relied on indirect environmental measures (i.e., the general lack of personality resemblance of adopted individuals) as indices of shared environmental effects. Bouchard and McGue corrected this problem in their 1990 study by examining the reared-apart twins' personality traits with reference to specific features of their rearing homes.[43]

The reared-apart twins completed the California Psychological Inventory, developed by Bouchard's Berkeley mentor Harrison Gough. This inventory measures "folk concepts" or "aspects and attributes of interpersonal behavior that are found in all cultures and societies, and that possess a direct and integral relationship to all forms of social interaction."[44] The specific form that was used included self-report true-false items organized into eighteen scales such as Dominance and Tolerance. Sample items are "I like to be the center of attention" and "I get pretty discouraged sometimes." The twins also completed the Moos' Family Environment Scale, a form assessing ten dimensions of the rearing family, such as Conflict and Independence.[45] This scale presents a series of true-false statements about the rearing family such as "There was a feeling of togetherness in our family" and "We fought a lot in our family." Genetic analyses of both scales were conducted, as were analyses of how the rearing family affected the twins' personalities. The participants were forty-five MZA twin pairs and twenty-six DZA twin pairs. The DZA twin sample included three opposite-sex twin pairs.

Both MZA and DZA twins scored lower than the inventory's reference sample on seven Family Environment Scale items, especially Expressiveness, Independence, Intellectual and Cultural Orientation, and Active Recreational Orientation. Both twin groups also scored higher than the reference sample on Moral-Religious Orientation, Organization, and Control. The twins also showed greater variability in some scores than did the reference group. This seemed surprising because the twins' scores did not differ from those of their spouses who were not adopted.

There were two possible explanations for these sample differences. First, the reference sample seemed to include some children, whereas the MISTRA sample included only adults. Second, it was possible that the high percentage of British twins (40 percent) affected the findings.

The increased variability we observed for the scores on five of the Family Environment Scale categories (Cohesion, Expressiveness, Conflict, Independence, and Achievement Orientation) increased our chances of finding meaningful correlations between the personality traits and the home environment scales.[46] Restriction in the range of adoptees' rearing environments in some studies has been criticized because it reduces the chance of finding associations among variables, but this would not be a factor in ours. The fact that the twins' scores did not differ from those of their nonadopted spouses suggested that our twins came from a wide range of family backgrounds.

The personality data were organized into five factors: Extraversion, Emotional Stability, Flexibility, Consensuality, and Femininity. Gough had reported four factors similar to our first four, but our fifth one (Femininity) had been reported in some previous studies. The Family Environment Scale was organized into three factors, Cohesion-Conflict, Positive Constraint, and Encouragement of Individual Growth.

Co-twin correlations for the ten family environment scales and three family environment factors were positive but not substantial. The MZA correlations ranged from 0.09 (Control and Expressiveness scales) to 0.38 (Independence scale), while the DZA correlations ranged from −0.23 (Moral-Religious Orientation) to 0.42 (Conflict). It appeared that, on average, the MZA twins' homes were more alike than the DZA twins' homes, but the difference was not statistically significant. Combining the MZA and DZA data let us estimate the maximum amount of selective placement (extent to which co-twins had been placed in similar homes). The mean of the pooled primary scale correlations was 0.17, and the mean of the pooled factor correlations was 0.19, showing that selective placement was modest. However, the important question was whether similarity in the twins' rearing homes was associated with their personality similarity. First, we had to see how similar their personalities were.

The mean MZA twin personality correlation was 0.45 (range: 0.10 to 0.64), and the mean DZA correlation was 0.18 (range: −0.28 to 0.53). The intraclass correlations were modest for some MZA scales, but they were larger for the more reliable factor scores. The average heritability was 0.49; in fact, the heritabilities for the separate scales were significantly greater than zero for almost every personality scale. This analysis concurred with our 1988 personality study showing that personality is about 50 percent heritable.

Correlations were computed between the personality and family environment scales and factors, although only the factor correlations are displayed in Table 7-2. Factors have greater reliability than separate scales because they are based on multiple outcomes.

Table 7-2.   Correlations between the California Psychological Inventory and Family Environment Scale
Factor Scores

Personality Factors	Family Environment Factors		
	Cohesion-Conflict	Positive Constraint	Encouragement of Individual Growth
Extraversion	−0.14[a]	−0.03	0.18[a]
Emotional stability	0.16[a]	0.07	0.10
Flexibility	0.09	−0.09	−0.07
Consensuality	0.49[a]	0.16[a]	0.19[a]
Femininity	−0.11	−0.02	−0.04

a. $P<.05$.
Source: Adapted from Bouchard and McGue, "Genetic and Rearing Environmental
Influences on Adult Personality: An Analysis of Adopted Twins Reared Apart," *Journal of
Personality* 58 (1990): 263–292.

Six of the fifteen correlations were significant, but only the one involving Consensuality and Cohesion-Conflict was substantial (0.49). This
meant that the more one sees the world as others see it, the less conflict
there was in the childhood home. However, these correlations must be
squared to obtain the proportion of variance in the personality measure
associated with variance in the environmental measure. Doing so indicated that about 25 percent of the variance in Consensuality could be
explained by the variance in Cohesion-Conflict. The amount of explained
variance in the other five significant correlations ranged from only 2.0
percent to 3.6 percent. This indicated that, overall, the rearing home environment has little affect on adult personality. Few significant correlations
between co-twin differences on the personality and family environment
measures emerged, demonstrating that whether or not the twins' rearing
homes had similar or different features was unrelated to their personality
similarity as adults.[47]

The most striking finding from this analysis was that the personality
heritability of 45 to 50 percent agreed with those from studies of twins
reared together, both children and adults. The California Psychological
Inventory is also very different from the Multidimensional Personality
Questionnaire we analyzed in 1988, but we obtained comparable genetic
estimates across the two studies.

None of the personality analyses suggested that twins reared apart
were more alike than twins reared together, as Shields had shown in 1962.
The data are the data, but some observations can be meaningful. When I
meet twins, I often find that MZT co-twins behave more similarly when

they are separated, making it hard to know which twin is which. But when twins meet me together, their tendencies toward extraversion-introversion or dominance-submission start to show. In contrast, I rarely observed these behavioral changes among the MZA pairs, probably because they lacked extensive interactional histories. For example, whether I spoke individually or jointly to the MZA fireman twins Mark and Jerry, they both seemed to take over the conversation with their loud speech and playful style. When I was with either or both of the MZA Scottish twins Caroline and Margaret, their gentle manner and respectful demeanor (and strong accent) made them indistinguishable (and often incomprehensible). Perhaps current self-report personality inventories are insensitive to subtle changes in MZT twins' behaviors because these inventories reflect behavior averaged over time. Future MZA and MZT twin studies might ask twins to compare their personality traits to those of their co-twin, as well as provide the usual self-report.

1990

The years leading up to 1990 brought several twin pairs to Minneapolis for their ten-year follow-up study. This was an opportunity for me to meet some twins who had been assessed before I had arrived in Minnesota. I saw the Jim twins again after not having seen them since 1979, on the set of Chicago's WLS-TV program *Friday Night*. They seemed as similar as ever. I also met the MZA male twins whose sexual orientation had been so difficult to classify—and it still was.

Some of the new twin pairs we studied in 1990 were also memorable. The twins I recall most clearly were elegant blonde Australian women, Judy and Cara, who had met through mistaken identity. In the late 1980s and 1990s, Australia had only two department store chains, David Jones (DJs) and Myer. Judy was a fashion buyer for DJs, and Cara was a fashion buyer for Myer, in their respective Brisbane stores. The twins found each other when fashion representatives visiting each store had asked, "Why are you two-timing, working for rival chains?" After this had happened several times, the representatives realized the women were twins and arranged for their reunion. According to Nick Martin, who brought them to our attention,

> it was a beautiful story of [the] genotype channeling them toward the same very specific niche . . . I believe that Bouchard and I met them for dinner within a year of their being reunited and were amazed (at least I was) at their similarity of dress, hairstyle, postures, and tastes. They wore the same sort of jewelry, smoked the same brand of mentholated cigarettes, and even

spoke with the same voice, although one had an English accent because of her upbringing. I took them with me on a national TV program on twins, and as a result we found about six other pairs.

Judy described the bouquet of flowers she had given to her sister in honor of their reunion. There were white flowers mixed with flowers of the "palest pink possible." That shade of pink was their favorite color, even before they met.

By the end of 1990, 107 reared-apart twin pairs had completed the MISTRA's assessment. And in 1990 alone, reports about the MISTRA had appeared in twenty-six publications, including *World Book Encyclopedia*,[48] *Der Spiegel* magazine,[49] and the *Philadelphia Inquirer*.[50] Scientific papers in a variety of medical and behavioral areas were being published. We also started a new and unexpected collaboration with the periodontal faculty.

CHAPTER EIGHT

Dental Traits, Allergies, and Vocational Interests (1991–1992)

This study provides new evidence of a marked genetic component to dentate status and dental caries experience and confirms previous reports of acknowledged inherited contributions to tooth size, malalignment, occlusion, and morphology.

—JoAnn C. Boraas, L. B. Messer, and M. J. Till

The Dental Assessment

Pediatric dentist Michael J. Till's career began at the Naval Air Academy station in southwest Texas where he transported patients' files to the dental office. Till, retired from the University of Minnesota at the time of this writing, deserves full credit for the dental component added to the MISTRA in 1980. Till had read about the MISTRA in the campus newspaper and saw the potential for dental research. When I met him in 2009 at the University Marriott Hotel, he recalled the "fun days" when twins came to his clinic.

When the MISTRA dental study began, several reared-together twin studies had reported genetic influence on number of teeth, dental caries, tooth eruption, and dental spacing.[1] Farber's review of the early MZA twin studies revealed a strong resemblance in the twins' dental structures such as tooth size and shape.[2] But according to Till, dentists in the 1980s thought that dental health was most closely tied to professional treatment and personal care. Fortunately for the study, most of the reared-apart twins predated the use of fluoride (a substance that prevents and even reverses tooth decay) and sealants (thin plastics that bond to the tooth's surface and prevent erosion). In the absence of dental interventions, the reared-apart twins were ideal subjects for examining genetic and environmental influences on caries and restorations. "The patterns we saw leaned toward genetic effects," Till said. He recalled MZA co-twins who followed different diets but showed few dental differences.

The MISTRA'S first dental paper appeared in 1988, and is discussed in this chapter along with 1991 findings from the periodontal (gum) examination we added to the twins' assessment schedule in 1986. A 1993 dental paper, an extension of the first, is also summarized here.

Dental exams were scheduled on Wednesday mornings and took about forty-five minutes to complete. Till's waiting room and examination cubicles in the pediatric clinic were decorated with pictures of animals and toys, intended to calm children's fears. I am sure that this scenery calmed some of our adult twins as well while they completed dental history questionnaires.

The research reported in the first dental article was a master's thesis project completed by Dr. JoAnn Boraas. The study included ninety-seven participants from forty-four reared-apart twin pairs and three reared-apart triplet sets. Some twins had missing data because of severe gagging, lack of teeth, full banding (metal parts used to secure braces to the teeth), or lack of consent, so the number of pairs varied across measures.

This exploratory study focused on dental morphology (form and structure), abnormal alignment, lesions, malocclusions,[3] and restorations rather than on rare dental conditions such as accessory cusps or shovel-shaped incisors. Soft- and hard-tissue examinations were also conducted. The interrater reliability for 35 percent of the radiograph diagnoses of cavities on adjacent teeth was 99.7 percent. Full-mouth study models of teeth were also made for each twin.

Most twins were each examined by two dentists, either faculty members or dental residents who are licensed dentists. These examinations were performed initially by Till and Dr. Louise Messer, and later by Boraas and Dr. John Conry. The dental examiners did not know the twins' zygosity, but Till said that if the twins looked a lot alike and one presented a dental feature of interest they "might have looked harder at the other twin" to see if there was a match.

Till was surprised by the first set of findings, and remarked, "I did not know they would be as alike as they were." Fifteen of the seventeen dental variables correlated significantly for the MZA twins, whereas only three correlated significantly for the DZA twins. Furthermore, three MZA correlations significantly exceeded the corresponding DZA twin correlations. The distribution of the variables was unaffected by age and sex, although age was the best predictor of number of teeth present.

The MZA twins showed significant resemblance in many dental measures despite any differences in diet and treatment. The twins' mean age of 40.6 years would have allowed these rearing factors to show maximal difference effects, but they did not. Genetic influence on measures such as salivary factors, oral flora, tooth eruption time, and tooth eruption sequence may have explained the MZA twins' similar history of cavities. No explanation for the lack of genetic influence on overbite and overjet was available; in fact, this finding conflicted with previous twin study findings. Till thought this finding was the biggest surprise.[4]

Dental terms are exotic, such as "Carabelli's trait" and "premolar grooves." Carabelli's trait is an extra cusp or pointed structure on a first molar; premolar grooves are flat elevations on the premolar teeth. Both were examined for twin resemblance in antimeres, homologues, and heterologues. Antimere teeth are the matching teeth appearing on a person's left and right sides of the mouth (e.g., two first permanent molars, one on the left and one on the right). Homologue teeth are teeth with similar positions, structures, functions, or characteristics (e.g., incisors). Heterologue teeth are teeth with different structures, positions, functions, or characteristics (e.g., molars differ from incisors in structure, position, and function).

Resemblance in antimere symmetry concordance (resemblance) was the same for MZA and DZA twin pairs for both Carabelli's trait and premolar grooves, suggesting an absence of genetic influence. However, MZA homologous concordance was approximately twice that of DZA concordance for these two traits, this time indicating the contribution of genetic factors. Heterologous concordance was also higher for MZA than DZA twins, indicating the strength of environmental influences. Lack of mirror imaging (trait reversal) was indicated by the similar values for homologous and heterologous concordance within the two twin groups. Reared-together twin studies have also failed to find evidence of mirror-imaging in these dental measures.

Just for fun, our dental colleagues put one MZA twin's upper jaw (maxillary) plaster model over the co-twin's lower jaw (mandibular) model to check the fit. It worked almost perfectly, showing that the twins' teeth had evolved and rotated in similar ways. Till said that the DZA twins' models were "all over the place."

Boraas's 1988 paper was the first to address dental findings in reared-apart twins. She confirmed what so many parents had told me about their identical twin children's matching teeth. Graduate dental programs at Minnesota and elsewhere referred new students to the MISTRA studies, and they still do. Boraas's work earned her the 1988 American Academy of Pediatric Dentistry Graduate Student Research Prize.

In a larger updated analysis including forty-six MZA twin pairs and twenty-two DZA twin pairs, every measure showed greater MZA than DZA twin resemblance. However, the Surfaces Restored Index was the

Table 8-1. Initial and Updated Comparisons of Dental Parameters in MZA and DZA Twin Pairs

Parameters	MZA		DZA	
	n (pairs)	r_i	n (pairs)	r_i
Dentate status				
Teeth present[a]	28	0.62[d]	10	−0.19
	46	0.45[c]	22	0.04
Teeth present[a] (excluding molars)	28	0.69[d]	10	0.06
	46	0.49[c]	22	0.11
Treatment status				
Teeth restored	28	0.66[d]	10	0.09
	46	0.57[c]	22	0.30
Teeth restored index	28	0.65[d]	10	0.51[b]
	46	0.61[c]	22	0.31
Teeth restored index (adjusted)	28	0.74[d]	10	0.47
Surfaces restored[a]	28	0.71[d]	10	−0.04
	46	0.46[c]	22	0.20
Surfaces restored index	28	0.72[d]	10	0.33
	46	0.67	22	0.17
Surfaces restored index (adjusted)	28	0.77[d]	10	0.46
Treatment/caries status				
Surfaces restored or carious index (adjusted)	28	0.79[d]	10	0.34
	44	0.58[c]	22	0.26
Tooth size				
Maxillary incisors	13	0.94[d]	2	0.06
Mandibular incisors	19	0.63[d]	6	0.33
Malalignment				
Rotation/displacement index	26	0.43[c]	7	−0.27
Rotation/displacement index (adjusted)	26	0.43[c]	7	−0.09
Occlusion variables				
Overbite	23	0.03	6	−0.15
Overjet	23	0.06	5	0.31
Arch width				
canine-canine	24	0.81[d]	4	0.92[c]
molar-molar	14	0.69[d]	4	0.76[b]

a. MZA > DZAs.
b. $P < .05$.
c. $P < .01$.
d. $P < .001$.
Source: Adapted from Boraas et al., "A Genetic Contribution to Dental Caries, Occlusion, and Morphology as Demonstrated by Twins Reared Apart," *Journal of Dental Research* 67 (1988): 1150–1155; and Conry et al., "Dental Caries and Treatment Characteristics in Human Twins Reared Apart," *Archives of Oral Biology* 38 (1993): 937–943.

only measure in which the MZA and DZA twins differed significantly, possibly because the larger sample was still modest in size. Every trait correlation was significant for the MZA twins, while none were significant for the DZA twins. The initial and updated analyses are summarized in Table 8-1.

The updated dental trait heritabilities ranged between 0.52 and 0.82. The Surfaces Restored Index's heritability equal to 1.00 possibly reflected sampling error.[5] Interestingly, all the MZA correlations fell somewhat since the 1988 analysis, and most of the DZA correlations increased. It is possible that the MZA correlations were overestimated and the DZA correlations were underestimated in the previous analysis that included smaller numbers of twins. But the big picture did not change—this second study underscored the importance of examining older twins for whom dental problems were more likely present, allowing for more sensitive tests of genetic effects.

Conry, who completed the updated analysis, speculated that the genetic transmission of oral structure may be key to the MZA twins' similarity in caries experience.[6] People with shorter upper jaw (maxillary) arches are at greater risk for cavities. The reared-apart twins were not examined on a site-by-site (location) or quadrant-by-quadrant (upper or lower right or left area) basis, which would have helped identify the role of tooth morphology in dental decay.

The twins' behaviors might also illuminate the genetics of dental disease. Genetically based intellectual factors related to understanding health-related issues, and personality factors related to vigilance in dental care could be important. Unrelated individuals might achieve different success levels in preventing dental disease despite following similar dental regimens.

Meanwhile, in the mid-1980s we added measures of periodontal disease to the study. Periodontitis is a common cause of adult tooth loss, and about three-fourths of Americans experience some periodontal symptoms.[7] We began bringing twins to Moos Tower's seventh floor immediately after their dental examinations.

The Periodontal Clinic

In August 1986, periodontal graduate student Bryan Michalowicz was about to go on vacation when he got a call from his advisor, Dr. Bruce Pihlstrom. Pihlstrom said that they needed to submit a research proposal to the National Institute of Dental Research[8] for studying periodontal traits in reared-apart twins. It rarely happens, but the proposal (an RO1 grant, which supports specific projects based on investigators' interests and competencies) was funded upon the first review.

Michalowicz hadn't heard of the MISTRA until Pihlstrom's call, but it came at a good time, just as he was searching for a thesis project. Few periodontal studies of reared-together twins had been done by 1986. A 1958 German study of six- to twenty-nine-year-old twins had reported genetic influence on calculus (hardened dental plaque or tartar).[9] However, a 1969 study of twelve- to seventeen-year-old twins failed to find genetic influence on several periodontal measures, including calculus.[10] A problem with these studies was their use of relatively young twins who may not have passed through the risk period for periodontal disease. Once Pihlstrom and Michalowicz had decided to study adult twins reared apart, they recruited adult twins reared together via David Lykken's twin registry. This work would be a first.

When the study began every reared-apart twin was examined individually by the same two periodontists. After about the sixth set, Michalowicz told Pihlstrom that because some measures, such as inflammation, were judged subjectively, the possibility of bias from impression of twin type was a concern. That is, suspecting that twins were MZA (or DZA) could cause examiners to unintentionally reduce (or widen) co-twins' recorded differences. (This was not a problem for evaluating radiographs or plaque composition, which can be done blindly.) According to Michalowicz, Pihlstrom was a "meticulous" investigator and took a preemptive approach to potential criticism. His solution for avoiding bias was to cover the first twin using bibs stapled together to create a mask. "This was always a fun thing because you could hear a voice, but not see a face." Once Michalowicz was trained and interrater reliability was high, each twin was seen by either Michalowicz, Pihlstrom, or their colleague Jim Hinrichs, so masking was discontinued.

The first periodontal article appeared in 1991 in the *Journal of Periodontology*.[11] The sample included sixty-three MZT twin pairs, thirty-three same-sex DZT twin pairs, and fourteen MZA twin pairs. Attachment loss, probing depth, and gingival and plaque indices were obtained from the surfaces[12] of a representative set of six teeth, known as the Ramfjord teeth. Sigurd Ramfjord, a Norwegian investigator and Pihlstrom's mentor at the University of Michigan, had devised this system which reduced assessment time from forty-five minutes to ten. The six teeth reflect the mean periodontal status of the individual. Twins with fewer than five Ramfjord teeth present were omitted from the study.

The genetic analyses of attachment loss were performed on mouth means. Dorothy Aeppli, a co-investigator and biostatistician in the Biometry Division of the University of Minnesota's School of Public Health, used bootstrap sampling (the drawing of multiple samples from a population to estimate the replicability of the results)[13] to derive confidence intervals (estimates of the range of values of an unknown population measure) for these values because of their sensitivity to non-normality. Seven hundred samples were drawn from the MZT and DZT groups and combined randomly. The correlations and heritabilities were then computed for each sample. The same procedure was used for the MZA twin pairs.

Pihlstrom recalled, "I have very vivid memories of our first analysis. I almost fell off my chair; I could not believe it. Bryan [Michalowicz] was with me. The heritabilities were about 50 percent. I was very happy that we could make a contribution to the field. Our paper changed the way people thought about periodontal disease." The findings, presented in Table 8-2, were later confirmed by a Virginia Commonwealth University reared-together twin study in which Michalowicz collaborated.[14] Both the MZA and MZT correlations were consistently higher than the DZT correlations, demonstrating genetic effects.

The heritabilities for attachment loss, probing depth, gingivitis, and plaque ranged between 0.38 and 0.82 (twins reared apart) and 0.38 and 0.51 (twins reared together). These findings explained the inconsistencies among extant genetic studies of periodontitis. That is, previous work had focused on the microbiota (microscopic organisms in a particular environment) of plaque, whereas the MISTRA results highlighted the effects of hosts' (i.e., twins') genetic influences on disease. The MZT and MZA twins' oral bacteria were not more alike than that of the DZ twins, but the extent and severity of their periodontal symptoms (response to the bacteria) were more alike. These findings brought unexpected media attention to our periodontal team.

The second periodontal paper appeared later in 1991.[15] The study combined sixty-two MZT, twenty-five DZT, and thirty-three MZA twin pairs in an analysis of alveolar bone height. Alveolar bones are ridges containing sockets that are located on the bones that hold the teeth. Genetic effects on this measure had never been examined.

A device holding each twin's head in place was used to obtain panoramic radiographs.[16] Bootstrap sampling was used to estimate the between-pair and within-pair variances, intraclass correlations, heritabilities, and confidence intervals as in the previous periodontal analysis. These values are summarized in Table 8-3 (the actual values of these statistics were not provided in the article). The study showed that alveolar bone height has a significant genetic component.

An important point from this study was that the genetic mechanisms associated with alveolar bone height might be tied to periodontal pathology (bone loss) or to anatomical development (bone thickness). This

Table 8-2. Twins' Mean Values, Variances and Intraclass Correlations, and Heritability Estimates for the Periodontal Measures

Parameter	n (pairs)	$\bar{X}$(SD)[a]	r_i (90% CI)[b]	H Together[c]	H Apart[d]
Attachment loss (mm)				0.48 (0.21–0.71)	0.38 (0.01–0.79)
MZT	43	−1.0 (0.57)	0.49 (0.28–0.70)		
DZT	20	−0.9 (0.47)	0.08 (0.00–0.30)		
MZA	12	−0.5 (0.57)	0.38 (0.01–0.79)		
Probing depth (mm)				0.51 (0.12–0.68)	0.69 (0.48–0.86)
MZT	63	2.9 (0.34)	0.54(0.34–0.68)		
DZT	33	3.0 (0.33)	0.16 (0.00–0.40)		
MZA	14	3.0 (0.50)	0.69 (0.48–0.86)		
Gingival index				0.40 (−0.17–0.66)	0.82 (0.69–0.89)
MZT	63	1.1 (0.26)	0.58 (0.44–0.67)		
DZT	33	1.2 (0.29)	0.37 (0.05–0.62)		
MZA	14	1.4 (0.54)	0.82 (0.69–0.89)		
Plaque index				0.38 (0.02–0.56)	0.46 (0.13–0.69)
MZT	63	−0.1 (0.39)	0.39 (0.18–0.57)		
DZT	33	−0.1 (0.37)	0.06 (0.00–0.30)		
MZA	14	0.3 (0.43)	0.46 (0.13–0.46)		

Note: H = Heritability.

a. MZT and DZT twins did not show mean differences on any of the four measures ($P<.10$).

b. The r_i and confidence intervals (CI) were obtained from the bootstrap distribution (r_i = median).

c. Heritability ($2 − [r_i$MZ − r_iDZ]$) was estimated by the median of the bootstrap samples.

d. Heritability (r_i MZA) was estimated by the median of the bootstrap samples.

Source: Adapted from Michalowicz et al., "Periodontal Findings in Adult Twins," Journal of Periodontology 62 (1991): 293–299.

Table 8-3. Intraclass Correlations, Heritabilities, and Confidence Intervals for Alveolar Bone Height of MZT, DZT, and MZA Twin Pairs

	n	r_i^a	90% CI[b]	h^{2^a}	90% CI of h^2
MZT	62	0.70*	0.53–0.80	0.36	−0.15–0.77
DZT	25	0.52*	0.25–0.70		
MZA	33	0.55*	0.35–0.74	0.55	0.35–0.74

a. Median values of the bootstrap samples.
b. 5th and 95th percentiles of the bootstrap distribution, $P<.05$. CI: confidence interval.

Source: Adapted from Michalowicz et al., "A Twin Study of Genetic Variation in Proportional Radiographic Alveolar Bone Height," *Journal of Dental Research* 70 (1991): 1431–1435.

conclusion makes sense in relation to previous findings of genetic influence on skeletal dimensions[17] and on periodontal pathology, as shown in the initial 1991 article. This second periodontal article had less of an impact on the field than the first, but it was important work in another sense—if the alveolar bone height had not shown significant genetic influence, it would have detracted from the initial study.

Findings from the first 1991 MISTRA article also led several groups to study genetic susceptibility to cytokine (immunological agent) production. The now-editor of *Peridontology*, Ken Korman, referenced the study as a basis for developing cohorts to investigate host susceptibility. According to Michalowicz, a seminal 1997 article of Korman's linking a specific gene to inflammation was inspired by the MISTRA research.[18] As a result, Pihlstrom and Michalowicz were asked to author a genetics chapter for the most prestigious periodontal textbook *Carranza's Clinical Periodontology.*[19] Pihlstrom also was asked to present the twin study data at a symposium, "Genetics of Periodontal Disease," at the 2001 meeting of the International Association of Dental Research, in Chiba, Japan.

Michalowicz misses the scientific excitement and interactions with the twins now that the study has ended—this was a common theme among the MISTRA colleagues. Therefore, I was surprised that Pihlstrom felt differently. He explained that the team went as far as it could go—posing questions, providing answers, and getting confirmation from other investigators. "While one always misses the excitement of scientific discovery it's rare that a research project has a definite beginning and end like this one. In that sense, I'm glad that we were able to bring it to a definite conclusion," he said. The Minnesota periodontal group would publish several more articles in 1999 and 2000 and would win additional awards. In fact, the first 1991 article was cited under the section "Advances in

Pathogenesis of Periodontal Disease" in a special 2009 supplement to the *Journal of the American Dental Association,* "150 Years of Progress."[20]

Like his dental counterpart Boraas, Michalowicz won the American Academy of Periodontology's 1987 national competition for outstanding graduate student research. He received the Balint Orban Award for that work, which by then included thirty reared-apart twin pairs. "I was dumbstruck—some real giants in the field said that we quantitated findings that they had suspected for years," Michalowicz recalled.

Regardless of the accomplishments, there were also regrets. Both Michalowicz and Pihlstrom acknowledged their inability to assay the plaque without destroying the sample for other analyses. Having serum would have allowed them to look at the twins' reactions to antibodies, testing their theory that response to bacteria is genetically mediated. This, and identifying genes linked to periodontitis, would have been the next logical steps in their research program. But this would have required the expertise of genetic epidemiologists interested in periodontal diseases, and few people are qualified to take on such tasks. The search for genes tied to life-threatening conditions like cancer and diabetes are given greater priority. One can live with periodontitis. Nevertheless, one of the benefits of revisiting the MISTRA investigators has been rekindling their excitement in reared-apart twin data that have yet to be analyzed. Some planned analyses in periodontology and other areas will be described in the final chapter.

Pihlstrom may stay involved in future analyses of the reared-apart twins, but at a distance. He relocated to the National Institute for Dental and Craniofacial Research, in Bethesda, Maryland, in 2002, and was acting director of the Extramural Division of Clinical Research, a position he held until 2007. He is now an independent oral health research consultant. One of his missions is promoting research activities among young scientists, and he encourages them to apply for RO1s.

Allergies and Antibodies

Allergies are common medical conditions involving abnormal reactions to otherwise harmless substances, such as lobster and house dust.[21] Blumenthal had always been interested in genetic and environmental factors affecting atopic disease (allergy predisposition). Before the MISTRA got started, he had discussed twin research with Lykken, although they had never collaborated. Understandably, he saw the MISTRA as a unique opportunity to explore factors affecting asthma, rhinitis (nasal inflammation), skin-test response, total serum levels of immunoglobulin E (IgE, proteins that include antibodies elicited by allergens), and specific levels of IgE as measured by the radioallergosorbent test (RAST, an allergy test done using a blood sample).

Previous reared-apart twin studies did not systematically study response to allergens, but allergic reactions had been observed among twenty-nine of the early MZA twin pairs.[22] The conditions included eczema, urticaria (raised itchy skin that usually indicates an allergy), heat spots (eruption of small vesicles in warm weather), asthma, hay fever, bronchitis (inflammation of the main air passages to the lungs), nasal polyps, sinusitis, frequent colds, and unspecified allergic reactions. Approximately half the cases were concordant, including six of eight pairs with two or more allergies, suggesting genetic effects.[23] Reared-together twin and family studies had also indicated genetic effects on allergic conditions.[24]

In 1985, the MISTRA had reported genetic effects on IgE, as discussed in Chapter 4. That work included twenty-six MZA and ten DZA twin pairs.[25] Six years later, Blumenthal had access to fifty-three MZA twin pairs (twenty-three male and thirty female) and twenty-one DZA twin pairs (five male and sixteen female).[26] The analyses were done in combination with data from thirty-four MZT and twenty-nine DZT twin pairs recruited from the Minnesota Twin Registry, and seventy-six MZT and eighty-two DZT twin pairs from the Finnish National Public Health Institute. The mean ages of the reared-apart Minnesota twins and reared-together Finnish twins were similar (MZA: 38.91 ± 12.89, DZA: 43 ± 10.22, MZT: 35 ± 13.00, DZT: 38 ± 13.00), but the reared-together Minnesota twins were younger (MZT: 29 ± 11.00, DZT: 30 ± 13.00). The prevalence rates for asthma and seasonal rhinitis in both Minnesota twin groups were similar to those reported in population studies.[27]

Data sources included the twins' medical examinations, blood samples, and skin testing. The IgE levels of most twins were determined by double-antibody radioimmunoassay, a sensitive test for measuring antigens in the blood, although the paper radioimmunosorbent test (PRIST) was used to measure total IgE response for twins in the Finnish sample; the two methods are comparable, so the data were pooled. Specific serum IgE levels were measured by RAST. Concordance rates for seasonal rhinitis and asthma for reared-apart and reared-together twins from the Minnesota studies are presented in Table 8-4.

The MZA-DZA concordance difference for asthma was the only value to reach statistical significance. Had the samples been larger, they might have provided the power for detecting other meaningful differences. The values were also lower than those cited in Blumenthal and Bonini's 1990 review,[28] possibly due to methodological differences. The intraclass correlations were statistically significant for all twin groups, with the exception of the DZT twins from Minnesota, as shown in Table 8-5.[29]

Biometrical analyses of the serum IgE data did not show differences between reared-together twins from Minnesota and Finland, so the data were combined. The genetic effect was estimated as 0.564, and the non-

Table 8-4. **Probandwise Concordance Rates for Seasonal Rhinitis and Asthma for the Minnesota Twin Samples**

	Seasonal Rhinitis			
	MZA	DZA	MZT	DZT
Number concordant	9	2	8	3
Number discordant	12	5	10	8
Percentage concordant	60	44	62	43
	Asthma			
	MZA	DZA	MZT	DZT
Number concordant	4	0	2	0
Number discordant	1	2	1	2
Percentage concordant	89[a]	0	80	0

Note: Concordance was only studied in pairs with one or more affected twins.
a. $P < .05$ concordance.
Source: Adapted from Hanson et al., "Atopic Disease and Immunoglobulin E in Twins Reared Apart and Together," *American Journal of Human Genetics* 48 (1991): 873–879.

Table 8-5. **Intraclass Correlations for Immunoglobulin E Level**

Minnesota n (pairs)	r_i	95% CI
MZA (49)	0.640[a]	0.442–0.779
DZA (21)	0.486[a]	0.087–0.751
MZT (34)	0.422[a]	0.106–0.661
DZT (27)	0.258	−0.123–0.573
Finland		
MZT (76)	0.560[a]	0.384–0.696
DZT (82)	0.365[a]	0.152–0.530

a. $P < .05$.
Source: Adapted from Hanson et al., "Atopic Disease and Immunoglobulin E in Twins Reared Apart and Together," *American Journal of Human Genetics* 48 (1991): 873–879.

shared environmental effect was estimated as 0.436. A shared environmental effect was not indicated because the twins reared apart were more alike than the twins reared together. In addition, a trend toward greater skin-test and RAST concordance in MZA (55 percent, 50 percent) and MZT (70 percent, 50 percent) twin pairs than DZA (50 percent, 0 percent) and DZT (28 percent, 33 percent) twin pairs was observed. The small sample sizes possibly prevented the differences from reaching statistical significance, but it may be that some antigen sensitivities are influenced by environmental factors.

The first study of IgE levels in twins reared apart showed a genetic effect for total serum IgE level with little effect from the shared family environment. This was evidenced, in part, by the similar total IgE levels for the MZA and MZT twins. However, examining the RAST and skin-test data by specific antigen did not indicate genetic effects. More might have been said about genetic effects on these antigens in particular, and on allergy predisposition in general, had the twins been selected for atopic disease. Such a sample would have shown a greater variety of symptoms and symptom severity.

Vocational Interests

There were many medical "firsts" from the MISTRA, as shown by the studies in dentistry, periodontology, and immunology. There were also psychological "firsts" occurring simultaneously. One was our study of vocational interests.

Psychology graduate student Dan Moloney worked on the MISTRA between 1985 and 1988, administering tests and processing data. He came to the University of Minnesota because Bouchard "gave a great talk on the twins" at St. John's University, and Moloney was captivated. He often went to the airport to pick up the new pairs and recalled how easily and naturally the reunited twins got along.

An important question was whether the heritability of vocational interests would match the 50 percent we had found for personality traits. Moloney predicted that the heritability of vocational interests would be lower—and he thought that family influences would play a part. His biggest contribution to the MISTRA was his analysis of the vocational interest data, work that earned him his PhD degree.[30]

Moloney's study built upon Bouchard's preliminary 1986 analysis of vocational interests. Bouchard had shown genetic influence on the Strong-Campbell's six General Occupational Themes. Five years later, data were available for fifty-two MZA twin pairs and twenty-seven DZA twin pairs. The larger sample also allowed us to look at whether family rearing factors and home facilities (e.g., artwork or gardening equipment) affected vocational interests. This would be the first vocational interest study to use twins reared apart and one of the few to use adult twins. Previous studies had included mostly younger subjects, which was problematic since vocational interests do not stabilize until about age eighteen.[31] Moloney's would also be the first such study to apply biometrical modeling, and to examine the effects of family factors on vocational interests.

In keeping with the MISTRA's goal of within-study replication, vocational interests were assessed by two measures: the Strong Vocational Interest Blank–Strong-Campbell Interest Inventory (SVIB-SCII) and the Jackson Vocational Interest Survey.[32] In the first section of the Strong, twins indicated "Like," "Indifferent," or "Dislike" for 281 items concerning occupations, school subjects, activities, leisure activities, and types of people. In the second section, twins indicated their preference for one activity over another in each of 30 pairs. In the third section, twins responded "Yes," "No," or "Undecided" to 14 personality items that could be self-descriptive. Their answers yielded scores on 6 General Occupational Themes, 23 Basic Interests Scales, and 207 Occupational Scales. Moloney analyzed only the Basic Interests and General Occupations in his article.

The Jackson survey included 289 paired-comparison statements concerning work activities. Twins chose the more personally interesting activity in each pair, providing answers that yielded 34 scales with 17 items each. The other two measures included in the study were the Family Environment Scale and Physical Facilities Checklist, described in Chapters 5 and 7.

The vocational interest data went through numerous statistical manipulations. Three factor analyses were performed to see if the variables formed a smaller number of independent and coherent subsets. The first factor analysis was applied to the combined Basic Interest Scales and Jackson scores; the second was applied to the ten Family Environment scales; and the third was applied to the forty-one Checklist items.

Mean scores on the General Occupations and Basic Interests Scales were similar for MZA and DZA twin pairs and slightly lower than those reported in the inventory manual. Mean scores on the Jackson were also similar for the two types of twins and similar to the Jackson norms. The only exception was the significantly lower Adventure scale score for the DZA twins. The Adventure scale taps people's enjoyment of novel situations and the seeking out of unusual or dangerous situations. This difference may have reflected the twins' older age, relative to the Jackson sample that included high school and college students.

The interest scales were organized into ten factors: Enterprising, Academic Orientation, Artistic, Investigative, Work Style, Realistic, Social, Adventure, Medical, and Conventional. All six occupational scales were included, as were others identified in earlier work. The Family Environment Scale yielded three factors: Cohesion versus Conflict, Positive Restraint, and Encouragement of Individual Growth. This was the same solution reported by Bouchard and McGue in their 1990 personality study, based on a slightly smaller sample, described in Chapter 7.[33] Moloney's analysis also reduced the home facilities to four factors—Material Possessions, Cultural, Scientific/Technical, and Mechanical/Outdoor—the same ones obtained in the information processing study.

The series of analyses indicated considerable genetic influence (approximately 40–50 percent) on vocational interests. The mean MZA intraclass correlations were 0.38 (General Occupations) and 0.39 (Basic Interests), with scales ranging from 0.12 (Sales) to 0.57 (Science). The mean DZA intraclass correlations were 0.01 (General Occupations) and 0.05 (Basic Interests), with scales ranging from −0.27 (Domestic Arts) to 0.33 (Merchandising). The mean heritabilities for Occupations and Basic Interests were 0.35 and 0.37, respectively. In most cases, a general model (one that included genetic and environmental effects) fit the data structure better than a model that included only environmental effects. The general model was rejected only for Domestic Arts and Office Practices due to their large negative correlations.

The Jackson showed a pattern similar to that of the Strong, increasing our confidence in the findings. The mean MZA intraclass correlation was 0.43, with scales ranging from 0.20 (Independence) to 0.69 (Creative Arts). The mean DZA intraclass correlation was 0.11, with scales ranging from −55 (Physical Science) to 0.67 (Professional Advising). The mean estimated heritability for the Jackson was 0.44. The general model did not fit the Physical Science and Professional Advising scales because the DZA correlations were not equal to half the MZA correlations. The same sets of analyses were performed on the ten interest factors.

The mean MZA and DZA intraclass correlations for vocational interests were 0.50 and 0.07, respectively, and the mean heritability was 0.50. The general model failed only for Academic Orientation because of the large correlational difference between the MZA and DZA twin pairs.[34] Overall, the analysis showed that occupational interests were substantially guided by genetic potentials. But it was our final set of analyses that were most provocative and corroborated the genetic findings, shown in Table 8-6.

We found little evidence that rearing impacted vocational interests. Only three correlations between the three family factors (Cohesion-Conflict,

Table 8-6.   Intraclass Correlations, Heritabilities, and Genetic Tests for the Ten Vocational Interest Factors

Scale	MZA r_i	DZA r_i	Heritability ± SE	χ^2 for test of: No Genetic Effect (3 df)	General Model (2 df)
Enterprising	0.41	0.30	0.50 ± 0.12	**10.04**	2.21
Academic orientation	0.73	0.19	0.82 ± 0.06	**17.04**	**6.58**
Artistic	0.52	−0.07	0.50 ± 0.11	**13.03**	2.12
Investigative	0.68	0.02	0.66 ± 0.09	**18.00**	1.92
Work style	0.25	−0.03	0.22 ± 0.14	2.76	0.48
Realistic	0.44	−0.09	0.41 ± 0.12	9.85	1.90
Social	0.54	0.02	0.52 ± 0.11	**12.50**	1.27
Adventure	0.54	0.04	0.53 ± 0.13	**10.44**	2.43
Medical	0.47	0.14	0.49 ± 0.14	**9.10**	2.19
Conventional	0.38	0.17	0.38 ± 0.13	*6.28*	*0.29*

Note: No Genetic Effect Model: $\chi^2 > 7.82$ is significant at .05; General Model: $\chi^2 > 5.99$ is significant at .05. Statistically significant χ^2 values are shown in bold; statistically nonsignificant χ^2 values that differ significantly are in italic. df: degrees of freedom; SE: standard error of the mean.

Source: Adapted from Moloney et al., "A Genetic and Environmental Analysis of the Vocational Interests of Monozygotic and Dizygotic Twins Reared Apart," *Journal of Vocational Psychology* 39 (1991): 76–109.

Positive Constraint, and Encouragement of Individual Growth) and ten interest factors were statistically significant. The strongest relationship was between Artistic Interests and Encouragement of Individual Growth—but only 5 percent of the individual differences in the former were explained by the latter! Moreover, the direction of the relationship was implausible—it was unlikely that greater Encouragement of Individual Growth *reduced* Artistic Interests.

The same theme of negligible family influence on vocational interests emerged when we looked at links between the home facilities factors (Material Possessions, Cultural, Scientific/Technical, and Mechanical/Outdoor) and interest factors. Few significant correlations emerged, and in only one case did a facility factor (Cultural) explain more than 10 percent of the individual differences in an interest factor (Artistic). Furthermore, prestudy contact between the twins had little effect on their vocational interest resemblance—correlations between the ten interest factors and contact measures ranged between −0.03 (total contact time) and 0.11 (time together before separation).

Moloney remembers staring at the computer with Bouchard, studying the statistics that reflected the negligible family effects on vocational interests. "We went over and over it, but our analyses were correct. Bouchard finally said that we needed to let the data tell us what was there—that was the idea behind the MISTRA."

Moloney's study had both theoretical and practical implications. Consistent with previous studies, genetic influence was found to substantially shape vocational interests. Studies showing vocational interest resemblance between parents and children from intact biological families could not truly claim that children's interests were based on what their parents did or how they raised them. Of course, family environments may change over time with consequences for children's behaviors, and such effects have been analyzed using intact biological families.[35]

We did find that the DZA twins were less alike in vocational interests than the DZT twins described in the twin literature. This finding recalled Tellegen's suggestion that common rearing may induce behavioral similarity between siblings when they are not genetically identical. The nature of social relationships between DZ twins, in general, have been neglected relative to those of MZ twins. But if we are to understand how genes and environments work together, it will be necessary to give DZT and DZA twin relationships higher research priority.

Our analysis left about 50 percent of the variance in vocational interests unexplained by genes and shared environments, so we looked toward nonshared environmental factors. This area is murky, and discovering what these factors are has been a goal of behavioral geneticists for some time. In 2000, University of Virginia psychologist Eric Turkheimer discussed this "gloomy prospect," underlining the difficulty of finding trait-relevant nonshared environmental events because unique experiences affect behavior in unsystematic ways.[36] The guidance of parents, teachers, and other mentors can significantly affect the career paths that children eventually choose. Reading a great book or going to the theater can also inspire interest that may turn into a profession. How these influences operate, and why they vary across individuals poses a formidable challenge in behavioral genetic investigations.

1991 to 1992

The years 1991–1992 added eleven new reared-apart twin pairs to the study (two MZA and nine DZA) for a total of 118 pairs. We also conducted follow-up studies, bringing back seven pairs who had been assessed previously. I was thrilled to meet Barbara and Judy, the twins I reunited as a graduate student who had visited Minnesota two years before I arrived. They showed the same closeness and familiarity of sisters who had grown up together. It was just as Bouchard and DiLeonardi had observed at their first meeting at the Minneapolis airport in 1980.

In September 1991, I accepted a faculty position at California State University at Fullerton. I had been with the MISTRA for nine years, the first three as a postdoctoral fellow and the last six as a research associate. Bouchard had stepped down as department chair, freeing him to run the study more directly. It was time for me to establish an academic niche of my own. The thought of leaving the MISTRA saddened me, although I had no time to dwell on such feelings then. Knowing I would soon be gone, Bouchard had me schedule four twin pairs back to back during my last four weeks in Minneapolis. We had never assessed so many twins spaced so closely together. It was an exhausting but fitting farewell.

CHAPTER NINE

Creativity, Work Values, and Evolution (1992–1993)

AVID T. LYKKEN WAS BRILLIANT and funny, frank and controversial. He enjoyed hearing other people's ideas and had many of his own, some hotly contested. He deprecated lie detection[1] and advocated parental licensure, the issuing of permits to couples who met government standards for reproducing.[2] Lykken was also a skilled writer and storyteller. He supplemented his scientific concepts and conclusions with real-life examples, many drawn from his experiences with the reared-apart twins.[3]

Lykken was also a clever methodologist. He showed how statistical power increased by 20 percent by studying twins reared apart versus twins reared together.[4] In twin research, he was famous for introducing *emergenesis,* a concept he detailed in a 1992 article in *American Psychologist* that remains controversial to this day.[5]

Emergenesis: Lykken's Legacy

Emergenesis refers to genetically influenced traits that do not run in families. Emergenic traits are thought to emerge out of complex configurations of polymorphic genes that come together by chance in an individual.[6] According to Lykken, emergenesis explained extraordinary musical talent, mathematical ability, and athletic prowess in families in which musicians, mathematicians, and athletes were absent or ordinary. Individuals born in later generations would lack these talents because genetic segregation would dissolve the gene combinations underlying the unusual trait. Lykken reasoned that such processes might explain Triple

Crown champion Secretariat's running speed and Indian mathematician Srinivasa Ramanujan's numerical genius. Secretariat's speed surpassed that of his distinguished lineage, and Ramanujan owned just two math books, both in a foreign language. The skills of such horses and people may differ qualitatively, not just quantitatively, from those of others.

Emergenic traits include any complex behavior that appears rarely in families, not just unusual talents or skills. The unique behaviors of several of our MZA twin pairs are illustrative of emergenic traits. There were female co-twins who giggled incessantly, female co-twins with affinities for dogs and horses, and male co-twins with outstanding mechanical skills; these male twins each separately diagnosed a faulty wheel bearing on Bouchard's car. Few DZA twins showed such similarities. Lykken noted that these observations were only "suggestive in the 'context of discovery'"[7]—as I indicated, the important information was the marked MZA-DZA difference in the size of the intraclass correlation for a given behavior. That is, a high MZA (or MZT) correlation, coupled with a low DZA (or DZT) correlation, flagged a possibly emergenic trait. Lykken concluded that emergenic traits could only be detected with twin studies because MZ twins share all their genes (and, consequently, their complex gene configurations), whereas DZ twins share only half their genes on average.[8] It would be rare (though possible) for nonidentical twins to inherit the same multigene combination.

The MISTRA analyses suggested an emergenic quality to several of the twins' measured traits. These traits included the alpha midfrequency (an electroencephalogram spectrum parameter), the well-being scale (from the Multidimensional Personality Questionnaire), and the rate of electrodermal habituation (physiological response to loud sounds). Lykken's studies of twins reared together added arts and crafts interests to the list of possible emergenic traits, and data from the Swedish reared-apart twin studies added extraversion.

In his 1992 paper, Lykken included a section called, "Emergenesis versus Epistasis,"[9] probably anticipating objections from colleagues. Epistasis, a standard concept in genetics, refers to interactions among several nonallelic genes, genes located on different chromosomes or on different places within the same chromosome. In contrast, emergenesis goes beyond gene interaction to include a large number of genes and to describe observable features "at the molar level, as configurations of partly genetic traits."[10] Lykken reasoned that most complex traits are quite a bit removed from specific genetic events, so emergenic characteristics can be thought of as composites of lower level dispositions, working in concert with environments. For example, athletic talent may require a certain balance of speed, musculature, and motivation plus opportunities and training. One may think of emergenesis as epistasis writ large. Of course, major genetics advances have been made since 1992, especially with the unraveling of the human genome in 2001. Scientists are now searching for genes predisposing people to complex traits such as schizophrenia, autism, and cancer, with mixed success. Finding specific genes linked to these disorders is difficult because genes interact with each person's unique genetic background and environment—and there are many genes from which to choose.

Lykken speculated that chance combinations of genes underlying emergenic traits could be qualitative steps in the evolutionary process. Such "emergenic evolution" would require long time spans and would supplement, not replace, evolutionary changes linked to accumulating micromutations (small changes in DNA that may be harmful, beneficial, or neutral to the organism and population).[11] Evolutionary perspectives on human behavior were gaining attention in the 1990s, and it was exciting to think that twins reared apart could contribute to this awareness. It turned out that MZA and DZA twins were valuable resources for testing other evolutionary-based hypotheses, as I will describe in this and subsequent chapters. Thus, emergenesis was an interesting and creative concept that generated new ideas about behavior and ways to test them.

Earlier in this book, I suggested that comparing the different editions of Plomin's *Behavioral Genetics* could track progressive changes in the field. The 1990 edition did not reference emergenesis, but the three editions from 1997 and after did, calling it "an extreme version of epistasis."[12] Emergenesis is Lykken's legacy, but epistasis remains a vital concept in genetic research. For example, models assessing the capacity of viruses to replicate in the absence and presence of drugs had greater predictive power if they included multiple epistatic effects (i.e., interactions among mutated genes).[13] Where multiple epistatic effects end and emergenesis begins is a key question.

Reassessing Creativity

Emergenesis showed up in a 1993 creativity paper from the project.[14] This study was led by Niels Waller, the first author on the religiosity paper discussed in Chapter 7. Waller had been invited to comment on British psychologist Hans Eysenck's target article on creativity, published in *Psychological Inquiry* in 1993.[15] Eysenck viewed creativity as reflecting personality and cognitive factors working together interactively, rather than additively. At that time, twin studies had found low heritabilities for creative thinking (devising something new or original)[16] and ideational fluency (producing ideas that meet certain requirements), but none had examined creative personality (displays of energy, flexibility, independence, sensitivity, and openness).[17] In fact, creativity in any of its manifestations had never been studied in reared-apart twins.

The Creative Personality Scale embedded within Harrison G. Gough's 300-word Adjective Check List was completed by the reared-apart twins. The scale is a thirty-item measure of trait creativity based on responses from over 1,700 individuals, many from fields requiring creative activity. Twins endorsed items they believed were self-descriptive (e.g., reflective and unconventional).[18]

Creativity data were available for forty-five MZA twin pairs, one MZA triplet set, and thirty-two DZA twin pairs. The intraclass correlations were 0.54 (MZA twins) and −0.06 (DZA twins)—the marked twin group difference in the size of the correlations was consistent with emergenesis. Waller concluded that creativity was genetically influenced but did not run in families. Waller also challenged Eysenck's view of psychoticism as a creativity component because Eysenck's twin correlations did not fit the pattern expected for emergenic traits.

Interests and Talents

The continued development of the Minnesota Twin Registry and MISTRA enabled additional analyses combining twins reared apart and together. In 1993, Lykken published the first reared-apart/reared-together twin study of interests and talents.[19]

A mostly environmental view of the origins of interests and talents was prevalent in the early 1990s. A 1991 paper by research psychologist Itamar Gati indicated that genetic effects explained less than 5 percent of the variance in vocational interests.[20] Our vocational interest paper by Dan Moloney, published the same year, moved the figure closer to 50 percent.[21] Many other questions were addressed by Lykken in the 1993 paper on the heritability of recreational interests,[22] such as:

1. Do vocational interests, leisure-time interests, and talents inter-correlate, and do they produce interest factors?
2. Do MZT twin intraclass correlations provide good heritability estimates of interests and talents?
3. Are interests and talents emergenic?

The reared-apart twin sample used in the interest analysis included fifty-three MZA twin pairs (nineteen male and thirty-four female), thirty-six DZA twin pairs (eleven male and twenty-five female), and one MZA triplet set (male). The interest inventory was introduced into the study when it was already under way, so only about half the twins completed the forms in the laboratory; twins who had been to Minnesota completed them at home and returned them by mail. The reared-together twin sample included 924 twin pairs, in which 618 pairs were female and 524 pairs were MZ. These twins received an inventory packet by mail. A group of 198 pairs (forty-nine MZ male, fifty-three MZ female, forty-four DZ male, and fifty-two DZ female) completed the forms again three years later.

The composition of the reared-together twin sample exemplified another of Lykken's contributions, known as the *Rule of Two-Thirds*.[23] In 1987, Lykken showed that volunteer twin samples in many studies are generally composed of two-thirds MZ twins and two-thirds female twins.[24] MZ twins may be more invested than DZ twins in being twins and in participating in twin-related activities. It is also well known that females are generally more willing research volunteers than males.

The twins completed four different measures created by Lykken:[25]

1. The *Occupational Interest Inventory* included 100 item composites that tapped broad aspects of occupational interest (e.g., skilled trades such as appliance repair, auto mechanics, and carpentry). Twins were told to assume equal pay and equal status across all occupational groups. They indicated "Like," "Dislike," or "Indifferent" for each one, with regard to how much they would enjoy the type of work and that field's working conditions.
2. The *Minnesota Leisure-Time Interest Test* included 120 items describing a range of recreational activities (e.g., fishing, enjoying nightlife, or going on safari). Assuming no time, money, age, or health limitations, twins indicated the frequency with which they would engage in such activities (1 = never to 5 = as often as possible).
3. The *Minnesota Talent Survey* was a forty-item inventory of familiar talents. An example was "*Carpentry:* (1) You can make furniture, cabinets, etc., (2) You can hang a door, use power saws, build a doghouse, etc., (3) You can do minor repairs using hand tools, or (4) You are unskilled with hammer or saw." Twins chose the alternative that best fit their self-perception.
4. The *Self-Rating Inventory* consisted of thirty-one items concerning qualities not directly assessed by the first three measures. An example is abstract intelligence: the ability to solve intellectual

problems, to understand complicated issues, to figure things out. Twins compared their traits and abilities to those of others on a five-point scale (1 = lowest 5 percent to 5 = highest 5 percent).

In addition to these, the Multidimensional Personality Questionnaire was available for all reared-apart twins. This questionnaire was also included in the packet sent to reared-together twins.

The ranges and mean values of the intraclass correlations for the interest factor scores did not differ between reared-apart male and female twin pairs, so the data were combined. We found that genetic influence explained over 30 percent of the variance in occupational and leisure interests, whether we looked at the separate inventory items or at the factors composed of related clusters of these items. Organizing the data into larger scales and superfactors yielded average heritabilities of 48 percent and 53 percent, respectively.

The average intraclass correlations for the MZA and MZT twins were nearly identical at the item level—0.34 and 0.32, respectively. At the factor level the MZT twins showed somewhat greater resemblance and less variability than the MZA twins—the average correlations were 0.49 and 0.42, respectively. A difference in the factor structure (derived from the reared-together twin data) may have been responsible for this finding— many MZA twins were raised outside the United States and may have had different interest opportunities. Overall, our results contrasted sharply with the less than 5 percent genetic contribution reported by Gati two years earlier. Our results were also consistent with those from our 1991 vocational interest study. Lykken's interests analysis was another successful effort at replication within the MISTRA.

Each of the three questions posed at the beginning was answered:

1. Factor analysis organized the data into thirty-nine factors and eleven superfactors. The superfactors and their reliabilities (interrelations among the test items) are listed in Table 9-1.
2. The MZT correlation appeared to be a more reliable and conservative estimate of heritability than the value obtained by doubling the difference between the MZT and DZT correlations. That is because the formula overestimates narrow heritability due to MZ twins' shared nonadditive genes.
3. Emergenesis characterized 67 percent of the 291 items and 62 percent of the fifty interest-talent factors. Arts and Crafts was exemplary—the MZT correlation was high, while the DZT correlation approached zero. Such traits would fit the definition of emergenesis.

Table 9-1.   Eleven Superfactors Based on the 39 Interest-Talent Factors

Superfactor	Alpha (reliability)
Intellectual and educated	0.90
Breadth of interest	0.84
Self-esteem	0.71
Adventurous versus harm-avoidant	0.88
Solidarity	0.65
Artificer versus athlete	0.82
Religious orientation versus sensual indulgence	0.89
Personal attractiveness and charm	0.55
Agrarian activities	0.86
Male physician	0.69
Female physician	0.73

Source: Adapted from Lykken et al., "The Heritability of Interests: A Twin Study," *Journal of Applied Psychology* 78 (1993): 649–661.

Our answer to question 3 was especially interesting because many MZA twins' jobs and activities were similar but not exactly the same. The reared-apart twin firemen, Mark and Jerry (Figure 9-1), both installed electrical equipment, but one worked with burglar alarms and the other with fire-suppression systems. Both twins loved music, but Mark preferred rock and roll, and Jerry preferred country and western. Both twins were interested in forestry, but Marked had worked in the field, while Jerry had studied forestry at school. The twins were also football fans, although Mark favored the Dallas Cowboys and Jerry favored the Washington Redskins. The twins lived about sixty miles apart in New Jersey when they met, so their team preferences did not reflect their hometowns. The twins said that despite these differences they "liked each others' styles."

No one would claim that there is a gene predisposing individuals to favor burglar alarms over fire alarms, or the Dallas Cowboys over the Washington Redskins. Most important is that just by being themselves Mark and Jerry showed exactly what Lykken was talking about in his paper—the idea that particular interests seem less heritable than the dispositions underlying them.[26] What persuaded Mark to take on forestry in an applied way and what made Jerry pursue it in the classroom probably reflected their nonshared experiences. A huge challenge for behavioral geneticists is to identify those nonshared experiences. Mark and Jerry also show that how twin researchers define similarities and differences, and whether they focus on specific traits or broad tendencies, affect heritability estimates.

Lykken also talked about a "cafeteria of experience." Choice of experiences and reactions to them are partly determined by one's physique, ability, and temperament. But opportunities must also be available, and some opportunities may be more appealing at one time than another. Given the complex pathways from genes to behavior, it still amazes me that MZA twins can be so similar in what they do and what they like. But it is not their similarities alone that are impressive, it is their similarities relative to those of other genetically and environmentally related family members. It would be impossible to explain MZA twins' similarity and adopted siblings' lack of similarity without reference to genetic factors.

Interests and talents have certain qualities that make them important and meaningful to us. Our data also suggested that these same qualities extend to the work we choose to do. Our research exploring the origins of work values gave us insight into how and why we select some professions over others.

Figure 9-1. Firemen twins Jerry Levey (left) and Mark Newman were reunited in 1985 at age thirty-one. A year later, Jerry is enjoying a Budweiser, the twins' favorite brand of beer. Note the pinky finger underneath the glass—both twins held a glass this way. (Photo credit Nancy L. Segal.)

Workplace Values

In 1992, theories about what people valued in their jobs focused on environmental events, such as family experiences and occupational socialization. Available theories at that time did not consider genetic influence, reflected by the empirical studies reporting environmental links between work values and gender, and education and experience. Together with our colleagues Richard Arvey and Lauren Keller, with whom we had collaborated previously, we analyzed the twins' work values.[27]

The sample included twenty-three MZA twin pairs and twenty DZA twin pairs. This sample was small relative to those included in other analyses we conducted at this time because the inventory we used—the Minnesota Importance Questionnaire—was a late addition to the study.[28]

The questionnaire included 190 paired-comparison items and 20 items requiring absolute judgments of the importance of each work outcome. Twins answered the paired-comparisons with reference to the base question: "Which is *more important* in my *ideal* job?" A sample item is: "(a) I could be busy all the time, or (b) The job would provide an opportunity for advancement." Twins also answered "Yes" or "No" to absolute judgments with reference to the root phrase: "On my *ideal job,* it is important that . . ." A sample item to which they applied that phrase is "I could make decisions on my own."

Twins also provided their current job so that we could assess the similarity of their occupations. Five of the thirty-two twin pairs who provided this information held very similar jobs to their co-twin, and all were MZA pairs. We also coded the twins' jobs for occupational level or category, such as blue collar versus white collar, and other features. Blue-collar (e.g., flight attendants) and white-collar (e.g., attorney) jobs differ, but they may be similar in complexity such as in their hierarchies of authority and range of responsibilities. Similarly, two flight attendants or two attorneys may hold the same type of job, but their jobs may differ in terms of their number of bosses and assigned tasks.

The twins' job levels were generally not the same—both twins in four out of nineteen MZA pairs and two out of thirteen DZA pairs held blue-collar positions. These data were not complete, but it seemed unlikely that similarity in work values would be associated with similarity in job level. Previous studies had suggested that parents' socioeconomic status affected their children's work values. However, in their 1989 chapter on information processing, McGue and Bouchard showed that the co-twins' rearing parents' socioeconomic levels were not very similar.[29] The present sample included a subset of the larger sample, so it was unlikely that this measure would influence twin resemblance in work values. However, within-pair differences in parental socioeconomic status could lead to differences in work values—a twin from a high-status family might value creativity more than a co-twin from a lower status family who might invest more in sick leave.

The Minnesota Importance Questionnaire items were organized into twenty individual scales and six factor scales. The score variances did not differ between the MZA and DZA twins, but the mean Autonomy score was significantly higher for the DZA than MZA twins. The DZA twins also scored higher than the MZA twins on the individual scales of activity, compensation, creativity, independence, and responsibility. If these were DZT twins, I might have explained this finding with reference to DZ twins' generally lower investment in their twin relationship and possibly greater desire for individual achievement. There is no obvious explanation for these mean score differences in reared-apart twins.

The correlations for five of the six factor scales, shown in Table 9-2, were significant for the MZA twins, but only one (Achievement) was significant for the DZA twins. Correlations for ten of the twenty individual scales were significant for the MZA twins, but only two were significant for the DZA twins. More striking were the median work value correlations of 0.42 for the MZA twins and 0.16 for the DZA twins, and the median individual scale correlations of 0.34 for the MZA twins and 0.20 for the DZA twins (not shown in the table). These results were our first indication that what we value at work is influenced partly by our genes. It was unfortunate that the Minnesota Importance Questionnaire was not available for a larger twin sample—the lack of statistical power may have explained why only two individual scale correlations (company

Table 9-2. MZA and DZA Intraclass Correlations for the Minnesota Importance Questionnaire (MIQ) Work Value Factor Scales

Factor Scale	MZA	DZA
Achievement value	0.43[a]	0.41[a]
Comfort value	0.43[a]	0.17
Status value	0.42[a]	0.24
Altruism value	0.14	0.15
Safety value	0.40[a]	0.07
Autonomy value	0.41[a]	0.13

a. $P < .05$.

Source: Adapted from Keller et al., "Work Values: Genetic and Environmental Influences," *Journal of Applied Psychology* 77 (1992): 79–88.

policies and human relations aspect of supervision) showed a significant MZA-DZA difference.

The heritability estimates (based on model fitting and corrected for attenuation) ranged from 0.37 (Altruism) to 0.68 (Achievement), with a median estimate of 0.46. Our relatively low heritability for Altruism was at odds with the 0.53–0.56 estimate reported in the literature.[30] Perhaps our measure captured a different aspect of altruism or was less reliable.

Our findings showed that approximately 60 percent of the variance in work values was tied to environmental factors and measurement error. People are not born with work values; these values must be acquired from work experiences and other life events. It may be that genetic factors underlying intellect, personality, and temperament predispose us to favor certain work outcomes and circumstances. It is also likely that job satisfaction (analyzed by members of our research team in 1989) is affected by how much work values are actualized while on the job, and whether opportunities are available to pursue one's ideal job.

Our findings made sense considering the accumulating evidence of genetic influence on social and religious attitudes we saw in the literature as well as in our own studies. We felt that our results could help organizations and companies understand why improved work conditions and other perks may not be embraced with the same enthusiasm across employees. In June 2010, I asked our collaborator, Arvey, to reflect on these findings when I saw him at the International Congress of Twin Studies in Seoul.

Like most researchers, Arvey described additional measures he wishes we had gathered from the twins. He was especially interested in details about the twins' work histories, such as those of the reared-apart twin volunteer firemen Mark and Jerry. Calling the two men a "rare base rate," Arvey wondered about the processes that independently led each twin to his job. Jerry, who had always wanted to be a fireman, had chased fire trucks as a child. Mark became interested in firefighting when his friends thought it would be fun to try, but he became committed to the service after saving a woman's life.[31]

Evolutionary Perspectives

The new discipline of evolutionary psychology emerged out of sociobiology in the late 1980s and early 1990s. The key concept of sociobiology was that of natural selection acting through differential reproductive success. As such, sociobiology focused on fitness maximization, or behavior based largely on survival and gene transmission by reproduction. In contrast, as I explained in Chapter 5, evolutionary psychology is concerned with finding mechanisms that evolved to meet the challenges and demands of human existence, such as telling friends from foes and distinguishing safety from threat. Thus, it focuses mostly on explanations that consider behavioral and cognitive functions with reference to survival and reproduction (i.e., ultimate explanations). However, explanations of behavior based on immediate causal events—proximal events that activate psychological mechanisms—also interest evolutionary psychologists.[32]

Evolutionary psychology and behavioral genetics have some common goals, yet their different foci have kept them largely apart.[33] As described briefly in Chapter 5, evolutionary psychology is concerned mostly with species uniformities, whereas behavioral genetics is concerned mostly with individual differences. However, behavior geneticists have shown that virtually all measured traits display genetic variation, causing evolutionary psychologists to ask why meaningful genetic variation exists. Various explanations for trait variability have been proposed, such as mutations (gene changes) and nonadditivity (genetic variance resulting from interaction among genes that is not eliminated by selection), and continue to be debated. Evolutionary psychologist and University of Minnesota graduate Steven Gangestad believes that life history theory, the view that humans and nonhumans direct environmental resources toward activities that will benefit their growth, survival, and reproduction, can offer answers.[34] Behaviors that are optimal at one time may change as a function of environmental situations (nutritional availability), personal circumstances (an individual's age), and other factors. Human intellectual, personality, and hormonal systems have evolved such that certain behaviors are more favorable under some circumstances than others.

There have been efforts to bring behavioral genetics and evolutionary psychology closer together. In 2001, Bouchard and University of Texas psychologist John Loehlin attempted to reconcile evolutionary and behavioral genetic perspectives on personality.[35] They suggested that basic emotions and motivations such as anger, fear, nurturance, and curiosity vary across a broad range because different levels of these traits would not be detrimental to fitness, except at the extremes where they would be selected against. Genetic variation in such traits could reflect the different environmental conditions that Gangestad discussed.

Given the intellectual divide, few researchers attend meetings of both the Human Behavior and Evolution Society and the Behavior Genetics Association. This is unfortunate because (1) behavioral genetics provides informative methods for testing evolutionary-based hypotheses, and (2) evolutionary psychology offers behavioral genetics another theoretical perspective for interpreting findings.

I was introduced to sociobiology in the late 1970s as a graduate student. My mentor at the University of Chicago, the late Daniel G. Freedman, was writing *Human Sociobiology: A Holistic Approach* at that time.[36] Many of his students, including me, attended his informal weekly seminar on the subject. Freedman's book, published in 1979, appeared four years after E. O. Wilson's controversial book *Sociobiology: The New Synthesis*, which had given a name and set of concepts to a large body of research.[37] *Sociobiology* was a comprehensive review of findings on sociality, and made a strong case for a biological basis to social behavior. Wilson's last chapter on the biological basis of human social behavior became quite controversial.

W. D. Hamilton's 1964 inclusive fitness theory of altruism (altruism will be selected for when the behaviors benefiting a recipient exceed the cost to an actor) may have had the greatest impact on sociobiological (and evolutionary psychological) research of any scientific work in this area.[38] Hamilton asserted that altruism should be directed more often toward close kin (i.e., individuals likely to carry common alleles) than distant kin as a way of indirectly transmitting one's genes to future generations. In general, one should be predisposed to help a sister over an aunt, and an aunt over a cousin—sisters share half their genes on average, by descent, whereas nieces and aunts share one-quarter and cousins share one-eighth.

Hamilton defined *inclusive fitness* as an individual's reproductive success, enhanced by the individual's effects on relatives other than offspring. Of course, such behaviors would not occur consciously. No one helps anyone else for the purpose of preserving his or her own genes, but people act as though they do—helping others feels good in an immediate sense, one reason why such behavior may be maintained. Identification of immediate events affecting the display and continuity of social closeness, cooperation, and other beneficial behaviors between relatives are also important. It seemed that using inclusive fitness theory to understand human social relationships would not detract from the significance of everyday influences on social behavior, but would provide another way of interpreting that behavior.

The implications of Hamilton's reasoning for MZ and DZ twin relationships were striking. Perhaps MZ twins' unusual closeness could be understood in an ultimate sense—that is, it would pay to act more kindly toward one's MZ twin than one's DZ twin because that would be like "helping" one's own genes. It would also add a "why" to the twin's behavior. My 1982 doctoral dissertation—a study of cooperation, competition, and altruism between twins—was undertaken with these themes in mind.

I always believed that twins reared apart would offer unique tests of evolutionary-based hypotheses.[39] Canadian psychologists Chuck Crawford and Judith Anderson agreed, as shown in their 1989 article on the topic.[40] They suggested grouping MZA twins according to hypotheses about specific behaviors or rearing conditions and comparing their developmental pathways. For example, some evolutionary psychologists have predicted that female sexual maturity should occur earlier in father-absent homes than in father-present homes.[41] They have reasoned that it would be a better life history strategy for girls from father-absent homes to leave their disorganized environments to start families of their own. The idea of relating different behavioral outcomes to different life experiences is exactly what the MISTRA was all about—our goal (as stated in the Introduction) was to identify associations between differences in the twins' life histories and the twins' behavioral differences. There were some wonderful opportunities to use the MZA and DZA twins in evolutionary-based analyses.

The late evolutionary psychologist Linda Mealey claimed that for evolutionary psychologists "kinship, via the effect of inclusive fitness, constitutes a core construct of relevance to all social interaction."[42] Twin studies exemplify this view, especially studies of social relationships between MZA and DZA co-twins, a topic I review in Chapter 12.

Several years after arriving in Minnesota, I met Linda Mealey, a psychology professor at St. John's University in St. Cloud, Minnesota. She and I became close friends and colleagues and continued our association after I left Minnesota for California. Linda was interested in how genetic and environmental variables affected reproduction-related variables, such as age at marriage and number of children. She asked Bouchard for access to the reared-apart twin data, and he agreed—Bouchard was careful about releasing his files outside the department, but he was generous and encouraging when he trusted colleagues and believed they were serious about their work. In 1993, Linda and I published the first paper analyzing reared-apart twin data in the context of evolutionary theory.[43] We showed that while some behaviors related to reproduction may be genetically influenced, they do not affect the number of children.

Our sample included fifty-five MZA twin pairs and twenty-seven DZA same-sex twin pairs. The mean ages were 38.2 years (standard deviation [SD] = 14.5) for the males and 42.2 years (SD = 10.7) for the females, so not all twins had completed their reproductive years. The twins had also been raised in modern societies that had transitioned from high fertility and mortality to low fertility and mortality, probably reducing the variance of some measures. Small, statistically significant relationships may have been larger without these constraints. Linda and I drew our data from the Life History Interview and the Briggs Life History Form.[44] The intraclass correlations for our seven outcome measures are displayed in Table 9-3.

These values suggested that genetic factors influenced age at first marriage. It turned out that place of birth, a factor that (naturally!) is constant for co-twins, had a significant effect on age at first marriage. Genetic effects were also suggested for age at first date, paralleling what we found for age at first marriage and what others have found for age at first intercourse. Among males, age at first marriage was also associated with parents' religious affiliation. The high DZA correlations for timing of children suggested an environmental effect outside the family but shared by the twins—perhaps the prevailing cultural expectation was that people should start their families by a certain age. The lack of genetic influence on number of children surprised me. When Linda and I began our work, there were no twin studies on family size. In later years, twin studies estimated the heritabilities for number of children to be 0.32 for males and 0.34 for females.[45]

Our goal, mostly exploratory, was to see if personality and health characteristics (e.g., extraversion and teenage health) were related to reproductive events (e.g., age at first child and number of children). The individual findings from that study were less meaningful than the big picture. Our data suggested that males' reproduction-related behaviors were more affected by genetically influenced measures of personality and health than were females.' For example, in males later age at first marriage was associated with low activity level (−0.35) and poor childhood health (−0.44).

Table 9-3. Intraclass Correlations for Reproduction Outcome Measures

Measure	MZA (n = 25–47)	DZA (n = 15–26)
Age at marriage	0.76	0.53
Age at first child	0.19	0.64
Age at second child	0.38	0.55
Number of children	0.06	0.10
Age at first date	0.33	−0.02
Dating frequency	0.33	0.40
Not want children	0.33	0.15

Note: n = pairs.
Source: Adapted from Mealey and Segal, "Heritable and Environmental Variables Affect Reproduction-Related Behaviors, but Not Ultimate Reproductive Success," *Personality and Individual Differences* 14 (1993): 783–794.

Females' reproductive outcomes were influenced more by family dynamics than were the males'. For example, females with multiple marriages had experienced parent-child conflict and family instability. The only important reproduction variable—reproductive success—was directly related to childhood health and only for males.

The outcomes of our study conformed to evolutionary-based predictions. That is, males are more likely to have their reproductive capacities reduced under adverse conditions such as poor health than are females. Males with less favorable sexually dimorphic characteristics are also less likely to attract potential mates than males with favorable characteristics. Thus, we concluded that while proximal or immediate developmental mechanisms may have evolved in accordance with evolutionary expectations, they might not be relevant in modern societies.

The MISTRA researchers completed other evolutionary-based analyses of the reared-apart twin data during the study's later years and beyond. It was important to incorporate this perspective into our work because of rapidly growing interest in this area. Bouchard tells people that he started studying evolutionary psychology because I encouraged him to. He was only partly right—he also knew that it was becoming an important perspective in the field, one that would add meaning to our findings. In fact, the word evolution eventually appeared in the titles of seven of our publications. Evolutionary considerations were also discussed in other papers, such as Lykken's emergenesis paper reviewed previously[46] and our 1990 IQ paper published in *Science*.[47]

My friend Linda Mealey passed away in 2002 at the age of forty-seven. Her condition was diagnosed as cancer, and it spread quickly. I still resist the urge to call her when interesting topics arise, especially related to twins.

Personality and Cognition

Invitations to write book chapters increase when laboratories are productive. The growing number of empirical papers from the MISTRA probably led to the 1993 publication of several chapters and a book, *Twins as a Tool of Behavioral Genetics,* coedited by Bouchard and German geneticist Peter Propping.[48] Because Bouchard's chapters on personality and intelligence published in other collected works surveyed many studies in the field, not just the MISTRA, they will not be reviewed here in full. Instead, I have summarized them briefly, highlighting material on the reared-apart twins. Some of the MISTRA findings reported in the chapters were new because they were preliminary analyses on their way to becoming full-length papers. Sometimes older data were used in new ways.

Bouchard authored an overview of genetic and environmental influence on adult personality in a volume edited by Joop Hettema and Ian Deary.[49] The first part of his two-part treatise summarized the major model fitting results from twin, adoption, and extended family studies on the Big Five personality traits. The Big Five emerged as a dominant personality paradigm in the early 1990s. Big Five traits are easy to remember if you think of OCEAN: Openness (imaginative, inventive versus narrow, simple), Conscientiousness (organized, efficient versus disorderly, careless), Extraversion (sociable, dominant versus retiring, withdrawn), Agreeableness (cooperative, sympathetic versus quarrelsome, cold), and Neuroticism (calm, stable versus distraught, unstable). The second part of his chapter critiqued material that has been discussed throughout this book, so I will focus on the first part of his chapter.

The first of Bouchard's two tables displays model fitting results from a meta-analysis of reared-apart twin data from Minnesota and Sweden, an analysis originally done by John Loehlin (Table 9-4).[50] Shared family environments make modest contributions in both models. The data also show the difficulty in choosing between models requiring special twin and sibling environment parameters and nonadditive genetic effects. Special twin and sibling effects occur when the behavior of one twin or sibling affects the behavior of a co-twin or co-sibling. The late behavioral geneticist David Rowe also observed "sibling mutual influence"—pairs of same-sex nontwin brothers and sisters who liked each other or shared friends were more alike in delinquency than those who disliked each other or did not share friends.[51]

Bouchard's second table showed the MZA, MZT, DZA, and DZT Big Five correlations based on personality data from a Swedish twin study and various samples from the Minnesota reared-apart and reared-together

Table 9-4. Alternative Models for Twin Data on the Big Five Personality Traits

Big Five Trait	Additive Genes	MZ Environment	Sibling Environment	Additive Genes	Epistasis	Equal Environment
Extraversion	0.36	0.15	0.00	0.32	0.17	0.02
Neuroticism	0.31	0.17	0.05	0.27	0.14	0.07
Conscientiousness	0.28	0.17	0.04	0.22	0.16	0.07
Agreeableness	0.28	0.19	0.09	0.24	0.11	0.11
Openness	0.46	0.05	0.05	0.43	0.02	0.06

Source: Adapted from Bouchard, "Genetic and Environmental Influences on Adult Personality: Evaluating the Evidence," in *Foundations of Personality,* ed. P. Joop Hettema and Ian Deary, 15–44 Dordecht: Kluwer, 1993).

twin studies. Table 9-5 shows only the weighted mean correlations based on these samples. The MZA data suggested an average heritability of about 0.50, and the lack of difference between the MZA and MZT twins suggested a shared environmental effect of zero. However, the 0.50 heritability left plenty of room for environmental influences unique to individuals. Nonadditive genetic effects were indicated for extraversion and neuroticism because the DZA and DZT correlations were less than half the MZA and MZT correlations, suggesting emergenic effects on these traits.

Bouchard often said that the absence of shared environmental effects on personality was "counter-intuitive, but true." It was certainly one of the most provocative and controversial findings from our study. The fact that other investigators were finding the same thing using other instruments and samples increased our confidence in the findings. I accept these results, based as they are on the twins' self-reports. We also asked the twins' spouses and companions to complete the Adjective Check List to describe the twins' personality, information that is not yet analyzed. It is likely that these data would have shown somewhat less MZA co-twin similarity than that found from the twins' self-reports. A previous reared-together twin study reported that peer ratings of the twins' personalities indicated genetic influence across the different traits, although less than that derived from the twins' self-ratings.[52]

If the twins had rated themselves relative to their co-twins, I wonder if we would have captured what Shields suggested—that MZA twins are more alike than MZT twins on some personality traits because MZA twins did not develop social roles within their twinship. As I've written

Table 9-5. Weighted Mean Correlations for the Big Five Personality Traits for Minnesota Twins Reared Apart and Together

Big Five Trait	MZA	MZT	DZA	DZT
Extraversion	0.51	0.53	−0.03	0.17
Neuroticism	0.54	0.47	0.27	0.15
Conscientiousness	0.50	0.57	0.09	0.35
Agreeableness	0.51	0.42	0.10	0.18
Openness	0.60	0.43	0.31	0.18
Mean	0.53	0.48	0.15	0.20

Note: The combined samples included the following pairs: MZA (n=61), DZA (42), MZT (n=99), and DZT (n=99) who completed the California Psychological Inventory); and MZA (n=52), DZA (n=33), MZT (n=553), and DZT (n=459) who completed the Multidimensional Personality Questionnaire.

Source: Adapted from Bouchard, "Genetic and Environmental Influences on Adult Personality: Evaluating the Evidence," in *Foundations of Personality,* ed. P. Joop Hettema and Ian Deary, 15–44 (Dordecht: Kluwer, 1993).

elsewhere in this book, people interacting with twins usually find that twins behave more similarly when they are apart than when they are together. However, we did not detect this effect in the MISTRA self-report personality data.

Plomin and McClearn's *Nature, Nurture, and Psychology* summarized major behavior genetics advances that had occurred during the previous decade.[53] At its 1992 meeting, the *American Psychological Association* had named genetics as one of the themes that best reflected present and future psychological research.[54] The MISTRA probably had a lot to do with that—the book's editors wrote that McGue's chapter fell within what they considered "the front lines of genetics research."[55]

A striking feature is the series of graphs reproduced in Figure 9-2 that show IQ intraclass correlations from past and present reared-apart twin studies.[56] The correlations ranged between 0.64 and 0.74 for the three previous studies, and 0.69 and 0.78 for the more recent MISTRA and Swedish studies. The weighted average correlation was 0.73, using a total of 162 MZA twin pairs. The similar finding based on the three earlier

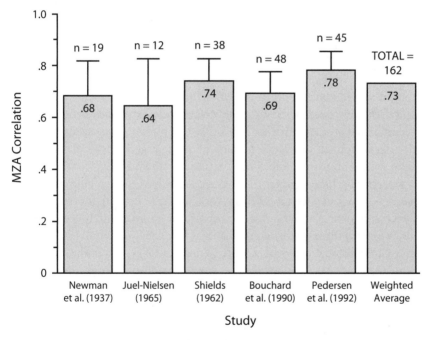

Figure 9-2.   MZA Twin IQ correlations from five studies. Adapted from McGue et al., "Behavioral Genetics of Cognitive Ability: A Life-Span Perspective," in *Nature, Nurture, and Psychology,* ed. Robert Plomin and Gerald E. McClearn, 59–76 (Washington, D.C.: American Psychological Association, 1993). *Note:* Bars at the top indicate standard errors.

studies and the MISTRA was robust, as I indicated in Chapter 5, but it was more so with the addition of the forty-five Swedish pairs.

The MZA twin correlation directly estimates heritability. Thus, McGue noted that IQ heritability was about 75 percent, considerably higher than the 50 percent figure provided by other kin comparisons. Because most MZA twins were adults, and because the results were consistent across studies, he concluded that the large MZA IQ correlation probably reflected increased genetic influence over time, rather than biased sampling or assessment.

McGue's reasoning fits nicely with my own work on virtual twins, the same-age unrelated pairs I have been studying since the early 1990s. The virtual twin IQ correlation, which directly estimates shared environmental effects on behavior, is 0.28 (n = 140), leaving the remaining 0.72 accounted for by genetic factors, nonshared environmental factors, and measurement error.[57] These results appear to mirror those from the MZA twins for the following reason: recall that a subgroup of the virtual twins (n = 43 pairs), who were very young children when I first studied them, showed a drop in their IQ correlation from 0.30 to 0.11 at their second testing in later childhood.[58] This change suggested a reduction in shared environmental effects on IQ over time, with both genetic and unique environmental factors becoming more important. It is likely that when virtual twins are assessed as adolescents and adults their IQ correlation will approach zero, as reported in other adoption studies.[59] If this were the case, it would correspond to the MZA IQ findings of about 0.75 genetic and 0.25 nonshared environmental variance plus error. However, based on accumulated studies of twins and other kinships, a more accurate partitioning of adult IQ variance may be 60 percent genetic, 35 percent nonshared environmental, and 5 percent measurement error.[60]

Bouchard's 1993 chapter "The Genetic Architecture of Human Intelligence" did not include new MISTRA twin data.[61] Instead, it provided evidence supporting a hierarchical structure of approximately ten primary abilities with three major peaks: General Visualization, Fluid Intelligence, and Crystallized Intelligence, with General Intelligence at the top. General Visualization refers to mental manipulation of figural information, Fluid Intelligence refers to genetically based abilities, and Crystallized Intelligence refers to skills acquired through education and experience. Memory span and vocabulary are examples of the ten primary mental abilities that cluster under their relevant factors (i.e., Fluid Intelligence and Crystallized Intelligence, respectively). Bouchard also called for meta-analytic studies of intelligence and an end to ad hoc criticism of individual studies. In this context, he revisited some of the objections to his reared-apart twin studies that I detailed in earlier chapters, most notably Chapter 3.

Bouchard and Propping's book, *Twins as a Tool of Behavioral Genetics*, focused on what twin studies had revealed about general intelligence and personality traits. It resulted from a 1992 Dahlem workshop held in Berlin on the subject: "What Are the Mechanisms Mediating the Genetic and Environmental Determinants of Behavior?" Dahlem conferences are unique in that background papers, written around discussion topics, serve as the basis for small group discussions. MISTRA data were not presented, but some interesting historical notes on twins were embedded within Bouchard and Propping's introduction.

They wrote that the idea of studying twins went back many years, to before Galton's time. Saint Augustine, in *The City of God,* used twins to refute astrological claims. But, as discussed earlier, it was Sir Francis Galton who is famous for developing the twin method for formal scientific inquiry in 1875.[62]

1992 to 1993

In August 1993, we began our collaboration with colleagues at the Jean Mayer U.S. Department of Agriculture Human Nutrition Research Center on Aging (Energy Metabolism Laboratory) at Tufts University. Now twins would fly from Minneapolis to Boston to complete a five-day analysis of body size measures, food intake, and energy expenditure. This five-year study, funded for one million dollars by the U.S. Department of Health and Human Services, assured us that separated twins would continue to be identified and assessed. Finding financial support was always our biggest difficulty (as is described in Chapter 14), and we never knew if the study would continue for two years or one year—or at all.

We added five new twin pairs to the study in 1993, two MZA and three DZA opposite sex sets, as well as four spouses and partners. We also studied seven follow-up twin pairs (four MZA and three DZA), as well as four spouses. We presented seventeen conference papers and invited lectures. In California, I began working on twin studies of odor identification and sensitivity, using the University of Pennsylvania Smell Identification Test.[63] I sent forms to Minnesota for the reared-apart twins to complete.

The first reared-apart female twin pair I had studied in 1982 was one of the four MZA twin pairs who returned to Minnesota in 1993. The twins sent me their photographs, and it was striking but not surprising to see how alike they still looked and how similarly they had aged. The twins reminded me of a photo Bouchard had hung in all of his offices showing a pair of beautiful elderly MZ female twins (Figure 9-3). The photo had been a gift from identical twin photographers, Kathryn M. Abbe and Frances M. Gill, and had appeared in their stunning volume, *Twins on Twins*.[64] Better than any study, the picture captures essential elements of the aging process—the graying hair and matching creases in their skin suggest that physical changes are largely influenced by genetic factors. A small inset of the twins looking so similar at a younger age underlines the idea of genetically based physical development, similar to what I noticed about the Minnesota pair. Bouchard loved this photograph, and he relished photographing reared-apart twins beside it.

Abbe and Gill also gave Bouchard a unique set of slides showing themselves together at many different ages. The images of these twins as infants,

Figure 9-3.   Bouchard's favorite photo: identical twins Genevieve and Eloise Reed at age ninety-four. (Photo courtesy Kathryn M. Abbe.)

Figure 9-4. MZA twins Keith (left) and Jake as infants, at age eleven or twelve (Keith) and ten (Jake), at age twenty-four on their first assessment day in Minnesota, and at age fifty-five during a taped interview for Keith's son's school project. Keith is right-handed, and Jake is left-handed. Note the opposite positioning of the handles of the twins' coffee cups. (Photos [infant, childhood, and adult years] courtesy of Keith and Jake. Photo credit [Minnesota study] Thomas J. Bouchard Jr.)

children, young women, and beyond suggested a rare time-lapse photography in which the individual ages before viewers' eyes. In this case, it was two individuals, and they were growing up exactly the same way. Bouchard often opened his twin lectures with these slides, which regularly captivated his audiences. When we positioned the MZA twins' separately shot childhood and adult photos next to each other, we saw the same thing. The genetically influenced unfolding of physical growth and development is well known, but MZA twins make this process especially striking, as shown in Figure 9-4.

CHAPTER TEN

Family Environments, Happiness, Sensation Seeking, and the MMPI (1994–1997)

ETWEEN THE YEARS 1994 and 1997, the MISTRA published papers on a number of new research topics. The twins showed that current perceptions of the past are genetically influenced, people have happiness set-points, and practice does not always lead to perfect performance. They also showed that there was genetic influence on the personality correlates of psychopathology on the Minnesota Multiphasic Personality Inventory (MMPI), and that the same genes affected impulsivity and sensation seeking. By the start of 1994, nearly 130 pairs had been studied.

All in the Family

Graduate student Yoon-Mi Hur (now a faculty member at Mokpo National University in South Korea) joined the MISTRA in 1990 after a two-year stint in the University of Minnesota's psychometrics program. She was charming, funny, and exceedingly smart. After graduating from Minnesota in 1993, she returned to South Korea to teach classes, conduct research, and develop the South Korean Twin Registry. "The striking behavioral similarities I witnessed during the assessment and analyses convinced me of the importance of genes in human behavior," Hur recalled. Her first MISTRA paper out of seven, co-authored with Bouchard, examined twins' perceptions of their childhood environments.[1]

The genetics of the family environment drew considerable research attention in the late 1980s and early 1990s. It sounded contradictory, but evidence supported genetic influence on family environment measures and on how we construct and perceive our environments. Parents who enjoy reading and have books and magazines at home are likely to have intelligent children—but these parents also transmit genetic factors associated with high intelligence to their sons and daughters. Some children will thrive in educationally stimulating environments and seek them out, while others may find them somewhat overwhelming and prefer to learn in quieter spaces.

Research on the genetics of family influences began with the late psychologist David Rowe's 1981 and 1983 studies showing that adolescent MZT twins held more similar perceptions of parental support (i.e., acceptance or rejection), but not parental control (i.e., permissiveness or restrictiveness), than DZT twins.[2] His results were replicated in Sweden using the retrospective reports of adult twins reared apart and together.[3] In 1995, the MISTRA published the first analysis of reared-apart twins' perceptions of their family environments using multiple indicators. One measure was the Block Environmental Questionnaire, which assesses parental characteristics.[4] The other measure was the Family Environment Scale described in Chapter 7. Hur used the same parenting dimensions described in the previous studies in order to test the generality of these findings.

Data were available for over one hundred reared-apart twin pairs, fifty-eight MZA and forty-six DZA. The standard version of the Block included ninety-two items describing parental characteristics and the family context. Six scale scores were generated (Maternal Acceptance-Rejection, Paternal Acceptance-Rejection, Cohesion, Maternal Intellectual-Cultural, Paternal Intellectual-Cultural, and Organization) based on the responses of 276 twins and their spouses. The data were also reduced to two major parent-perception factors: Support (parental support and acceptance) and Organization and Cultural Orientation (parental restrictiveness and control). Factor analysis of the ten Family Environment Scales (Cohesion, Expressiveness, Conflict, Independence, Active Recreational, Achievement Orientation, Intellectual-Cultural, Moral Religious Emphasis, Organization, and Control) produced the same two major factors that we found for the Block.

The support-related scales in both the Block and Family Environment Scale showed relatively high MZA correlations (e.g., Cohesion: 0.42; Independence: 0.39), while the control-related scales showed relatively low MZA correlations (e.g., Organization: –0.07; Moral Religious Emphasis: 0.18). The pattern of correlations in Table 10-1 demonstrated that we replicated Rowe's previous findings of genetic influence on support and the absence of genetic influence on organization; thus, the reared-apart twin sample was not atypical in terms of family perceptions. Within-study

Table 10-1. **MZA and DZA Intraclass Correlations for the Block Environmental Questionnaire and Family Environment Scale**

Block Environmental Questionnaire		
	MZA	DZA
n (pairs)	39–44	31–37
Factor		
Support	0.51[a]	−0.24
Organization and cultural	0.12	0.31[b]

Family Environment Scale		
	MZA	DZA
n (pairs)	58	46
Factor		
Support	0.31[a]	0.17
Organization and cultural	−0.03	−0.19

Note: The Block Environmental Questionnaire was added one year after the study began, so it was available for fewer twins than the Family Environment Scale.

a. $P < .01$.

b. $P < .05$.

Source: Adapted from Hur and Bouchard, "Genetic Influences on Perceptions of Childhood Family Environment: A Reared Apart Twin Study," *Child Development* 66 (1995): 330–345.

confirmation was provided by comparable results from the two questionnaires. Modeling showed that, for adults, Support during childhood was affected by additive genetic and nonshared environmental factors, whereas Organization was mostly affected by the nonshared environment; that is, genetic factors played a modest role in how adults viewed parental control during childhood. A model fit to the combined data showed that genetic factors explained 44 percent of the variance in Support and 28 percent of the variance in Organization.

Hur speculated that genetic effects on Support reflected reactive genotype-environment correlation, that is, that MZA twins probably elicited matched responses to their behaviors from their respective rearing family members. However, it was also possible that the MZA twins processed, interpreted, and/or recalled information the same way, so even if their recollections were distorted (as most people's are to some degree) they were distorted in the same manner. As Hur pointed out, retrospective bias may be partly genetically based.

Hur also suggested that the common rules and standards of Western families could explain the reduced heritability for Organization. Parental rule-setting is universal, but most of the twins came from Western cultures. Of course, some parents are more permissive than others. Another possibility is that some children and adolescents reject parental authority in most forms, so even indulgent parents seem restrictive in their children's eyes.

The Roots of Happiness

David Lykken was enormously interested in what makes people happy—*lykken* means "the happiness" in Norwegian. Lykken's twin analyses showing genetic influence on happiness drew considerable attention.[5] One of his most striking findings was that one MZA twin's happiness at time 2 was closely associated with his or her co-twin's happiness at time 1, showing a heritable, stable component to that trait. However, Lykken also believed happiness (including his own) could be raised, at least momentarily, by doing things one liked to do.

Studies on the roots of happiness had been ongoing for years when Lykken began this research. Everyone wants to be happy, but not everyone is, so scientists had tried finding the life events associated with happiness. A 1995 study by David Myers and Edward Diener showed that higher social status and higher wages, factors expected to raise happiness, did not.[6] Instead, it seemed that people are able to cope reasonably well with their misfortunes and still maintain a characteristic degree of happiness. At the same time, not everyone was equally happy. Myers and Diener suggested that happiness was affected by social relationships, religious faith, cultural factors, and personal goals.

Lykken used twins reared apart and together to explore genetic influence on human happiness. His book on the subject was an outgrowth of his 1996 twin study conducted with Auke Tellegen.[7] They first examined the happiness levels of 2,310 reared-together twins using a contentment measure from Lykken's Self-Rating Inventory. Twins were asked, "Taking the good with the bad, how happy and contented are you on the average now, compared with other people?" Responses ranged from 1 (lowest 5 percent of the population) to 5 (the highest 5 percent of the population). Lykken found that 86 percent of the twins placed themselves in the top 35 percent. Lykken suggested, albeit tentatively, that natural selection might have favored happy people who were likely to mate, have children, and become our ancestors.[8] This could be true, but only to an extent because natural selection would not have favored habitually happy people who might have overlooked threats and physical dangers.[9] It may also be that many twins (especially MZ twins) are happier and more secure than others because of their close companionship. A Danish study found a lower suicide risk among twins than nontwins, which the investigators explained by twins' close social ties.[10] It is unfortunate that Lykken's analysis was not applied to nontwin individuals.

In another analysis, Lykken replaced his single-item measure with the well-being scale from Tellegen's Multidimensional Personality Questionnaire. Educational attainment, social status, income, and marital status explained just trivial amounts of the happiness variance. Even Tellegen's traditionalism scale that correlated moderately with religious commitment correlated only 0.05 with well-being, meaning that religious people are not happier or unhappier than nonreligious people. This finding challenged the view that embracing religious beliefs predisposed people toward happiness. But Lykken's findings on the heritability of well-being drew more attention—he was the first researcher to show that genes partly explained individual differences in happiness.

The Multidimensional Personality Questionnaire had been taken twice by seventy-nine MZT twin pairs and forty-eight DZT twin pairs at the mean ages of twenty and thirty years. The correlation between their well-being scores obtained at the two different ages was 0.50. There is another informative calculation that can be done with twin data called a cross-twin, cross-time correlation. Here, twin A's score at one age is correlated with twin B's score at another age, and vice versa. If this statistic is higher for MZ than DZ twins, it means that the stable part of the trait is genetically influenced.

Lykken found that the MZT twins' cross-twin, cross-time correlation of 0.40 was equal to 80 percent of the 0.50 retest correlation (0.40/0.50). However, the same correlation for the DZT twins was about zero. These results suggested that genes affected what Lykken called "the happiness set-point" or stable part of happiness. The happiness set-point is each person's characteristic happiness level that might fluctuate depending on daily events and experiences. Subsequent research has supported the idea of a genetically influenced happiness set-point, although individual differences in returning to one's baseline level have been observed.[11] The near-zero DZT and 0.44 MZT happiness correlations, based on the first questionnaire administration, suggested that happiness might be emergenic.

The Multidimensional Personality Questionnaire was also available for forty-four MZA twin pairs and twenty-seven DZA twin pairs. The estimated heritability for well-being from our 1988 personality study was 0.48.[12] Fortunately, twenty-six reared-apart twin pairs had taken the questionnaire twice about 4.5 years apart, yielding a retest correlation of 0.67. Assuming a long-term well-being stability of 0.60, Lykken showed that the heritability of their stable happiness component was also 80 percent (0.48/0.60), and that the heritability of their momentary happiness was about 50 percent. It seemed that an MZ twin's happiness was a better predictor of his co-twin's current or future happiness than was the co-twin's educational achievement, status, or income.

Intraclass correlations for the well-being scale are displayed in Table 10-2. They included data from some new reared-apart twin pairs that had been studied since the publication of our 1988 personality article.

The similar MZA-MZT correlations suggested that shared environments do not affect how happy people become. Most importantly, Lykken showed that people have a characteristic well-being level. But daily events would not significantly alter the usual happiness level to which people revert when the glory of success or the despair from grief subsides. This information seemed potentially valuable to patients and to therapists trying to understand and improve their clients' quality of life—but this information could be misconstrued, especially if Lykken's next words were not read carefully.

Lykken concluded, "Trying to be happier [may be] as futile as trying to be taller."[13] However, a close reading of the study shows that if people tried to determine what made them happy, and minimized what made them unhappy, then despite their genetic backgrounds their happiness levels could be elevated—albeit not permanently—as long as they were doing things they enjoyed. In fact, Lykken regretted that quote, noting in his 1999 happiness book, "That pessimistic conclusion is not impelled by the data and, in fact, I believe it is wrong."[14]

Lykken's happiness research was cited in the *New York Times,* the *London Times,* the *Manchester Guardian,* and in Italian, German, and South American periodicals.[15] He called the coverage "unprecedented." The happiness set-point concept was embraced by a number of researchers, including Ed Diener, Paul Costa, and Robert McCrae. The three had found that happiness levels were stable, and that people generally did not maintain

Table 10-2.   **MZA and MZT Intraclass Correlations for Well-Being**

Twin Type	n (Pairs)	r_i (Standard Error)
MZA	75	0.52 (± 0.10)
DZA	36	−0.02 (± 0.17)
MZT	647	0.44 (± 0.03)
DZT	733	0.08 (± 0.04)

Source: Adapted from Lykken and Tellegen, "Happiness Is a Stochastic Phenomenon," *Psychological Science* 7 (1996): 186–189.

unusually high or low moods.[16] They also acknowledged that severe psychological problems or continual bad luck could override the happiness set-point. This makes sense because extreme situations have a greater impact on behavior and mood than ordinary daily events. Lykken's estimated happiness heritability of 50 percent was questioned by psychologist Howard Weiss, who suggested that genetic influence on individual differences in happiness could be as low as 25 percent or as high as 75 percent.[17]

Tellegen's take on the happiness research emphasized within-person variability despite the genetic effect: "There's a range of oscillation around a given person's set-point. This means that you can be an emotional Pavarotti . . . and it will still average out."[18] Lykken elaborated on the nature of the happiness set-point by asking if it is just an average of repeated measures or "is there a true homeostatic process that is activated by any deviation from the value characteristic of the individual?"[19] That is, perhaps when someone experiences a pleasant or unpleasant event the body works to restore that person to his or her characteristic happiness level.

The media attention led Lykken "to speculate more freely" on his findings than he might otherwise have done.[20] He remarked on the contented style of people doing work that brought them pleasure, singling out the clever plumbers in his favorite shop and the skillful garbage collectors in his neighborhood. "The people in my examples either have above-average set-points or they transcend their set-points by doing their jobs with skill and good humor."[21] He also urged people to act on their happiness feelings, recognizing that money and status many not increase happiness and can even lower it.

Lykken had advice for parents: "Nurturing the child's innate pro-social proclivities, which include the inclination toward constructive endeavor, constitutes the most important responsibility of parents, the socialization of their children."[22] In other words, effective parenting means being aware of, and responsive to, children's talents and creativity. Finding genetic influence on the happiness set-point or on any other behavior never denied the crucial roles that families played. Everyone associated with the MISTRA believed this.

Practice Effects

It was surprising to find genetic influence on practice, something parents pressure their children to do when they are learning a new task. Most parents encourage their children to repeat the alphabet, replay musical scales, or work at whatever skills they have to get better. Most people assume that "practice makes perfect," but the nature and outcomes of practice are more complex. The same amount of practice may affect two individuals differently, depending on their commitment, motivation, and ability. Author Malcolm Gladwell wrote that one has to practice for 10,000 hours before becoming an expert.[23] Some people might need that much practice, but a few may be experts from the start. Galton, father of the Twin Method, told the story of a young man who claimed first place in a national running race without formal training or experience.[24] It seems practice and guidance can refine natural talents, but they cannot create them.

By the mid-1990s, several reared-together twin studies had reported a genetic influence on motor skills, but the effects of practice over more than a single day had not been examined.[25] Our studies showed a genetic component to improvement following practice by engaging the twins in a multiday motor skill acquisition task. The late Professor Paul (Bill) Fox directed this phase of the assessment, which was the first of its kind in the history of reared-apart twin studies.

A student assistant arrived in the laboratory every Thursday, Friday, and Saturday morning of the assessment week to individually escort twins to a special testing room. The psychomotor battery included a hole steadiness test (to examine involuntary hand movement), the Purdue Pegboard Test (to assess gross movements of the fingers, arms, and hands, and also fine fingertip dexterity), and the Rotary Pursuit Test (to measure ability to keep a stylus on a moving target). Data were available for sixty-four MZA twin pairs and thirty-two DZA twin pairs.[26]

The Rotary Pursuit apparatus resembled an old-fashioned record player. A disk placed on the top of a rectangular box was rotated in a clockwise direction, at a constant speed of sixty revolutions per minute. Holding a metal stylus, twins were instructed to keep contact with a metal spot on the moving disk, while the length of time on target was recorded. Each of the twenty-five trials in each thirty-minute session lasted for twenty seconds, and trials were separated by ten-second breaks.

The twins' responses were organized into five blocks per day, with each block consisting of five trials. The MZA and DZA twins did not differ in their performance levels, and both groups improved considerably during the first day. They also improved after a break from the activity between days one and two, and two and three. Variability within each twin group increased over the three days because practicing from day to day improved some twins' skills more than others.

The MZA twins' correlations were stable and showed a slight increase over time, whereas the DZA twin's correlations were unstable and irregular. The higher MZA correlations indicated significant genetic influence on performance, but there were more interesting features of these data.

The first trial on day one showed a higher heritability for the percentage of time on target (0.66) than the other four blocks on that day. Fox suggested that individuals rely on their current abilities when attempting a new task, and MZA twins would be more highly matched than DZA twins in this regard. And, except for day one, genetic influence increased as the trial blocks progressed—the highest heritability (0.74) occurred on day three on the fourteenth trial block. The MZA twins maintained a high level of similarity, whereas the DZA twins generally drifted apart. Even more striking, the MZA twins' similarity across trial blocks did not differ from the block-to-block similarity of a single individual, which was not the case for the DZA twins. A purely environmental model for all fifteen trials was rejected.

Table 10-3 shows the intraclass correlations for the slope (change in performance across days). The MZA twins' higher slope correlations were increasing, while the DZA twins' lower correlations were decreasing. Model fitting indicated a heritability of 0.66 on performance (time on target) and 0.40 on reminiscence (improvement). Nonadditive genetic factors were suggested because of the relatively high MZA correlations.

Everyone improves with training—in fact, the lowest-scoring twin on day three outperformed the highest scoring twin on day one. But not everyone improves to the same degree. Fox suggested that practice sessions on this task enhanced the twins' environmental similarity, reducing existing differences between MZA twins more than between DZA twins. When environments are uniform, genetic differences contribute more to behavioral differences among people. Conversely, when environments are different, genetic differences become less salient. Because environmental similarity

Table 10-3. Intraclass Correlations for the Slope and Reminiscence for the Rotary Pursuit Test

Day	Measure	MZA (64 pairs)	DZA (32 pairs)
1		0.56	0.24
	Slope		
2		0.69	0.17
3		0.72	0.11

Note: Day 3 was added after the study began, resulting in 58 MZA twin pairs for related measures.

Source: Adapted from Fox et al., "Genetic and Environmental Contributions to the Acquisition of a Motor Skill," *Nature* 384 (1996): 356–358.

enhances heritability (the proportion of variance associated with genetic differences), the declining DZA correlations reflected genetic effects on performance and practice.

People were quite taken by these new findings. They had practical appeal and could help them understand why they might do well on some tasks with little practice and only slightly better on others despite lots of practice. The study was reported by Reuters news service, whose article included an interview with one of the authors, then University of Kansas psychology professor Scott Hershberger, who had spent a year at Minnesota. Hershberger claimed, "Since the identical twins [were] building upon a common genetic substrate . . . practice [was] going to have the same effect for them."[27]

The genetic influence on the effect of practice in sports performance has not been considered, but would be expected. Identical twin Olympic athletes Jiang Tingting and Jiang Wenwen (synchronized swimming) and Mark and Bob Bryan (tennis) are known for their extraordinary performances, but few nonidentical co-twins both perform at elite levels.[28] The MZ twin athletes' rigorous and consistent practice could minimize slight ability differences between them, increasing the heritability of physical skills. Similar processes may apply when twins pursue academic activities, especially those requiring repetition or rote learning. Teenage identical twins Erin and Becky Glendaniel of Delaware have both participated in national spelling bees in different years.[29] We found a high heritability for spelling, as discussed in a later chapter.

Personality and Psychopathology

In 1996, a group of MISTRA colleagues examined the Minnesota Multiphasic Personality Inventory (MMPI) personality indicators of psychopathology, studied for the first time in reared-apart twins.[30] The MMPI is a widely used personality and mental health inventory, developed in 1940 by Starke R. Hathaway and J. C. McKinley.[31] Interest in personality-psychopathology associations and the genetic underpinnings of these associations was high at the time.

The article's lead author was David DiLalla, Southern Illinois University psychologist and former student of Irving Gottesman.[32] DiLalla met Bouchard at the 1987 Behavior Genetics Association meeting in Minneapolis when he was a graduate student at the University of Virginia. "Gottesman introduced us. I'm sure I appeared kind of silly. I was in awe of the whole thing—the MISTRA had rock star status. And Bouchard was such a striking figure." After a postdoctoral position at the University of Colorado and a clinical internship in Denver, DiLalla joined Southern Illinois University in Carbondale.

> I was interested in the genetic and environmental correlations between personality and psychopathological traits, but I couldn't gather these data in Carbondale. It was lucky for me that the MISTRA's MMPI data hadn't been spoken for. The other plus was Bouchard's collaborative generosity. Gottesman arranged for us to analyze the data, and Bouchard trusted us to develop our ideas and interpretations. But he read the manuscript and made contributions.

Other contributors to the MMPI study were University of Colorado behavioral geneticist Greg Carey, another former student of Gottesman who had been DiLalla's postdoctoral mentor, as well as Gottesman and Bouchard. Carey knew Bouchard from his graduate student years in Minnesota, and he recalled that Bouchard significantly influenced his thoughts about the origins of behavior. Carey was a postdoctoral fellow at the University of Washington in St. Louis when Bouchard began the MISTRA. He told me, "[The study] was not a screwball idea. I had concerns about how many twins [Bouchard] would find and if they would be willing to come to Minnesota for one week. But I was fascinated by the Jim twins. Case studies can generate great hypotheses, and Tom accomplished a great deal more."

The MMPI results were available for sixty-five MZA twin pairs and fifty-four DZA twin pairs (thirty-eight same-sex and sixteen opposite-sex). The MMPI includes over 500 behavioral style and preference items, rated as "true," "false," or "can't say." The twins' responses were computer scored for the ten clinical scales (e.g., Depression and Hypochondriasis), the three validity scales (e.g., Lie and Frequency), and the thirteen Wiggins content scales. The Wiggins content scales (e.g., Family Problems and Authority Conflict) covered thoughts, experiences, and behaviors associated with psychopathology. Gottesman had studied these scales in 1977 using adolescent twins reared together and found evidence of both genetic and environmental effects.[33]

Intraclass correlations for the ten MMPI Clinical Scales ranged from 0.29 to 0.64 for the MZA twins, and from 0.03 to 0.23 for the DZA twins, consistent with a genetic influence. A nonadditive genetic influence was suggested for the Frequency scale because the DZA correlation (−0.02) was much less than the MZA correlation (0.52), and because it did not fit the model's assumption that only additive genetic effects were important. The Wiggins scales behaved like the clinical scales in that the MZA twins showed greater resemblance than the DZA twins. Intraclass correlations ranged from 0.23 to 0.65 for the MZA twins and from −0.12 to 0.34 for the DZA twins. Only two scales (Religious Fundamentalism and Feminine Interests) didn't fit the additive genetic model.

According to DiLalla, there were no real surprises in the results. The overall finding of 44 percent genetic variance in the MMPI's clinical and content scales agreed with previous studies, and the results came from what DiLalla called a "fantastic resource." In Carey's view, the study "joined the nexus of behavioral genetic research that sputtered to life in the '60s and '70s and truly came to life in the '80s and '90s."

An interesting and novel feature of DiLalla's work was the multivariate profile analysis, looking at the score elevation and tracing the peaks and valleys of the twins' MMPI scores. The average score elevation looks at each twin's average scale score, while the profile shape looks at the difference of each twin's MMPI scale from the average. This analysis showed that genes affected both the average score elevation (how high or low twins scored overall) and the profile shape (the form of psychopathology, that is, whether twins scored high or low on the same scales). Such findings had been reported for twins reared together, yet they were more striking among twins who had always been apart. But DiLalla was cautious in interpreting that data because the group of reared-apart twins was a small, nonpsychiatric sample. He suggested that certain profile configurations found in the study did not necessarily signal specific psychiatric problems that were more or less genetically influenced. Still, the scales associated with psychotic behavior (such as bipolar disorder) seemed more heritable than those associated with neurotic behavior (such as disruptions in memory, awareness, and identity).

The authors noted that regional associations in the MMPI had been previously reported, a factor that could have enhanced the twins' similarity. This seems unlikely because, in most cases, both the MZA and DZA co-twins had been raised in the same country, and the DZA twins were still less alike. However, DiLalla and his colleagues wisely gave us a look at the scores of the MZA twins raised in different countries. Their within-pair differences of 8.5 and 5.1 T-score points were, respectively, equal to and below the MZA twin group average of 8.6.[34] Thus, the culture of rearing does not necessarily affect personality or the predisposition to psychopathology. For comparative purposes, the investigators cited MZA twin pairs with differences above the group average, as large as 16.4 and 17.2. In one case, the twins became discordant for major affective disorder with psychosis, and in the other case a head injury five years before assessment had probably caused neurological damage in one twin. These last two cases showed that MZA twins raised in the same culture could differ in personality and psychopathology for a variety of reasons.

Studying a large group of MZA twins raised in different countries would be the best approach to understanding how cultural factors affect behavior. But twins raised apart are rare, and twins raised in different cultures even more so. The MISTRA had only six such pairs, four MZA and two DZA. In 2008, Yoon-Mi Hur and I studied a pair of twenty-eight-year-old MZA female co-twins of Korean descent, raised in South Korea and the United States, respectively. We found both striking similarities (e.g., identical IQs and nearly identical self-esteem scores) and interesting differences (e.g., weight difference of 11.86 pounds and dissimilar sports participation) between them. These twins did not take part in the MISTRA.[35]

The Minnesota investigators would revisit the MMPI in 1999. Meanwhile, other personality traits and associations among them were explored, such as impulsivity and sensation seeking.

Impulsivity and Sensation Seeking

Hur's second study used reared-apart twins to see if the association between impulsivity and sensation seeking could be partly explained by the same genes.[36] *Impulsivity* is behavior expressed without thought or deliberation in response to objects or events.[37] *Sensation seeking* is a behavior that entails a search for new, intense, and complex experiences, and a willingness to take risks to acquire them.[38] People high in impulsivity tend to be high in sensation seeking. When Hur began her analysis in the mid-1990s, genetic effects of 0.40 for impulsivity[39] and 0.36 for risk-taking had been reported.[40] Biological correlates common to these traits, such as monoamine oxidase level, had also been described.[41] Based on these findings, Hur reasoned that a genetic connection between impulsivity and sensation seeking was likely.

The measure of impulsivity was the Control scale of the Multidimensional Personality Questionnaire, and the measure of sensation seeking was Marvin Zuckerman's Sensation Seeking Form V. This form is organized into four subscales, namely Thrill and Adventure Seeking, Experience Seeking, Disinhibition, and Boredom Susceptibility. The twin sample included fifty-seven MZA pairs and forty-nine DZA pairs (Table 10-4). With the exception of Thrill and Adventure Seeking, a genetic influence was indicated, especially by the relatively low DZA correlations. The amount of genetic variance shared by Control and the Sensation Seeking scales was 55 percent, supporting the expected link between impulsivity and sensation seeking.

Table 10-4.   Intraclass Correlations for Sensation Seeking Measures and for Control

Scale	MZA	DZA
Thrill and adventure seeking	0.47[a]	0.48[a]
Disinhibition	0.50[a]	0.10
Boredom susceptibility	0.43[a]	0.16
Experience seeking	0.54[a]	0.28[b]
Control	0.51[a]	0.05

a. $P < .01$.
b. $P < .05$.

Source: Adapted from Hur and Bouchard, "The Genetic Influence between Impulsivity and Sensation-Seeking," *Behavior Genetics* 27 (1997): 455–463.

A significant feature of this study was that it demonstrated a well-reasoned idea about two personality traits, impulsivity and sensation seeking, based on observed relationships between these two traits and their likely biological underpinnings. Of course, males' sensation-seeking tendencies exceed those of females, making an argument for conducting analyses separately by sex. But Hur's modest sample size precluded organizing the twins in this way.

Hur's work had practical implications. Impulsivity had been linked to problem behaviors such as substance abuse, conduct disorder, and suicide attempts. Some individuals acting on impulse may inadvertently endanger themselves and the people around them. Impulsive behavior could be a warning sign to parents and teachers of behavior that goes beyond reasonable risks. However, some people depend on heightened levels of intellectual stimulation, emotional excitement, or physical danger to feel content. Matching experience to temperament is everyone's challenge.

While Hur was completing her 1997 study, the MISTRA's analyses of vocational interests and job satisfaction continued. The 1994 studies in these areas were extensions and replications of earlier work.

Replications: Vocational Interests and Job Satisfaction

Graduate student Deborah Betsworth's 1992 PhD dissertation[42] built upon Dan Moloney's 1991 study of vocational interests,[43] discussed in Chapter 8. Bouchard provided Betsworth with scores for a slightly larger number of reared-apart twins than Moloney had used. Her article appeared in 1994.[44]

Betsworth gathered data from twins reared together, twins reared apart, adoptive parents and children, and biological parents and children. The participants had already completed the Strong Interest Inventory, but their data were rescored to yield the scales comprising the Hansen Combined Form Scales. She did this because the Hansen scales include all twenty-six scales common to the different versions of the Strong. The scales she used included six General Occupational Themes, seventeen Basic Interest Scales, and two special scales (Academic Comfort and Introversion/Extroversion); the special scales had not been examined in our earlier study. However, Betsworth omitted the Adventure scale from her analysis because of its low reliability. The median correlations for the eight different kinships are shown in Table 10-5.

Several features of these data are worth noting. The higher MZT than DZT, and higher MZA than DZA correlations demonstrated genetic influence. However, the lower MZA than MZT correlations for the General Occupational Themes and Basic Interest Scales suggested shared environmental effects. Analyzing all eight kinships simultaneously yielded a heritability of 0.36, lower than the 0.40 to 0.50 reported in Moloney's paper. Betsworth also reported an environmental effect of 0.64 for vocational interests (0.09 shared and 0.55 nonshared), whereas we had previously found an environmental effect of 0.50 (all nonshared). Betsworth suggested that Moloney's use of three vocational interest measures rather than one explained the discrepancies between the two studies. We had actually reported a range of heritabilities for the different measures: 0.37 for the Basic Interest Scales, 0.44 for the Jackson, and 0.50 for the ten vocational interest factors generated by items in these instruments. Thus, Betsworth's 0.36 based only on the Strong agreed with Moloney's 0.37.

Betsworth's median correlations for the biological family members were just slightly higher than those of the adoptive family members who shared no common genes. Perhaps studying vocational interests concurrently in parents and children produced misleading results. People's interests change with age, and popular activities in one generation may be outmoded in another generation. Studying twins overcomes this problem because of their common age, and studying twins reared apart overcomes the shared environmental confounds that plague family research.

Replications and extensions of the MISTRA's earlier work also involved a survey of job satisfaction and work values.[45] Richard Arvey continued to collaborate on this project, and University of Minnesota industrial relations professor Brian McCall, University of Pennsylvania economist Paul Taubman, and University of Minnesota graduate student Marcie Cavanaugh were added.

Arvey replicated our earlier findings twice using two samples of twins reared together. The first sample included ninety-five MZT and eighty

Table 10-5. Median Intraclass Correlations for Vocational Interests

Scale	MZT (1,960 pairs)	DZT (1,212 pairs)	MZA (59 pairs)	DZA (33 pairs)	Adopted Parent-Child (283 pairs)	Adopted Sibling (63 pairs)	Biological Parent-Child (332 pairs)	Biological Sibling (60 pairs)
General occupational themes	0.48	0.23	0.31	0.07	0.10	0.11	0.15	0.15
Basic interest scales	0.47	0.21	0.33	0.05	0.08	0.08	0.13	0.14
Academic comfort	0.54	0.24	0.46	0.25	0.11	0.04	0.21	0.22
Introversion/extroversion	0.50	0.24	0.52	0.07	0.06	0.24	0.18	0.08

Source: Adapted from Betsworth et al., "Genetic and Environmental Influences on Vocational Interests Assessed Using Adoptive and Biological Families and Twins Reared Apart and Together," *Journal of Vocational Behavior* 44 (1994): 263–278.

DZT male twin pairs from the Minnesota Twin Registry. Our 1989 paper had analyzed these same data for thirty-four MZA twin pairs, yielding a job satisfaction heritability of 0.30.[46]

As discussed earlier, intrinsic job satisfaction refers to opportunities to use one's abilities and talents, extrinsic job satisfaction refers to one's working conditions, and general satisfaction refers to overall contentment with one's work situation. Intraclass correlations from the replicated analysis are shown in Table 10-6.

Note that the MZA-MZT intrinsic satisfaction correlations did not differ, despite differences in rearing, gender, and sample size. Both MZ correlations exceeded the DZT correlations, but all three were low for extrinsic satisfaction. The MZT general satisfaction correlation was lower than the corresponding MZA correlation. Our 1989 findings of genetic effects on intrinsic satisfaction and lack of genetic effects on extrinsic satisfaction were confirmed. Genetic effects on general satisfaction were suggested, but the estimated 0.16 heritability in our replication (see below) was lower than the 0.30 heritability in our 1989 study. The variances of this measure across the two samples were similar, so this difference may have been associated with unknown features of the two samples.

The reared-together sample was large enough to let Arvey estimate the genetic and environmental variance in job satisfaction. The best model for intrinsic satisfaction showed that 23 percent of the variance was explained by genetic factors, and the best model for general satisfaction showed that 16 percent of the variance was explained by genetic factors. A genetic effect on extrinsic satisfaction was not indicated by these data, consistent with our previous analysis.

When extrinsic and intrinsic job satisfaction are analyzed at the same time, the possibility that both are genetically influenced but to different degrees is raised. Lower genetic influence on extrinsic than intrinsic job

Table 10-6.   Intraclass Correlations for the Three Job Satisfaction Measures

Scales	MZA	MZT	DZT
Intrinsic satisfaction	0.315[a]	0.29[b]	−0.02
Extrinsic satisfaction	0.109	0.09	−0.01
General satisfaction	0.309[a]	0.19[a]	0.01

a. $P < .05$.
b. $P < .01$.

Source: Adapted from Arvey et al., "Job Satisfaction: Environmental and Genetic Components," *Journal of Applied Psychology* 74 (1989): 187–192; Arvey et al., "Genetic Influences on Job Satisfaction and Work Values," *Personality and Individual Differences* 17 (1994): 21–33.

satisfaction would make sense because most people like having caring bosses and good benefits. Greater variability, some genetically based, should characterize intrinsic job satisfaction because people value opportunities for creativity and achievement differently.

Arvey's second replication (reported as Study 2 in the same paper) used male twins from the National Academy of Sciences-National Research Council's sample of white male twin veterans.[47] The sample sizes were huge—1,152 MZT twin pairs and 1,055 DZT twin pairs. These twins completed sixteen job importance items and one general job satisfaction item in a 1974 questionnaire specific to that study. The MZT correlation (0.21) for general job satisfaction significantly exceeded the DZT correlation (.05), although both were significant. The MZT twins' correlations were higher on all seventeen measures, significantly so for ten of the sixteen job importance items (e.g., "provided much free time" and "represented a challenge").

One exception to the finding of genetic influence concerned Family Business, for which the similarity of the MZT (0.42) and DZT (0.39) twins hardly differed. Of course, genetic influence on this item was not expected because most people would value their family's business to some degree due to family ties, in addition to (or instead of) its intrinsic interest. After eliminating this variable, a 0.27 genetic component to overall job satisfaction was found, close to our 1989 finding of 0.30. Arvey also found a 0.35 genetic estimate for the remaining fifteen work values. This finding was important because it replicated our 1992 study, using a different instrument and different twin sample. The fact that Family Business did not show a genetic effect indicated that the analyses discriminated among the different work values.

These replicated studies were important, given the criticism our 1989 job satisfaction paper had evoked from several industrial organizational investigators. The fact that the studies were conducted with different samples and one study had administered a different instrument increased confidence in the findings. But none of these studies were perfect. The model did not consider nonadditive genetic effects, and both replication samples were male. Nevertheless, the results were encouraging, and Arvey believed the information would be useful to employers hoping to improve their employees' work lives. The genetic effects, while significant, were not substantial, inviting opportunities for change from within the job culture.

It was also apparent that a genetic perspective was starting to seep into the minds of researchers who had not previously considered this view. A widely cited 1993 article by University of Georgia social psychologist Abraham Tesser reviewed evidence for the heritability of social attitudes, and he argued for bringing genetic perspectives to psychological theory and experimentation.[48] At the same time, Tesser was aware of the slow acceptance of a genetic view of attitudinal differences by his sociology colleagues. Nevertheless, twin studies of earning power,[49] social attitudes, and religious interests[50] were proliferating in the mid-1990s.

Increased interest in genes and behavior can also be explained by the Human Genome Project (1990–2003), aimed at identifying all 20,000–25,000 human genes and sequencing the three billion DNA subunits.[51] Parallel advances in molecular genetic techniques made it possible to search for genes tied to complex behaviors and diseases. The press closely covered progress in these areas such that a genetic viewpoint was permeating the consciousness of the public as well as the social scientists.[52]

Chapters and Papers, 1994 to 1997

Looking over Bouchard's curriculum vitae for the years 1994 through 1997 shows that MISTRA-related chapters in edited volumes outnumbered MISTRA-related empirical articles about 2.5 to 1.0. I suspect that the chapters were accumulating quickly because Bouchard received so many invitations to contribute to psychology handbooks, annual reviews, and conference proceedings. Bouchard preferred analyzing data, but he had trouble turning down interested colleagues. In those years, the team assessed eleven twin pairs new to the study and twelve twin pairs who had been studied before, for about five per year on average, which was less than had been accomplished in several previous years. The pool of reared-apart twins might have been dwindling, but as I will show in the last chapter new sources of reared-apart twins are surfacing.

There was a total of fourteen MISTRA chapters or review papers, mostly on intelligence and personality, published between 1994 and 1997. They are too detailed to summarize fully, but I have prepared a selective sampling of key material. (A complete list of MISTRA publications appears on the Web site.)

Other Significant Work

A 1994 highlight was Bouchard's essay, "Genes, Environment and Personality," published in a special issue of the journal *Science* on genes and behavior.[53] His review of historical developments in personality research showed that, until the 1980s, the relatively small reared-together twin studies yielded heritability estimates of 50 percent. Since then, larger samples, reared-apart twin and adoption studies, and model fitting techniques had reduced that figure only slightly to just over 40 percent. With common environments explaining 7 percent of the variance, and nonshared environment and measurement error equally divided among the remainder, two-thirds of the reliable personality variance could be tied to genetic factors. Graphs showing the same gene-environment breakdown for the Big Five personality factors across three independent replications that included twins reared apart and together told this important story. Bouchard made an impressive case for the genetic and environmental effects and structure of personality.

One of Bouchard's points, often lost in discussion, was that finding nonshared environmental effects on personality did not mean that such events affected personality traits in systematic or predictable ways. Parenting style could, for example, be a cause of children's behavior in some cases, but a consequence in others. Permissiveness by parents might encourage independence in some children, but might result from rebelliousness in others. This observation recalled the "gloomy prospect" discussed in Chapter 8.

Bouchard also defined the "next big hurdle" in personality research as that of attempting to understand the function of individual personality differences in an evolutionary context. "The purpose of this variation is undoubtedly rooted in the fact that humans have adapted to life in face-to-face groups."[54] Knowing why people differ in personality would transform behavioral genetics from a descriptive to an explanatory discipline. We would know why we differ, not just that we differ. Siblings may differ in personality because they inherit different genes, but also because they occupy different places in the family. Research has found that later-born children are more rebellious or risk-taking than older, more mature children in the family, possibly due to their need to secure parental resources that might go to their elder siblings.[55] Other evolutionary-based research has examined the personality correlates of fertility and mate desirability.[56]

Also in 1994, Arvey and Bouchard authored a book chapter summarizing the MISTRA's studies of job satisfaction and work values.[57] The MISTRA had completed enough reared-apart twin research on work-related traits to fill a chapter. That chapter offered a model showing how genetic and environmental influences might affect variables studied by industrial organizational psychologists; this model is displayed on the Web site. Arvey believes that the model is still relevant, but he would add outcome variables such as leadership, work design (physical aspects of the job), salary, financial well-being, financial risk, and occupational switching. He would also add a path indicating a direct reciprocal relationship between what were labeled Genetic Differences and Environmental Differences, because genetic expression is affected by environments and environments reflect genetic differences. For example, a person's artistic potential requires opportunities for expression, and such workplace opportunities reflect a person's interests and talents.

Arvey also speculated that some variables in his model might eventually be expanded to include specific genes associated with work-related behaviors. I will discuss the impact of molecular genetic advance on reared-apart twin studies in the final chapter.

Several chapters written by Bouchard in 1995 and 1996 were not about the MISTRA in particular, but they were influenced by the MISTRA's findings. His chapter in the 1995 *International Handbook of Personality and Intelligence* called for bringing behavioral genetic and evolutionary perspectives to longitudinal behavioral studies.[58] He suggested that repeated measures on twins and adoptees would disentangle the genetic and environmental confounds inherent in most longitudinal analyses. Bouchard's late friend and colleague Ron Wilson showed us this with his 1980s longitudinal twin studies in Louisville—Wilson's concept of genetically influenced "spurts and lags" in mental development are still famous. Wilson found that MZT twins showed similar patterns of intellectual growth and stability during childhood, while DZT twins showed patterns that differed. The IQ similarity in adult MZA twins was even more compelling in light of these findings because Wilson showed that intellectual changes during development, not just scores at a given time, had a partial genetic basis.[59] It is likely that the adult MZA twins underwent similar intellectual growth patterns in childhood and adolescence, ending up alike when we studied them as adults.

The importance of viewing behavior from an evolutionary perspective is a recurrent theme in many of Bouchard's chapters. He believed that traditional life-course approaches did not consider the adaptive nature of individuals' life histories. Bouchard also showed special interests in traditionalism and tolerance, identifying Robert Altemeyer's Right-Wing Authoritarianism Scale as the best contemporary measure of such traits.[60] Most scientists in the 1980s believed that authoritarianism was largely social or cultural in origin, but Bouchard favored an evolutionary explanation. He stressed the universality of following rules and conventions, and the fact that parents set standards for their children to follow. Right-wing authoritarianism became a focal point of Bouchard's work in the late 1990s and, subsequently, the origins of what he called the "Traditional Moral Values Triad"—authoritarianism, conservatism, and religiousness.

A footnote to Bouchard's chapter, "Genetics and Evolution: Implications for Personality Theories," caught my eye: "I believe that social scientists will eventually give up this naïve [environmentally driven, standard social science] model in the face of evidence."[61] Bouchard asserted that Table 4 in our 1990 *Science* IQ paper,[62] showing genetic influence on nearly thirty psychological traits, was the clearest refutation of the idea that human behavior was mostly environmental in origin. He asked why the criticism seemed "interminable," and tried to answer the question himself: "All decisions by human beings are made on the basis of information that satisfies rather than being conclusive. A natural consequence of this fact is that it will always be possible to argue that there is not sufficient scientific knowledge about a topic to make an unalterable decision."[63]

Bouchard published seven book chapters and reviews in 1997. These publications summarized current findings on intelligence, personality, and other psychological measures from the MISTRA and elsewhere. One of his papers, published in *The Sciences*, addressed the implications of reared-apart twin studies for human reproductive cloning.[64] Human reproductive cloning had attracted considerable attention following the 1996 cloning of Dolly the Scottish lamb.[65] I had also used the reared-apart and reared-together twin findings to assess its possible behavioral consequences.[66]

Bouchard and I agreed that the lack of perfect similarity between MZA co-twins on every measured trait meant that clones and donors would not be exactly alike in behavior. And unlike twins, clones and donors would belong to different generations, offering them access to different opportunities and experiences. In separate papers, we both mentioned that clones and donors would not share intrauterine environments as did twins. In my writings I also reminded readers that MZ twins' shared prenatal environments mostly produced differences between them, so clones and donors might actually be more alike in traits such as birth weight than MZA or MZT twins. In fact, the degree of similarity between clones and donors could vary across traits as we had been finding for the MZA twins. In accordance with Experience Producing Drive Theory it was reasonable to suppose that clones and donors might be driven toward similar people, places, and events within their respective environments.

I did not agree with Bouchard's statement that "clones are simply identical twins by another name." Identical twins are clones by definition (genetically identical organisms), but clones are not identical twins because they do not share their time of conception, prenatal environment, parents, or generation.[67]

The MISTRA data were integrated into the chapters, tables, and charts of widely used textbooks in behavior genetics and psychology.[68] A graph with IQ findings that first appeared in the 1997 behavioral genetics primer by Plomin et al. would be reprinted with updates in later editions.[69] The MZA IQ data were now organized into "old" and "new" studies, as shown in Figure 10-1. The "old" studies were based on reviews by Bouchard and McGue,[70] and amended by Loehlin,[71] and included the findings from Newman et al., Shields, and Juel-Nielsen.[72] The "new" studies were those by Bouchard et al. and by Pedersen et al.[73] The somewhat higher heritabilities provided by the "new" (0.78) versus "old" studies (0.72) most likely reflected participants' older ages. The heritability of IQ had been shown to increase over time, probably because small genetic effects become more important as individuals gain greater environmental control.[74] The graph also showed that IQ heritability increased with the degree of

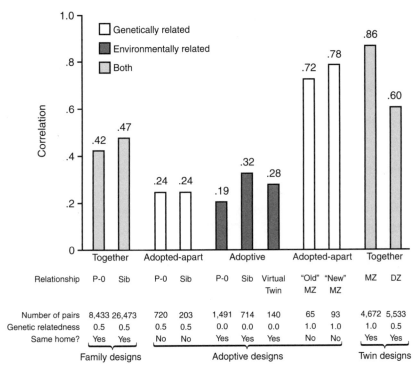

Figure 10-1. Average IQ correlations across different pairs of relatives. (Adapted from Plomin et al. 2008.) Updating the "new" MZA twin correlation yields a value of 0.75 (n = 119), based on data from Pedersen et al. (1992) and Johnson et al. (2007). Johnson's paper, which reports general intelligence findings for the full MISTRA MZA twin sample, is reviewed in Chapter 13. Pedersen's result (n = 45, r_i = 0.78) used the first principal component; the Johnson group's result (n = 74, r_i = 0.73) used the *g* factor score. The virtual twin data are from Nancy L. Segal, "Twins: The Finest Natural Experiment," *Personality and Individual Differences* 49 (2010): 317–323.

genetic relatedness between people; that is, full siblings who share 50 percent of their genes on average, by descent, are more alike in IQ than half-siblings who share 25 percent. This pattern of similarity has been repeated in several reviews and remains a robust finding.

Looking Ahead: 1998 and Beyond

In 1998, the number of empirical papers from the MISTRA increased, and the numbers held steady even after the last pair of new twins (number 137) was studied in April 1999; Bouchard studied the last pair of follow-up twins a month later. This upward trend was partly due to the continuing collaborations with Susan Roberts and Paul Fuss at Tufts University in Boston. Roberts received a federal grant in 1993 to study the twins' body composition and nutrition, letting Bouchard assess more new twins and reassess those who had visited Minnesota previously. New graduate students wrote dissertations on the twins' ego development and religious interests, work they eventually turned into publications.[75] And the new reared-apart twins expanded the databases, allowing for further analyses of continuing topics such as intelligence and personality, and analyses of new topics such as social relationships and body asymmetries.

In April 2010, I visited Minnesota a second time and met again with Meg Keyes, Bouchard's former student and assistant. Keyes had worked with Bouchard when the Jim twins were found, and again for six years as associate director of the project (1992–1998) after I had left. She recalled the "incredibly long hours" that each assessment took and the long preparation time before each assessment. One day, she and graduate student Katie Corson were assembling the twins' inventory booklets, a labor-intensive task. Bouchard left for lunch, and as he was passing a McDonald's restaurant, a young homeless man asked him for change. Bouchard said he could not give him money, but he could give him a job. The young man spent the rest of the afternoon making booklets with Keyes and Corson.

At the end of 1997, Bouchard sent his usual annual report to his primary funding source at that time, the David H. Koch Charitable Foundation. It was an unusually thick (1.25 inches) volume covering twin recruitment, twin assessment, professional activities, scientific papers, and newspaper articles published between 1995 and 1997. Two major articles about the study had appeared in the *New Yorker*[76] and in *Psychology Today*,[77] and a chapter had appeared in a popular science book,[78] all of which were appended to the report.

But it was the "Director's Comments" that caught my eye in 2010 because they included the first formal sign that the MISTRA was winding down:

> The recruitment of new twins to this program will most likely cease in the summer of 1998 after nearly nineteen years. The reasons for ceasing recruitment of new twins are two-fold. The first is that funding for the center has declined. The second is that the number of new twins being located each year has declined.

It is still hard to believe that the MISTRA no longer exists except as data waiting to be analyzed. Had I read those words in 1997 it would have seemed completely unimaginable that the MISTRA would end in the near future. It was such a vital program that shaped the careers of many colleagues and enriched the lives of many twins. "Twin Weeks" were fascinating, overwhelming, and exhilarating. There was rarely time for personal matters when twins were in town, but nothing else was as important. Findings from the MISTRA had widely infiltrated the psychological field, changing our thoughts on how genes and environments affect behavior. When the study ended there would be no place to send newly reunited pairs or separated twins in search.

In his 1997 statement, Bouchard acknowledged the financial support of the Koch Charitable Foundation, the Tufts University Nutrition and Aging Laboratory, and the University of Minnesota Periodontal Group. Since the first Koch Foundation grant was made in 1985, these sources were among those that had covered the twins' airline fees and hotel expenses. Various medical costs, such as the echocardiograms and allergy tests, were subsumed by the different departments and no one received salaries.

Federal funding was especially difficult to obtain because the number of twin pairs was never certain. Federal granting agencies, such as the National Science Foundation and National Institutes of Mental Health, require detailed participant descriptions, including age, gender, and minority status. This was just not possible with the reared-apart twins who could appear at any time. "This smothers creativity," Bouchard said. "The private foundations were a blessing because they can afford to take risks." In accepting support from the Pioneer Fund support in 1981 Bouchard took a calculated risk that the research would weather the controversies surrounding that source, as I will discuss in Chapter 14.

The history of reared-apart twin studies remained contentious throughout the MISTRA's years. The Cyril Burt affair and concerns over how gene-behavior relationships might interfere with good parenting and social programs were foremost in some grant reviewers' minds. Ratings Bouchard received on federal grants could be Excellent or Poor—this wide range and the comments associated with them most likely reflected some reviewers' biases to a large degree.

When Bouchard talked to me in April 2010 about ending the study when he did, he cited lack of funding and the decreasing number of reared-apart twins, but he also mentioned personal fatigue. "I worked eighteen hours a day when twins were in the lab and then I slept for two days." "What if you had gotten a five million dollar grant?" I asked him, "Would the MISTRA have ended when it did?" He paused, then recalled his long conversations with Lykken over the need for a comparison group of twins reared together and the importance of developing the Minnesota Twin Registry. But I think we both knew that a large grant would have extended the life of the MISTRA, a child that Bouchard had nurtured for years and did not seem quite ready to let go despite the work involved. Whenever I tell Bouchard about a new reared-apart pair he says I should study them.

CHAPTER ELEVEN

"Larks" and "Owls," Ego Development, and Authoritarianism (1998–2002)

 OME PEOPLE get up early and work best at six in the morning ("larks"), while others like to sleep late and work into the night ("owls"). Most people know which type they are, but don't know how they got that way. In 1998, Yoon-Mi Hur and Bouchard examined "morningness" and "eveningness"—and these tendencies, like most measured traits, showed genetic effects. This finding, which occurred relatively late into the study, was understandably less surprising than the detection of a genetic influence on habits, fears, and medical traits that were suggested with our earliest pairs. This shift in thinking began with the information processing and ophthalmology findings in 1984 and 1985. Genetic effects on speed of response and on visual acuity had been surprising and exciting during the early stage of the study. This shift was reinforced by the MISTRA's early 1990s findings of a genetic influence on less frequently measured traits such as religious involvement and work values, and by similar findings from other laboratories.

Fourteen scientific papers appeared between 1998 and 2002. Other new topics examined during those years included ego development, headache frequency, dietary preferences, and authoritarian tendencies. The MISTRA investigators also reported new findings on topics studied previously, such as creativity and religiosity.

Morningness-Eveningness

When Bouchard's graduate student Hur analyzed the reared-apart twins' morningness-eveningness data, only one other such twin study was available.[1] That 1992 investigation had found heritabilities of 0.56 for males and 0.48 for females from reared-together pairs.[2] Given that the MZA and MZT twins showed the same degree of similarity in personality and job satisfaction, Hur suspected that the MZA twins would also show matching wake-sleep cycles. Had this analysis been conducted when the MISTRA began, she might not have been so sure.

Scores on the Morningness-Eveningness Questionnaire[3] were available for fifty-five MZA twin pairs, fifty DZA twin pairs, two hundred and five MZT twin pairs, and seventy-nine of the reared-apart twins' spouses. The questionnaire included thirteen items, such as "At what time in the evening do you usually feel tired and, as a result, in need of sleep?"

The MZA correlation of 0.47 was close to the values reported in the previous study. The MZT correlation of 0.57 was somewhat above the MZA correlation, suggesting that shared rearing environments explain only a small amount (10 percent) of individual differences in preference for the morning or evening.

What was surprising was the unexpectedly high morningness-eveningness correlation (0.45) for the DZA twins. Perhaps some DZA twins' schedules were not initially to their liking, but they had to acclimate due to their working conditions, family obligations, or other matters. Another possible explanation for this result was assortative mating or mating between spouses who matched in their waking and sleeping time preferences. Positive mate assortment for morningness-eveningness among the spouse pairs in our sample was found, but not enough to explain the DZA twins' resemblance.

When the data from the three twin groups were analyzed simultaneously, the heritability of morningness-eveningness was 50 percent, consistent with the 1992 study. There was also interest in whether age affected this trait—perhaps younger twins slept later or older twins went to bed earlier—but age had little effect. It seems that we become "morning" and "evening" people because of how our individual circadian system is structured, not because we saw our mother get up early or our father sleeping late. Sleep-wake patterns also become less regular as we age, a pattern of change that could be partly genetically controlled.

The Morningness-Eveningness Questionnaire was completed on or about the third day of the assessment week. Perhaps the twins should have completed this form before they arrived so we would have known when we could expect their best performance! Assuming that the MZA and DZA twins were equally divided among larks and owls, our failure to do so probably did not affect the data.

Ego Development

By 1998, various investigators on the project had published several personality studies, but not the twins' ego development scale. This was a timely topic because some personality researchers were examining relationships between ego development and the Big Five personality traits, as well as relationships between ego development and cognitive skills.

Psychologist Jane Loevinger is famous for her comprehensive research on adult ego development.[4] She saw the ego as a "lens" for viewing the social world and ego development as the changes in those views. She characterized it as a "master trait" that organizes many specific personality traits. More specifically, Loevinger viewed ego development as a developmental process that unfolds in stages during childhood, then stabilizes during adolescence and adulthood. She explained that "the search for coherent meanings in experience is the essence of the ego or ego functioning . . . The ego maintains its stability, its identity, and its coherence by selectively gating out observations inconsistent with its current state."[5]

Loevinger recognized different levels of ego development. The least mature levels are characterized by presocial, impulsive, self-protective, and ritualistic behaviors. The most mature levels are characterized by conscientious, individualistic, autonomous, and integrated behaviors. The modal level of ego development, based on American samples, is characterized by reference to the expectations of other people regarding rules for personal conduct and social values.[6] Individual differences in ego development levels can be observed at all ages after fourteen, so Loevinger's theory could be applied easily to the adult reared-apart twin sample.

In 1994, Minnesota graduate student Denise Newman completed the first study of reared-apart twins that addressed genetic and environmental influences on ego development.[7] Newman, who worked directly with Auke Tellegen, said, "I was interested in ego development, and ego development had an instrumentation that could be addressed within a behavioral genetic framework. It was Loevinger's brilliance that enabled that possibility, and it was of course Bouchard's uncanny knack for designing a study with lots of different measurements in it, knack (with maybe Tellegen's influence) that allowed me to realize the project was possible."

Newman also looked at whether ego development was distinct from cognitive ability, especially verbal skills, an issue also raised by Loevinger and colleagues.[8] This was an important feature because the instrument, the Washington University Sentence Completion Test, relies on verbal fluency,[9] a feature that could confound ego development measurement. However, while verbal fluency tests are usually administered under timed conditions, the Sentence Completion Test is not. As Loevinger and colleagues noted, the valid variance in ego development should not be fully accounted for by intelligence. Previous associations between ego development, general ability, and the Big Five trait of Openness to Experience led Newman to examine the extent to which ego development provided unique information about an individual.

The Sentence Completion Test is a projective test (a method in which subjects respond to unstructured or ambiguous terms or images)— Loevinger believed that measuring ego development required projection of the subjects' own frame of reference.[10] The test also comes in male and female forms. Sample items for males and females are:

> Female: A girl has a right to _____.
> Male: A good father _____.

The cognitive tests Newman used included the Wechsler IQ test and the verbal subtests of the Hawaii Ability Battery. The sentence completion responses were rated independently by individuals who were blinded to the twins' age, sex, and zygosity. The score distributions for all 248 people (forty-five MZA twin pairs, twenty-eight DZA twin pairs, nine individuals from DZA opposite-sex pairs, and ninety-three of the twins' spouses, children, and companions) were similar to those from other adult samples.[11]

The MZA intraclass correlation of 0.50 suggested that half the variance in ego development is genetically influenced. The corresponding DZA correlation was 0.22. When Newman recalculated the correlations after statistically removing the effects of verbal ability and IQ, the values fell only slightly to 0.45 and 0.41, respectively, for MZA twins and 0.21 and 0.17, respectively, for DZA twins. Ego development could, therefore, be considered as separate from intellect, a finding confirmed in the biometrical analysis. Genetic influence on ego development was 0.54,[12] and individuals' nonshared experiences were nearly as important.

The twins' ego development similarity could not be explained by similarities in their rearing environments. Only one measure (mothers' education level) correlated significantly for both MZA ($r_i = 0.45$) and DZA ($r_i = 0.56$) co-twins. Selective placement can inflate resemblance between adopted apart relatives, giving greater weight to environmental effects than is warranted. However, mothers' education explained less than 1 percent of the variation in ego development.

These results were exciting. Newman also concluded that the data affirmed the presence of the "black box" of variance.[13] That is, idiosyncratic things that happen to people explained about half the variance in ego development. However, the specific events (e.g., going to college or losing a spouse) that raise or lower ego development levels were unknown—hence the uncertainty.

Newman wondered to what extent genetic and environmental influences on ego development were constant or variable across ages, a question she could not answer with her modest sample. She also wondered how comparable her findings were to those from other personality studies, a question she could answer. Previous personality studies, including the MISTRA's, suggested that most personality traits showed a 50 percent genetic effect with little shared environmental influence, as Newman found for ego development.

Openness to Experience (imaginative, inventive versus narrow, simple), the Big Five personality trait with the largest additive genetic component, was the only Big Five trait that had been associated with ego development.[14] Loevinger's modal classification spans two levels, conformist and self-aware. Individuals at the conformist level value group acceptance and can delay or modify their impulses. Such individuals might tend toward the "narrow, simple" pole of Openness to Experience. In contrast, those at the mature, self-aware level are more individualistic and autonomous and might be found closer to the "inventive, imaginative" pole. The possibility that common genes affect ego development and Openness to Experience, particularly at different ages, would be worth pursuing.

The distinction Newman found between ego development and cognition was consistent with a meta-analytic study of findings from forty-two investigations. Reasons to support the conceptual and functional distinction of ego development and intelligence include the higher scores given to shorter sentence completions, the irrelevance of speed of response, and the fact that most adults possess the vocabulary to express significant ego development features.[15]

Newman sees ego development as a "compelling and central aspect" of personality development. "There is a very extensive empirical literature to support a very rich theoretical story ... ego develops from infancy and well into adulthood; something that is not fully formed at birth becomes so formed by early adulthood and changes still a bit more across the lifespan." The similarities she observed in the twins reared apart are more impressive in light of these remarks.

The Headache Study

New studies of the twins' physical conditions were also progressing in the late 1990s. A study on migraine headaches came about because a specialist was interested.

The MISTRA's collaborator on the headache study was Dr. Dewey Ziegler from the University of Kansas Medical Center's Department of Neurology.[16] Ziegler wrote to Bouchard in April 1989 to say that the reared-apart twins would be informative participants in a study of factors affecting migraine headache, and he proposed a collaboration. Bouchard put Ziegler in touch with David Lykken who could provide reared-together twins, and a research agreement was reached in October.

I immediately thought of the Jim twins when I learned about the headache study because both men had similarly described their severe migraines, which had begun in their teens. Their similar symptoms suggested that headaches could have a genetic basis. The reared-apart Korean twins whom I discussed earlier also experienced headaches, albeit of different frequency and severity from one another. However, their matched complaints, and the fact that their biological mother had suffered migraines are consistent with genetic effects.

Several reared-together European and Australian twin studies conducted between 1956 and 1995 had found that genes explained 50 percent of the variance in headache susceptibility.[17] However, two United States studies, including one by Ziegler in 1975, failed to find genetic effects.[18] Farber's 1981 review had identified four out of five headache-concordant pairs scattered among the early MZA twin investigations,[19] but no one had formally studied headaches in reared-apart twins.

Ziegler's study included twenty-three MZA, one hundred and three MZT, twenty DZA, and fifty-one DZT twin pairs. The reared-together twins came from the Kansas and Minnesota registries, and they had volunteered in response to notices about a headache study. The reared-apart twins were MISTRA participants, so they were not recruited with reference to headache predisposition. Only female twins were included in the study because headache prevalence (the frequency of individuals expressing a trait at a particular time) was low among the male twin respondents, a sex difference that has been well documented.[20]

A telephone interview was administered to each twin beginning with the question, "Have you ever had repeated headache (apart from blows on the head or during acute illness) that you would consider more than mild?" If answered affirmatively, clinical details about their headaches were requested.

Headache resemblance was higher for MZT (0.52) than DZT twins (0.00), reflecting genetic influence. In contrast, the MZA twins (0.52) were only slightly more alike than the DZA twins (0.46), a possible result of the small sample. Because the MZA correlation directly estimates genetic influence, it was concluded (albeit, tentatively) that 52 percent of the headache variance was associated with genetic factors—this was the same value Ziegler obtained by model fitting. The lack of difference in the MZT and MZA correlations suggested that shared environments did not affect headache frequency—instead, environmental contributions to headaches appeared unique to individuals, possibly related to emotional stress, fever, sun exposure, or dehydration.[21]

The findings applied to women, not to men, and they did not distinguish between headaches with and without aura (the presence of feelings and signs that proceed a headache). Despite these limitations, a genetic component to migraine headache was indicated, although the relatively high DZA correlation urged a cautious interpretation. Knowledge about factors affecting headaches could potentially benefit the thousands of affected individuals attempting to make sense of their symptoms.

Headaches, both severe and mild, can have many sources, such as eating certain foods, eating irregularly, or not eating enough. Headaches, dizziness, and joint pain are among the symptoms associated with allergic reaction to gluten, a protein found in most grains, breads, and cereals. A pair of our MZA male twins suffered from "irritability" and other difficulties, suggesting a food allergy. In fact, these tall, thin British gentlemen had been experiencing the same symptoms from their allergy to gluten. However, when they arrived in Minnesota only one twin had determined that eating wheat products was the cause. Upon becoming a vegetarian and eliminating wheat from his diet, this twin's health and spirit improved dramatically. His twin brother agreed to make the same dietary changes when he returned home.

One month later, Bouchard received a letter from one of the twins saying that both were feeling better and were scheduled for allergy testing. The visit of these twins was meaningful in other ways. The letter read, "So we grow more, even more alike . . . I think that we are now quite close in our understanding and empathy . . . Without the basis of our visit [to Minneapolis] I do not think that we would have ever spent sufficient time together for this to have happened."

Meals and Snacks

There was interest in the twins' dietary preferences, but not just because of their possible allergies to certain foods. Eating is a fundamental and pleasurable human behavior. Knowing whether certain foods are selected or rejected because of genetic factors, cultural habits, family practices, body size image, or all four were questions that the reared-apart twins could potentially answer.

Children growing up together have limited freedom to eat what they like, but once they become adults they are free to choose. Adults can also decide how much and how often they want to eat. Sharing meals with the MZA twin pairs showed that favorite foods, quantities, and meal times were often matched. The fireman twins, Mark and Jerry, both craved Chinese food and very rare steak. The giggle twins, Daphne and Barbara, co-invented a signature cocktail that they called "Twin Sin," made by mixing one ounce of vodka, one ounce of blue curaçao, one ounce of crème de cacao, and a half ounce of cream—they thought it was the greatest. Oskar, raised in Germany, was instantly enthusiastic about the spicy foods that Jack, his Trinidad-raised brother, offered him. These observations suggested genetic effects on food preferences, even the possibility that genetic factors can override cultural food practices.

Existing findings on twins' dietary choices were mixed when Hur, Bouchard, and Elke Eckert began looking at the diet data in 1998.[22] Their review of the research showed that estimates of genetic influence on nutrient and beverage intake ranged from about 0.30 to 0.50, and one study had found genetic influence on complex carbohydrate intake only. Relationships between twins' dietary similarities and the amount of contact time between them were also in dispute. The MISTRA had the data to revisit these questions using sixty-six MZA and fifty-one DZA twin pairs.

The twins completed the Food Frequency Questionnaire developed for the National Heart and Lung Institute Twin Study.[23] The questionnaire's interview format was modified to allow the questions to be answered by self-report rather than by personal interview. The form's sixty-seven items requested information on the frequency of eating foods included in standard American diets (e.g., milk and cheese) and on the timing of meals and snacks. However, twins also listed their preferred foods that were not included in the survey. Participants' height and weight were also obtained in the laboratory, measures that were converted into the body mass index (BMI = weight in kilograms/height in meters^2). Age correlated only moderately (0.17 to 0.20) with various dietary variables such as calories, protein, and fat showing that older people ate more than younger people, but not a great deal more.

Hur compared similarities between the pairs of MZA twins, DZA twins, and spouses across three dietary categories: nine nutrients (e.g., calories and protein), two eating frequencies (e.g., meals and snacks), and six beverage intake frequencies (e.g., whole milk and coffee). The MZA twins (0.30 to 0.35) were more alike in three of the four dietary categories than the DZA twins (0.08 to 0.22) with one exception: the DZA twins' nutrient intake showed greater similarity than that of the MZA twins (0.35

versus 0.22). Other than sampling fluctuations, this result could not be explained. Model fitting yielded average heritabilities of 0.30 (nutrient intake), 0.30 (meal frequency), 0.33 (snack frequency), and 0.32 (beverage frequency). Thus, what we eat and how often we eat appear moderately influenced by genetic factors.

An important point is that certain foods must be available if both reared-apart twins are to eat them. Oskar's German culture did not provide the spicy foods he eventually found so appealing. Other foods seem to have acquired tastes. An Australian twin would enjoy spreading Vegemite or Marmite on toast,[24] condiments that would probably receive a "No, thank you" from an American counterpart who had never tasted them and knew their origin. In a separate case study, Hur and I also discovered a shared distaste for fish in reared-apart Korean co-twins we had studied. Fish was less commonly eaten in the area of the United States where one twin was raised, but it is a large part of the Korean diet. Perhaps the smell or texture of fish were unpleasant for the Korean-raised twin, and could be for the American twin as well. These ideas could be tested using larger twin samples.

The diet data produced some counterintuitive results. Hur did not find a link between body size and amount of food intake, suggesting that metabolism rather than quantity consumed is largely responsible for body weight and fatness. This finding was consistent with the outcome of a clever 1990 twin study conducted by University of Laval researcher Claude Bouchard—no relation to the MISTRA's director.[25] In this study, twelve MZT male twin pairs abstained from exercise for eighty-four days while on a diet exceeding their normal intake by 1,000 calories. At the end of the study, everyone had gained weight, but the amount gained, which varied from 9.5 to 29.3 pounds, was more similar within twin pairs (for co-twins) than among twin pairs. Metabolism seemed to mediate weight gain more significantly than diet.

One might suppose that the twins' time together influenced their dietary preferences, but it did not: the mean correlation between their contact and the seventeen dietary measures was zero. What the twins ate, and when, were generally products of their genes and their unique experiences. These same factors appear to be at play when family members eat out together and can order freely. There are often as many different meals as there are diners.

A personal story told to us by one of the MZA female twins suggested a unique experience that could affect one's dietary habits. When the thirty-six-year-old twin and her sister came to Minnesota for the assessment, the twin who was five feet three inches tall and weighed 123 pounds admitted that she had always felt too heavy. But when she met her twin sister, who stood five feet four inches and weighed 130.5 pounds, she was surprised to find that her sister looked "great." This experience made her rethink her views about her own body size.

Voices

According to family and friends, my fraternal twin sister and I are nearly indistinguishable on the telephone, so twin studies of voice quality have been of great personal interest. Early studies showed that MZT co-twins' voices are nearly identical with respect to fundamental frequency (characteristic highness or lowness of the human voice) and fundamental frequency range, although later studies showed overlap in the level of MZT and DZT twin similarity.[26] Similar tone and pitch were indicated for twenty out of twenty-one early MZA twin pairs for whom such observations were made.[27] Shields noted that voice similarities are "frequently" detected among DZT twins and sibling pairs, suggesting a contribution from genetic factors combined with regional and cultural influences.[28] A 1995 review concluded that genetic effects clearly influence voice quality, assuming that function is related to genetically influenced physical structures.[29]

Reared-apart and reared-together twins' fundamental frequency and range were the subjects of a 1998 master's thesis by Michael Hammer at the University of Kansas.[30] Twins were recorded while reading Grant Fairbanks's "Rainbow Passage,"[31] with the second sentence analyzed due to its high correlation (0.99) with the full paragraph. Based on a relatively small sample (forty-nine MZT, eight DZT and fourteen MZA twin pairs), the intraclass correlations for both frequency (0.53, 0.58, 0.59) and range (0.30, 0.43, 0.51), respectively, were quite similar. However, vocal discrimination between related and unrelated pairs (generated randomly from the twin sample) was suggested. These results contrasted with what Farber had called the "stunningly alike" pitch, tone, and overall vocal characteristics observed (but not studied systematically) among the majority of fifty early MZA pairs.[32] Conclusions from the small sample that included the MZA twins are tentative, at best.

Authoritarian Attitudes

Psychological studies of authoritarianism were started at Berkeley in the 1950s by the German emigré sociologist and philosopher Theodor W. Adorno and colleagues. These studies were intended to understand the endorsement by many German citizens of Hitler's fascist regime and their participation in his anti-Semitic programs and policies. The authoritarian personality was characterized by conventionalism, aggression, submission, cynicism, and admiration of power and strength. One conclusion of that study, summarized in *The Authoritarian Personality* (1950), was that authoritarian personalities originated with harsh, punitive, and controlling parents whose children projected these tendencies onto minorities or other stigmatized groups.[33] The view that authoritarianism was traceable to rearing environments was evident nearly forty years later in Altemeyer's *Enemies of Freedom* (1988).[34]

The origins of authoritarianism were particularly interesting to Bouchard who had attended the University of California–Berkeley as an undergraduate and graduate student between 1959 and 1966. Bouchard had been an active participant in the free speech movement at that time and was even arrested on one occasion for his activities. At the University of California–Santa Barbara, where Bouchard was an assistant professor from 1966 to 1969, he and philosophy professor Merrill Ring organized an extensive series of antiwar marches.[35]

Authoritarianism was also intriguing to Bouchard's graduate student Kathryn Corson (formerly McCourt). Corson had originally planned to study ingroup-outgroup phenomena in nonhuman primates at Minnesota but changed her mind because a good measure was unavailable. "But right-wing authoritarianism seemed related, and Bob Altemeyer was so convinced that it [the origin of authoritarianism] was all parent to child through the environment. Many behavior geneticists also thought that attitudes were all about rearing environment and not genetic influence, so it was fun to take it on," Corson recalled fifteen years later.

Few behavioral genetic studies of social attitudes were available in the 1980s. John Loehlin and Robert Nichols failed to find genetic influence on political and religious attitudes in their 1976 landmark study of adolescent twins.[36] However, their result might have reflected the twins' young age and exposure to their parents' views while still living at home. Thoughts about the roots of authoritarian attitudes showed little change for the next ten years. Then, the 1986 Martin et al. twin study of social attitudes drew surprised attention to findings of significant genetic influence on conservatism, radicalism, and tough-mindedness.[37] That paper prompted Bouchard to add Altemeyer's thirty-item Right-Wing Authoritarianism Scale to the MISTRA's assessment schedule,[38] which he obtained from David Lykken who was distributing it to his registry twins. Bouchard also added the Wilson-Patterson Conservatism Scale[39] to the assessment, but the results were not published until 2003.

The Right-Wing Authoritarianism Scale is a self-report inventory with nine response categories ranging from +4 (very strongly agree) to −4 (very strongly disagree), with an intermediate response of 0 (exactly and precisely neutral). Sample questions include "It is important to protect fully the rights of radicals and deviants," and "Obedience and respect for authority are the most important virtues children should learn." In 1986, the scale was administered to new twins and to twins returning for their follow-up visit, and mailed to twins who had been assessed previously. Data were available for forty MZA twin pairs and forty-two DZA twin pairs. Data were also available for 423 MZT twin pairs and 434 DZT twin pairs.

The first authoritarianism article to come from the MISTRA appeared in 1999[40] and was based on Corson's 1996 doctoral dissertation.[41] Corson (McCourt during this study) began by noting that higher authoritarianism was significantly associated with fewer years of parental education (reared apart: −0.36, reared together: −0.37) and lower parental occupational status (reared apart: −0.40, reared together: −0.30). Higher authoritarianism was also linked to lower cognitive ability (−0.37) in the reared-apart twins; ability data were unavailable for the reared-together twins. When these different correlations were recalculated (variously removing the effects of ability, education, and occupational status), they dropped somewhat but remained significant. For example, high authoritarianism was still tied to low parental education after removing the effects of cognition on authoritarianism.

The correlational pattern among the four twin groups was somewhat unusual. The higher MZA (0.69) and MZT (0.63) than DZA (0.00) and DZT (0.42) correlations showed genetic effects. However, the DZT twins showed modest resemblance, while the DZA twins showed none. If we relied on the reared-apart twin data, then the genetic effect would be 0.69 because the MZA correlation directly estimates heritability. On the other hand, if we used the reared-together twin data, then the genetic effect would have been 0.42 (based on doubling the MZT-DZT correlational difference). These conflicting bits of information had to be reconciled by way of model fitting.

Model fitting[42] showed a genetic effect of 50 percent. It also showed that unique environmental effects plus measurement error explained 35 percent of the authoritarianism variance and shared environmental effects explained 15 percent. McCourt observed that "like witnesses at a crime scene" the four twin types provide different information about the origins of right-wing authoritarianism. Most importantly, she showed that the traditional view of authoritarianism, in which rearing by authoritarian parents leads to authoritarian children, was untenable. McCourt explored this issue further, using retrospective measures of the rearing environment from the Block Environmental Questionnaire and Family Environment Scales described in earlier chapters.

McCourt organized the reared-apart twins and their spouses according to rearing by biological or nonbiological relatives. Four environmental measures—achievement orientation, moral-religious emphasis, organization, and control—correlated significantly with authoritarianism (0.22 to 0.35) for twins raised by biological relatives. This might suggest that family environment factors drive authoritarian traits in children, perhaps through parental rearing practices and/or by parental modeling. However, the correlations between authoritarianism and the family environment measures were negligible for the twin adoptees, showing that the family environment was not associated with this behavior.[43] Without the reared-apart twins, the wrong conclusion (i.e., authoritarian attitudes come from within-family dynamics) would have been reached.

The lack of social influence on authoritarianism was further shown by the lack of association between right-wing authoritarianism and the twins' contact prior to assessment. Once again, Lykken was correct in his view that psychological research with twins gets at behaviors' underlying causes better than psychological research with nontwins. Bouchard's 1999 study on religious beliefs would confirm this view.

Intrinsic and Extrinsic Religiousness

In November 1998, the John M. Templeton Foundation funded a three-day workshop in Berkeley, California, on religious beliefs. The invitees were researchers with access to relevant but unpublished twin data. Bouchard's paper on intrinsic and extrinsic religiousness from that workshop became one of twelve contributions to a 1999 issue of *Twin Research* devoted to twin studies of religion, values, and health.[44] Professor of Human Genetics and Psychiatry and Reverend Lindon Eaves, who authored the introduction, called the collection "a small landmark in the study of behavioral genetics"[45] because prevailing social science views held that religious beliefs were acquired within the rearing family. Psychology textbooks at that time were surprisingly devoid of chapters on religiousness, given its association with personality, depression, and physical health.

Bouchard's paper was the second MISTRA publication on religiosity; the first had appeared in 1990.[46] Bouchard saw religiousness as a significant and complex psychological construct—higher levels predicted better

234 BORN TOGETHER—REARED APART

mental and physical health,[47] and reduced delinquency and drug abuse, yet increased religiosity was also associated with increased prejudice and intolerance.[48]

This second religiosity study focused on intrinsic religiousness, the significant religious values that may have personal meaning (e.g., central influence of religion in one's life), and extrinsic religiousness, the utilitarian religious values that may enhance social status or self-concept (e.g., social benefits of religious participation). The distinction between the two was made in 1967 by psychologists Gordon Allport and J. Michael Ross,[49] among others. Bouchard examined the roots of these religious tendencies in thirty-five MZA twin pairs and thirty-seven DZA twin pairs. However, this study went beyond that purpose in following Edward O. Wilson's view that by "traditional methods of reduction and analysis science can explain religion but cannot diminish the importance of its substance."[50] Bouchard addressed the issues of replication, measurement, parsimony, and heuristics, although consilience[51] (i.e., unity of knowledge) was "unquestionably relevant but beyond the scope of this paper."[52]

This study was an attempt to constructively replicate the MISTRA's 1990 finding of genetic influence on religious interest and commitment. The reared-apart twins completed the Age Universal Religious Orientation Scale, a modified version of the Allport and Ross Intrinsic-Extrinsic scales. The Allport and Ross scales had been used to measure intrinsic and extrinsic religious orientations in adults. In 1983, its authors, Richard L. Gorsuch and G. Daniel Venable, rewrote the twenty items from the Intrinsic-Extrinsic scales in simpler language to allow for research with children and adolescents.[53] The MISTRA introduced other changes to accommodate a wider variety of religions and to maintain a consistent format across some MISTRA inventories.[54] Sample intrinsic items are "I enjoy reading about my religion" and "I try hard to live all my life according to my religious beliefs." Sample extrinsic items are "It doesn't much matter what I believe as long as I am good" and "Although I am religious, I don't let it affect my daily life." The Age Universal Scale was added to the study in the late 1990s, so a relatively small number of twins had completed it by 1999. The twins' scores on selected California Psychological Inventory scales as a check on the social desirability of their responses on the religiosity scale were also examined.

With regard to parsimony, Bouchard noted that religious behaviors were rarely studied by psychologists because they assumed that such behaviors were part of the personality domain. However, associations between measures of personality and religious behaviors were small. The heuristic value of studying religious behaviors comes from the potential insights into numerous individual and societal circumstances (e.g., physical health and delinquency).

The data indicated significant genetic influence on intrinsic religiosity (0.43) and extrinsic religiosity (0.39). The possibility that these results could be explained by the adopted twins' placement into families with similar religious practices was ruled out. Knowing that social desirability (the tendency by some individuals to answer in ways that would be seen as desirable by others) might affect the responses, Bouchard correlated the twins' two religiosity scores with relevant scales from the California Psychological Inventory, namely, the Good Impression and Dicken Social Desirability and Acquiescence Scales. The only significant correlation was between the Good Impression Scale and intrinsic religiosity, but it was small (0.18). The twins seemed to have answered truthfully without trying to convey a favorable impression.

A curious finding was that the three contact measures (time together before separation, total contact time, and total time apart) correlated significantly with the within-pair difference in extrinsic religiosity for the DZA twins, but not for the MZA twins. This meant that a greater amount of contact between the DZA twins was associated with smaller differences in extrinsic religiosity between them. If, for example, reunited DZA co-twins attended religious services together because they enjoyed the attention their twinship attracted, then their contact time would increase, and their extrinsic religiosity difference would decrease. However, none of the previous analyses had detected such associations, so this finding deserved attention. A closer look at the data showed that only early contact, not later contact, affected the DZA twins' similarity in extrinsic religiosity. Secondly, several of our contact measures were approximations because several pairs had completed the inventories by mail and could have had varying amounts of contact after leaving Minnesota. It was also possible that the contact findings occurred by chance, because they had not emerged in other analyses.

Three features of this study stand out. The first is that intrinsic and extrinsic religiosity appeared to be distinct religious dimensions. The correlation between them was only 0.04. Therefore, it is not possible to talk about whether or not someone is "religious"; it is important to consider specific religious behaviors, for example, those that are intrinsic and extrinsic. This conclusion was supported by the modest positive correlations between the California Psychological Inventory's social maturity scales and intrinsic religiosity, demonstrating intrinsic religiosity's buffering of individuals against difficult psychological conditions. Bouchard did not find meaningful associations between intrinsic and extrinsic religiosity and personality traits as anticipated if religious behaviors are distinct from personality measures. The only possible exceptions were a modest negative association between intrinsic religiosity and Aggression, and a modest positive association between intrinsic religiosity and Traditionalism, consistent with expectations based on the nature of this measure.

The second outstanding feature of this study was the finding of significant, but modest, genetic influence on both the intrinsic and extrinsic scales. This was further evidence against a longstanding social view of the origins of religious attitudes and values. It seems counterintuitive that genes would affect religiosity more than family factors, but the data tell a more truthful story than our beliefs about how the world should work. Genetic effects on religiosity were replicated in the study (using a different assessment measure), but the expectation that intrinsic religiousness would show greater heritability than extrinsic religiousness was not confirmed. This was surprising because our 1989 study of job satisfaction found genetic effects on intrinsic satisfaction but not on extrinsic satisfaction, suggesting that the more personally significant aspects of work activities and interests have a partial genetic basis.

The third outstanding feature of this study was the failure to replicate the emergenic effect found for religiosity in the 1990 MISTRA study headed by Waller and Kojetin. This does not mean that an emergenic effect was not there—it means that additional replications with larger samples would be required before we can conclude that one was not present.

In the ten years that followed publication of the special *Twin Research* issue, twins showed up more frequently in studies conducted by political scientists, economists, and game theorists,[55] researchers who had not thought previously about how genetic factors might affect their measures. Twins provided the perfect opportunity for them to test their new ideas with new data.

Creative Accomplishment

Creativity involves considerable mental effort and sacrifice, behaviors that vary across individuals. The underpinnings of creative activity have interested psychologists for some time, although possible genetic effects have been largely overlooked. Plomin's 2008 behavioral genetics textbook briefly reviews just ten twin studies of creativity that show very modest genetic effects. Possible overlap between creativity and general intelligence has been held responsible for the genetic effects on creativity in some cases.[56]

Having access to extensive data from the MISTRA's reared-apart twins enabled the extraction of subsets of information that could answer interesting questions. This approach was discovered serendipitously by Bouchard, given the wide array of inventories that were administered. One question was, "Are the correlates of creativity and high levels of accomplishment genetic in origin?" In an address delivered to the 1995 National Research Symposium on Talent Development, Bouchard presented reared-apart twin data that provided an affirmative answer, work that was subsequently published in 1999.[57]

Bouchard began with Frank Barron's well-known 1965 work on creativity that listed personality traits characteristic of productive scientists, based on nine different research programs.[58] Barron had also completed twin studies showing genetic influence on verbal measures of creativity and esthetic abilities, but not on esthetic preferences.[59] Bouchard reproduced Barron's list, adding the MISTRA's measure of each personality trait, as shown in Table 11-1.

Table 11-1. **Personality Traits of Productive Scientists and the Corresponding MISTRA Measure**

Barron's Trait	MISTRA Measure
Ego strength	Ego Strength Scale[1]
Emotional stability	Negative emotionality (factor)[2]
Independence	Independence Scale[3]
Control	Self-control[3]
Liking for abstract thinking; drive for comprehensiveness in explanations	Thinking vs. feeling[4]
Personal dominance and forcefulness of opinions	Social potency[2]
Nonconformist thinking	Traditionalism[2]
Preference for dealing with things other than people	Holland Investigative Theme[5]

Note: MISTRA measures come from the following sources: [1]Minnesota Multiphasic Personality Inventory; [2]Multidimensional Personality Questionnaire; [3]California Psychological Inventory; [4]Myers-Briggs Type Indicator; [5]Strong-Campbell Interest Inventory. The MISTRA did not have measures for "special interest in pitting oneself against the unknown, so long as one's own efforts can be the deciding factor" and "liking for order, method, [and] exactness together with an interest in the challenge presented by contradictions, exceptions and apparent disorder."

Source: Adapted from Bouchard and Lykken, "Life Achievement in a Sample of Twins Reared Apart: Estimating the Role of Genetic and Environmental Influences," in *Talent Development III. Proceedings from the 1995 Henry B. and Jocelyn Wallace National Symposium on Talent Development,* ed. Nicholas Colangelo and Susan G. Assouline, 81–97 (Scottsdale, Ariz.: Gifted Psychology Press, 1999).

The findings were remarkable. Nearly every MISTRA creativity measure showed genetic influence in the 0.40 to 0.50 range, based on the MZA correlations. In contrast, the DZA correlations ranged from −0.05 to 0.38. Several traits, such as Thinking versus Feeling, appeared to be emergenic, given a high MZA correlation (0.57) and low DZA correlation (−0.01). These results agreed with those in the 1993 creativity paper reviewed in Chapter 9.[60] They also added to the extant literature showing a wide range of social environmental factors, such as level of organizational encouragement and emphasis on teamwork, that may enhance or impede creativity.[61] Challenging and supportive workplace environments can increase creative activity, but individual differences among employees require other, possibly genetically based explanations.

Genetic influence was also evident on four other creativity measures that were used, namely the Creative Temperament Scale (from the California Psychological Inventory), the Creative Personality Scale (from the Adjective Check List), the Esthetic Judgment Scale (from the Comprehensive Ability Battery), and the Holland Artistic Theme (from the Strong-Campbell Interest Inventory).

Bouchard found an absence of genetic influence on the Barron-Welsh Art Scale, an instrument that assesses artistic sophistication by having subjects indicate "like" or "dislike" of thirty-two different pen and ink drawings. Interestingly, several previous studies of young twins had reported higher DZT than MZT correlations, findings that Bouchard called "surprising and paradoxical."[62] Certainly, the MZA twins' observed similarities in home decoration and personal adornment, as well as on the creativity measures, made the art scale findings hard to believe. I also recall interviewing MZT male co-twins who paint pictures together but cannot recall which twin had done what in the completed works.

Barron also showed that several Minnesota Multiphasic Personality Inventory (MMPI) scales were high among creative writers, exemplifying the assumed link between tendencies toward psychopathology and talent. But he never considered whether these scales were genetically based. In the MISTRA, four scales from the MMPI (psychopathic deviation, psychasthenia, schizophrenia, and hypomania) showed substantial genetic effects, and a fifth (hysteria) showed moderate genetic effects. Perhaps assumed links between touches of "madness" and talent have some basis in fact.

It seems that psychologists have come full circle with respect to their take on creativity and talent. Research in this area actually began with Sir Francis Galton's nineteenth-century inheritance perspective. In his 1864 book *Hereditary Genius,* Galton tracked the accomplishments of fathers and sons via their reputations, and concluded that eminence runs

in families.[63] He came to the same decision when he compared the biological and adoptive sons of eminent figures—the abilities of adoptive
sons did not measure up to those of their adoptive fathers as was true of
biological sons. Galton eventually convinced his initially skeptical halfcousin, Charles Darwin, that "genius" was transmitted biologically from
parent to child and was not just the product of hard work.[64] But psychology moved away from this view for many years with the introduction of
Watson's behaviorist perspective in the 1930s. Today, no one would say
that creative talents do not require nurturance, but most would agree
that there are vast individual differences in potential skills. Some people
have to work harder to achieve the same goals.

Bouchard wished that he had included some standard creativity tests,
calling their omission "a clear mistake," even while he did not find these
tests completely convincing. "It would have given us greater representation of so-called good creativity tests."

Personality and Psychopathology

A personality inventory that was a first for reared-apart twins was the
Myers-Briggs Type Indicator.[65] The Myers-Briggs measures four bipolar
dimensions derived from Jungian personality theory: Extraversion versus
Introversion, Sensing versus Intuition, Thinking versus Feeling, and Judging versus Perceiving. The MISTRA's 1998 estimates of genetic influence
on these dimensions ranged from 0.40 to 0.60, consistent with what
others had found.[66] Possible emergenic effects for Extraversion versus Introversion and Thinking versus Feeling were also observed. If replicated,
these findings would predict low levels of parent-child similarity even
though these traits are highly heritable, because parents and children do
not share the complex gene configurations that underlie emergenic traits.

The reared-apart twin sample grew and developed over time. It was
always interesting to compare findings from the different-sized samples
that were available at different stages of the study. Obtaining comparable
results could offset criticisms that the small samples precluded meaningful findings. For example, the California Psychological Inventory, first
analyzed in 1990, included forty-five MZA twin pairs and twenty-six
DZA twin pairs. These data were reexamined in 1998 using additional
twins, for a total of seventy-one MZA twin pairs and fifty-three DZA twin
pairs, as well as ninety-nine MZT twin pairs and ninety-nine DZT twin
pairs.[67] The earlier and later analyses yielded average heritability estimates of 0.50 and 0.46, respectively, for the primary scales (e.g., Sociability, Dominance, and Communality). The later study also examined the

Vector Scales (Internality, Norm-Favoring, and Self-Realization) and Special Purpose Scales (e.g., Work Orientation, Leadership Potential). Both studies showed that family rearing factors and contact between twins had little influence on the adult personality measures. The MZA twins were as similar as the MZT twins.

More important than within-study replication was between-study replication. The California Psychological Inventory scale heritabilities were slightly higher than those reported by Nancy Pedersen for the Swedish reared-apart twins studied at the Karolinska Institute,[68] but the reasons were not obvious. However, the MISTRA's findings were consistent with findings from large-scale reared-together twin studies, such as those reported by psychologists Lindon Eaves, Kerry Jang, and John Loehlin.[69] Across-study consistency should have quelled criticisms that the reared-apart twins were unrepresentative or aberrant.

The MISTRA also produced some first-time analyses of psychopathology measures. One was a 1999 heritability study of the MMPI's Harris-Lingoes and Subtle-Obvious Subscales.[70] The Harris-Lingoes subscales were created by Robert E. Harris and James C. Lingoes in 1955 to overcome the overlap among six of the MMPI's multidimensional clinical scales (i.e., Depression, Hysteria, Psychopathic Deviate, Hypomania, Paranoia, and Schizophrenia) by organizing them into smaller subscales. These subscales were intended to improve the interpretation of specific behavioral and emotional problems linked to increases in the clinical scales. For example, Hypomania was divided into Amorality, Psychomotor Acceleration, Imperturbability, and Ego Inflation.

The Subtle-Obvious subscales were developed by Daniel N. Wiener and Lindsey R. Harmon in 1948 because some items seemed to discriminate among diagnostic categories but might not seem psychopathological to the person completing them, hence the "subtle" and "obvious" scales.[71] Wiener and Harmon reasoned that someone magnifying their problems might overendorse "obvious" items as compared with "subtle" items. Similarly, someone hiding or downplaying their problems might not endorse the obvious items, but would overendorse the subtle ones.[72] This new scheme involved the same scales reorganized by Harris and Lingoes, with the exception of Schizophrenia.

Although the Subtle-Obvious subscales were intended to improve diagnostic efficacy, their usefulness has been questioned. In 1999, psychologist David DiLalla reasoned that if these subscales were substantive then genetic variance would be expected.[73] DiLalla, who had taken the lead in our first MMPI study in 1996,[74] also took the lead in this second one. According to one of his coauthors, Greg Carey, this study was important for clinicians to know about.

DiLalla's analysis included the same 111 twin pairs (sixty-five MZA and fifty-four DZA) as in the 1996 study. The heritabilities ranged from 0.23 to 0.61 for the twenty-eight Harris-Lingoes subscales. However, the surprise was finding genetic influence on the five Obvious subscales (0.37 to 0.56) and on four of the five Subtle subscales (0.27 to 0.35). Genetic effects were surprising because previous studies had shown that the Subtle-Obvious scales did not meet their goal of improved diagnostic discrimination and showed little relationship with other relevant behavioral scales. However, DiLalla was convinced that genetic effects on the Subtle-Obvious scales made these scales meaningful, but perhaps not in ways that had been supposed. He recalled that in 1974, the late psychiatric geneticist Seymour Kety responded to Thomas Szasz's view of schizophrenia as mythical by stating, "If schizophrenia is a myth it is a myth with a strong genetic component."[75] DiLalla applied this same reasoning to the MMPI's Subtle scales.

DiLalla and I had a great time exchanging stories about the MISTRA during a telephone conversation in July 2010. He said that this 1999 paper was one of his favorites:

> The goal was really psychometric; it was not a twin thing. Behavior geneticists had been accused of heritability hang-ups, but we used the twin method to investigate substantive questions. But I am humble about the impact of this work—it would take other, larger samples with more validity markers to replicate our findings. But the MISTRA twins were a fantastic resource. I greatly appreciated Bouchard's willingness to make the data available to a young investigator—it had a strong and positive influence on my professional development.

As the sample grew, it was clear that the study's initial goal—determining whether the twins' life history differences were linked to current behavioral and physical differences between them—did not cover all the types of investigation that were possible with the data. In other words, the MISTRA data could address many intriguing behavioral questions beyond those indicated in its "mission statement." Some interested psychology faculty and students who were not directly involved with the MISTRA "borrowed" the data to test ideas of their own. A paper by Robert (Bob) Krueger and his former student Kristian Markon was a good example of this kind of collaboration.

Krueger was first exposed to the MISTRA in the early 1990s as an undergraduate student at the University of Wisconsin. He took a class from Dr. Al Harkness, a visiting professor who had graduated from the University of Minnesota. "The class had a Minnesota flavor," Krueger recalled. "And the MISTRA was hard to miss if you were interested in individual differences." Krueger met Bouchard in 1998 when he arrived in Minneapolis for his job interview. "We just hit it off. I admired his work, but I was a bit intimidated by him at the time." Krueger got the job and loved the collaborative spirit that the department offered. The idea for a paper on personality and psychopathology came about through a casual conversation after class with Krueger's student Kristian Markon. "We knew that Bouchard had the data we needed."

Markon and Krueger used Tellegen's Multidimensional Personality Questionnaire or MPQ (personality) and the MMPI (psychopathology) data in creative ways. Previous research had shown that normal and abnormal behaviors are correlated, but no one knew why. Markon and Krueger found that associations between normal and abnormal personality traits resulted mostly from shared genetic factors and partly from shared environmental effects.[76] For example, they found that genetic correlations between paranoia (MMPI) and Achievement (MPQ), and between Social Introversion (MMPI) and Well-Being (MPQ) were 0.53 and −0.47, respectively. This research encouraged future study of why personality and psychopathology are related, looking at nervous system processes that may be common to both.

Such studies are vital to progress in the personality field and were possible because Bouchard shared his data (albeit carefully) with interested colleagues. Of course, those of us who worked directly with the twins saw the data come alive in ways that it never could for those seeing it only on a computer screen. In 2010, I asked Katie Corson, the author of the authoritarianism paper, to come up with an interesting memory or observation from her time working on the MISTRA. She remembered giving the University of Pennsylvania Smell Identification Test to twins.[77] This is a scratch-and-sniff test that presents a series of odors with four alternative choices for identification. (I had used this smell test in research with reared-together twins in California, and decided that reared-apart twin data would be a great complement to my work—another example of wanting to study "everything possible" with the reared-apart twins.) The interesting question for me was whether reared-apart twins would show the same level of resemblance in odor identification as the reared-together twins who, presumably, had been exposed to similar odors during their lifetime.

Corson recalled, "One [reared-apart] twin would say, 'Ah, baked bread. That brings back such fine memories!' And then I'd be testing the other twin [independently, in a separate room] and when she came to the same [item] she said, 'Lovely! Is there anything that stirs the mind like the smell of baked bread?' I don't even think bread was the 'correct' answer."

Periodontology: Not All Genetic

Most journals do not welcome negative findings, but negative findings may be informative. After our colleagues Bryan Michalowicz and Bruce Pihlstrom found genetic influence on periodontal measures[78] and on alveolar bone height[79] in 1991, they failed to find genetic effects on periodontal bacteria and temporomandibular joint symptoms in 1999[80] and 2000.[81] The few available twin studies of these traits generally did not indicate genetic effects, but the sample sizes were small, some subjects were young, and questionnaires sometimes replaced clinical examinations. Michalowicz and Pihlstrom, therefore, believed that methodologically superior studies of periodontal bacteria and joint symptoms using reared-apart and reared-together adult twins were worth doing, but they were not terribly surprised by their findings.

The analysis of periodontal bacteria involved looking at dental plaque samples for the presence of *Prevotella intermedia, Porphyromonas gingivalis, Aggregatibacter actinomycetemcomitans, Eikenella corrodens,* and *Fusobacterium nucleatum.* The sample included twenty-one MZA, seventeen DZA, eighty-three MZT, and forty-eight DZT twin pairs. Most twins showed the early stages of periodontal disease, and oral bacteria were frequently detected. However, co-twin concordance for particular bacterial species was low in both reared-apart and reared-together MZ and DZ twin pairs. And the MZA twins were as similar as the MZT twins, as they often were on psychological measures. The overall message of the periodontal study was subtle but powerful: individuals will not develop periodontitis in the absence of bacteria, but disease development is not inevitable in its presence. Most remarkable was that shared family environments do not affect the presence of oral bacteria in adults—instead, random events unique to each individual appear to play the biggest role.

These findings contrasted with those from the 1991 study, showing genetic influence on clinical and radiographic measures of periodontal disease. Therefore, other genetic factors possibly linked to the immune system had to explain the twins' similar periodontal disease susceptibility.

Temporomandibular joint symptoms include joint-area pain, joint noises, tooth clenching, and tooth grinding. Slightly more than one-fourth of twins in the 242 pairs that were studied (forty-eight MZA, thirty-five DZA, ninety-eight MZT, and sixty-one DZT) had experienced one sign or symptom, most commonly joint noises. These data were based on a clinical evaluation and a medical/dental questionnaire. The MZA twins were as alike as the MZT twins across measures, showing once again that shared family environments did not play a major role. The heritability estimates, based on the MZA correlations, ranged from negligible for clenching (−0.01) to low for arthritis (0.29). Thus, joint symptoms appear to be nonfamilial.

Both sets of findings seemed surprising, even though Michalowicz and Pihlstrom were not surprised. It made sense that MZA and MZT twins should harbor more similar types of oral bacteria than DZA and DZT twins. And given our previous genetic findings on dental structures and personality traits, I expected the oral expression of nervous habits, such as tooth clenching and tooth grinding, to show genetic effects. But the data told a different story in both cases.

Pihlstrom maintained that the findings were interesting and added to our knowledge base. Michalowicz suggested that this research was ignored by other investigators—the negative genetic findings did make it into the journals, but the data did not dazzle their colleagues as had the 1991 findings of genetic influence on periodontal disease measures. I suspect that if they had found genetic influence on bacteria and/or joint disorder, their work would have received greater notice.

Many behavioral science colleagues and critics may not have known about the periodontal studies and the lack of genetic influence on some measures. That is understandable because psychologists are unlikely to conduct searches in the dental literature. But that was unfortunate because the MISTRA investigators were often accused of looking for genetic factors, emphasizing the twins' similarities and ignoring their differences. This was not the case—we were interested in results of any kind on any topic that was studied. We did not decide how the data turned out, *the twins did.*

1998–2002

The last annual report Bouchard prepared spanned the years 1995 to 1997, probably because after 1999 the only funding sources were private donors and the Whitfield Institute, which ceased to exist in 2005. Furthermore, the last twin assessment took place in April 1999. Bouchard began dividing his time between teaching and research at the University of Minnesota, and skiing down the slopes of Steamboat Springs, Colorado. He retired fully in 2009, at which time he relocated permanently to Steamboat Springs. However, MISTRA activities continued even after the last twin pair went home. Bouchard created files documenting each twin pair's discovery and testing histories, and organized the hundreds of photographs that had been taken of the twins. His students processed data from many tests and inventories that had not been analyzed. Research team members published findings on social relationships, mental ability, personality, sexual development, and moral values, to name a few.[82]

CHAPTER TWELVE

Twin Relationships, Social Attitudes, and Mental Abilities (2003–2005)

OUTSIDE A SHOPPING MALL, thirty-eight-year-old Marty and Stephanie stared at each other in a bewildered daze, touching each other's faces and hair as if they were their own. After several minutes they joined hands, jumping up and down with glee. Thirty-four-year-old Jim and Trent exited their cars on a stretch of Texas highway. They approached one another slowly, shook hands, asked the other simultaneously how they were "after all these years," then started laughing. Reunited identical triplets Bob, Dave, and Eddy met one another on two occasions when they were just nineteen—first Bob and Eddy, then Dave and Bob and Eddy. They described their moments of meeting as "ecstatic shock."[1]

I have videotapes of the first reunions between MZA twins Marty and Stephanie, Jim and Trent, and several other sets. I never tire of watching these tapes or hearing their stories. The first jubilant moment when the twins recognize each other is overwhelming. Reunions of separated twins have also grabbed public attention because they appeal to the deep-seated sense that family members belong together.

What people call "the twin bond"—identical twins' extraordinary understanding, intimacy, and rapport—most likely comes from the twins' perceptions of their matched abilities, personalities, and temperaments. This view comes from studies of reared-together twins, set within different theoretical perspectives and based on twins of varied ages and gender.[2] These studies consistently show closer MZ than DZ twin relationships, as would be predicted from MZ twins' greater physical and behavioral resemblance. Such findings have begun to affect decisions about separating young adopted twins, compensating a twin for a co-twin's wrongful death, and even deciding if identical twins' identical test scores reflect independent efforts or cheating.[3]

The three early MZA twin studies did not systematically assess the nature and quality of the twins' evolving relationships. The investigators did, however, append wonderfully descriptive accounts of the twins' life histories to their quantitative findings, some of which included information about the twins' relationships. They did this because they were intrigued by the human interest aspects of their cases as well as by the science. Newman et al. claimed that their nineteen pairs would provide writers with plenty of material for good stories.[4]

According to Newman et al., MZA twins Edith and Fay, age thirty-seven, "had become very fond of each other and enjoyed impersonating each other."[5] Betty and Ruth, age twelve, "were interrupted while dancing on a table top in one of the examination rooms . . . In all these high-spirited performances Ruth seemed to be the leader, but Betty was entirely cooperative."[6] Shields's twins Madeline and Lilian, age thirty-six, "bought themselves identical dresses when they next met, as if they wanted to make up now for the pleasures of twinship which had been denied them."[7] Juel-Nielsen's twins Palle and Peter, age twenty-two, said, "We saw something very familiar in each other, and this familiarity was almost 'weird.' "[8]

Forty of the fifty-four early MZA twin pairs for whom social relationship information was available grew close to one another after meeting. This was evidenced by their frequent contact following reunion, satisfaction with their relationship, and other factors. Twins from fourteen of these early MZA pairs did not become close, and information was vague or missing for the remaining twenty-two sets. But the finding that nearly 75 percent of the pairs had bonded closely indicates that the length of shared time does not necessarily decide how twins' relationships progress. Unfortunately, comparable information on DZA twin pairs was unavailable.[9]

Twin Relationship Survey

It was apparent to the MISTRA researchers that meeting a twin was a significant, life-changing event for our participants, regardless of their zygosity. Most twins were adoptees and were delighted to hear new details about their biological family, and to acquire in-laws, nieces, and nephews about whom they had not known. They were also excited to learn more about their medical life histories. My graduate studies, which combined twin research and evolutionary psychology, convinced me that a formal study of MZA and DZA twins' social relatedness would be meaningful on both theoretical and practical levels. Aside from testing the hypothesis that MZA twins would show closer social relations than DZA twins, the findings could help us and the twins understand their feelings with regard to meeting and being with one another.

The hours spent with the Minnesota twins were great opportunities to watch their relationships unfold. The MZA twins generally showed a better "fit" than the DZA twins, as if they had known one another all their lives. Their common understandings and shared laughter came more easily for them than for the DZA twins, revealing a greater sense of "we." But it was important to systematically record and analyze these observations to give them scientific significance. When I arrived in Minnesota in 1982, I asked Bouchard if a protocol was in place to capture the twins' relations with one another. He said there wasn't, but he encouraged me to create one. The result was our fifty-two page Twin Relationship Survey, first administered in 1983.

The survey appeared initially as a thick stack of green and white fanfold computer paper, then acquired a leaner look as a spiral-bound booklet with a pink cover. The number of questions grew after the first few administrations because the twins volunteered information on topics we had yet to consider, such as how the twins' adoptive siblings felt about the newly found twin. The survey's final version contained sections on the twins' rearing-family situations, satisfaction in the rearing home, search for biological relatives, and meetings with the twin. Some twins completed this survey during their follow-up visits, and several answered it by mail. Most twins genuinely enjoyed this part of the study because it connected meaningfully to why they were participating in the project. They loved learning about their similarities and differences on the behavioral and medical tests, but their relationship with their twin touched them on a deeper level.

The Twin Relationship Survey posed two key questions concerning the *closeness* and *familiarity* that twins felt toward their co-twin. Each question was answered with reference to the *time of their first meeting* (recalled) and the *time of their study participation* (current), for a total of four questions. Their answers ranged from (1) greater than best friends to (6) less than someone I meet for the first time.

Twins also answered two questions with reference to the current closeness and current familiarity they felt toward any unrelated siblings with whom they were raised. This set of questions was one of the most informative features of the study.

Bouchard grumbled about how much file drawer space the survey consumed, so I understood his delight when he finally mailed them to me in

California. The surveys now occupy considerable space in my laboratory, but I am grateful for the volume of information we collected because I have used these data many times.

In 2003, twenty years after creating the Twin Relationship Survey, I wrote the paper I'd always wanted to write—a study of social closeness and familiarity between reunited twins.[10] The analysis used data from forty-four MZA twin pairs, thirty-three DZA twin pairs, and seven individual twins. Based on Hamilton's inclusive fitness theory (reviewed in Chapter 9), I expected the MZA twins to express significantly greater closeness and familiarity than the DZA twins, and they did. The current ratings for both MZA and DZA twins exceeded their initial ratings, probably because the twins had had a chance to be together and become closer and more familiar over time. The twins' closeness scores exceeded their familiarity scores, both when they met and currently, but the familiarity that they felt for one another also increased with time.

The twins' answers were anticipated, but fascinating still—the differences in ratings between the MZA and DZA pairs were greatest at the highest levels of closeness and familiarity (i.e., closer/more familiar than a best friend). Furthermore, the proportion of DZA twins endorsing the highest level of *current* closeness (at the time of testing) was less than the proportion of MZA twins endorsing the highest level of *initial* closeness (at the time of reunion). Some DZA twins took longer to achieve the high level of closeness that many MZA twins experienced almost immediately. It is unlikely that this was because the reunited MZA and DZA twins had different expectations about how they would get along—aside from researchers, many people place importance on twinship rather than on twin type.[11] That is, they equate "twinness" with "sameness" or "closeness," but this view will not make DZ twins alike or socially close.

The four social relatedness measures showed negligible or slight associations with the six contact measures (e.g., days before separation or total contact time), except for two small but statistically significant correlations. Current familiarity showed a 0.16 correlation with days before separation, but the relationship between them was in a counterintuitive direction, that is, more time together was associated with reduced familiarity. Time from reunion to assessment showed a 0.21 correlation with current closeness, indicating that twins studied soon after their first meeting were closer than those studied later. However, many factors (e.g., the twins' work responsibilities and our work obligations) affected the scheduling, thereby reducing the meaningfulness of this finding.

A wealth of information lies in the simple contrasts between people who vary in genetic and environmental relatedness. Comparing the social closeness between full siblings and half-siblings, or between half-siblings and step-siblings can say something about whether genetic relatedness plays a role. The reared-apart twins' unrelated siblings were true research treasures in this regard. It turned out that the twins' current closeness and familiarity ratings were higher for the co-twins they had recently met than for the adoptive siblings they had always known. These results were more striking than the twin comparisons because they were not what logic would suggest. It makes more sense for lifelong siblings to be closer than reared-apart twins meeting for the first time, but the data held a different message, one that agreed with evolutionary predictions.

The next step was to figure out the reasons behind the MZA-DZA twin differences in social relatedness. It was expected that similarities in the twins' personality traits, interests, values, and/or education would be tied to their social relatedness, but that was not the case. Perhaps the twins' *perceptions* of their similarities, rather than their objectively measured self-reported traits, triggered the levels of connectedness they expressed. A 1991 study showing that relatives' perceived personality similarity predicted the degree of support and conflict between them affirms this possibility.[12] My former University of Chicago thesis advisor, the late Daniel G. Freedman, put it best when he suggested that recognition of common features may foster a "sense of 'we' between ourselves and our fellow tribesmen. Recognition of this sense triggers a series of emotions whose net effect is tribal unity and the increased chance for altruism."[13]

Since the MISTRA ended, my colleagues (including Bouchard) refer newly reunited reared-apart twins directly to me. University of Minnesota psychology professor Mike Miller put me in touch with Nina, a twenty-four year old Korean-born MZA female twin raised in the United States. Nina met her twin sister for the first time in Seoul at age twenty-one. I heard the details of their reunion at *Between*, a trendy restaurant in the Itaewon section of Seoul, when I visited South Korea in 2010. The twins' first meeting occurred in a taxi cab that took the twins from the university campus to the train station—the American twin, who was taking classes, first had to spot the cab that carried her sister. En route to their birth city of Busan, the Korean-raised twin indicated that she wanted to hold her sister's hand and then "cuddle together" while they fell asleep. The American-born twin said that while it would be strange to cuddle with someone she'd met for the first time, it felt normal and natural with her twin.[14]

This fascinating remark beautifully captured our fundamental human tendency for social closeness with someone like us. I wish I could have worked it into the survey.

Personality and the Family Environment

Many MISTRA's later analyses built upon earlier ones. By 2003, links between the articles examining the twins' responses on the Family Environment Scale were apparent. In 1990, Bouchard and McGue found that genetic factors had a modest effect (.31) on the recollection of family cohesion (how much family members were concerned, committed, and helpful toward each other). They also showed that about 25 percent of the variance in consenuality in adulthood (how much a person sees the world as others see it, as measured by the California Psychological Inventory) could be explained by cohesion or conflict (openly expressed anger) in the childhood home. More consensual adults came from more cohesive homes.

In 1995, Hur and Bouchard, using an enlarged reared-apart twin sample, found significant genetic influence on memories of family cohesion (0.35, based on the Family Environment Scale and 0.44, based on the Block Environmental Questionnaire). However, they found relatively little genetic influence on the recall of organization (importance of structure and planning) or cultural orientation (level of political, intellectual, and cultural activities) in the childhood home. Then, in 2003, Krueger, Markon, and Bouchard tested the idea that personality heritability might explain the heritability of recalled family environments.[15] That is, maybe happier people are more likely to remember pleasant than unpleasant childhood events. Since the family environments of reared-apart twins are not shared, this study also let them see if the co-twins' different family environments (the nonshared variance, in this case) explained their current personality differences.

Beginning with psychologist David Rowe's 1981 twin studies, a recurrent and provocative behavioral genetic finding was that recollections of the family environment are under partial genetic control.[16] The difficulty was that no one knew how these recollections were influenced. Krueger wanted to figure this out. He used a range of environmental measures (i.e., the Family Environment Scale, Minnesota-Briggs History Record, Block Environmental Questionnaire, and Physical Facilities Questionnaire) and organized the scores into two factors (Status: socioeconomic and intellectual/cultural status; and Cohesion: cohesion versus conflict in the rearing home). The personality measures were the three Multidimensional Personality Questionnaire higher-order factors (Positive Emotionality, Negative Emotionality, and Constraint). Data were available for fifty-two MZA twin pairs and thirty-eight DZA twin pairs.

As expected, genetic influences on family environment measures *were* explained by genetic influences on personality traits. For example, genetic influence on constraint (emotional control) and on lack of negative emotionality (not feeling aggressive or alienated) explained 40 percent and 60 percent of the genetic effects on recalled cohesion, respectively. Thus, genetic factors predisposing people to control their emotions and to lack negativity are the same genetic factors that lead them to recall, or believe they recall, a cohesive childhood family environment. Krueger also found that positive emotionality explained 100 percent of the genetic effects on status (childhood family standing). That is, genetic factors underlying positive emotions predispose people to recall family environments as having been high in socioeconomic, intellectual, and cultural status.

Krueger's other key result was that the co-twins' differing perceptions of their family environments had little impact on current personality differences between them. In other words, if one MZA twin recalled a low-conflict home and his or her co-twin recalled a high-conflict home, these different perceptions were not associated with the twin's differences in emotionality. But the twin's personalities were not exactly alike, so their differences had to come from events that they did not share. I was intrigued by Krueger's proposal that there may be a "personality set-point," analogous to Lykken's happiness set-point discussed previously.[17] If so, minor daily events, such as catching a bus or losing a bet, might cause temporary fluctuations around people's characteristic positivity, negativity, and constraint levels. Perhaps we caught some twins on a day when such minor events had occurred.

I liked this study because of its simple design and sophisticated reasoning. (It is also one of Krueger's favorites.) Krueger also included an insightful discussion of the objective and subjective elements of the twins' answers. This discussion was necessary for making sense of how heritable personality traits could explain heritable family recollections. Answers to personality and rearing questionnaires reflect both subjectivity and objectivity. However, if the twins' responses were more subjective, then perhaps their personalities affected the way they recalled their childhood homes. Happy, upbeat twins might have focused on pleasant events, whereas sad, depressed twins might have remembered the bad times. Alternatively, if the twins' answers were more objective, they might have actively influenced the nature of their rearing homes. Twin peacemakers might have promoted congenial home atmospheres, whereas twin troublemakers might have created conflict.

Krueger's was an earnest attempt to uncover links between different genetically influenced behaviors. Further attempts at constructively replicating his findings are, hopefully, forthcoming.

More recent to this writing, Krueger has focused on how unusual circumstances in people's lives can impact genetic and environmental effects on personality.[18] Reports of either very high or very low parental conflict by adolescent reared-together twins showed that their positive emotions were affected by their shared environment. This finding is important, but it must be reconciled with findings of personality resemblance in some of the adult reared-apart twins who were raised in especially different and unusual circumstances. Active genotype-environment correlation—the seeking out of environments compatible with inherited characteristics—probably best explains the twins' matched personality traits. Resiliency, in particular, explains why MZA twin Roger Brooks, who bounced around from home to home, showed the same sunny personality as his twin brother Tony Milasi, who was raised in a warm Italian family. According to Krueger, the biggest behavioral mysteries are posed by MZA twins such as Jean and Joan, both of whom took music lessons—the twin who had received less family pressure to perform turned professional, but the opposite outcome was also possible. Understanding why and how rearing circumstances produce one result over another remains a true challenge.

Social Attitudes: Conservatism and More

Irving Gottesman celebrated his retirement with a festschrift held at the University of Minnesota in June 2001. The resulting 2004 volume, edited by Gottesman's former student Lisabeth F. DiLalla, included a chapter by Bouchard summarizing the MISTRA's findings on social attitudes.[19] On the topic of authoritarianism, he reminded readers, "Although we were pushed into the domain of genetic influence on attitudes by Martin et al.'s (1986) work with the W-P [Wilson-Patterson] Conservatism Scale, the first attitude-like questionnaire on which we published data was the Multidimensional Personality Questionnaire's traditionalism scale."[20]

Our 1988 personality study reported an MZA correlation of 0.53 for traditionalism, based on forty-four MZA twin pairs.[21] A 2003 paper and the 2004 festschrift chapter updates showed a remarkably stable figure (0.52), based on seventy-four MZA twin pairs, with the latest MZT correlation based on a study of 626 sets equal to 0.61.[22] The numbers reflected substantial genetic influence on traditionalism. In fact, the updated mean MZA correlations for the Multidimensional Personality Questionnaire's eleven personality scales and three higher-order factors (0.46 and 0.50) closely matched those based on the 626 MZT twin pairs (0.46 and 0.52).[23] In addition, the estimated mean heritabilities from the reared-together study (0.44 and 0.49) were extremely consistent with the MZA intraclass correlations which directly estimate heritability. The data on traditionalism and the other personality scales proved to be important to the analyses of the Wilson-Patterson Conservatism Scale.[24]

The Wilson-Patterson Scale was brought into the study in 1986. Bouchard also added Altemeyer's Right-Wing Authoritarianism Scale to the assessment at that time, but for some reason the authoritarianism data were analyzed first. (Bouchard said he was a "moron" not to have included such inventories in the first place.) At that time, the few attitudinal studies based mostly on young twins showed little genetic influence on social attitudes,[25] so researchers, including Bouchard, were not motivated to pursue this domain. Martin et al.'s 1986 twin study on the topic left him no choice.

The reared-apart twins completed the same twenty-eight-item version of the conservatism scale as the Virginia Commonwealth University twins,[26] not the fifty-item version used by Martin et al. The briefer form allowed comparisons between MZA and MZT twins, and was better suited to our crowded assessment schedule. The findings were published in 2003,[27] with an update in Bouchard's 2004 chapter.

The conservatism scale captured a significant and distinct attitudinal dimension: conservatism. This was shown by the high correlations of conservatism with Altemeyer's Right-Wing Authoritarianism Scale (0.72) and Tellegen's traditionalism scale (0.58), based on 338 reared-apart twin and nontwin participants. At the same time, the Wilson-Patterson showed low correlations (−0.16 to 0.17) with the Multidimensional Personality Questionnaire's other personality scales, such as Absorption and Alienation. It also showed a low, negative correlation with the IQ scores (−0.23). The fact that both the personality scales and IQ scores were not strongly correlated with conservatism showed that the conservatism scale had discriminant validity—that is, that it was measuring a behavior that differed from both personality and intelligence. Bouchard also found that childhood rearing measures were unrelated to conservatism among twins who had been adopted, with "Importance of Religion" to the mother being the only exception (−0.22). However, the similarity in this measure between co-twins was minimal, and any resemblance between them did not affect their resemblance in conservatism.

It is exciting when new findings replicate existing ones. That is because there is a sense that the real answer is at hand. Replicating Martin's (heritability 0.62) and the Virginia group's findings for conservatism (heritability 0.65 for males and 0.45 for females) was important because most people believed that this attitude came mostly from the rearing family environment. Finding that the MZA and DZA conservatism correlations were 0.59 and 0.21, respectively, and that the genetic estimates ranged from 0.56 to 0.59, were significant breakthroughs. A successful constructive replication had been completed—but there was more to come.

In 2004, Bouchard revisited the Wilson-Patterson Scale by organizing its twenty-eight items into three factors we labeled Sexual Conservatism, Social Conservatism, and Militarism, as well as a Total Conservatism score based on all twenty-eight items. Again, it was found that Total Conservatism correlated highly with traditionalism (0.60), but not with the other Multidimensional Personality Questionnaire scales. As expected, the three factors and total score correlated highly with right-wing authoritarianism (0.62, 0.42, 0.51, and 0.73, respectively). These findings demonstrated convergent validity among the measures; the scales that should theoretically be related to one another were related. The three factors and total score also showed the expected lack of correlation with general intelligence (−0.21 to −0.14). These findings showed discriminant validity among the measures; the scales that should theoretically be unrelated to one another were unrelated.

The four MZA intraclass correlations (0.51 to 0.62) exceeded the four DZA intraclass correlations (−0.05 to 0.35), consistent with genetic influence on the specific factors comprising conservative attitudes. However, the near zero DZA correlation (−0.05) for Militarism was a surprise low that was hard to explain. The only corroborating evidence available were the low DZT (0.23) and full sibling (0.20) correlations for Militarism in the Virginia study. Militarism could conceivably be an emergenic trait, influenced by unique gene combinations. If so, it would not be unusual to see army volunteers and conscientious objectors within the same family.

The within-study replication was important because it confirmed conservatism as a distinct social attitude, but did so in a new way by means of the three factors and a total conservatism score. This work also showed the benefit of having direct access to both the twins' data and to their life histories—the findings gave scientific meaning to the twins' experiences, downgrading the explanations based on coincidence or fabrication that some critics had claimed. The firemen twins, Mark and Jerry, were completely against women serving as volunteer firefighters. The giggle twins, Barbara and Daphne, who were so talkative on most issues, were totally uninterested in politics and fell silent when the topic came up. The British twins, Irene and Jeanette, both crossed out "tolerate" and replaced it with "respect" on a questionnaire item concerning other people's religions.[28] These glimpses into the twins' minds often came about casually over lunches and coffee breaks, and we made notes of these observations. Bouchard thought it was best to avoid controversial topics with the twins to keep the atmosphere congenial.

Bouchard's 2004 chapter also provided updated results for religiosity. The MISTRA's within-study replications and those of other investigators showed that the genetic influence on religiosity stayed at about 0.50. The widespread belief that religiosity in adulthood was a product of family rearing during childhood was under revision.

The idea that social attitudes are partly shaped by genetic factors is still hard for some people to accept. This is probably because parents and children are seen together at religious institutions, social activities, and community events. It makes intuitive sense that children's social attitudes should be shaped by those of their parents. In fact, the MISTRA found that among intact biological families the moral religious orientation and intrinsic religiosity were substantially correlated (0.53). Again, because biological parents and their children share both genes and environments, these causal factors cannot be separated. Adoptive parents and children who share no genes in common provide informative tests of relationships between family background and religiosity. The 1999 study of religious behavior reported a negligible relationship between moral religious emphasis in the childhood home and intrinsic religiosity during adulthood (0.10) among the adopted twins.[29]

Children grow up and draw conclusions of their own, filtering information through their own personalities, perceptions, and experiences. The Virginia group found only age-related differences in conservatism until the young reared-together twins turned twenty. As young adults, these twins could express their own views more freely, allowing their genetic tendencies to emerge. That is, children usually follow their parents' religious practices until they are old enough to form their own beliefs and act on them. Laura Koenig, one of Bouchard's dissertation students and the only one to study only reared-together twins, showed the same effect.[30] She did not find a genetic influence on retrospective religiousness (religious activities and interests adults recall as children), but she did find a genetic influence on current religiousness (religious activities and interests adults have at present).[31]

Koenig arrived in Minnesota in 2001 after the data collection had ended, but she said, "I loved hearing Tom's stories about the different pairs and what they were like." She often uses MZA twins Oskar (raised Catholic in Nazi Germany) and Jack (raised Jewish in Trinidad) as "a great example of how religious affiliation is environmental, and how religious importance can be influenced by genes . . . There is no gene for religiousness, but the genetic effects on personality and such can influence people's beliefs. The reared-apart twins were a great way to make that point."[32]

The rearing home's religious emphasis, parents' education, and other family factors were just not there when it came to social attitudes and religiosity in adulthood. For those who maintained that they were, this situation exemplified what Bouchard called "an argument," not evidence.[33]

Reading and General Intelligence

Wendy Johnson arrived at the University of Minnesota in the fall 2000 as a new graduate student in the Department of Psychology. Bouchard suggested that she work with Matt McGue since Bouchard would soon be retiring. "But [Bouchard] is still here," she told me in October 2009, implying that he enjoyed the MISTRA too much to leave.

Johnson earned her PhD in 2005, then worked for Bouchard and McGue as a postdoctoral fellow for a year and a half. As of 2010, she has been a research fellow and reader at the University of Edinburgh, Scotland, analyzing cognitive ability data from the Minnesota and United Kingdom samples. Understanding the genetic and environmental structure of intelligence and personality is her passion. Over the years, Johnson and I have coauthored several articles and a chapter using the reared-apart twin data and cohosted a symposium.[34] But it wasn't until that October day that I heard her reflections on the MISTRA.

Johnson said, "I have never met a single reared-apart twin, but I would love to." Bouchard was no longer gathering data in 2000, so Johnson knew the pairs only as identification numbers in computer files. She probably knew the files better than anyone, but working directly with twins might help her answer questions she still wants to address: Is there something special about being a twin that affects behavior? Why do twins recover from low birth weight better than nontwins? Such questions reflect the currently changing behavioral-genetics trends—away from estimating heritabilities and toward finding the psychological and biological mechanisms underlying behavior.

Johnson was first author on three papers that combined tests and inventories within and between the domains of general intelligence, special mental abilities, reading performance, and personality. Her work produced new ideas about the structure of intelligence. One of her first papers concerned the Stroop Color-Word Test.

The Stroop Color-Word Test has been of psychological interest since its introduction in 1935.[35] It is a test of mental attention and flexibility that assesses how well people can inhibit or stop one response to say or do another response.[36]

The 1978 version of the Stroop,[37] added to the MISTRA in 1986, presents participants with three pages. The first page displays color words (green, red, and blue) printed in black ink, the second page displays rows of Xs printed in various colors, and a third page displays color words printed in different ink colors (e.g., the word *red* would be printed in green). Interference on this test refers to whether a word's meaning, such as *red*, affects the subject's ability to name the color if it is printed in green.

The color-word interference score is determined by the number of colors on page three that are read aloud correctly in forty-five seconds. This score has been hypothesized to reflect individual differences in verbal processing. Interference is greatest during the elementary school years when automaticity (performing an activity using little focused attention) with color words is new, but performance improves over time. Reading skill has also been linked to Stroop test performance but mostly in younger populations and clinical samples. Other Stroop measures have been studied, such as the word score (number of words on page one read aloud correctly) and the color score (number of colors on page two read aloud correctly).

Only two twin studies using the Stroop test were available when Johnson began her analyses. Greater MZT than DZT twin resemblance was found, but the samples were small, and the twins were elderly.[38] Thus, the MISTRA was the first study to consider genetic effects on Stroop test performance in a middle-aged twin sample, and to relate Stroop scores to mental ability, reading, and personality. This was also the first time that data from the two reading tests, the Slossen Oral Reading Test and the Woodcock-Johnson Reading Mastery Test, were used.[39]

Reading tests were added to the MISTRA in the late 1980s in collaboration with Professor Jay Samuels in the Department of Educational Psychology. This work began when Bouchard was hosting a visitor from abroad who wanted to meet Samuels. The three met in Elliott Hall, and Samuels asked Bouchard if he had included a reading component in the assessment schedule. In the mid-1980s, there were some tape recordings made of the twins in various settings, but not the more informative tests of word recognition, reading speed, and comprehension that interested Samuels. "Tom realized that this was an opportunity to do something," Samuels recalled. In the weeks that followed, Samuels and I assembled three oral reading passages, a spelling test, and two reading tests that were used in educational assessments. According to Samuels, "We did it [the reading component] a gorgeous wonderful way. We chose passages that could be read at advanced high school or college levels. We did not use a multiple-choice format—we had the twins read the passages out loud and tell us what they remembered [known as active recall]. Doing two things at the same time—deciding and comprehending—gets to the issue of reading fluency."

Samuels and I also designed a spelling test. We selected thirty-seven words from Dr. Richard Venezky's computer-generated list that could either be spelled phonetically (e.g., department) or had unique letter combinations that were not rule-related (e.g., echo). We thus assessed rule mastery and visual memory. Samuels called the data "an international gold mine." Johnson made great use of this gold mine to produce her three studies. Her paper on genetic and environmental influences and correlates of the Stroop test utilized the Wechsler IQ scores, selected special mental ability tests, and the two standard reading tests. It included fifty MZA twin pairs, thirty-seven DZA twin pairs, as well as twins' spouses and companions for a total of 271 participants. It remains the largest study of its kind.

Genetic influence was found on every Stroop test measure, ranging from 0.35 for interference to 0.50 for words.[40] The Stroop was not developed with the idea of assessing genetic and environmental influences on performance, a feature yielding results that were both unbiased and persuasive. Johnson also found that most of Tellegen's personality scales showed little relationship to Stroop performance. This was somewhat surprising because previous studies had shown a relationship between Stroop test performance and impulsivity. Interestingly, the IQ score, most mental ability measures, and the reading test scores were significantly correlated with Stroop test performance. It was possible that the twins' similarities in mental abilities were responsible for the similarities in their Stroop scores; however, the twins' correlations hardly changed when the effects of the mental performance scores were statistically removed. Thus, the different Stroop measures are valid ability constructs, in and of themselves.

Johnson's interests led her to consider a second problem: Is the genetic factor structure (i.e., the different ability components or dimensions) of general intelligence and reading performance the same for children and adults? This analysis also offered an opportunity to look at the heritabilities of reading and word recognition.[41] In order to maximize the difference between our general intelligence and reading measures, she chose three fluid ability tests from the special ability battery—pedigrees, flexibility of closure, and induction.[42] These three tests reflect abilities that are not closely tied to formal education, whereas reading is a learned skill. The reading measures included the two word-recognition tests (Slossen and Woodcock), the three reading passages, and the spelling test that Samuels and I had assembled.

Happily, in 2009 I found old copies of the spelling words and reading passages in my files. In the 1980s and early 1990s, I could almost recite them by heart after having listened to the twins repeat them so many times. The following list includes some of the words and sentences from the spelling tape, exactly as the twins would have heard them.

- Department—He worked in a department store—Department
- Echo—I heard the echo—Echo
- Nuisance—The small noisy child was a nuisance—Nuisance

The person on the tape reading them was Bouchard. Twins were instructed to write each word on an answer sheet once it had been repeated.

Twins then read three passages aloud and told us everything they remembered about what they had read. The first sentences from each passage are reprinted here to provide a sense of the topics we covered:

- A medical problem that seems to afflict women more than men is sensitivity to cold.
- Popular opinion holds that success at work depends upon continually pushing for what you want and refusing to take no for an answer.
- When researchers first began to study reading, many ideas about its nature were generated from the method of introspection.

The twins' scores on the spelling test were the number of words they spelled correctly. Their scores on the reading passages were created by assigning values to the number of different points they presented in each passage during their retelling; their tape-recorded sessions were rated by independent judges. This approach to reading comprehension relies on active rather than passive recall and is generally equivalent to the more commonly used multiple-choice method.

Johnson found that the genetic factor structure of general intelligence and reading performance was the same for adults and for children. A strong relationship between general intelligence and reading performance in these adult twins was also found. Interestingly, the twins' reading comprehension skills were linked to their general intelligence but not to their reading performance. It could be that, in adulthood, recognizing words does not guarantee text comprehension—some people can read fluently without grasping the concepts behind what they read. The participants' spelling skills were linked to both their general intelligence and to their reading performance, not surprisingly as words with both phonetic and nonphonetic letter combinations had been included. Words with nonphonetic letter combinations are harder to spell, so it made sense that the more intelligent, better readers were also better spellers.

The heritabilities for the reading measures were higher than those estimated for children in prior studies (0.21 for spelling to 0.45 for word recognition).[43] Our values were 0.77 for the Slosson, 0.74 for the Woodcock, 0.76 for spelling, and 0.51 for reading comprehension. This was not very surprising because the heritability of general intelligence increases with age. But the relatively high DZA correlations on the Woodcock (MZA: 0.72, DZA: 0.70), Slosson (MZA: 0.73, DZA: 0.60), and reading comprehension (MZA: 0.36, DZA: 0.59) were puzzling because DZA twins are expected to be only half as alike as MZA twins. Of course, higher than expected DZA twin resemblance on some mental ability measures had been observed in the past. None of the possible explanations we could think of, such as assortative mating or selective placement, could be confirmed.

These intelligence and reading studies are good examples of how the MISTRA's rich data files enabled many types of analyses, over and beyond the heritability studies. In contrast, the investigators of the three early reared-apart twin studies focused mostly on the twins' behavioral similarities and dissimilarities. This observation is not intended to detract from the contributions made by these early studies. Clearly, the breadth and diversity of their tests were less than those of the MISTRA, and the sophisticated quantitative methods that allow genetic and environmental dissection of measured traits were unavailable. The MISTRA was able to explore many avenues of inquiry because of its comprehensiveness. Here is another example, also from Johnson's work: the conclusion of her third article is stated in its captivating title "Just One g."[44]

Johnson's third analysis addressed continuing controversies within psychology, namely, the identification of a general intelligence factor called "g" and its measurement. Since the beginning of the modern mental testing movement in 1905 with French investigators Binet and Simon,[45] researchers have debated the evidence for a general intelligence factor versus separate mental abilities as well as the best methods for intellectual assessment. General intelligence, or g, refers to a shared factor that underlies human abilities and explains why tests of different skills (e.g., vocabulary and comprehension) are correlated.[46] Competing models recognize separate abilities or talents that function independently or somewhat independently.[47] The MISTRA investigators reasoned that finding similar g factors based on different clusters of mental ability tests would demonstrate that there is, in fact, "just one g."

Three different mental ability batteries had been completed by the 436 MISTRA twins, spouses, and others: the Wechsler IQ test, the Hawaii Ability Battery, and the Comprehensive Ability Battery.[48] Here, the twins were treated as separate individuals without reference to their relatedness. In a combined analysis, the three g factors correlated highly, ranging from 0.99 to 1.00, values that are rarely seen in psychological research. Based on this finding, there appears to be a single g—of course, this g does not capture the full range of abilities, nor does it pinpoint the biological processes underlying human intellect. But the findings made a strong case for including g in future models of intelligence. According to Johnson,

"These results provide the most substantive evidence of which we are aware that psychological assessments of mental ability are consistently identifying a common component of general intelligence."[49] Bouchard worded this conclusion more forcefully in his 2009 paper, asserting that "the previously widespread belief that different intelligence tests yield estimates of quite different intelligences is simply false."[50]

Johnson and Bouchard used the twins' and spouses' mental ability data to probe the structure of human intelligence in other ways.[51] They compared the fit of the data to the three extant major intelligence models: the Cattell-Horn fluid-crystallized model, the Vernon verbal-perceptual model, and the Carroll three-strata model. This was one of the few MIS-TRA analyses that specified a hypothesis at the outset—the Vernon model was expected to fit the data best. Beyond that, the work was exploratory in nature, although it generated other hypotheses. Bouchard waited years to do this analysis—statistical techniques were too rudimentary when the study began, and the sample needed to grow.

The Cattell-Horn model recognizes two types of intelligence: crystallized (the intelligence acquired from learning and culture) and fluid (the genetically based capacities unrelated to experience). The Vernon model recognizes a general intelligence factor and two main ability groupings: verbal-educational and special-practical-mechanical. The Carroll model includes a general intelligence factor, broadly specialized abilities, and narrowly specialized abilities that relate to a specific domain in the second group. As expected, the Vernon model fit the MISTRA data best, although Johnson and Bouchard enhanced it by adding memory and image-rotation factors. They called it—appropriately—the Verbal-Perceptual-Image Rotation Model, noting its consistency with the idea of coordinated function across brain regions and the importance of brain laterality (specialization of mental function across the brain's left and right hemispheres) in mental performance. The g factor contributed substantially to the verbal, perceptual, and image-rotation components, which then contributed to eight more specialized skills (verbal, scholastic, fluency, number, content memory, perceptual speed, spatial, and rotation). More will be said about this model in the next chapter.

Johnson replicated this model in a 2005 study using Thurstone and Thurstone's 1941 data from 710 Chicago schoolchildren.[52] She replicated it again in 2007 using a battery of forty-six tests available for 500 professional seamen from the Royal Dutch Navy.[53] And she did once more in 2008 using a different five-test battery and sample.[54] The MISTRA twins had launched a continuing research program—it was usually the other way around, with the MISTRA testing new methods and findings with the twins.

Tony Vernon, professor of psychology at the University of Western Ontario in London, Canada, is an expert in the study of intelligence and editor of the journal *Personality and Individual Differences*. According to Vernon, "[The Verbal-Perceptual-Image Rotation Model] is the first 'new' model of the structure of intelligence to come along in a long time. It showed itself to be a better fit to the data than Thurstone or Cattell or P. E. Vernon, though it was mostly closely aligned with the Vernon model."[55]

I never thought I would say this, but the fact that the original *g* findings on the model were based largely on reared-apart twin data was inconsequential. Data from good nontwin samples could have—and have—accomplished the same thing.

Johnson made an interesting point as we ended our interview. Unlike many other MISTRA colleagues, she said Bouchard may have compromised the scientific rigor of the study by publicizing the MZA twins' unusual similarities. "You don't need quirky stuff—it does not establish anything about behavior. The anecdotes gave detractors something to attack. You need to show striking observations more systematically. Of course, I say this now with 20/20 vision of hindsight which Bouchard could not have had at that time." Johnson referenced a group picture of identical twins in which the children's hands are positioned similarly within pairs, but differently between pairs. It appears in a 1982 introductory genetics textbook by the late geneticist Edward Novitski.[56]

Some people might claim that the twins in the picture simply followed the photographer's instructions regarding their hand placement, but the similarities were mostly within the pairs. One might also suggest that each pair's parents had instructed them on how to hold their hands when they were being photographed. However, Johnson speculates that while we are all socialized to fit into our environments, no one instructs us on how to hold our hands. Of course, we really don't know what the twin children were told to do, but as Bouchard said in his last lecture, observing similar hand postures in MZA twin pairs is the best answer to objections that hand holding is a learned behavior. That answer is shown in Figure 12-1.

Meaningful information is stored within each pairs' signature habits. But contrary to Johnson, one could argue that it was appropriate for Bouchard to discuss these habits publicly. Rare similarities between MZA twins are provocative, suggesting genetic effects, possibly emergenic in nature. The fact that the same physical and behavioral quirks are more often found in MZA than DZA twin pairs suggests, but does not prove, that genetic influence is at work, providing a rationale for further study. It is also the case that the MZA twins' unusual observations were not publicized exclusively by Bouchard.

Comment

The Association for Psychological Science publishes a slim journal called *Current Directions in Psychological Science*. Articles appear on a mostly invitation-only basis, although interested contributors can bring potential topics to the editor's attention. In a 2004 article, Bouchard identified several key trends and big questions.[57] He noted that behavior geneticists had always assumed that genetic influence would vary from trait to trait, and that behaviors such as social attitudes would show little heritability. But the two recent surprises have been the generally moderate level of genetic influence across most traits. According to Bouchard, "It seems reasonable to suspect that moderate heritability may be a general biological phenomenon rather than one specific to human psychological traits, as the profile of genetic and environmental influences on psychological traits is not that different from the profile of these influences on similarly complex physical traits and similar findings apply to most organisms."[58]

Figure 12-1. Five MZA twin pairs shown with CBS host Lesley Stahl on the set of *48 Hours*, November 15, 2003. Note the similar hand and leg positions of the twins seated in the front row. The male twins to the left and the female twins in the center of the second row did not participate in the MISTRA. (Photo credit John P. Filo, CBS News.)

Bouchard also asserted that the name of the field—behavior genetics—is an "unfortunate misnomer."[59] The studies are neutral with respect to genetic and environmental influences. Now that the heritabilities of most traits have been established, interest in uncovering the underlying molecular and environmental mechanisms is paramount.

CHAPTER THIRTEEN

Sexual Development, Fluctuating Asymmetry, Body Size, and the Structure of Intelligence (2006 and Beyond)

AM LOOKING AT THE CALENDAR as I write this last chapter on the MISTRA's findings. It is July 1, 2010, and I know that later today thirty-five-year-old Hanan Hardy will travel to Morocco to meet her twin sister Hassania for the first time. The twins, who appear to be MZ, were separated at birth because their biological mother could not care for them. Hanan was reared in the United States by their mother's close friend and enjoyed middle-class privileges; Hassania remained in Morocco and was sold to another family when she was just one week old, living in poverty most of her life. Hanan's adoptive family kept her birth details hidden, but Hanan learned the truth several weeks earlier from her twin sister who found her on Facebook. Hassania knew she had a twin, but she had been unable to find Hanan without that vital resource. The MISTRA's reared-apart sample might have been much larger if the Internet had been available for public use in the 1980s.

In the "old days," we would have done our best to bring Hanan and Hassania to the university, hiring a translator to help Hassania with tests and interviews. The twins' dramatically different rearing situations would have put genetic explanations of behavior to the strict tests our critics had clamored for. Based on other MZA pairs with very different backgrounds, we probably would have found some striking behavioral similarities between the Moroccan twins. We would have also learned more about how their homes, communities, and cultures mixed with their genetically based proclivities to produce differences between them.[1]

Reared-apart twins are no longer visiting Minnesota, but I keep track of all the cases I discover. I conduct "mini-assessments" with some of them, just as Hur and I did in 2008 for the Korean twins. I also hope to study Hasan and Hassania some day, albeit at a distance. Most of the MIS-TRA investigators also miss the excitement and frenzy of those whirlwind twin weeks, but they are making the most of the available data. Many papers appeared in the poststudy period, and there are more to come.

Sexual Development

During one of their premeeting telephone calls, Hanan and Hassania told each other that they weren't feeling well, and learned that they had started their periods at the same time. According to Hassania, they believed that their matched cycles and physical complaints were amazing. In spite of their menstrual discomfort, I could tell that they were having a good time discovering things they had in common.

The twins' coordinated menstrual timing was not surprising. No one had studied menstrual synchrony in twins, although reared-together twin studies have reported genetic influence on age at menarche, the onset of menstruation (MZT r_i: 0.65 to 0.97 and DZT r_i: 0.18 to 0.50).[2] Farber found a 9.3-month age difference in menarche for twenty-eight MZA female twin pairs scattered throughout the early studies. She also noted that the twins described similar symptoms, both common (e.g., irregularity and emotionality) and uncommon (e.g., fainting and vomiting) as did Hanan and Hassania.[3] However, a formal study of menarche in reared-apart twins had not been conducted until 2007.[4]

The MISTRA had relevant data for twenty-seven MZA female pairs and thirty-one DZA female pairs, taken from the Sexual History Timeline. The same data were available for thirty-three MZT female twin pairs and fourteen DZT female twin pairs from Lykken's Minnesota Twin Registry. I had a particular interest in the potential findings on age at menarche, due to some relevant work in evolutionary psychology, as I will explain later in this chapter. I analyzed the data in 2007 in California with Dr. Joanne Hoven Stohs, my colleague in the department of psychology. Stohs had never before worked with twins and acquired appreciation for genetic effects on behavior by doing so.

The four-group (MZA, DZA, MZT, DZT) design confirmed our expectation of genetic influence on age at menarche. The MZA twins (r_i: 0.56) were more alike than the DZA twins (r_i: 0.16), and the MZT twins (r_i: 0.70) were more alike than the DZT twins (r_i: 0.41). The MZT and DZT twins were also more alike than the MZA and DZA twins, respectively, suggesting shared environmental effects, possibly through diet or exercise.

I wondered about features of the reared-together twins' cohabitation that may have led to their synchronous menstrual timing. A 1971 study by biological psychologist Martha McClintock showed that female college students living in the same dormitory acquired menstrual synchrony over time.[5] The significant factor in McClintock's results was that the women had spent time together, but the underlying mechanism was uncertain. Of course, menstrual synchrony is not the same as age at menarche, but cohabitation could affect these measures in similar ways. Farber noted that twins who had met prior to puberty had a more similar age at menarche than twins who had met later, suggesting that contact during adolescence could affect this measure. However, she did not examine associations between age at menarche and contact frequency.

The mean ages at menarche were 12.50 years for the reared-apart twins and 12.86 years for the reared-together twins, similar to the age of 12.70 years reported for the general population.[6] However, our MZA twins reached menarche significantly earlier (12.24 years) than our MZT twins (12.80 years), a finding for which we had no explanation.

When Stohs and I began our study, a large body of work had been generated on the Belsky-Draper hypothesis.[7] This evolutionary-developmental hypothesis predicts that girls from father-absent homes should experience menarche earlier than girls from father-present homes, because it would be biologically and psychologically advantageous for them to leave their disorganized environments to begin families of their own. The presence of a stepfather and lower levels of parental investment have also been linked to girls' earlier age at menarche, whereas parental warmth and approval have been linked to later menarche. Research evidence has both supported and challenged these findings.[8]

I was skeptical of the Belsky-Draper hypothesis because I favored twin research showing genetic effects on age at menarche. Furthermore, a 2006 study by former University of Virginia graduate student Jane Mendle showed that the daughters born to twin mothers did not differ in age at menarche if one daughter was raised by a stepfather. The daughters of each twin were cousins, but they would be genetically equivalent to half-siblings if their mothers were MZ twins. Fortunately, data to further test the ideas generated by this body of work were available from the MISTRA's Twin Relationship Surveys. Questions concerning parental understanding, sense of belonging in the family, and childhood happiness and anxiety were relevant to our goal.

None of the childhood satisfaction and adjustment measures had a significant bearing on age at menarche, except understanding by father. We showed that greater paternal understanding was associated with *earlier* age at menarche, contradicting the Belsky-Draper hypothesis. Our find-ings were more consistent with research linking favorable living condi-tions, possibly greater resource availability, to earlier menarche.[9] Thus, the data supported a genetic explanation of individual differences in age at menarche. Parents who achieve earlier sexual maturity may be the ones to engage in risky sexual behavior, transmitting these tendencies to their daughters.

In 2009, Stohs and I went on to study genetic effects on age at first inter-course using the MISTRA twins.[10] Age at first intercourse had never been studied in reared-apart twins although several reared-together twin stud-ies were available. These studies had found genetic effects on this mea-sure, but the extent of genetic influence varied widely (0.00 to 0.72 for males and 0.17 to 0.49 for females). Age also made a big difference in the degree of genetic influence—most studies found higher heritabilities for younger twins than for older twins who also experienced their first inter-course at later ages. This finding probably reflected an easing of sexual re-strictions among the more recent, hence younger, cohorts at the time of the study. A more permissive sexual climate would allow greater freedom for expressing individual differences in sexual behavior.

Stohs and I approached our study the same way we approached our study of age at menarche. Using data from the Sexual Life History Timeline, we examined resemblance for age at first intercourse for thirty-four MZA twin pairs, twenty-five DZA twin pairs, and twenty-three individual twins. We then examined age at intercourse in relation to the timing of other behav-iors, such as age at first kiss. We also examined life history events consid-ered meaningful within evolutionary and developmental frameworks, such as peer and family relationships. We limited this second set of analyses to females because of our previous work on age at menarche.

The twins' mean age at first intercourse was 18.80 years. Consistent with previous twin studies, older twins engaged in their first intercourse at later ages (19.50 years) than younger twins (17.60 years). Also as ex-pected, the MZA twin pairs (0.34) showed significantly greater resem-blance than did the DZA twin pairs (0.22). These values did not change when we separately examined the MZA males (0.39, n = 13 pairs) and females (0.32, n = 21 pairs). Thus, the heritability of age at first inter-course, expressed directly by the MZA correlation, was 0.34, consistent with the findings from reared-together twin studies.

Some evolutionary-based studies have found that adverse family factors predicting earlier age at menarche also predict earlier age at intercourse. However, in 2002, psychologist David Rowe showed genetic influence on both as well as a significant genetic correlation (0.72) between them, challenging an exclusively family-dynamic interpretation of the findings. That is, genetic transmission may affect the timing and association between these measures. Some developmental psychologists see the connection between age at menarche and sexual activity as contingent upon peer relationships and the distancing of parents and children during adolescence and young adulthood. Again, items in our Twin Relationship Survey helped make sense of these associations.

Not surprisingly, twins who had intercourse earlier in life experienced their first kiss, first marriage, and first child at earlier ages than those who had intercourse later in life. The more interesting findings were that twins who were less happy than their childhood peers and less fulfilled in their childhood homes had intercourse at younger ages than their more contented and fulfilled counterparts. These results were consistent with developmental perspectives, but could also reflect genetically based personality traits that propel these individuals toward earlier sexual activity. The quality of the twins' relations with their parents was unrelated to age at first intercourse, suggesting the greater effects of peer relations on early sexual activities.

Our research on menarche and first intercourse demonstrated the utility of using behavioral genetic designs for examining evolutionary concepts and findings. As indicated earlier, these disciplines have functioned separately for long periods, but there is evidence of a rapprochement between them.

Fluctuating Asymmetry

If lines are drawn down the center of our bodies, it is unlikely that any of us are physical mirror images. Hand preference, foot size, and wrist circumference are not exactly the same on our left and right sides. These departures from physical equivalence, known as fluctuating asymmetry (FA), have been associated with genetic and environmental stressors,[11] such as inbreeding and mutations (genetic), and pesticides and food deficiency (environmental).[12] Fluctuating asymmetry has interested evolutionary psychologists because higher levels are thought to reflect increased stress susceptibility and reduced developmental stability. For example, women have been shown to prefer the scents of low FA men to the scents of high FA men, especially during females' high fertility phases.[13] Increased fluctuating dermatoglyphic asymmetry has also been associated with greater genetic risk for schizophrenia.[14]

In the late 1980s, Bouchard added a battery of anthropometric measures to the MISTRA assessment schedule. The addition was not done with

FA in mind because evolutionary-based studies exploring associations between FA and human psychological traits did not appear until the early 1990s.[15] Fluctuating asymmetry was, however, of interest to behavioral ecologists, human biologists, and psychiatrists in the 1980s.[16] The anthropometric measures were added to the MISTRA's assessment schedule mainly because extensive physical measurements had never been made on twins reared apart. However, we noted mirror-image effects in the twins' physical traits in order to explore questions of physical asymmetry at a later time.

In fact, there was a precedent for doing such work. In 1937, Newman et al. had recorded his MZA twins' sitting height, head length, head width, and cephalic index, as well as the usual height, weight, and fingerprint measures.[17] The only significant correlation Newman reported was between differences in the twins' weight and differences in their physical environment (0.60). However, as a biologist, Newman was also interested in physical asymmetries: "A good many pairs show[ed] mirror-imaging in eye defects, tooth anomalies, in master-eye, in a number of anthropometric measurements, and in motor and strength tests of the two hands."[18] However, the only documentation of these data is found in the twins' separate case histories included at the back of their book—only a handful of these measures were examined systematically.

Newman et al. found no difference in the MZA (n = 19 pairs) and MZT (n = 50 pairs) twin pairs' correlations for standing height, sitting height, weight, head length, and head width. However, the mean within-pair weight difference (5.87 pounds) between the MZA (9.90 pounds) and MZT twins (4.03 pounds) was statistically significant, a finding they variously explained by differences in the MZA twins' diet, climate, and care while they were growing up. The height similarity of the MISTRA's reared-apart twins ($r_i = .96$) was quite comparable to that of reared-together twins ($r_i = .94$), based on a 2011 analysis. In contrast, the weight similarity for the MZA twins ($r_i = .69$) was relatively less than that of the MZT twins ($r_i = .87$), suggesting shared environmental effects on body weight.[19] These analyses used a subset of mostly female MZA twin pairs (n = 29, 72 percent female) and a comparison group of MZT twin pairs (n = 49, 76 percent female), studied in collaboration with Tufts University researchers. The relatively low female MZA weight correlation is consistent with our early findings and those of other researchers.

Our array of seventy-seven anthropometric indices let us look at FA heritability and other features as they became popular research topics. In 1997, researchers reported that people with higher FA had lower IQs, a finding that led to attempts at replications. The degree of association between FA and IQ varied across studies, which used fairly small samples, so we attempted a study of our own.

The twins were asked to partially remove articles of clothing during the anthropometric assessment that was conducted by two examiners in a private room. One examiner made the measurements while the other examiner recorded them.[20] The metal calipers and other instruments were often cold, causing some twins to laugh or gasp slightly. But they accepted these procedures with the same good humor that they showed throughout the week. Some twins even thought the anthropometric assessment was interesting and fun.

I was a frequent anthropometric examiner along with a graduate student assistant. This was an interesting session because it revealed the separate physical similarities in the MZA twins that together contributed to their generally matched appearance. We literally hugged some of our heavier twins in the process of measuring their body circumference. We spotted the same clefts on the chins of MZA twins Trent and Jim, and the same receding hairlines on the big heads of the fireman twins, Mark and Jerry. I wish we had performed these procedures on the nineteen-year-old MZA male triplets Bob, Dave, and Eddy who visited Minnesota in 1980 before we conducted anthropometry studies. A photo of the three, displayed in Lykken's former laboratory, revealed that they had mirror-image smiles—one triplet's mouth curled up higher on the side opposite to that of his two brothers. One of the triplets was left-handed, and we might have found other reversed physical features among them, such as birthmarks and moles. We ended up with anthropometric data for eighty-eight twin pairs, sixty spouses, and twenty-seven nontwin relatives.

Johnson, Bouchard, and I concluded that there was a problem with most studies that had measured genetic influence on FA. The problem was that the studies had used FA measures of only one trait. We pointed out that single measures might not capture the FA of many traits affected by the same stressors. In other words, stress might affect head height *and* head width *and* arm length. A literature survey found that the estimated heritability of FA, based on a single trait, is 0.03.[21] In contrast, one exceptional study that looked at parent-child resemblance for FA, based on an eight-trait composite, showed a moderate heritability (0.38), although this figure was possibly inflated due to assortative mating.[22] However, the difficulty with that study was the confounding of genetic and environmental influence, something that would not be problematic with reared-apart twins. We reasoned that if the heritability of a composite based on many traits was higher than that of a single trait, then the FA of each of the many single traits must be affected by the same factors. In other words, the effects of stress on the FA of each trait could be small but might "add up" across traits. We also reasoned that the factors affecting the FA of the traits may have a genetic basis.

We created a ten-trait composite that included reliable measures such as foot breadth, knee height, and ear length.[23] We also created three additional FA indices, one measure based on the absolute difference between left and right sides for each trait, another measure that statistically adjusted for the direction of trait asymmetry, and a measure that statistically adjusted for each twin's variability in the single trait measures. Our results matched our reasoning. The three indices showed low heritability for the ten single traits (0.00 to 0.17), but higher heritabilities for the ten-trait composite (0.27 to 0.30). The use of multiple traits for studying the heritability of FA was a better approach than the use of single traits, as called for by Belgian biologist Stefan Van Dongen.

Van Dongen said, "The determination of h_{DI}^2 [the heritability of developmental instability] is one of the most challenging in evolutionary biology."[24] This is because FA may not accurately reflect developmental instability because it does not capture all sources of stress on the individual. The reared-apart twins, just by letting us pinch them with calipers and wrap them in tape measures, were up to the challenge.

In 2008 we completed another study of FA, one that failed to replicate the reported negative relationship between FA and general intelligence.[25] Some researchers had linked a larger left-right side difference in physical traits to lower intellect, although one contradictory study found greater physical asymmetry among males with higher IQs. The twins' intelligence test scores (a summary measure based on forty-two mental ability tests) and the anthropometric data were used to test this idea. In order for this relationship to hold, there had to be a genetic correlation between FA and ability, that is, the same genes that affected FA had to also affect intelligence.

We did not find this. We did find that FA was heritable, something we had shown in the previous study. We also showed, both in this analysis and in previous IQ analyses, that intelligence was heritable. However, we did not find a genetic link between the FA and intelligence measures as shown by the near zero correlations between them (−.01 to .04). Thus, FA and intelligence appear to be affected by different sets of genes.

These results made sense. That is because FA is a more likely reflection of a person's reproductive fitness or capacity to have children, and that has not been tied to intelligence. People at all IQ levels can have families. We were confident in our results because the sample was larger than previously studied samples, and because intelligence was assessed in more than one way.

An important next step in this research program would be to determine if more physically asymmetrical MZA twins are less healthy and/or less reproductively successful than their more symmetrical co-twins. My late colleague, Linda Mealey, had already linked increased physical attractiveness to reduced facial asymmetry within pairs of MZT twins.[26] This was a great technique because it separated the effects of FA from other physical attractiveness indicators, such as age and hair color that are matched for MZ twins. However, Mealey did not find that the more facially symmetrical twins recalled better parental treatment from childhood through age sixteen than their less facially symmetrical co-twins.[27] She suggested that childhood asymmetry may differ from later asymmetry due to developmental changes. The greater number of physical and behavioral measures currently available for the MISTRA twins would allow many informative analyses along these lines. For example, it would be possible to see if the more symmetrical MZA male co-twins were healthier or had fathered more children than their less symmetrical co-twins.[28]

Body Size, Nutrition, and Health

In 2009, the first set of results from the collaborative health and nutrition study, conducted with Dr. Susan Roberts at Tufts University, became available. In April 2010, I visited Roberts and her project manager Paul Fuss at their downtown Boston campus. I wanted to learn more about this research that had begun after I had left Minnesota.

On August 18, 1993, the first of thirty-seven MZA twin pairs arrived at Tufts's Human Nutrition Research Center. They came to participate in a four-day study of genetic and environmental influences on energy metabolism or body fat mass. Fifty MZT twin pairs, mostly recruited from the New England area, also took part. As Fuss explained, the study focused on individual differences in calorie intake versus energy expenditure, "and what hangs in the balance is body weight and body composition [amounts of fat, muscle, and bone]." The study's practical significance would be the identification of factors associated with body fat mass, leading to better treatments for metabolic conditions.

I spent about forty-five minutes with Roberts until she left for a series of academic meetings. She is a small, slim woman with a British accent who loves her job and works hard at it. Roberts studied nutrition as an undergraduate student at the University of London, served as a research technician in Africa, and earned a PhD at Cambridge University for her work on mathematical models of energy expenditure. She arrived in the United States as a postdoctoral fellow at the Massachusetts Institute of

Technology, where she developed interests in weight regulation. This culminated in the collaborative reared-apart/reared-together twin study that she called a "stepping stone" toward finding effective weight-control interventions.

Roberts told me she learned about the "famous MISTRA" from the professional literature in 1990 and soon after arranged to visit Bouchard in Minnesota to suggest a joint project. The MZA twins struck Roberts as "ideal research subjects" for the study she envisioned. Her initial goal was to study MZA twins and adoption triads composed of adopted children, their adoptive parents, and their biological parents. This plan was ultimately not feasible because adopted children's biological parents are difficult to find, especially their fathers, so this group was replaced with reared-together twins.

The research arrangement worked well for everyone—Roberts's 1993 five-year grant of more than one million dollars paid for twins to visit Minnesota for the five- to seven-day assessment, then fly to Boston. By the time twins left Minneapolis, they would have recovered from any jet lag they might have had initially, something that would have interfered with Roberts's findings. The twins' were housed and fed in rooms next to the laboratory so the data could be gathered under highly controlled conditions. Twins received a $260 stipend for their time as well as an opportunity to tour one of America's most beautiful cities. "We brought in every pair that Tom gave us," Roberts said. "We could have gone on longer, but our grant cycle ended."

Roberts did not collect data from the twins herself, but she greeted them all and found them to be "delightful." "There was a real joy in their reunion, and no strife between them," she told me. As part of the protocol, the twins independently selected all of their meals on the first day and were especially pleased when they picked the same items. She recalled that twins in one of our British pairs each wrote down two items that were not on the menu—hot chocolate and bananas—even though there was no place on the menu to write alternative choices. These twins had traveled to the United States on Virgin Atlantic Airlines and were so excited about coming that they wrote to the airline's founder, Sir Richard Branson, to tell him. They received a letter back and showed it proudly to the Tufts University staff.

Roberts, who had had considerable experience with research participants, observed that the twins were "more into [the study] than nontwins. They feel special. And the MZAs were definitely more into it than the MZTs . . . But they could not try to be alike on our measures," Roberts assured me. The twins slept in separate rooms in the somewhat sterile, dormitory-like quarters of the Nutrition Center, and never ate seated together, although they ate in the same dining room. Every procedure and questionnaire was completed while the twins were apart. A possible caveat was that the twins' body composition, food intake, physical activity, and energy metabolism were studied under controlled conditions rather than at home in their regular setting. This situation, and their possibly similar array of food choices from the somewhat limited menu, may have slightly inflated the heritabilities of the findings. Furthermore, the majority of both MZAs and MZTs were female, limiting the generalizability of the results. "It's hard to get men," Roberts said. Most medical and behavioral studies, including the MISTRA, enroll more females than males for several reasons. Women are more likely to seek medical attention, women may gain greater enjoyment from the social aspects of research, and the sex difference in longevity yields a higher proportion of women in all adult age categories.

After interviewing Roberts, I spent the rest of the day with project manager Paul Fuss, hearing about the study, touring the laboratories, and inspecting the equipment. I also looked through their photographs of the MISTRA twins, now familiar figures but in unfamiliar settings. Fuss said that the twins charmed him. "What struck me was that they were strangers to us, yet they were so willing to come here. They took a real leap of faith, based on Bouchard's encouragement and their trust in him." Like Roberts, Fuss sensed that the MZA twins "felt even more special than the MZTs . . . they understood their value as MZA twins: it was a unique opportunity for them to contribute to science."

Fuss specifically mentioned the switched-at-birth Canadian twins Brent and George, and George's brother Marcus, who had accidentally grown up as George's twin[29] (brief mention of these twins' compelling story can be found in Chapter 1). The three had been placed in the same temporary foster home as babies. When the elderly couple caring for them became overwhelmed by their responsibilities, they decided to move Brent and George to a different home, but they inadvertently moved George and Marcus. The twins' mother returned to claim them when they were two months of age, never suspecting that a mistake had been made; consequently, Brent went home with the adoptive family most likely intended for Marcus. The switch was discovered when the twins and Marcus turned twenty and a student who saw Brent at a college club meeting mistook him for George. According to Fuss, "George was very sensitive to Marcus. They came to Tufts shortly after the switch was discovered." Fuss also remarked on how physically different Marcus was from the MZA twins Brent and George.

The Tufts University protocol was comprehensive, using only state-of-the-art procedures. The complete list of tests and procedures, organized into the five categories of nutrient intake, body composition, energy expenditure, metabolic parameters, and substrate oxidation, is available on this book's Web site.

Twins could consume no food or beverages after 7:00 P.M. on Sunday, the day they arrived, because testing began the following Monday. Their food intake was strictly monitored to precisely measure their energy uptake and energy expenditure. Each day began at 6:30 A.M. when the researchers recorded participants' fasting gown weight and vital signs. The day ended after dinner, leaving their evenings free with one exception— they could not eat and could only drink water after 9:00 P.M. Breakfast, lunch, and dinner were scheduled for 8:00 A.M., 12:00 noon or 12:30 P.M., and 5:00 P.M., respectively, except on Thursday, when their insulin test required them to fast between 8:00 A.M. and noon for the collection of timed blood samples. The various laboratory tests and clinical procedures occupied the mornings and afternoons. Although there was some flexibility to the schedule, the strict ordering of the tests could not be changed because some later tests depended on the completion of earlier ones. Twins knew that they could decline to participate in any part of the study, as allowed by informed consent procedures, but few did.

The body composition assessment received the most attention from the investigators. One morning, the twins lay on a cot with leads (used to record voltage) attached to their right hand and foot. An electrical current passed between them, relaying information about their quantity of body fat to an attached monitor. Later in the week, they sat in a tank of warm water and submerged their heads five or six times for a measure of body density. Body fat is less dense than water, so someone with more body fat weights less under water. However, bone and muscle are denser under water, so someone with more muscle weighs more under water.[30] (Twins were told to bring bathing suits for this part of the study.) Twins would also lie on a padded table twice over a forty-minute period for a full body scan that measured their fat distribution and bone density.

The most amazing apparatus was the BOD POD, a white jellybean-shaped capsule that could assess body density (body volume plus body weight) more accurately and in less time than underwater weighing. The device relies on the displacement of air rather than water for body composition calculations. Figure 13-1 shows a pair of reared-apart twins in the BOD POD, seemingly ready to launch into outer space.

The "bubble" was less dramatic than the BOD POD, but also informative. The bubble was a clear, lightweight canopy placed over the twins'

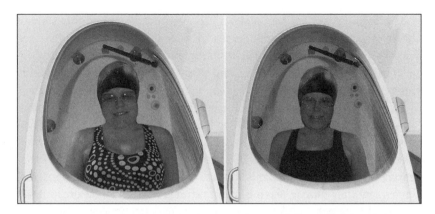

Figure 13-1. MZA female twins Jennifer Mitchell (left) and Margaret Williams, in BOD PODS. These British twins met for the first time at age fifty-seven after one discovered a time of birth recorded on her birth certificate—the unique indicator in Great Britain that one is a twin. They instantly felt like "old friends" and in correspondence to Bouchard listed similarities in "food, clothes, shops, religion, music, nail-biting, and excessive use of the telephone." The twins celebrated their seventieth birthday together at a party held at Jennifer's home in May 2011. (Photo credit Paul J. Fuss.)

heads before breakfast to measure their resting energy expenditure, or the thermic effect of feeding. When a person consumes calories, his or her energy expenditure increases so that the body can assimilate nutrients. Twins could breathe normally and watch television or read while this thirty-minute procedure took place. However, on one day the assessment continued after breakfast until noon, with the bubble on for twenty minutes out of every half-hour interval.

Throughout the four days of testing, twins sampled specific liquids and drank "palatability beverages." The liquids were part of a taste test in which different amounts of milk, cream, and sugar had been combined. Twins rated the pleasantness and sensory qualities of these liquids accordingly. The palatability drinks, ingested before lunch on three separate days, tested the effects of same-volume low fat, fat plus carbohydrate, and zero calorie concoctions upon food intake. The twins' meals were carefully weighed and measured, as were the bits of food they left behind on their plates. Anthropometric measurements were also taken on the first morning, and urinalyses were requested at preset intervals.

I knew many of the participating pairs, such as female twins Debbie and Sharon who were memorable for their religious similarities and differences discussed in Chapter 7. Debbie wrote, "We had THE best time there. We would go back in a heartbeat!" Sharon agreed: "Well, ditto on everything Debbie said. We LOVED IT. Everyone there made us feel so special—like we were the first and only twins they ever studied. They took a ton of blood work, and at the end Susan went over it with us showing how closely matched we were on things like cholesterol, considering that Debbie was macrobiotic at the time."

I asked Roberts to comment on Debbie and Sharon's resemblance because one twin was eating mostly grains and vegetables on her macrobiotic diet. Roberts was not surprised by their similarity because cholesterol level has a demonstrated heritability of 55 percent. The fact that Debbie was macrobiotic was inconsequential. Roberts also recalled a twin pair composed of one "junk food addict" and one "healthy eater" who matched across most measures except for body weight.

British twins Mary Holmes and Elaine Allin, whose religious backgrounds were also described earlier, had visited Boston for the study. Mary wrote about the twins' experiences in her wonderful 2008 book, *Being You*: "They were totally obsessed with taking our vital signs . . . It appeared that if a hair was out of place vital signs had to be taken."[31] Mary went on to describe the twins' last evening in Boston once the tests ended. All dressed up and joined by Mary's spouse, Tony, the twins spent hours at the bar of the Jacob Wirth restaurant, enjoying Tropical Sunrises because the bar had run out of their favorite, Bailey's Irish Cream. Mary described the rest of that evening. "I fell into bed but did not sleep. The room spun, I felt horribly sick. Stultified by alcohol I stumbled blindly to the bathroom. As I was throwing up I thought, with a measure of glee, *analyse that*."[32]

What Mary did not know until the next day was that her vital signs had been closely monitored for good reason. She had had a thyroidectomy a few years prior, and the Tufts University physicians discovered that her thyroid function was highly underactive, dangerously slowing down her metabolism. She was advised to seek medical attention when she returned home where she was put on medication. "I felt numb realising now why they had stopped me from doing some of the physical tests. I felt grateful and guilty simultaneously . . . Even though the intense research had been a chore and the experience often disagreeable, I felt an overwhelming debt of gratitude to Tufts University for their skilled and meticulous care."[33]

The staff also looked out for other twin pairs with specific needs. One of the few MZA twin pairs that was not part of the MISTRA had differed dramatically in their radiation exposure. One twin had spent time in Chernobyl, assisting victims of the 1986 nuclear power disaster. Even though the radiation emitted by the scheduled body scan was equivalent to just two days of natural background radiation exposure, the Tufts University physicians omitted it in her case out of caution.

There are many reasons for people to be grateful to Tufts University for findings that may significantly improve peoples' lives. In 2009, Roberts's colleague, Dr. Sonya Elder, examined genetic and environmental influences on cardiovascular disease, the leading cause of death in the United States.[34] Significant genetic influence was found on all the risk factors she measured. These risk factors included plasma lipid variables (56 to 77 percent), blood pressure (38 to 45 percent), and glucose and insulin measures (43 to 52 percent). Many people think that high-fat diets and sedentary lifestyles are the main reasons why some people develop heart disorders, but Elder challenged this view by concluding that genetic variation in the risk factors she measured is the primary reason why some people have the disease and other people do not. But she maintained that small dietary and lifestyle changes could significantly reduce cardiovascular risk in people with a family history of heart disease.

Elder also wondered whether the metabolic syndrome, which involves increased cardiovascular disease risk, hypertension, glucose intolerance, and visceral fatness and affects over 34 percent of American adults, was influenced by the same factors as cardiovascular disease. She determined that waist circumference, plasma glucose, plasma triglyceride concentration, and diastolic blood pressure were affected by the same genes, possibly those relating to insulin resistance. Insulin resistance is a possible underlying cause of the metabolic syndrome, so cardiovascular disease and the metabolic syndrome could have a common origin.

The Federation of American Societies for Experimental Biology annually hosts small research groups to discuss results from ongoing projects. These summer sessions are held in various locations around the world. In 2009, Elder presented a study on the twins' eating behaviors at one of these meetings.[35] Her study differed from Hur's previous work that had focused on the twins' nutrient intake. Instead, Elder targeted the twins' hunger, disinhibition, and restraint. *Hunger* refers to feelings of being hungry and the behavioral consequences of these feelings. Hunger differs from *disinhibition,* which is a decrease in dietary self-control due to emotions, alcohol, or other events. *Restraint* refers to the purposeful limitation of food intake that ignores physiological cues. Factors affecting these three eating behaviors could help, or hinder, weight-conscious individuals in their quest for a desired physique. The information was obtained from true-false items in the Three-Factor Eating Questionnaire.[36]

Disinhibition was assessed by items such as "I usually eat too much at social occasions, like parties and picnics." Restraint was assessed by items such as "I deliberately take small helpings as a means of controlling my weight." Hunger was assessed by items such as "I am usually so hungry that I eat more than three meals a day." Another part of the questionnaire asked about the frequency of related eating behaviors.

Elder showed that a person's environment was the most important influence on disinhibition and on restraint. Disinhibition is a strong predictor of weight gain and can cause some people to add forty pounds between twenty and fifty years of age, probably because metabolism begins to slow down. Roberts was especially excited by the Disinhibition results. The finding that disinhibitory eating was largely learned gave Roberts confidence that effective behavioral interventions to curb this type of eating are likely. She explained that the learned component of disinhibition is the reward, the dopamine surge that follows this type of eating. But she was surprised by the results, expecting cultural norms to have played a greater role in disinhibition—cultures affect social conventions such as appropriate meal times and acceptance of food from others.

It may be prudent to be more cautious than Roberts in thinking about finding ways to control disinhibitory eating. Many learned behaviors, such as closing a car door and stopping at a red light, would be difficult to change. The effectiveness of eating-control interventions may rely partly on genetically influenced personality traits such as conscientiousness and agreeableness and thus would need to be tailored to each individual's behavioral profile.

It was surprising to find that Disinhibition did not show genetic influence. Disinhibitory eating would seem to have an impulsivity component, a behavior with demonstrated genetic effects (0.40).[37] In reconciling these results, Roberts referred to Elder's finding that some people are more aware of their hunger than others; the internal locus for hunger had a substantial genetic component (0.50).[38] Roberts suggested that impulsivity may be situation specific and might not apply to eating situations. This is an interesting idea, but one that needs testing. Impulsive eating might lessen at formal dinners or family gatherings where eating habits can be observed, but it may increase at home or at work when no one is watching.

Roberts wished that her twin research could have continued as a longitudinal study rather than a cross-sectional one.[39] "I am an intervention person," she said, meaning that studying people over time would help in the development and monitoring of dietary controls. Roberts was also excited, but overwhelmed by the quantity of accumulated data, confident that ten more papers could be written. She listed the heritability of food preference, energy intake, satiety, and physical activity as future topics, with the goal of exploring common genetic links between physical activity and body fat. She takes pride in having brought methodological strength to her area of research.

Roberts seemed "hooked" on MZA twin studies and, like most investigators, regretful that she had not gathered more data at the time of the study. What more could have been added? Fuss suggested that if the study were conducted today, the researchers would have included additional genotyping components for linking DNA markers to body composition characteristics and chronic illness susceptibility. This would help to identify people at risk for cardiac and metabolic diseases, allowing preventative measures to be introduced more quickly.

In summing up his experiences with the MZA twins, Fuss said, "I can say without exception that there were no bad experiences. [Working with the MISTRA twins] was a life-changing experience. It was unusual in that you knew the twins so well in such a short time. More than any other study I have worked on, the data were truly humanized." Fuss also enjoyed his role as "travel guide and tour agent" for many twins who were visiting Boston for the first time.

During interviews with Roberts, Fuss, and many other MISTRA investigators, I found that the focus often shifted away from the research to the twins' life stories. For many of these researchers, it was probably the first time that they experienced the bringing together of great scientific stories and dramatic life events. "This study was hard to top," Fuss confessed. He is no longer in touch with the twins as before, but he loves receiving their holiday cards.

Facial Expressivity

The efforts of many individuals enriched the breadth and scope of the MISTRA. One such contributor to the study was psychologist Paul Ekman from the University of California–San Francisco. Ekman is renowned for his work on the universal linkage of human emotions and facial expressivity. Because of him, eighteen MZA and ten DZA twin pairs watched movies while research staff watched movies of them watching movies. Other contributors to the study were psychiatrist Kenneth Kendler and his colleagues from Virginia Commonwealth University in Richmond.

MZA twins Roger and Tony conveyed as much emotional content with their faces as with their words. They were expressive and responsive in conversations, making it possible to track their emotions as the topics changed. Lucky and Dianne, Daphne and Barbara, and Sharon and Debbie were just as demonstrative. These twins variously smiled broadly, rolled their eyes, and shook their heads. Twins in some other pairs were harder to "read," because they showed fewer facial emotions during their interactions with the staff.

As recently as 2007, little behavioral genetic work had been done on individual differences in facial expressivity. The MISTRA's Emotional Reaction Study, designed by Ekman, was the first twin study to assess genetic and environmental influence on spontaneous emotional expressions.[40] During the informed consent procedure on the first assessment day, we told the twins that we would film them during one activity only, but we would not say which one. We assured them that we would tell them once the activity had ended.

Ekman selected three short films designed to elicit emotional reactions. Twins first watched three one-minute clips of pleasant subjects, which included a gorilla playing at the zoo, ocean waves hitting a beach, and a puppy playing with a flower. These clips were followed by two two-minute films, one of men hurt badly in an accident and one of a medical training scene involving burn treatment and surgeries. A concealed video camera captured the twins' responses.

The Facial Action Coding System designed by Ekman and his colleague Wally Friesen allows for the analysis of forty-four different action units (expressions). Two certified judges viewed the films, each rating the expressions of just one co-twin in a pair to avoid bias. For ease of analysis with our small sample, the judges organized the action units into two positive emotions (happiness and surprise) and three negative emotions (sadness, anger, and disgust).

Genetic influence was found on the variability in positive emotional expressions such as surprise but not for happiness. In contrast, genetic effects on the variability in negative emotional expressions were not found. It is likely that most of the twins showed similar signs of sadness, anger, or disgust when viewing the accident victims or burn patients, overwhelming any individual differences. It was also found that response duration was more genetically influenced than response frequency. Perhaps people react similarly to some events as they unfold, but vary in the time taken to express or dampen their emotions. Regardless, the heritability of the facial expressivity measures showed a wide range (35 to 75 percent), so additional work with larger samples is needed.

This study reinforced my observation that the MZA twins' emotions and emotional expressions matched when they first met. Looking closely at some twins' reunion tapes, I could see that the facial expressions of joy, shock, interest, and disbelief were alike between co-twins. However, I was especially interested in the reunion experience of Jack Yufe (the

MZA twin raised Jewish in Trinidad) who met his twin brother Oskar Stohr (raised Catholic in Nazi Germany) at age twenty. This event was not taped, but Jack recalled that he was slightly embarrassed to see someone "wearing" his face.[41] It may also be that Jack and Oskar's initial facial expressions and his co-twin's perceptions of his expressions shaped the cool tone of their twinship at that time. A wonderful film, *Oskar and Jack,* shows the twins together for the first time in Germany, but it does not capture their moment of meeting.[42]

Oskar and Jack did not meet again until they came to Minnesota at age forty-six. When they arrived at the Twin Cities airport on separate flights, each twin wanted to see his brother before his brother saw him— just as it was twenty-six years earlier.

General Intelligence and Special Abilities

Studies of general intelligence were a mainstay of the MISTRA's research program, and not just because the origins of intelligence had a long tradition in individual differences research. It was because ongoing controversies over genetic explanations of ability, the structure of g, and the nature of sex differences in some mental skills focused research attention on intelligence.[43] Everyone was interested in the MISTRA's findings, even those who criticized the ideas and methods. But what gets published also reflects who is in the laboratory and when. Because former graduate student and postdoctoral fellow Wendy Johnson was interested in the origins of general intelligence, she pursued these interests often and from several angles.

Key articles in Johnson's later series of intelligence studies were replication of evidence for "just one g"[44] and replication of the Visual-Perceptual-Image Rotation model of mental ability structure,[45] referenced in Chapter 12. Another key accomplishment was a 2007 analysis of genetic and environmental influences on the Verbal-Perceptual-Image Rotation model.[46] This was the most complete MISTRA study on intelligence since data collection ended. It included seventy-four MZA twin pairs and fifty-two DZA twin pairs, for a total of 126 pairs.[47]

The Verbal-Perceptual-Image Rotation model is composed of four levels or strata. They include general intelligence or g as the fourth stratum, three broad categories called Verbal, Perceptual, and Image Rotation as the third stratum, eight specific abilities (e.g., Number Content Memory and Fluency) as the second stratum, and specialized skills that may reflect specific learning experiences or events as the first stratum. The strata are arranged hierarchically with g at the top. The second strata factors are variously linked to the third strata factors; for example, Fluency is associated with Verbal, and Number is associated with both Verbal and Perceptual.

The portion of genetic variance associated with the factors at each strata was high and consistent across measures (69 to 79 percent). The only exception concerned Content Memory, a second strata factor that showed relatively little genetic influence (.33). Content Memory includes immediate and delayed recall of information, as tested by the ability to recall pictures of common objects immediately after and some time after seeing them. It also includes remembering meaningless and meaningful associations between things, as tested by the ability to recall pairs of figures and numbers, and pairs of items and descriptors. It is possible that Content Memory is affected more by experience than by genes. The best waiters and waitresses are those who easily remember the orders from a table of eight. Memory skills may develop the longer one is a restaurant employee, but it is also possible that people with good memories seek positions that let them use their talents.

The proportion of genetic variance shown by g was a curious number (0.77). Anyone who recalls the Cyril Burt controversy involving Burt's possibly fabricated reared-apart twins, assistants, and data knows the significance of this number. Burt's alleged fraud was suspected because several replications of his MZA IQ analyses yielded correlations of 0.771.

Johnson's paper had an impact on the way psychologists thought about intelligence. Professor Tony Vernon believes that "Tables 6 and 7 in this article will become classics," based on the strong evidence for genes shared among the Verbal-Perceptual-Image Rotation factors. In thinking about her article, Johnson said, "The main response I got was that everyone wanted to know what heritability we had gotten for the g factor, making me realize how much that particular tidbit was buried within the paper." In fact, this figure (0.77) occurred in the last line of a substantial table, and was referenced only briefly in the results. I'm referring to it now because it was exactly what Burt had found: a 0.77 heritability means that 77 percent of the general ability differences among people are associated with genetic differences between them. It also means that about 23 percent of the differences are associated with differences in their environments, plus measurement error. Recall that studies of intelligence based on other behavioral genetic designs tend to produce a lower estimate of genetic influence because they estimate heritability indirectly. The MZA correlation estimates heritability directly.

The MZA and DZA g factor correlations were also omitted from the article, but I obtained them from Bouchard when I visited Minnesota in

October 2009 (MZA: 0.73, DZA: 0.47). I imagine that other readers wanted them as well. The MZA *g* correlation was nearly identical to the estimated heritability of 0.77. Bouchard also provided the twins' WAIS IQ correlations (MZA: 0.62, DZA: 0.50). The larger MZA than DZA correlation was consistent with genetic influence on IQ, but the MZA value and MZA-DZA difference were lower than what was found for the *g* factor correlations. This may reflect the greater reliability of the *g* factor score, but other explanations are possible.

By 2010, Johnson had thought more about other aspects of her study since its original publication:

> I've come to understand much more clearly how very little genetic correlations can actually tell us about how systems of traits come together. If a genetically influenced disease causes cognitive decline and that disease occurs in a sample, there *will* be a genetic correlation between cognitive function and the disease, even if it's the disease that causes the cognitive problem directly, without any overtly common genes between cognitive function and the disease.

For example, inherited eye disorders, such as the macular dystrophies, cause visual loss in children, teenagers, and adults.[48] Knowledge of impending blindness understandably causes depression and apathy, behaviors that could interfere with mental performance. The connection between the eye disorder and either depression or lowered ability could be conceivably, but incorrectly, explained by shared genetic factors.

Johnson continued, "So today, I might separately examine the heritability of *g* and the patterns of genetic correlations, with specific emphasis on all their possible interpretations." I am sure that discussion of these issues will affect how researchers interpret their findings in the future. Even genetic appearance can be deceptive. Johnson has since addressed these topics in subsequent research papers.[49]

Although it is not reported in Johnson's article, the IQ differences between MZA co-twins are of interest, relative to those from previous MZT and MZA twin studies. The average IQ difference between MZT twins is 6 points, although the range can be considerable.[50] The average within-pair IQ differences for twins in the three previous studies varied from 7.25 to 14.00 points, with a range of 1 to 24 points for individual pairs. The within-pair difference for MZA twins (n = 70 pairs) in the MISTRA was 7.07 (standard deviation = 5.83), with a range of 0 to 29 points. These findings further underline the prenatal and postnatal environmental effects on general intelligence, the importance of assessing cognitive ability using different samples, and the need to include multiple ability measures in psychological research. The DZA within-pair IQ difference for the MISTRA twins (n = 53 pairs) was 8.78 (standard deviation = 7.09), with a range of 0 to 25. The average DZT twin difference is 10 points, but also varies across studies.[51]

Bouchard included a simple, but extraordinary table in his 2009 review paper of research on g.[52] The table lists the MZA general intelligence correlations from the three early twin studies, the Swedish Adult Twin Study of Aging, and the MISTRA. Collectively, these studies provide further support for the finding that individual differences in intelligence have a substantial genetic basis. The weighted mean of the IQ correlations from these five different studies, conducted in four different countries, is 0.74 (n = 187 pairs). This was another example of constructive replication, as was Johnson's article reporting a value of 0.77 for the g factor heritability, in which Johnson used different measures of the twins' intelligence levels than the other studies. Results from different psychological investigations rarely come that close.

Because of the quality, breadth, and availability of the twin and spouse data, Johnson and Bouchard also used it to explore sex differences in mental skills as well as relationships among general ability, specific abilities, and interests. Some of this work did not have a "twin angle"—nontwins could have been used in some analyses, assuming they had completed the same extensive test battery.

Sex differences in special mental abilities, but not in general intelligence, have been observed for decades. Males tend to excel in visual and spatial tasks, while females generally excel in verbal and perceptual speed tasks.[53] These are average differences only—there is plenty of overlap among the sexes, making it impossible to know someone's sex from his or her test scores. A given male could perform above the female mean on a verbal fluency test, and a given female could perform above the male mean on a mental rotation test. In fact, our highest scorer on the Shepard-Metzler Rotation task, an activity in which males typical excel, was a female twin.

Building upon her Verbal-Perceptual-Image Rotation model studies, Johnson examined the structure of mental abilities after statistically controlling for the effects of general intelligence.[54] She relied on data from the forty-two mental ability tests comprising the Hawaii Ability Battery, Comprehensive Ability Battery, and WAIS IQ test. Three underlying dimensions emerged—rotation-verbal, focus-diffusion, and content memory—each involving different abilities. People with different mental skills are found at different places along these dimensions. For example, people close to the rotation pole of the rotation-verbal dimension did better at spatial and rotation tasks than they did on vocabulary, spelling and verbal interpretation tasks, and vice versa.

Johnson found that males clustered toward the rotation and focus poles of the rotation-verbal and focus-diffusion dimensions, while females tended toward the verbal and diffusion poles. Females also clustered toward the "good memory" pole of the content memory dimension more often than males. None of this was surprising. These results matched the findings in the psychological literature showing small, but consistent sex differences in these measures. Of course, both males and females are expected to be found at any position along the poles, just not in equal numbers.

The more interesting results from this study concerned sex differences in the residual scores. Residual scores were derived by stripping the forty-two mental ability test scores of the effects of age, and both age and *g*. Once this was done, sex differences in the residual scores were *greater than* the sex differences in the original scores. The fact that sex differences in ability increased once *g* was removed suggested that *g* may represent a general problem solving ability that hides sex-related differences in specific skills. The residual scores also showed similar degrees of genetic influence (0.38–0.70), as did the original test scores (0.33–0.79), with Memory Content again showing the lowest heritability (0.38). This result suggested that residual abilities follow systematic patterns that are biologically rooted in the brain.

Johnson produced evidence that the tests did not measure the same things in the same way for people positioned differently along the poles. People presented with the same problem might try to solve it differently. One person might mentally rotate an image to determine its appearance from another angle, while someone else might draw a series of figures to try to find a solution. One person might take a "mental snapshot" of an image he or she wished to remember, while someone else might verbally describe the image to himself or herself.

The origins of sex differences in mental ability have yet to be fully known, but sex differences in brain structures, physiological functions, and neurological features might hold answers, the subject of a subsequent paper by Johnson and Bouchard.[55] Male brains are more lateralized than female brains, meaning that males' different mental functions are found more exclusively in the brains' left hemisphere (verbal) and right hemisphere (nonverbal). Females' brains are relatively less lateralized, so their verbal and nonverbal functions are distributed across both hemispheres to a greater degree than are males'.[56] Hormonal influences also affect mental functioning. For example, females show better spatial skill performance during the menstrual phase of their menstrual cycle compared to the midluteal phase, consistent with normal fluctuations of estradiol and progesterone.[57]

Biological measures could be examined in conjunction with psychometric measures. Substantial correlations have been reported between general mental ability, total brain volume, and volumes of gray and white matter in specific brain regions.[58] Johnson created two novel WAIS scores ([Block Design – Vocabulary]/Full Scale IQ and [Block Design + Information – Coding – Digit Span]/Full Scale IQ) that correlated highly with the rotation-verbal dimension (0.69). She suggested that these novel scores could be useful in biological brain studies.[59] For example, it may be that these scores, which are associated with peoples' positions along the rotation-verbal pole, reflect sex differences in brain structures and processes, an idea that could be tested with brain-imaging studies. In 2008, Johnson's group went on to show associations between the rotation-verbal and focus-diffusion dimensions and gray matter in two brain regions.[60]

There are many studies on the nature and origin of mental skills, interests, and occupational pursuits. However, these areas have remained largely separate from one another. Understanding associations between mental abilities and interest-occupation groups was the focus of the next MISTRA study.

There is a common belief that people are interested in activities in which they perform well. But the causal direction is unclear—are we interested in what we are good at, or are we good at what we are interested in? It is easy to understand how we might look for opportunities that allow expression of our best skills. MZA twins Tom and Steve (who were not in the MISTRA) were both weight lifters who owned their own gyms, one in New Jersey and the other in Kansas. Tamara and Adriana performed separate modern dance routines, one in New York City and the other on Long Island, until their chance reunion let them dance together.[61] The twins in both these sets had the body builds conducive to the physical pursuits that engaged them, as well as the resources and support. But exposure to activities is not enough. The fireman twins, Mark and Jerry, never adopted their mothers' interests in opera and ballet, openly showing disdain for these activities. The twins preferred going fishing, watching television, and drinking beer with their firehouse friends. Perhaps there were commonalities among these twins' interests and occupations. Johnson used latent class analysis to find out.

Latent class analysis is a statistical procedure that provides groupings of individuals, rather than groupings of variables. For example, many people are interested in athletics, but some people like noncompetitive activities such as individual weight-training or floor exercise. These people might also enjoy editing manuscripts or computer programming, occupations that are practiced indoors and are noncompetitive. Similarly, Johnson was interested in identifying groups of people whose interests and occupations had common features.[62] She was also interested in whether sex differences in mental skills affected sex differences across interest-occupation groups. MISTRA data from the Strong-Campbell Interest Inventory and Jackson Vocational Interest Survey were available for this purpose. Johnson also used the twins' mental ability test scores derived from the Verbal-Perceptual-Image Rotation model analyses discussed previously.

Johnson's study was exploratory in nature with no specified hypotheses or predictions. Using latent class analysis, she created eight interest-occupational groups, ranging from "adventure" to "personal care," but there was nothing magical about this number—her choice of groups generated by the data was somewhat subjective and practical.

Johnson found greater differences among interest groups in general intelligence than in abilities. Higher intelligence groups also showed greater diversity of interests than lower intelligence groups. More job options may, therefore, be available for smarter people who, as Johnson notes, probably capitalize on the features of their jobs that they enjoy most. In fact, most college professors love the intellectual challenge inherent in their occupation, but variously prefer its teaching or research opportunities.

Johnson also discovered greater sex differences in the twins' interests than in their abilities. Overall, fifty-six percent of men were classified into groups that included 1 percent of women, and 70 percent of women were classified in groups that included 7 percent of men. Interest-occupation groups that were especially sex-polarized were Adventure (0.01 women, 0.99 men) and Administration (0.94 women, 0.06 men).[63] Social pressures and biological factors, but probably both, could account for this finding. Selective attention to events in the environment may also contribute to these differences. We know that female infants prefer to look at faces and male infants prefer to stare at mobiles.[64] Male infants are also more successful than female infants on age-appropriate mental rotation tasks.[65] If and how these early sex differences lay the basis for later sex differences in verbal and spatial skills are unanswered. One possibility is that personality traits mediate our choice of activities. The data to test this idea exist, and maybe one day Johnson will get to them.

The Traditional Moral Values Triad

The MISTRA's poststudy period from 2006 and beyond included studies on many unrelated topics, as in the preceding years. There was value to this variety; it reflected the wide range of behaviors examined by the collaborators when the data were available and when they had the time to explore it. Throughout this book I have emphasized empirical twin analyses, but provocative themes were also found in some of the chapters published in volumes organized around special topics. Unfortunately, such volumes draw less attention because they often take longer to publish than journal articles, making the information somewhat dated, and these books are expensive. In two MISTRA-related book chapters on religious behavior and beliefs, Bouchard and his former student Laura Koenig brought name and definition to one of Bouchard's main interests—the Traditional Moral Values Triad.

It was unusual for Bouchard to think in threes after years of thinking in twos, but the research findings were responsible for this one adjustment. Psychologists had defined three major attitudinal and belief dimensions, namely, authoritarianism, religiousness, and conservatism, all of which the MISTRA had studied separately or in combination.[66] Bouchard united them in a bigger way as traditionalism or the Traditional Moral Values Triad. His justification was not just the 0.50–0.70 correlation among the various measures of these dimensions—he used evolutionary reasoning to explain why the three formed a likely and sensible cluster.[67]

In the early and final versions of his book chapters, written in 2009 and in 2010, Bouchard asked three simple but profound questions that he believes are confronted by children in modern society: (1) "Who is in charge?" (2) "What does he/she want?" and (3) "What do I do?" All three questions concern family and group relations, and probably arose as human society and human intelligence evolved.

Bouchard identified the adaptive human tendency to obey authority as the mechanism that could illuminate the three questions posed above. If the reference is the family, then the answer to question one is the parent or caretaker. In support of this idea, I recall an amusing but telling conversation between one of my colleagues and her belligerent seven-year-old son to whom she asserted forcefully, "I am the adult, and I make the rules." Alternatively, if the reference is the greater universe, then the answer is supernatural beliefs, God(s), or agents outside the visible world. Bouchard noted that such views were reasonable in light of available knowledge. In fact, he noted that his own "favorite entities, genes," regarded as having causal influence on behavior, were neither visible nor tangible until genetic advances made them so.

Bouchard asserted that obedience underlies traditionalism and is a likely adaptation, given its universality in childhood. Not all children are equally obedient, and some are defiant, but those who follow the rules are generally more socially successful than those who do not. Evidence suggesting that Traditionalism may enhance reproductive fitness comes from links between higher conservatism, higher fertility, and earlier child-bearing as well as genetic influences on fertility and social attitudes.[68] The studies on age at menarche and age at first intercourse, described earlier in this chapter and elsewhere, showed genetic effects. No one knows for certain how attitudes and fitness measures mesh, but Bouchard believes that twins can provide answers: longitudinal analyses of twins' reproductive fitness correlates and social attitudes could clarify connections between the two. Does having children enhance conservative attitudes in their parents, or does being conservative enhance childbearing? Longitudinal studies do not reveal causal connections, only experimental studies do—but twin studies are experiments that are created naturally.[69]

Bouchard and colleagues authored several chapters and reviews on intelligence, intelligence tests, heritability, and other topics between 2006 and 2010. A survey of organizational behavior showed that twin research had advanced since our 1989 job satisfaction paper, but many behaviors such as factors affecting job and occupational switching were still unexplored.[70] The job histories that were gathered from the twins, beginning with the part-time jobs they held while still in school, would enable such a study. Perhaps a MISTRA colleague reading this will be inspired to take a closer look.

Bouchard also authored a tribute to developmental behavioral geneticist Sandra Scarr, arguing for strong inference as a strategy for scientific advance.[71] Based on a 1964 article by John R. Platt,[72] strong inference includes the systematic application of alternative hypotheses, the design of multiple experiments, the carrying out of these experiments, and the repeating of this process. Bouchard identified quantitative genetic analysis as exemplary of the strategy of strong inference.

Birth Order

In 2008, psychologist Shirley McGuire from the University of San Francisco and I attempted a study that I had thought about for some time—a test of Frank Sulloway's birth-order theory using MZA twins.[73] Sulloway showed that firstborns tend to be traditional and conventional, while later-borns tend to be risk-taking and rebellious.[74] It appeared that a novel test of his model could be done using an MZA twin design because birth-order effects would be unconfounded by genetic influences on personality. Many co-twins occupied different birth-order positions in their separate rearing families. We reasoned that if MZA co-twins placed in different birth-order positions showed Sulloway's expected birth order and personality relationships, this would add to research demonstrating sibship position effects on personality. Birth order could then be considered part of the nonshared environmental influences on personality, partly explaining differences between co-twins. We used birth order and personality data from the MISTRA and from the Swedish Adoption Twin Study of Aging.

We found that co-twins in different birth-order positions did not show meaningful personality differences, but the sample sizes were too small to permit firm conclusions. In fact, the small numbers of twins in the various birth-order combinations reduced our comparisons to just same birth-order versus different birth-order groups. Moreover, our personality data were self-ratings rather than ratings made specifically in comparison with the co-twin, which are more sensitive to birth-order effects.[75] Other factors, such as twins' age at adoption, gender of siblings, age spacing, and rearing status of siblings (biological or adoptive) also needed to be considered. Some studies are theoretically compelling but practically undoable, and this may be one of them, at least at this time.

Handedness

The MISTRA's handedness data were not published at the time of this writing, but they were important to include in this book, given the generally higher proportion of left-handedness in twins than nontwins (14.5 percent versus 9.9 percent)[76] and the similar frequency of left-handedness in MZ and DZ twin pairs.[77] Increased left-handedness in twins has been variously linked to delayed zygotic splitting among approximately 10 percent to 25 percent of MZ twins, the increased prenatal adversities (e.g., premature birth) affecting both types of twins (but especially MZ twins), and associations between familial left-handedness and twinning.[78] However, a 2003 study questioned the higher rate of left-handedness in twins, having found similar rates among twins and their nontwin siblings.[79]

The MISTRA twins completed the Oldfield Handedness Inventory, a twenty-item self-report form that asks subjects how often they use their left or right hand to perform various unimanual (e.g., writing and drawing) and bimanual (e.g., peeling a potato and opening a bottle) tasks.[80] Ratings are made on a nine-point scale (1 = left always to 9 = right always).

Beginning in 1982, we assessed the twins' hand preference, both by observing them perform the tasks specified by the twenty items and administering the self-report form at another time. This procedure let us assess the validity of the self-report; item analysis for the first 113 individual twins showed inconsistencies in some items, although not necessarily in handedness classification. The analyses reported here used the behavioral assessment data except for cases in which only the self-report form was available.[81]

Handedness data were available for 247 twin individuals, 94 males and 153 females. The twins' handedness preferences were categorized using the Crovitz-Zener scoring and classification scheme (right: 14 to 30, mixed: 31 to 40, left: 41 to 70) based on the first fourteen items of our inventory.[82] There were 200 right-handers (81 percent), 24 left-handers (10 percent), and 23 mixed-handers (9 percent) among the MISTRA twins. Organizing the twins according to right-handedness and non-right-handedness yielded 47 (19 percent) non-right-handers, nearly twice as many as the expected 10 percent of non-right-handers in the general population. The proportions of non-right-handed twin individuals were similar for the MZA (16 percent) and DZA (23 percent) twins.[83] The proportions of hand-concordant and hand-discordant pairs, across handedness categories and overall, are shown in Table 13-1. The proportions of nonconcordant pairs did not differ between the MZA (24 percent) and DZA (35 percent) twins.[84]

The 24 percent hand-discordance among the MZA twin pairs matched the 25 percent figure reported in the literature for MZT twin pairs. The 35 percent hand-concordance of DZA twins is somewhat high but consistent with the equal number of non-right-handedness in both twin groups. Overall, these early results agree with previous findings of elevated

Table 13-1. Handedness Concordance and Discordance for MZA and DZA Twin Pairs

Handedness	MZA (%) 74 pairs	DZA (%) 55 pairs
Right-left	15	18
Right-mixed	8	15
Left-left	0	2
Left-mixed	1	2
Mixed-mixed	3	5
Right-right	73	58
Hand-concordant	76	65
Hand-discordant	24	35

left-handedness in reared-together twin samples. Our MZA handedness findings also agree with those of Shields and Juel-Nielsen who observed hand-discordance in 16 percent and 18 percent[85] of their samples, respectively; in contrast, 45 percent of twenty MZA twin pairs studied by Newman et al. (original nineteen pairs plus one pair identified after the study was published) were opposite-handed. Methodological differences may explain the discrepancy—Newman et al. assessed handedness by wrist tapping and finger tapping tasks, whereas Shields administered handedness items and a handedness questionnaire, similar to the MISTRA.[86] Juel-Nielsen did not specify his handedness assessment procedure.

The reared-apart twins' handedness data are relevant to the fundamental principle underlying twin methodology, namely, that the trait-relevant environments of MZ and DZ twins must be equivalent in order to examine the heritability of a trait. However, a subset of MZ twins differ in handedness because of delayed division of the zygote, a process that does not apply to DZ twins. Therefore, it would be inappropriate to use a conventional MZ-DZ twin comparison to assess genetic influence on hand preference, as I will illustrate.

In 1957, biologist David Merrell observed, "The discordance between identical twins proves the importance of environmental factors while the discordance between a left-handed child and his completely right-handed cultural and familial environment indicate the importance of innate factors in the development of handedness."[87] Subsequent family and adoption studies of handedness have shown genetic influence on hand preference,[88] but conventional twin comparisons would suggest otherwise—as would the data from the MISTRA.

Mental Ability Again

In late March 2011, Irving Gottesman sent me a new mental ability paper from the MISTRA, authored by Johnson and Bouchard.[89] This paper was neither a literature review nor an empirical analysis. It began with a concise survey of research on the structure of human ability and a brief description of the MISTRA's mental ability measures and findings from previous reports. A new finding concerned the adjustment of the sample's mean IQ score from 109.7 (standard deviation = 11.8; range: 79 to 140), based on 1995 norms, to 101.3 (standard deviation = 14.8; range: 61.1 to 139.9), based on the average rate of secular change.

But this new paper was unlike any other that Bouchard or anyone else from the study had published previously because it furnished the correlation matrix generated by the forty-two mental ability tests completed by the MISTRA participants. Johnson and Bouchard explained, "The purpose of this paper is to make the MISTRA dataset available to other researchers so that it can be used both to generate new ways of thinking about mental ability and to attempt to replicate findings generated in other datasets."[90] The inclusion of the data matrix was surprising at first because the MISTRA data were hard to come by and the data had never been publicly released—but Bouchard was all about replication, and the time was right. It was interesting to speculate as to what would be said by critics who claimed Bouchard was too protective of his data.

A second 2011 paper by doctoral student Jason Major at the University of Edinburgh, together with Johnson and Bouchard, used the reared-apart twins' mental ability test data to show why single-factor models do not adequately represent g.[91] Data supplementary to this article are available online.

Nearly Final Comment

It is almost impossible to believe that, by this point in the book, I have surveyed the MISTRA's entire publication list. The most satisfying part of this process has been the long conversations with friends and colleagues who couldn't resist revisiting this exciting and challenging time in their careers. It is gratifying to have rekindled the interest of some collaborators in data they had forgotten about or didn't know existed. Michalowicz will be exploring associations between oral diseases (e.g., tooth loss) and cardiovascular health (e.g., blood pressure) using data from his periodontal studies and the Tufts University body composition battery. He explained that relationships between periodontal disease and heart disease may arise through common genes. Hanson believes the twins' stress test data are unique and should be analyzed for measures such as heart rate and blood pressure at each three-minute stage. Few people complete a 21-minute graded exercise test, so the variability in these measures might reflect genetic factors, with implications for health and training.

Johnson wants to examine assortative mating for intelligence and the stability of g across test batteries. The collaborators at Tufts University are planning a paper on predictors of energy intake and dietary composition using the twin data, an effort led by doctoral student Lorien Urban. Sonya Elder, also from Tufts University, will be completing her study of the twins' eating behaviors. Bouchard is planning an analysis of the twins' creativity involving their drawings of a person and a house, captured on videotape. I hope to explore associations between the twins' spatial abilities and hand preference. Several articles and chapters on the heritability of behavior, general intelligence, body fatness, and religiosity are in press or under review.[92] I also hope to explore Bouchard's treasury of tapes if and when they are transformed to DVD. In addition to the Juel-Nielsen interview described in Chapter 3, I watched the only other tape that had been converted—a 1979 semistructured life events interview with one of the Jim twins by Tellegen and Gottesman. Such interviews were informative sessions, revealing significant features of the twins' lives and showing their movements and gestures as they spoke.

The ongoing and planned analyses of the reared-apart data show that, although the MISTRA may be complete, it is not really over. The impact of this project on research and reasoning about the origins of individual differences in intelligence, personality, attitudes, interests, values, talents, and so much more will undoubtedly persist far into the future.

CHAPTER FOURTEEN

Questions, Answers, and Twin Studies of the Future

N|o one could satisfy the MISTRA's critics while the study was in progress, but I have the benefit of time. Over thirty years have passed since the project began, and over ten years have passed since it ended. The bitter 1970s nature-nurture debates have largely (but not completely) subsided as evidence of genetic influence on behavior has accumulated. Most serious scholars have accepted the body of work produced by the MISTRA and related studies, and many individuals have rethought the significance of their own findings in light of this work. Researchers have moved on to explore new and interesting questions about factors affecting behavior, some of which I describe at the end of this chapter. What follows are summaries of the challenges, objections, and accusations voiced by the MISTRA's critics and responses to them. Some issues discussed earlier are revisited here because of their importance—and because some serious misunderstandings of twin research designs, findings, and implications remain.[1]

The MISTRA's Data Collection Procedures: Fair or Biased?

The MISTRA's data collection procedures were criticized based on assumptions rather than facts. Some critics assumed that the twins exchanged information during the assessment, the intelligence tests and personality inventories were flawed, and the occasional use of the same tester for both co-twins yielded biased data.

Beginning with the first assessment day and as part of the informed consent procedure, Bouchard routinely requested that the twins refrain from discussing the research activities until both had completed them. Everyone was confident that the twins and their companions understood the reason for this and fully complied.

To the extent that the staff and budget allowed, every effort was made to keep the data free from potential biases by following procedures set by Bouchard. Twins were always seated apart as they completed their inventory booklet in the MISTRA's laboratory or elsewhere. A staff member was always present during these sessions to answer the twins' questions privately, if any arose. Two staff members independently reviewed each twin's inventories for completion and clarity, noting questions that needed additional attention from the twins.

The use of separate examiners (unrelated to the study) and simultaneous testing of twins were strictly followed for the IQ testing because of its controversial nature and because the early reared-apart twin investigators had been criticized for sometimes testing both twins. Simultaneous and separate (or consecutive) testing by different examiners was in place for most activities, with some exceptions, such as the medical/psychiatric interviews administered to the early twin pairs and David Lykken's psychophysiological battery that the twins did in reverse order on different days. Kevin Haroian who tested both twins in Lykken's laboratory told me that "the computer controlled the presentation. We never saw any systematic differences between the twin tested on Monday and the twin tested on Tuesday." Several other exceptions included taking the joint twin photographs, videotaping a joint interview immediately after the individual interviews, and administering the special mental ability battery (due to concerns over examiner differences in administration).

Some tests, such as the general physical examination, chest x-ray, stress electrocardiogram, special mental ability battery, and psychomotor tasks, were administered to co-twins by the same physician, psychologist, or staff member. Testing related individuals can conceivably bias researchers' expectations for the second participant based on the performance of the first. However, what seems like reasonable inference can prove insignificant upon closer inspection.

Bouchard pointed out long ago that those who raised such objections were the same people who reexamined the data with full knowledge of the twins' IQ differences.[2] In other words, critics who categorized the early pairs by age at separation, contact, and other factors had access to these twins' IQ scores, so their categorization may not have been done blindly.

The burden of proof lies with the critics—bias must be demonstrated, not assumed. The critics of reared-apart twin studies never conducted a formal test of their assumptions, but I did. In 1991, I compared IQ intra-class correlations for MZT and DZT twin children (all of whom I tested myself) with twin children from a different sample (in which I tested only one twin). The intraclass correlations hardly differed between sample 1 (MZT: 0.84, n=68; .DZT: 0.54, n=34) and sample 2 (MZT: 0.88, n=28; DZT: 0.54, n=34). I concluded that when examiners follow well-prescribed administrative and scoring rules tester bias is negligible or absent.[3]

Several of the collaborators commented on the possibility of bias in their particular assessments. Paul Fuss, the project manager of the Tufts clinical nutrition study, explained that the same two testers recorded each twin's anthropometric measurements. Both examiners assessed each twin in re-verse order, and the data were averaged together. Fuss emphasized that testers did not check the results until data were available for both twins. The same individual recorded each twins' maximal oxygen uptake, but Fuss said it was difficult to see how an investigator could bias a machine.

Leonard Heston administered medical interviews to both twins until he left Minnesota in 1990. "I presented the questions in the same way to each individual—doctors learn to do this during their second year of medical school. There was a possibility of bias, but if so it did not operate in an important way." Heston's comment offers a realistic understanding of potential bias in the project's methods and its effects on the data. No data are perfect, but given the care with which each individual's informa-tion was gathered there is little chance that the MISTRA findings were inaccurate or misleading in any way. The lack of bias shown by my IQ test experiment most likely applies to findings in other behavioral do-mains. The MISTRA's findings generally showed excellent agreement with those from other twin studies, which would not have happened with poorly gathered data.

The intelligence tests, personality inventories, and most of the interest questionnaires that were administered had been used widely in prior re-search. The reliability and validity of these instruments had been well established. Bouchard's choice of these instruments was largely guided by their use in previous twin studies so that they could enable comparative findings.

The results from the IQ data analyses were extremely consistent with the findings from the three previous reared-apart twin studies and the study conducted in Sweden. Furthermore, twin data are more informa-tive in conjunction with data from other kinships varying in genetic and environmental relatedness. It is difficult to explain the much greater IQ similarity of MZA twins (0.74), relative to that of DZT twins (0.60), biological parent-child pairs (0.42), half-siblings (0.31), adoptive siblings (0.29–0.34), virtual twins (0.28), adoptive parent-child pairs (0.19), and cousins (0.15) without reference to genetic factors.[4] In fact, there has never been a convincing environmental explanation as to why genetically identical individuals meeting as adults are more behaviorally alike than unrelated individuals raised together. Research also shows that unrelated individuals raised together become less alike in intelligence over time.[5] A consistent result from the MISTRA's analyses was that features of the twins' rearing homes made negligible contributions to their behavioral resemblance. This point was often lost in some of the harsh media treatments of the MISTRA.

As an aside, when Bouchard delivered his last lecture to University of Minnesota students on April 16, 2010, I was there, as was my former postdoctoral colleague Kimerly Wilcox. When Bouchard showed the 0.77 MZA IQ (g factor) on the screen, Wilcox sent me a knowing smile. We both remembered that we had given Bouchard a t-shirt with the number ".771" printed across the front, as I mentioned earlier. Even this controversial figure associated with Sir Cyril Burt's twin study remains a robust finding.

Some critics argued that personality inventories do not faithfully capture the behaviors people express in real life. Of course, inventories are imperfect, but they are superior to observational data gathered on just a few unrepresentative occasions. Inventory respondents indicate traits, attitudes, and interests that are most characteristic of their "self," providing a summary view of their behavior over time. However, depending upon the investigators' goals, observational studies can be very informative. I am a long-time member of the International Society for Human Ethology, whose members study behavior by naturalistic experimentation and observation. High-quality ethological studies require a large number of subjects for testing hypotheses about very specific behaviors. The reared-apart twins were in Minnesota for only one week, so their time and ours had to be used very efficiently to learn as much about them as possible. Had the twins' personality and interest assessments been limited to a few observational sessions, the likely yield would have been unrepresentative or atypical material. Moreover, the MISTRA was exploratory in nature, so an observational approach was not suited to the study's goal. However, in addition to the standard interviews and inventories that were administered, the twins' facial expressions were recorded while they watched films, they were photographed in unposed standing postures on the first assessment day, and they were videotaped in unstructured individual and joint interviews.

Every major domain of behavior that was assessed, such as intelligence, personality, and attitudes, was accomplished by multiple measures. Within-study constructive replications generally produced comparable findings, which could only have occurred with good-quality data. A final point is that the standard measures that were used, such as the Wechsler Adult Intelligence Scale and Minnesota Multiphasic Personality Inventory among others, had been designed to assess individual differences in behavior *with no reference to genetic effects.* The fact that the MISTRA and other twin researchers found genetic influence on these measures further supports the unbiased nature of the data. Of course, despite effective safe-guards, biased data collection is possible in any psychological study.

In 1974 correspondence, James Shields (investigator of the 1962 British reared-apart twin study) addressed similar criticisms of his work that were raised by Leon Kamin (the individual who had ignited the controversy over Cyril Burt). Shields wrote, "The criticisms boil down to poor tests, experimenter bias, and insufficient separation of the twins. Even if these criticisms had as much force as Kamin claims, they would not lead to the conclusion of zero heritability, but rather that the degree of heritability cannot be estimated satisfactorily."[6]

The Reared-Apart Twins: Was the Sample Size Problematic?

The fact that the reared-apart twins comprised a collection of cases rather than a systematically gathered sample was always acknowledged by the MISTRA investigators. I used the term "sample" throughout this book for the sake of convenience only, as explained in Chapter 2.

Many critics claimed that the reared-apart twin sample was too small to generate valid findings. There is little question that twin samples composed of several hundred pairs or more are desirable in psychological research. However, the United States lacked a twin registry, which forced Bouchard to rely on recruitment methods that yielded a smaller number of pairs. Nevertheless, the quality of the twin pairs that were studied was excellent—the sets were separated earlier in life and reunited later than twins in the three previous reared-apart twin studies and in the Swedish study whose researchers benefited from registry access. The MISTRA twins were also older at the time of assessment than the twins in the investigations by Newman et al. and Shields.

Sample size can, and did, pose difficulties for some analyses. The smaller number of subjects sometimes prevented assessments of the differences among twins organized by sex and zygosity, as in Johnson et al.'s 2007 mental ability study.[7] The DZA twins showed higher than expected

resemblance on militarism and on some mental ability measures. Another problem linked to the modest sample size was the large variation in
heritability estimates, as in Johnson et al.'s 2005 study of intelligence and
reading performance.[8] These DZA twin findings could have reflected assortative mating, placement effects, or sample fluctuation. Placement
effects could usually be ruled out as explanations, but the DZA twins'
similarity on some measures could not be resolved completely; therefore,
a larger DZA twin sample would have been desirable. These limitations
were discussed in the publications, noting that the DZA twin pairs were
more often typical than atypical of DZ twins generally.

It is important, but also unappreciated, that heritability estimates are
more accurate and efficient when they are based on data from twins reared
apart than twins reared together, and can be derived from fewer numbers
of pairs. These points were developed by Lykken and his colleagues in an
unpublished 1981 manuscript.[9] Lykken showed that only fifty MZA twin
pairs, compared with four to five hundred MZT twin pairs and four to
five hundred DZT twin pairs, can estimate heritability with the same degree of confidence. That is because heritability is reflected directly by the
MZA intraclass correlation, whereas heritability is calculated indirectly
by doubling the difference between the MZT and DZT intraclass correlations. The MISTRA had studied eighty-one MZA twin pairs by the end of
the study, thirty-one more than the fifty MZA twin pairs specified by Lykken. Improving methods for estimating heritability was a goal of Lykken's
throughout his career.[10]

MZA Twin Resemblance: Genetic Influence or Selection of Similar Pairs?

In their 1937 book, Newman et al. recalled:

> The first case studied by us of identical twins reared apart gained consider-
> able publicity through no fault of ours, for the twins themselves gave their
> photograph and their life stories to an enterprising local reporter, who sent
> his news story to an American newspaper, from which it was copied far and
> wide. Since our name and address were given, we were deluged with all
> sorts of letters from twins and about twins, a few of which furnished valu-
> able clues.[11]

Bouchard's experience of identifying twins, especially in the early
years, did not differ greatly from that of Newman et al. with respect
to the press. The Jim twins were featured in national and international
newspapers, leading to other new cases. Bouchard's appearances on talk
shows and other media had the same effect. As the project progressed,

some twins were located through social services and reunion registries, sources that would not necessarily attract visually or behaviorally similar twins. The eighteen twin pairs who met through mistaken identity (seventeen MZA and one DZA) were very similar in appearance, but there is no connection between physical and behavioral resemblance, as has been discussed.

The methods by which MISTRA participants (and reared-apart twins in other studies) were identified have been criticized for attracting or favoring assessment of the relatively more similar MZA twin pairs.[12] That may have been somewhat true of the study by Newman's group because those investigators were only interested in studying MZA twin pairs, possibly excluding dissimilar MZA sets. But their possible exclusion of dissimilar MZA pairs is only an assumption, one I was guilty of until I read Newman's 1940 case report of a reared-apart female pair he identified after publishing his 1937 study. Newman noted that he had recently discovered a reared-apart male pair in which one twin was eager for research while his twin was "somewhat of a hoodlum and refuses to submit to examination." Newman wrote, "This is unfortunate in view of the fact that the two brothers now seem to be so different in their personality traits."[13]

Juel-Nielsen recruited only MZA twin pairs, but did so through a population registry; as a result, he was able to identify all possible pairs born in Denmark between 1870 and 1910, although he included several pairs born after 1910.[14] Shields's appeal for twins via the British Broadcasting Corporation yielded ninety-two pairs, which he reduced to forty-one MZA twin pairs after omitting duplications and exclusions (nineteen), no replies (ten), refusals (five), incompletely investigated cases (four), and dizygosity (thirteen). Shields also found three additional MZA twin pairs (for a total of forty-four) and two additional DZA twin pairs from other sources[15]

The charge that the MISTRA sought the more similar MZA pairs fails because Bouchard decided early on to study DZA same-sex and opposite-sex twin pairs. It is true that the majority of the separated twin pairs (59.1 percent) were MZA, whereas the natural twinning rate predicted that 30 to 35 percent of the pairs should have been MZ.[16] Of course, there is no way of knowing if twin separations occurred equally among MZ and DZ twins. It is conceivable (but unproven) that MZ twins are separated more often than DZ twins because of the greater prenatal hazards to which they are subject and their consequent poorer early health, which imposes greater emotional and financial burdens on parents.

It is likely that the outnumbering of DZA twins by MZA twins in the MISTRA also reflects MZA twins' greater ease of finding one another due to their matched appearance.[17] However, to the extent that there was an overrepresentation of MZA twins, it could be also argued that both the less visually similar pairs *and* dissimilar pairs were attracted to the study. That is probable, given that DZA twins (who did not look alike) also volunteered for the research. In fact, twins from the second pair, assessed two months after the Jim twins, were DZA females.

Many MZ twins, even those growing up together, are uncertain of their twin type, partly because they and their families magnify small differences between them. This phenomenon is well known to investigators studying twins. However, MZ twins misclassified as DZ by their parents or themselves receive similar behavioral ratings, consistent with their true zygosity as opposed to their perceived zygosity.[18] A number of the reared-apart twins were uncertain of their twin type after they met, as were we. Laboratory analyses of the twins' blood samples took time, so some twins finished the assessment and went home before they, or we, knew their true twin type.

It is possible to suppose, however, that the more physically similar MZA twins did visit the laboratory. The idea that twins who look more alike are more behaviorally similar than those who look less alike due to their more similar treatment by others has been raised.[19] If true, psychosocial factors rather than genetic ones would explain the resemblance we observed between them. However, such reasoning has been weakened by analyses showing that similar treatment by others does not cause MZ twins to be alike.[20]

Science rests on data, not dialogue. Just as Juel-Nielsen compared his registry and nonregistry twins and found no significant differences between them, the effects of various family characteristics (e.g., socioeconomic status, or rearing with a relative or nonrelative) and contact measures (e.g., age at separation or age at reunion) on the MISTRA twins' trait similarities were measured. Such factors contributed little to the observed variance in measured traits and little to the similarity between the twins. Some journalists, such as NBC's science correspondent Robert Bazell, complained that some MZA twins had had contact before being assessed, implying that this limited the genetic interpretations of the findings.[21] The investigators always emphasized that the variable contact across the twin pairs was beneficial because it allowed analysis of the extent to which contact was associated with similarity.

In October 2010, I discovered a letter in Bouchard's files written to him in February 1979 by reared-apart twin Roger Brooks. Brooks and his twin brother, Tony Milasi, had reunited fifteen years earlier after a twenty-five year separation, and were interested in participating in the MISTRA. Brooks had read about the study in the *New York Times* and after explaining his circumstances wrote, "As for the 'contamination' [the fact that we have been in contact since meeting], I strongly believe that a truly comprehensive study of the effect of the environment and heredity can be *enhanced* by carefully following the subsequent lives of these twins." Brooks had it right.

Media Attention: Bouchard Manipulated the Press and the Press Manipulated the Data

> This reporter [Lisa Lynch] never spoke with me to check her facts! The article was written *as though* I was interviewed. (Bouchard, November 20, 1996)

This handwritten note runs across the top of one of the most egregious articles written about Bouchard and the MISTRA.[22] Lynch's only factual words were those suggesting that the MISTRA was "one of the most controversial dispatches in the nature-nurture debate." The MISTRA saw other outrageous articles, notably one by John Horgan in *Scientific American* discussed later in this chapter. These two articles were more extreme than most, but they convey the kinds of criticisms to which the MISTRA was subject from time to time. A sampling of Lynch's statements (L) are listed below, followed by my responses (R) to them.

> (L) Bouchard studied intelligence with Arthur Jensen when Bouchard was a student at Berkeley.
> (R) Bouchard did not know Jensen in those years, nor did he conduct studies of intelligence. A footnote to one of Bouchard's 1998 papers reads, "Jensen had been on the Berkeley faculty in Educational Psychology (located in Tolman Hall, the same building as Psychology) while I was a student but, as far as I can recall, I had not met him."[23]

> (L) Bouchard manipulated the press because newspaper coverage attracted twins to the study. The press, in turn, manipulated the findings to imply that Bouchard's data had resolved the nature-nurture debate.
> (R) Reared-apart twins were found in many ways, not just through the media. Bouchard talked openly to members of the press because the findings were exciting and he believed it was important to explain them publicly. He was pleased that news reports attracted twins because as many pairs as possible were desirable for the data analyses, but he never sought media attention.

> (L) MZA twins Oskar and Jack, raised Catholic in Nazi Germany and Jewish in Trinidad, respectively, "had to be at least slightly interested in media attention or at least appearing as 'twin-like' as possible."
> (R) Oskar and Jack had many similarities, but each disparaged the historical and political views held by their brother, a sentiment that caused friction between them. They were hardly "twin-like" in that respect.

(L) Bouchard eventually backed away from the media because journalists alleged, based on our findings, that "we cannot change who we are."

(R) None of the MISTRA colleagues suggested that genes prevent behavioral change or improvement, only that not everyone benefits equally from the same experiences or interventions. Bouchard discussed the study with any journalist or media outlet interested in talking to him.[24]

A 1996 article on science writing by the late sociologist Dorothy Nelkin in the medical journal *The Lancet* continued some of Lynch's themes. Nelkin stated that the MISTRA investigators "sought press publicity for their studies of identical twins when their work was rejected by professional journals."[25] The source of this misinformation was Lynch's article. Ironically, Nelkin also stated "many accusations of inaccuracy can be traced to reporters' efforts to present complex material in a readable and appealing way."[26]

At the same time, many newspaper, magazine, and television journalists were informed, open-minded, and fair in covering the MISTRA. They include among others Edwin Chen (*New York Times Magazine,* 1979),[27] Constance Holden (*Science,* 1980),[28] Lew Cope (*Minneapolis Star Tribune,* 1983),[29] Lawrence Wright (*New Yorker,* 1995),[30] and Jill Neimark (*Psychology Today,* 1997).[31] Excellent television documentaries were produced by WGBH in Boston ("Body Watch," 1987) and WNET in Newark ("Innovations: What Makes Us Tick? The Biology of Personality," 1989).

Findings: The MZA Twins' Similarities Occurred by Chance

In 1995, *New York Times* columnist Frank Rich detailed some curious parallels between then President Bill Clinton and then House Speaker Newt Gingrich, born three years apart.[32] Both men had been favored eldest children, had had strong doting mothers, had participated in student protests, and had avoided the draft. The idea that two people near in age and of the same sex, chosen randomly, can match across different traits was a frequent counterargument to the possibility that some of the MZA twins' unusual similarities were genetically influenced. The critics' reasoning was that eighty-one MZA twin pairs completed approximately 15,000 questions, so many findings of similarity could have occurred by chance.

Bouchard agreed that two unrelated individuals from the same country could display some remarkable resemblances.[33] However, if chance was chiefly responsible for the MZA twins' behavioral similarities, then the DZA same-sex twins should have been just as similar, but they were not. In addition, none of the Clinton-Gingrich similarities are as rare or as striking as most of those displayed by the MZA twins. Finally, as mentioned, the effects of age and sex were removed from the data prior to analysis in order to control for these common factors.

MISTRA Publications: Scientific Journals versus Media Coverage

Bouchard kept regularly updated lists of the MISTRA's publications that he forwarded to anyone upon request. He also mailed packets of his publications to all individuals requesting them. That is why a 1993 *Scientific American* article by John Horgan provoked such an angry reaction from him. And that is also why a letter disputing Horgan's remarks was authored by Matt McGue and cosigned by sixteen behavioral scientists from eight institutions in the United States, Australia, Sweden, and the Netherlands; the letter appeared in a later issue of the magazine.[34]

Bouchard prepared an unpublished memo, "Accuracy in Science Reporting," in response to Horgan's piece that he circulated to his close colleagues. He also presented his remarks to a 1994 seminar, "Science and the Powers," in Stockholm, Sweden.[35] Horgan's charges were based largely on claims by Kamin. Misstatements about the MISTRA's publication history were also made by Professor Val Dusek (D)[36] as well as by Horgan (H),[37] as listed below, followed by a response (R).

> (D) With the exception of the Eckert et al.'s 1986 homosexuality paper, "the scientific data and methods of analyses upon which these conclusions are based have not yet been published in a referred scientific journal."[38]
>
> (R) Bouchard and his colleagues published five other scientific papers between 1981 and 1987, and several book chapters in professional collections.
>
> (H) The MISTRA twins were motivated to exaggerate their similarities for media attention or to please the investigators.
>
> (R) In his memo, Bouchard asserted that, "the twins would have to be pretty talented to exaggerate their similarities in IQ, special mental abilities, reaction time to a variety of tasks they have never seen before, responses to thousands of questions that they have never considered, as well as cardiovascular functioning, cavities, etc." In fact, many of the twins declined media opportunities in the interest of privacy.
>
> (H) The MISTRA presented anecdotes as evidence.
> (R) Bouchard countered that carefully chosen anecdotes were described in the context of considering plausible mechanisms behind them.
>
> (H) The MISTRA misrepresented the twins' contact frequency and rearing similarities.
> (R) Bouchard had sent a packet of MISTRA publications to Horgan, so Horgan should have been aware that selective placement did not explain the MZA twins' IQ similarities. Bouchard emphasized that the effects of con-

tact and upbringing were not downplayed, but rather were measured with reference to the twins' behavioral resemblance.

Project Funding: A Review of the Sources

Most people will be surprised to learn that the MISTRA operated more like a mom and pop business than a major scientific investigation—sometimes twin pair to twin pair. That was not the public perception—in 2007, psychology professor William H. Tucker wrote that the MISTRA was "assisted by millions of dollars in grant funding from numerous sources," but that was misleading.[39] The MISTRA received a total of $2,330,720 in research support over a twenty-five year period; some funds were awarded after the study ended in 1999, and some collaborators used their own awards to support only specific parts of the project. The largest single grant, awarded in 1996 when the study was close to ending, was for $155,455. The average funding per year was only $93,228; in contrast, Susan Roberts who studied the twins' body size and nutrition at Tufts University received $210,443 per year for five years. The MISTRA's different funding sources and the dollar amounts are listed in Appendix A, Table A-1.

Funds were shockingly modest in size, though steady enough to keep the MISTRA in business for twenty years. Fortunately, many medical costs were absorbed by the investigators working with us. Even when the project was close to $10,000 in debt, Bouchard kept it going, despite the fact that the cost of assessing one twin pair with spouses was $6,935, not including staff members' salaries.[40] Bouchard once used his own money to purchase camera film from a Seattle company that charged half the price of Kodak. (The film quality was awful.) Bouchard had once considered mortgaging his home, but his wife Pauline wouldn't stand for that. Due to some bookkeeping issues in the University of Minnesota accounts office, he had overspent his funds by $20,000, a deficit eventually covered by Pioneer funds.

There are three main reasons why funding for the MISTRA was difficult to obtain. The most significant reason was the timing of the study. Even though a genetic perspective was in the air in the 1970s and 1980s, many people viewed genetic explanations of behavior as discriminatory and neglectful of what good parenting and interventions could accomplish. Some reviewers were, therefore, concerned about the potentially explosive nature of findings that might support genetic influences on IQ and other behaviors. The second reason was grant reviewers' doubt that a sufficiently large reared-apart twin sample could be identified. Federal grant proposals require demographic details of potential subject pools, data that Bouchard could neither know nor predict because reunited twin pairs surfaced at any time. The third reason was that Bouchard, as he was the first to admit, did not "think big" when it came to grants, carefully crafting his budgets to match the number of assessments he could realistically complete.

In 1981, the financial backing of the MISTRA became contentious among academics, journalists, and the general public when Bouchard accepted a grant from the Pioneer Fund. The Pioneer Fund, based in New York City, had a reputation for supporting research with a racial bent. I will look at the background of the Pioneer Fund and its role in the MISTRA later in this chapter. First, it is important to know that, as principal investigator of the MISTRA, Bouchard received awards and donations from nine separate sources between 1979 and 2004—however, the publicity surrounding the Pioneer Fund left the false impression that that agency was the project's sole benefactor.

The MISTRA was also funded by grants awarded to the colleagues in periodontics (Pihlstrom and Michalowicz) and clinical nutrition (Roberts). The twins' travel, room and board, lost wages, and honoraria (approximately $5,100 per pair, with spouses, $2,600 without spouses) were covered by these grants, but the majority of funds supported the investigators' operating costs. These grants also supported assessments of reared-together twins with which we were not as directly involved. I have summarized these separate funding sources in Appendix A, Table A-2. A detailed summary of all yearly sources of MISTRA funding is presented in Table A-3.

Funding Sources

Initial Funds

There is a story behind every grant Bouchard received on behalf of the MISTRA. The University of Minnesota Graduate School was actually responsible for financially launching the MISTRA. As a well-respected tenured professor, Bouchard received several thousand dollars from the University of Minnesota's graduate school in March 1979 to study the Jim twins. There was no way to know what Bouchard would learn from the Jim twins or where those findings would lead, but universities can risk small sums of money for promising projects. It was a smart decision because the MISTRA ultimately enhanced the school's reputation for first-class research and productivity. Bouchard's scientific curiosity was also satisfied, something worth a lot to an investigator.

In the wake of the publicity surrounding the Jim twins, Bouchard had a casual chat with his department chair, John (Jack) Darley Sr. Darley told him, "You will find more twins, so you will need more grants." Darley telephoned the Spencer Foundation, a Chicago-based organization that supports research on educational issues and values. The next meeting of the awards committee was ten days away. Bouchard submitted a grant and received $32,000. At about this time, Bouchard also secured a $10,000 grant from the publishing house Harcourt Brace Jovanovich, and $5,000 from various business sources.

"Jack Darley knew lots of people," Bouchard told me. Bouchard could not recall exactly how the Harcourt funding came about, but it could have been a casual conversation with Darley in the corridor. In fact, Bouchard kept a "Jack Darley Grant Help" file that included Darley's many letters written to granting agencies on Bouchard's behalf. In it, I discovered an April 27, 1979 letter written by Bouchard to then University of Minnesota President Peter McGrath, in which Bouchard praised the faculty and staff who gave so generously of their time during the Jim twins' assessment.

Bouchard also submitted several grant proposals to the National Science Foundation. But as Irving Gottesman pointed out, a reared-apart twin study was "not their cup of tea."

The National Science Foundation

The National Science Foundation (NSF) was created by Congress in 1950 "to promote the progress of science; to advance the national health, prosperity, and welfare; to secure the national defense . . ."[41] It supports work in many fields, including mathematics, computer science, and the social sciences. But federal agencies tend to be quite cautious in allocating their resources. At one time, the NSF provided immediate funds for time-limited projects, such as a University of Minnesota study on people's response to the failed prediction that flooding would end the world on December 21, 1954.[42] Based on this precedent, Bouchard applied to the NSF for funds to study the Jim twins. However, the NSF no longer supported individually proposed projects that require urgent funds. Bouchard described this problem in a 1979 letter to Richard Atkinson, then director of the NSF. He noted that the Minnesota graduate school funding for the Jim twins came "on the basis of one phone call," and that the subsequent publicity generated additional pairs.[43]

The NSF did not fund Bouchard's 1979 proposal, "A Study of a Pair of Monozygotic Twins Reared Apart," submitted when the Jim twins were discovered. Excerpts from the three NSF reviews, which yielded two ratings of "excellent" and one of "fair," are reproduced below.[44] My assignment of reviewer numbers was arbitrary.

Reviewer 1 described the proposed work as "an unusual opportunity to obtain valuable developmental information ... although its analysis will not remake any general theories. (Excellent)

Reviewer 2 claimed that such "case studies carry weight that is all out of proportion to their general methodological status." (Excellent)

Reviewer 3 argued that it was "impossible to perform any statistical tests on these data, and therefore to rule out explanations of the findings other than those preferred by the investigators." (Fair)

Federal proposals demand enormous amounts of detailed preparation, so the fact that Bouchard assembled the materials within weeks of the March 1979 study of the Jim twins put him at a disadvantage. Recall that the Jim twins were found in February 1979 and studied in March of that same year. A letter from the NSF to Bouchard dated April 5, 1979 (less than one month later) brought news that his proposal had been declined.

A handwritten note scribbled onto one of the reviews, presumably by the grants officer, read, "By the time I got the award document through the process here the research had already been done. So the thing is moot (and was declined)." As it turned out, the research was *not* finished, so the Jim twins returned to Minneapolis five months later. Perhaps Bouchard should have revisited this proposal when he invited the Jim twins back. But even if timing had not been an issue, a favorable outcome was uncertain.

Reviewer 3 predicted a biased interpretation of the data, despite the fact that he or she recognized the uniqueness of the research opportunity elsewhere in the review. Furthermore, no study offers a "conclusive test of existing theories" as he or she demanded; rather, studies provide findings that confirm or challenge previous or existing ones, advancing knowledge in the process. Even Reviewer 1 who was generally positive claimed, "its analysis will not remake any general theories." Of course, the MISTRA and other studies ultimately did "remake" theories of behavior by showing both genetic influence and minimal shared environmental effects across virtually all measured traits.

Bouchard applied again for NSF funding in 1979, 1980, and 1982, but these attempts were unsuccessful. The widely ranging reviews of his initial and revised submissions mirrored the strong disagreement over what reared-apart twin data could contribute. His initial proposal received eight total ratings of excellent (4), very good (1), good-fair (1), and poor (2). His resubmission received seven total ratings of excellent (2), very good (2), good (1), good-fair (1), and very poor (1). One negative reviewer did not enter a rating.

The positive comments to the proposal were stunning. "It is the kind of study one often dreams about." "Its significance is enhanced as a result of the semi-demise of the Burt data." "This study is destined to become a classic in the field regardless of the particular results." One laudatory reviewer who admittedly knew "nothing about genetics," was excited about the MZA data, but was "not clear" on what the DZA data could contribute. On the negative side, the small sample, the assumed contact between co-twins, an inflated budget, and a slim chance of finding "anything new" were variously mentioned by the more negative reviewers. One feared that the work would "fan the controversy regarding heretibility [reviewer's incorrect spelling repeated several times] of intelligence . . . rejection is the only intellectually defensible course for NSF." This last comment contrasted sharply with another reviewer's belief that "if the investigators can indeed come up with twenty additional monozygotic pairs . . . NSF should consider putting up the whole $150,000 to let them do it."

In 1981, Bouchard received a $50,000 NSF grant for his work on the MISTRA. However, his 1982 proposal for continued funding was rejected. Once again, the reviewers' ratings displayed a wide range of opinions as to the merits of the work: Excellent (3), Very Good (2), Very Good-Good (1), and Fair (2). A sampling of their comments is insightful.

Reviewer 1: "This study eminently deserved support. It is concerned with a most important topic and it is going about the scientific task in a most informed and competent way. The results already achieved have been of great interest and I would anticipate the study, when extended may prove to be evidentially unsurpassable within the next fifty years or so." (Excellent)

Reviewer 2: "Using a variety of instruments to evaluate the same traits(s) is the wisest approach . . . I disagree with them sharply on which tests are appropriate and on how to evaluate information." (Very Good)

Reviewer 3: "This ongoing study has been reviewed frequently with mixed reactions and has received considerable publicity. Both factors make it difficult to be critical . . . At least three of the many questions that can be raised leave me luke-warm about this effort. First, the questions of self-selection . . . A second and related point, is that variables in the childhood environment that may be important are not assessed . . . A third concern is raised by the absence of a theoretical perspective and the reluctance to specify the questions that will be asked of these data." (Fair)

Negative feedback is not a bad thing when it is well reasoned and offered in the spirit of scholarly criticism. Bouchard relished these kinds of exchanges. But emotions and unawareness motivated some responses to a new reared-apart twin study. One especially insulting 1980 review suggested, "There is no chance whatever that this research, which throws the kitchen and bathroom sinks at a small number of MZAs, will [make] any advance at all over Shields [1962]—who, by the way, also studied adults, and more of them. I have actively resented the newspaper and magazine propaganda efforts of these investigators." As indicated earlier, another reviewer complained about the *small* sample size, then suggested that Bouchard first conduct a "feasibility study" to secure 150 MZA and 150 DZA twin pairs! Bouchard wrote in the margins, "Reviewer does not know what he/she is talking about?" That reviewer also expressed great admiration for Lykken, bemoaning the fact that Lykken's talents were not directed toward a richer data set. Another reviewer, who had complained about the lack of attention to the effects of childhood environment measures on behavior, seemed unaware of the many relevant questionnaires and inventories the twins completed from the start.

With reviewers so sharply divided, it is easy to understand the MISTRA's funding difficulties. Negative reviews often overtake positive ones when committees allocate limited funds on a competitive basis. Looking at the rating distributions of Bouchard's two grants confirms this view—in both cases, there were more excellents than poors and more excellent/very goods than fair/poors, but the negative ratings carried greater weight.

Although some reviewers' comments seemed unjustified, the MISTRA was not a perfect study. The twins were identified in numerous ways, forcing the investigators to assess the representativeness of the reared-apart twins by comparing their characteristics with those of reared-together twins. The number of DZA twin pairs was small, making some findings hard to interpret and some analyses impossible to complete. Childhood rearing factors were obtained retrospectively and thus were subject to possible distortions and inaccuracies. However, the analyses were conducted with the various caveats in mind, as do all investigators engaged in behavioral science research.

The Pioneer Fund

The Pioneer Fund was started in 1937 in New York City by Wycliffe Preston Draper. Draper was born in 1891 to a wealthy Massachusetts family.[45] He was a well-educated individual whose family's fortune let him pursue his interests in archeology, anthropology, and behavior without responsibilities or obligations. In the 1920s, Draper became interested in the genetic basis of intelligence and in eugenics—efforts to improve population quality by encouraging more intelligent individuals to reproduce more and less intelligent individuals to reproduce less. Eugenics had gained the attention of many psychologists and geneticists in the early

1900s, both in the United States and abroad.[46] In his will, drafted in 1960, Draper left five million dollars in research funds to the Pioneer Fund. Draper passed away in 1972. Over the years, the fund has supported projects on the hereditary basis of intelligence, personality, and social organization, with reference to both individual and group differences.[47]

The Pioneer Fund has a controversial past.[48] It was publicly accused of racist policies after the *Harvard Educational Review* published a 1969 essay, "How Much Can We Boost IQ and Scholastic Achievement?" by University of California–Berkeley psychologist Arthur Jensen.[49] Jensen suggested that the average fifteen-point IQ gap between black and white populations could be associated with genetic factors. Although Jensen had not been funded by Pioneer until 1973,[50] individuals critical of his essay discovered that the fund had supported previous research on race differences in intelligence. The story played out many times in the media.[51] Because of the Pioneer Fund's reputation for funding race-related research, its recipients allegedly supported racial discrimination and anti-interventionist policies with their work. The Southern Poverty Law Center included it in their list of hate groups.[52] Many academics, journalists, and others learned about the Pioneer Fund from the press.

The Pioneer Fund contacted Bouchard in 1980 or 1981—he had never heard of the fund prior to that time. His acceptance of their research grants intensified critics' charges and accusations that the MISTRA's program was driven by eugenics, motivated by politics, and flawed in design. Some MISTRA colleagues and students worried that the project and their good names would be hurt if Bouchard accepted Pioneer Fund support. Gottesman recalled:

> I brought [the Pioneer Fund's past and present] to Bouchard's attention. I felt that the study was strong enough to stand on its own and that we ran the risk of bad publicity if we accepted [their] funds. I would have turned it down and spent more time raising funds and writing grants. But I was not in a position to micromanage, and now I can't second guess what might have happened [had he declined the funds] . . . I was happy to get the benefits of the MMPI data and become a co-author on many papers, but I have not changed my mind about the Pioneer Fund. My name is on papers that acknowledge Pioneer Fund support, but that shows my confidence [in] the data.[53]

Gottesman also saw irony in the situation. The Pioneer Fund and the MISTRA's critics "got no reinforcement for any ideas about race differences in behavior because race never entered this project. We were concerned with the scientific study of individual differences . . . To my knowledge, no one connected to the project ever had a political agenda." The Pioneer Fund includes among its mission the study of group differences based on sex, social class, and race. The MISTRA's goal was to find associations between differences in the twins' life histories and the twins' behavioral differences.

Heston, who had once received a small Pioneer Fund grant, said there was "no reason for Bouchard not to accept the funds—he could not have done the study otherwise." Auke Tellegen, who was not a Pioneer Fund recipient, believed that accepting Pioneer Fund support was "politically risky," but that Bouchard needed the funds. McGue spoke for Lykken when he said, "David's argument was that we could take bad money and do good things with it."

Bouchard agrees with Lykken's statement and believes people can make their own judgments. "The left was killing us, which is why most of our funds came from private foundations." Bouchard was willing to accept money from any source, but he emphasized the responsibilities of acknowledging funding sources and describing exactly what the research accomplished. Bouchard also recalled his 1987 taping of the ABC's news program 20/20. The producers spent several days filming an MZA twin pair, then confronted Bouchard in a hostile manner about his Pioneer funding.[54] "I lost my cool—slightly. I told them that since I am being taped for TV they could ask me any questions they wanted, but they folded and went home. Unless they could uncover something dirty they were uninterested."

Former graduate student Susan Resnick, who worked on the MISTRA when it began, was "not happy" about the study's association with the Pioneer Fund. While working on the MISTRA, her support came from a National Institute of Health National Research Service Award, not from Pioneer. Resnick is a co-author on only one publication, the first preliminary description of the MISTRA's project design and findings, which appeared in 1981 prior to Pioneer Fund support.[55] She recalled, "Bouchard was very upfront about it—he felt that it was the only way to keep the study going."

Minnesota psychology professor Matt McGue had also weighed the implications of accepting Pioneer Fund support:

> The Pioneer Fund never influenced the study, and the study could never have been done without it. But there are legitimate concerns. The Pioneer Fund had a racial agenda. The 1980s was a more politicized time with respect to race, and some students worried that a Pioneer Fund association would "taint" them. True to his nature, Bouchard heard them out. My feeling then was that Bouchard was wrong to take it [the Pioneer Fund grant], but he proved to be right . . . what [Pioneer] got out of it was minimal.

University of Western Ontario psychology professor and editor of *Personality and Individual Differences*, Tony Vernon, also has received

Pioneer Fund support but was not associated with the MISTRA. Vernon believes that racist allegations against the Pioneer Fund were "questionable" at best, given that there has been "no solid evidence." Vernon and others also noted that the Pioneer Fund imposed no restriction on the investigators' procedures or publications.[56] According to MISTRA colleague Greg Carey, "Bouchard told me that the Pioneer Fund never told him what to write. I trust Bouchard, and I know when he says something he means it." Had Bouchard failed to find genetic influence on the behaviors that he studied, the Pioneer Fund would not have interfered with his reporting.

One of the benefits of writing this book has been the opportunity to obtain professional and personal perspectives from each investigator, not just about the science but also about how the science was done. Every colleague stands by the findings, including those who tried to dissuade Bouchard from accepting Pioneer Fund grants. The money partly supported the salaries of many project associates, secretaries, and research assistants, including mine. As Bouchard said in 2009, "If not for Pioneer we would have folded long ago."

The next MISTRA grant, obtained from the David H. Koch Charitable Foundation, was not awarded until 1985, a full three years later. That grant was presumably made possible by the Pioneer-funded work Bouchard had completed since 1982.

By the start of 1985, assessments had been completed on sixty-five reared-apart twin pairs, and the study had attracted considerable attention, including that of David H. Koch, who headed the Koch Foundation. Of course, without an offer of Pioneer Fund grants, Bouchard might have tried harder to get money from other sources, but he did try. His friend, businessman and developer William (Bill) I. Fine, who helped found the Fine Theoretical Physics Institute at the University of Minnesota, introduced Bouchard to many foundations in the Twin Cities, but nothing came of these efforts.

The David H. Koch Charitable Foundation

Twins are intensely interested in twin research, making them good donors as well as participants. David H. Koch, DZT twin and executive vice-president of Koch Industries,[57] a diversified company that operates oil refineries, manufactures chemicals, and owns cattle ranches, was one of them. According to Bouchard:

> I had never heard of David Koch until he wrote me a letter in 1984 or 1985 asking about Cyril Burt. I wrote him a two-page reply and received a letter back from him, asking me if I wanted to apply for a grant from his foundation. I should have looked into his background because I would have discovered

that he was a billionaire![58] I might have written a bigger grant [larger than $10,000 to 50,000 and for more than one or two years], but I never had the sense that a bigger grant was possible.

The Koch Charitable Foundation supports projects involving science, education, medicine, and the arts.[59] As shown in Appendix A, Table A-3, Koch made several grants to Bouchard between 1985 and 1996.

Correspondence between grantors and grantees reveals a project's future funding needs while highlighting its successes. In January 1992, Bouchard wrote to Koch inquiring about "emergency interim support" for a reared-apart twin follow-up study of aging that was "far superior to virtually all aging studies." Twenty pairs had been reassessed by that time, but the grants from the Seaver Institute (discussed in the next section) and the study's dental and nutrition colleagues would not let Bouchard keep to the ten-year follow-up schedule. He requested $73,895 from Koch to study twelve former twin pairs. The funds would have covered the twins' travel, lodging, and research expenses only; he did not ask for assistants' salaries. Bouchard also sent several articles to Koch, among them a publication in the *Executive Editor,* the journal of the National Association of School Boards. Bouchard wrote, "We are infiltrating the educational establishment!" meaning that educators were noticing the MISTRA findings. Prior to this letter, the last Koch grant was made in 1987; the next (and final) grant was made in 1996.

Bouchard wrote another letter to Koch in May 1995. This time, he wanted to know if he could continue to use the remaining $11,000 from the original grant even though the deadline had passed. Bouchard also noted that the Pioneer Fund had "over spent" and would not be funding research for several years. He explained that his available funds would be used up by July, and he hoped he could submit another proposal to Koch. Bouchard provided a long list of his accomplishments (e.g., presentation at the NATO Conference in the Netherlands; Distinguished Scientist Address at the American Psychological Association) adding, "We feel that our work, taken in conjunction with other behavior geneticists, has begun to completely transform the way in which human behavior is understood." It was a change from Bouchard's usual modesty. And he was able to use the remaining $11,000.

The Seaver Institute

The Seaver Institute, founded in 1955 by Frank R. Seaver, is based in Los Angeles, California. Seaver had made his fortune as head of Hydril, a Houston–based company that designs and manufactures products for petroleum drilling and production. The Seaver Institute supports research in science, medicine, education, public affairs, and the arts. It targets projects that are likely to help humanity, and it is willing to invest in projects unlikely to receive funding from other sources. Then President of the Seaver Institute, Dr. Richard Call, consulted with university officials to learn about potentially fundable projects of interest.[60] In the late 1980s, Call contacted Bouchard and met with him in Minneapolis to discuss grant support for the MISTRA. Five grants, totaling $250,000, were awarded in support of the MISTRA between 1988 and 1993.

The Whitfield Institute

The Whitfield Institute was a British charity established in 1999 by an anonymous donor.[61] The institute raised money with which it supported research. Bouchard was unaware of the Whitfield's existence until a colleague referred him to an associate of the institute who suggested that Bouchard submit a proposal. The proposal was approved in 2004, providing the final grant ($65,884) received by the MISTRA. According to Bouchard, the Whitfield grant enabled a great deal of data processing and analysis to be completed after the study ended. The Whitfield Institute closed in 2005 because the individual responsible for funding discontinued doing so.

Bouchard did not have a fortune to work with, but he made the most of the grants that came his way.

Twins Reared Apart Research: Looking Back and Looking Ahead

Because of its approach, its methods, its findings, and its timing, the MISTRA has substantially affected the way people think about the origins of behavioral and medical traits. Many scientists acknowledge the effects of genes on behavior.[62] The twins' reunion stories touch us deeply, an observation that constitutes vital information about the universal importance of family relationships in human social development.

The MISTRA's biggest contribution to psychology was showing that behaviors found to be familial, such as intelligence, personality, and religiosity, have substantial genetic components. The study also showed that shared environments have little effect on the behavioral resemblance of relatives living together. The limited effects of shared environments on behavior seem counterintuitive, but most people grasp this concept when they compare their own behaviors with those of their family members.

There have been misunderstandings of the findings. There have also been misunderstandings of behavioral genetics concepts in general. The biggest source of confusion comes from the meaning of the term *variance*.

Heritability, the variance in a trait due to genetic differences among people, applies to populations, not to individuals. Heritability estimates of 0.50 to 0.60 for alcoholism do not mean that every child born to alcoholic parents or every MZ twin with an alcoholic co-twin will become an alcoholic.[63] Having immediate alcoholic relatives increases one's risk of developing that disorder, but genes do not imply destiny. Gene-behavior relationships are probabilistic and indirect—the risk of becoming alcoholic in individual at-risk cases may be large or small. However, the value of knowing the relative risk of alcoholism lets individuals take preventative measures, such as avoiding or minimizing alcohol intake.

It is also important to emphasize that most behavioral genetic findings apply to individuals living within the normal range of human environments. The MISTRA did not study individuals from impoverished or abusive settings in which environmental effects can be quite salient. For example, a study of two-year-old twins found that children raised in deprived neighborhoods were at increased risk for behavioral problems, beyond any genetic liability.[64]

It is interesting to speculate on the impact the Jim twins might have had on psychological research had they met thirty years earlier than they did (in 1950) or thirty years later (in 2010). In the 1950s and 1960s, the Jim twins might have excited interest among academics questioning environmentalist views, but relatively few people were open to a genetic perspective at that time. When the Jim twins were discovered in 1979, the psychological climate had changed just enough so that many people were interested in what these twins might reveal about human behavior.

Had the Jim twins met in 2010, it is quite likely that they would have been of scientific interest, but they would probably not have attracted the worldwide attention that they did in 1979. By 2010, the heritability of most human behavioral traits had been established by countless twin, sibling, and adoption studies. (For this same reason, Cyril Burt's study might have stirred far less controversy had Kamin exposed Burt's suspicious correlations later than he did.) The irony is that the MISTRA inspired many of these studies. Regardless, the Jim twins would still have been valued research subjects in 2010 and beyond because of the increased focus on how environments affect behavior and the many advances made in the molecular genetics field.

Genes, Environments, and Heritability

Since about 2000, behavioral-genetic researchers have been paying greater attention to family and other environmental influences on behavior, and to how they work in concert with genetic potentials. University of Edinburgh research fellow Wendy Johnson believes that our understanding of gene-behavior relationships can be enhanced through twin studies of gene-environment transactions—that is, changes in genetic and environmental variation with changes in environmental effects, such as educational, occupational, and nutritional factors. Johnson's view makes sense.

This shift away from heritability estimation to more focused environmental analysis is understandable because we now know that most measured traits have a genetic component. However, the early reared-apart twin investigators also cared enormously about how environmental factors moderated gene expression. Newman's final 1940 reared-apart twin case included wonderfully speculative passages, material that rarely has a place in today's scientific journals given the emphases on statistical findings and participant confidentiality. He and his co-author Iva Gardner wondered if there are "thresholds of influence, and that, unless a certain threshold of difference in environment is reached, the organisms do not respond differently."[65] Their reasoning was based on the striking behavioral similarities he observed in his final pair, eighteen-year-old MZA twins Lois and Louise, despite their residential and educational differences.

In this 1940 case study, Newman also claimed that a common criticism of his 1937 study was that it emphasized environmental influence and minimized genetic influence. This comment is surprising given the prevailing environmentalist perspective of that time. He attributed this criticism to the educational specialties of his two co-authors. "Hence in our work we may have gone too far in the opposite direction." Throughout the course of the study, the biologist Newman was "much more impressed with the very great intrapair similarities of these twins, after they had been exposed to all sorts of environmental differences."[66]

Some investigators, Johnson included, have asserted that there is no longer a place for twin study estimates of heritability because of the increased focus on gene-environment relationships.[67] Clearly, the behavioral genetics field, which also includes studies of siblings, half-siblings, adoptees, and twin-family constellations has edged away from estimating trait heritabilities to assessing genetically based behavioral changes, genetic associations between different behaviors, and the genetic bases of environmental measures. The genetics of experience—that is, how people perceive and remember life events—promises to be a fascinating and informative area of investigation.[68] However, there are things we can still learn about the genetic basis of some traits.

Only one twin study has examined the genetic basis of romantic love styles, the tendency to fall in love quickly or slowly over time.[69] A lack of genetic influence and a shared family effect were reported. The only twin study of the heritability of materialism (the importance of owning and acquiring material possessions), conducted in 2009, also showed a lack of genetic effects, with the exception of a happiness dimension (contentment with one's current possessions).[70] Additional studies of these behaviors, using a variety of methods administered on several occasions, would be important for purposes of information gathering and replication. I wish Bouchard had administered love style and materialism questionnaires to the MISTRA twins, but it is impossible to assess every behavior in the same study.

Reared-apart twin studies have included mostly adults, but in 2006 I began the first prospective study of reared-apart twin children from China, as mentioned in Chapter 2. Genetic effects on intelligence, personality, and interests have never been studied using young twins adopted apart or together, but they can be estimated using these Chinese twin samples. Our understanding of traits such as fluctuating asymmetry, traditionalism, job satisfaction, and age at menarche would also benefit from studies tracking these separated twins as well as other unusual kinships, such as virtual twins (same-age unrelated siblings) and superfecundated twins (twins having the same mother, but different fathers).[71] Twin studies of behaviors that have been assessed rarely or not at all, such as adult romantic attachment, sleep quality, and disregard for rules, have appeared in 2011 issues of the journal *Behavior Genetics*,[72] but more would be welcome.

New Directions

Molecular genetics explores the effects of genes at the DNA level. Its techniques include linkage analysis and association analysis, among others. *Linkage* is the tendency for some genes to be inherited together because of their proximity on the same chromosome. *Linkage analysis* is used to map genes to specific chromosomes and to look for relationships between genotypes and phenotypes among related individuals. *Association analysis* involves direct tests of correlations between genotypes and phenotypes and can use populations. Genes or chromosomal regions thought to be relevant to a particular trait ("candidate genes") can be examined.[73] For example, a 2007 study looked at associations between cognition and genes associated with oxidative stress, thought to affect aging of the brain.[74]

Since the completion of the Human Genome Project in 2003 and the International HapMap project (a description of the common patterns of DNA sequence variation) in 2005, it has been possible to quickly scan the entire genomes of hundreds of people to search for genotype-phenotype associations. These efforts are called genomewide association studies (GWAS).[75]

Molecular genetic studies of medical disorders show that there are Mendelian (single gene) forms of complex conditions. Examples of such conditions include breast cancer, hypercholesterolemia, and Alzheimer disease. If an individual inherits the relevant detrimental gene for one of these disorders from his or her parents, the probability of developing the disorder approaches 100 percent. However, the Mendelian forms are quite rare, representing only about 2 percent of the cases. The overwhelming genetic contribution to these conditions comes from the polygenic (multiple gene) system in which each gene contributes to a probabilistic, rather than a deterministic, association with the disorder. This is especially true of psychopathology.

Molecular genetic advances have largely changed the complexion of human behavioral-genetic research and reordered its agenda.[76] Journal article titles in the 1970s focused on behavior, but many in 2011 focus on specific genes. However, some investigators believe that conventional twin studies are still making an impact in their areas of expertise. Susan Roberts, who headed the MISTRA's clinical nutrition study, said she is surprised when people "yawn" at heritability research because she believes that the reared-apart and reared-together twins she studied strengthened her work.

In an overview of behavioral and psychiatric twin studies delivered at the thirteenth International Twin Congress in Seoul, Professor Dorret Boomsma defined a significant role for classic MZ-DZ twin comparisons, even in the era of molecular genetic research.[77] She claimed that twins, especially behavior- and disease-discordant MZ twins, help identify genes underlying complex quantitative traits. Twins do this by controlling the genetic and environmental confounds inherent in biological parent-child relationships. It is also true that, despite years of study, little is known about *why* the heritabilities of height and other human traits have the values that they do. New techniques looking at genomewide gene expression promise to bring us closer to the answers.[78]

New areas of study have been defined by molecular genetic advances that have occurred since 2001 with the mapping of the human genome. The GenomeEUTwin Project is dedicated to finding genes linked to complex diseases by studying the DNA of hundreds of thousands of twin pairs.[79] This collaborative project includes researchers from Finland, Sweden, Norway, Denmark, the Netherlands, Italy, the United Kingdom, and Australia with ties to projects in Canada and Estonia.

Expectations for what genomewide association studies can accomplish should be reasonable. For example, single-nucleotide polymorphisms (SNPs, DNA sequence variations involving a change in a single nucleotide) associated with height explain less than 5 percent of the variation.[80] However, the heritability of height is close to 90 percent! About twenty common gene variants have been found for type 2 diabetes, and about seven have been found for schizophrenia, yet they explain very small percentages of the variance in these heritable conditions. The "missing heritability" may come from rare gene variants, structural gene variants, gene-gene interactions, gene-environment interactions, unknown gene variants, or combinations of these.[81] The genetic variation underlying general intelligence has also been linked to many genes with small effects.[82]

Interestingly, the search for molecular genetic correlates of disease and other traits parallels the search for nonshared environmental correlates of behavior. The environmental causes of complex human traits are "innumerable and essentially non-additive," and many small associations in both genomics research and in the social sciences cannot be replicated.[83] A great deal of work remains to be done with respect to linking specific genes to medical conditions, as well as to physical and behavioral traits.

Twin research can further activity in epigenetics, the study of changes in gene expression associated with factors unrelated to changes in DNA sequencing. In 2005, Mario F. Fraga, from Madrid's National Cancer Center, showed that the epigenetic profiles (patterns of chemical modification of the genes that affect gene expression) were more alike in younger than older MZT twin pairs.[84] Epigenetic patterns were also more alike in MZT twins who spent more rather than less time together. Gottesman has also conducted epigenetic twin studies in the area of psychopathology.[85] He has reminded everyone that the MISTRA showed that resemblance for some behavioral traits does not differ between MZA and MZT twins, so it will be important to reconcile this finding with those of Fraga.

Subsequent research has shown that specific environmental factors can affect the epigenome, thereby altering genetic expression, and that some such effects are heritable. For example, reduced male fertility associated with toxin exposure can be transmitted to later generations.[86]

In 2008, researchers identified copy number variations, differences in DNA segments, which may be linked to disease differences in MZT twins.[87] An international research team compared these characteristics in nineteen MZ twin pairs, ten of whom were free of Parkinson disease symptoms and nine who were discordant for the disease. Copy number variations were detected in both twin groups, but it is likely that they can offer insight into disease onset and progression. Studying copy number variations in disease-discordant MZA twins might tell us how environments affect the expression of specific conditions. Had this technology been available earlier, the MISTRA's MZA pairs who differed in narcolepsy, headaches, and depressive symptoms might have made contributions along these lines.

In the coming years, we are likely to see new behavioral genetic analyses of a widening array of behaviors, including dementia, obesity, autism, learning disabilities, schizophrenia, and bipolar illness. There will be increased efforts at finding endophenotypes, the internal phenotypes that bridge the gap between genes and complex behaviors and can help pinpoint their etiologies.[88] Endophenotypes, which could vary in form (e.g., neurophysiological, neuroanatomical, or biochemical), may offer simpler clues to the genetic bases of disease risk.[89] Gottesman and Shields popularized the term in 1973, and Gottesman has since asserted its importance in neuropsychiatric research.[90] Both quantitative and molecular approaches will be utilized in future behavioral genetic research—but twins' behaviors in natural and experimental settings will always excite and inspire.

Final Comment

I share stories of newly reunited twins with Bouchard, who told me, "An accumulation of such cases cannot do anything but help us make a persuasive case that something interesting is going on." He also admitted, "When I hear about a reunited pair it tugs at my heart strings." These are the pairs he won't be studying.

As a DZT twin, I knew from an early age that my twin sister Anne and I were very different in our behaviors and appearance, and I decided that there was "something" fundamentally different about us. We were hardly as alike as the MZ twins I knew in elementary school. When I learned in science classes about the effects of genes on behavior and the differential effects of environments on family members, our developmental differences made sense. Perhaps that is why the reared-apart twin findings seemed so reasonable, affirming my beliefs about the way people become who they are.

It may be surprising to learn that twins are still being separated, even though most adoption agencies appreciate the importance of keeping them together. During the last thirty years, advances in assisted reproductive technology have provided new sources of reared-apart twins. Frequently used techniques variously involve ovarian stimulation via fertility drugs, and the conception and implantation of multiple embryos into the mother's womb. Because some families are unprepared to manage or support multiple-birth children, parents sometimes arrange for twins' separate rearing. Parental divorce, foreign adoption, and accidental switching also keep some twins apart.[91] The good news is that better methods for reuniting twins, especially Internet resources, are available. And physicians working in the area of reproductive medicine are becoming better able to achieve successful pregnancies using single embryos rather than several.[92]

Had the Jim twins been discovered in 2001 or later, it is likely that studying their epigenetic profiles, copy number variations, and various molecular genetic characteristics would have been higher priorities than studying their shared occupations, heart conditions, and hobbies, the genetic components of which have been widely demonstrated. This is why the Jim twins would have had a different impact on thinking about behavior today than they had thirty years ago in 1979 when they found each other. Trying to tie the Jim twins' matched headaches and hobbies to specific genetic factors would not have produced the same high level of general fascination and debate as did the descriptions of their matched behaviors. However, Bouchard believes that reared-apart twins show us genetic influence on behavior in ways that no other source can, and that they will continue to do so. "It is so up front and personal with twins reared apart," he said. "You can see the effects right between the eyes."

The MISTRA's individual findings leave a big picture, one that it shares with past and present studies of twins and adoptees. It has "rearranged the furniture in psychology's house."[93] The so-called furniture or topics were not changed by behavior genetic studies, but the concepts, approaches, and explanations have been. Finding genetic influence on intelligence, personality, and many other human characteristics allows more realistic appraisal of similarities and differences among family members. The modest effects of common family influences on most behaviors—the events or experiences that make family members alike—offer greater understanding of parent-child and sibling resemblance and lack of resemblance. They also encourage efforts toward finding the nonshared environmental influences that significantly impact behavior and make family members differ.

About half the variation in most behaviors is explained by genetic factors, although some traits such as brain waves show greater genetic influence, and other traits such as job satisfaction show less. Environmental events, linked to individuals' life circumstances, can affect the expression of heritable traits such as intelligence and height. IQ gains have been reported for abused children adopted into high socioeconomic homes.[94] Poor nutrition may restrict the physical growth of a child or adolescent.[95]

Most important, the MISTRA has helped define the domains in which answers to questions about how behaviorally relevant genetic processes work are likely. Advances in molecular genetics and related fields are furnishing tools that can facilitate efforts in that direction.

We are moving toward a more informed view of what twin studies can and cannot accomplish. "Twin studies . . . refute both biological and environmental determinism. They do not negate the effect of the environment on behavior, nor do they overglorify the role of genes. They account for the uniqueness of each of us."[96]

Funding Sources

Detailed summaries of research funds awarded to the MISTRA on a yearly basis are included in Tables A-1, A-2, and A-3. The information in these tables was reproduced from Bouchard's grant records provided to him by the University of Minnesota's accounting office. This much financial detail is rarely provided or requested for any study, but it is presented here to satisfy the long-standing interests, questions, and criticisms associated with the MISTRA's funding sources. The largest single grant made directly to the MISTRA was for $115,455.

Table A-1. Funding for Bouchard as the MISTRA's Principal Investigator, Listed in Order of Amount

Funding Source	Award Amount (US$)
University of Minnesota Graduate School[a]	6,500
National Science Foundation	50,000
Business and industry (other)[b]	65,000
Whitfield Institute	65,884
Private donors	106,485
Spencer Foundation	181,300
Koch Charitable Foundation	185,000
Seaver Institute	250,000
Pioneer Fund	1,420,551
Total	2,330,720

a. The University of Minnesota Graduate School provided $3,800 (not listed here) to cover the Jim twins when they were discovered in March 1979.
b. Includes Harcourt Brace Jovanovich ($10,000).

Table A-2. Other Funding Sources for the MISTRA

Funding Source	Award Amount (US$)
National Institute of Health/National Institute of Dental Research (Pihlstrom)	216,123
National Institute of Health/National Institute of Dental Research (Pihlstrom)	308,730
Health and Human Services (Roberts)	1,052,213

Table A-3. Yearly Funding Sources for the MISTRA (Principal Investigator: Bouchard)

Source	End Date	Award (US$)	Year	Cumulative Year	Cumulative Total (US$)
University of Minnesota	1979 year	6,500.00			
Spencer Foundation	6/30/1980	32,000.00	1980	1979	38,500
Business and industry; other	12/31/1980	15,000.00	1980	1980	15,000
NSF Division of Integrative Biology and Neurosciences (INS)	6/30/1981	50,000.00	1981		
Pioneer Fund	8/26/1981	25,000.00	1981		
Spencer Foundation	6/30/1981	64,300.00	1981	1981	75,000
Pioneer Fund	7/14/1982	89,415.00	1982		
Spencer Foundation	11/30/1982	85,000.00	1982	1982	174,415
Pioneer Fund	8/31/1983	68,274.00	1983	1983	68,274
Pioneer Fund	4/30/1984	57,895.00	1984	1984	57,895
Koch Industries	2/13/1985	10,000.00	1985		
Koch Industries	2/13/1985	50,000.00	1985		
Pioneer Fund	7/31/1985	95,000.00	1985	1985	155,000
Pioneer Fund	7/31/1986	100,000.00	1986	1986	100,000
Koch Industries	6/30/1987	50,000.00	1987		
Pioneer Fund	7/31/1987	112,000.00	1987		
Pioneer Fund	7/31/1987	20,000.00	1987	1987	182,000
Pioneer Fund	6/30/1988	100,000.00	1988		
Seaver Institute	6/30/1988	50,000.00	1988		
Pioneer Fund	12/31/1988	10,000.00	1988	1988	160,000
Pioneer Fund	6/30/1989	100,000.00	1989		
Seaver Institute	6/30/1989	50,000.00	1989	1989	150,000
Pioneer Fund	6/30/1990	105,000.00	1990	1990	105,000
Seaver Institute	2/28/1991	50,000.00	1991		
Pioneer Fund	6/30/1991	100,000.00	1991	1991	150,000
Industrial donors	6/25/1992	50,000.00	1992		
Pioneer Fund	6/30/1992	105,000.00	1992		

Source	End Date	Award (US$)	Year	Cumulative Year	Cumulative Total (US$)
Beaver Institute	6/30/1992	50,000.00	1992	1992	205,000
Pioneer Fund	6/30/1993	105,000.00	1993		
Beaver Institute	9/30/1993	50,000.00	1993	1993	155,000
Pioneer Fund	6/30/1994	112,512.00	1994	1994	112,512
Koch Industries	6/30/1996	75,000.00	1996	1995	0
Pioneer Fund	6/30/1997	115,455.00	1997	1996	75,000
Private donors	12/31/1999	2,985.00	1999	1997	115,455
Private donors	12/31/1999	75,000.00	1999	1998	0
Private donors	12/31/1999	25,000.00	1999	1999	106,485
Private donors	12/31/1999	3,500.00	1999		
Whitfield Institute	3/31/2004	65,884.00	2004	2004	65,884
	Total MISTRA	2,330,720.00			
Other funding					
NIH/NIDR	8/1/1987–7/31/90	216,123.00			
NIH/NIDR	4/1/1993–3/31/1997	308,730.00			
IHS	8/1993–7/1998	1,052,213.00			

Note: Bouchard was also co-principal investigator (with Lykken) of several twin-related projects while the MISTRA was ongoing. Two of these grants supported development of the Minnesota Twin Registry (National Institute of Mental Health: $379,522; and Pioneer Fund: $20,000), and one grant supported a study of risk factors for criminality (Pioneer Fund: $99,621).

Glossary

Active genotype-environment correlation. The seeking out of environments and experiences compatible with one's genetic proclivities. Studious people are likely to be found at libraries and lectures, whereas artistic people might frequent museums and galleries.

Additive genetic variance. The genetic variance resulting from the independent effects of different genes adding up. Additive genetic variance is responsible for most of the genetic similarity between relatives in traits such as height.

Age-sex correction. Statistical procedures for removing the effects of age and sex or for various nonlinear or interactive effects of these variables on a trait. MZ twins and approximately two-thirds of DZ co-twins are the same age and sex, factors that can inflate trait similarity between them, just as it would between two unrelated same-age males or females. DZ male-female co-twins differ in sex, but being male or female could be associated with the level of a trait such as spatial skill, so age- and sex-correction would be appropriate for these twins as well. Data can be adjusted for the effects of age alone or sex alone.

Alleles. Different forms of a gene, such as the eye color gene (or allele) coding for brown, the gene (or allele) coding for green/blue, and the gene (or allele) coding for brown/blue.

Assortative mating. The tendency for individuals in couples to match on given traits. If these traits, such as intelligence or interests, have a genetic component then trait similarity between relatives such as DZ twins and full siblings can be enhanced, reducing heritability. Assortative mating does not affect MZ twin resemblance because MZ twins share all their genes. Assortative mating appears to be highest for social attitudes and values.

Attenuation correction. The upward adjustment of the correlation coefficient due to measurement error.

Biometrical modeling. Includes the class of statistical procedures that enable the simultaneous estimation of genetic, shared environmental, and nonshared environmental factors affecting variation in the traits of interest. These techniques can incorporate different kinships such as twins, their parents, and their children into the same model. Biometrical methods test how well a model fits a given set of data. For example, investigators compare the fit of several models and can decide if a model including genetic and nonshared environmental components fits the data better after the addition of a shared environmental component.

Correlation coefficient (r). A statistical measure of association between two things, such as height and weight, that varies between -1.0 and 1.0. This correlation is squared to obtain the proportion of variance in one variable (such as height) that is predictable from the variance in the other variable (such as weight).

Direct heritability estimates. Derived from the intraclass correlation of MZA twins or other relatives. The MZA intraclass correlation of 0.50 for a personality trait directly estimates the heritability of the trait because MZA twins share only their genes. Direct heritability estimates are higher than indirect heritability estimates, although the reason for this difference in unclear. The intraclass correlations for unrelated siblings or unrelated parent-child pairs directly estimate environmental effects because these individuals share only their environments.

Dominance. The interaction between two genes, or alleles, at corresponding locations on paired chromosomes. A child who inherited a dominant gene for type A blood from one parent and a recessive gene for type O blood from the other parent would have type A blood. A child would have type O blood only when he or she inherited two copies of the gene for type O, in which case there is no dominance effect.

Emergenic trait. A unique behavior or attribute resulting from interactions among complex gene configurations. Emergenesis explains why some genetically influenced traits, such as unusual musical talent or running speed, may not run in families. Emergenic traits can be identified by a very high MZ intraclass correlation and a very low DZ intraclass correlation. This is because MZ twins share all their genes and gene combinations, whereas DZ twins share half their genes, on average, and rarely inherit the same complex gene combinations.

Epigenetics. The study of chemical reactions that "turn on" or "turn off" certain genes at different points in time. For example, prenatal nutrition, stress, and toxins may affect gene expression that is controlled by the epigenome. Environmental toxins can lower male fertility, an effect that can be transmitted to subsequent generations.

Epigenome. A subset of genes whose functions are a consequence not only of their DNA sequence but also of the biochemical factors affecting their expression.

Epistasis. Interactions among genes at different chromosomal locations. Epistasis is similar to dominance but involves associations among genes or alleles at more than one locus.

Gene. A hereditary unit that occupies a specific place or locus on a specific chromosome. A gene is a segment of DNA (deoxyribonucleic acid) that codes for a certain chemical product that ultimately contributes to human characteristics.

Genotype-environment correlation. The co-occurrence of particular genetically based traits and environments. A person with an inquisitive mind would be likely to be found in libraries and museums.

Genotype×environment interaction. The different effects of the environment depending upon the genotypes of the individuals. A very bright child would probably enjoy an extracurricular opportunity to study math, whereas his less bright sibling might find the class uninteresting or even stressful.

Genetic correlation. The extent to which two traits, such as disinhibition and experience seeking, are influenced by common genes. Genetic correlation between two traits is indicated if the MZ cross-twin cross-trait correlation exceeds the DZ cross-twin cross-trait correlation. For example, if the correlation between the height of MZ twin 1 and the weight of MZ twin 2 is greater than the correlation between the height of DZ twin 1 and the weight of DZ twin 2, this suggests that height and weight are affected by some of the same genes.

Genotype. The genetic makeup of an organism; also, the set of genes relevant to a given trait.

Heritability. The proportion of trait variance in a population that is due to all sources of genetic differences among the members of that population, also called broad heritability. If the heritability of intelligence is estimated to be 0.70 then 70 percent of the variance, or individual differences in the population, is explained by genetic differences among the members of the population and 30 percent is explained by environmental differences among them plus measurement error. Heritability does not apply to individuals—it would be incorrect to say that 70 percent of an individual's intelligence is associated with genetic factors, because genes and environments are not separable at the individual level, only at the population level.

Indirect heritability estimate. Heritability based on the difference between two correlations. For example, if the MZT IQ correlation is 0.86, and the DZ correlation is 0.60, the difference between them is 0.26; the 0.26 value is then multiplied by 2 to obtain the heritability estimate of 0.52. This is because MZT twins share all their genes plus their environment, while DZT twins share half their genes plus their environment. The difference between the two correlations yields half the genetic effect; the difference is multiplied by 2 to obtain the full genetic effect.

Intraclass correlation coefficient (r_i). A statistical measure of association or resemblance between twins and other classes of relatives. The intraclass correlation normally ranges from 0.0 to 1.0, indicating no resemblance or perfect resemblance between relatives on a trait of interest. Negative intraclass correlations are possible, showing less systematic resemblance between relatives than individuals paired randomly; this could occur in the event of contrast effects for twins. The intraclass correlation, derived from analysis of variance, expresses the ratio of the between-group variation in a trait to the total variation in a trait. Between-pair variance refers to differences among the pairs in a sample, the within-pair variance refers to differences within each twin pair, and the total variance refers to their sum. If the trait under study is affected by genetic factors, the between-pair differences would be higher for MZ than DZ twins, and the within-pair differences would be relatively smaller; however, the total trait variance for the two types of twins is assumed to be the same. Genetic effects are shown if the correlation for MZ or MZA twins exceeds the correlation for DZ or DZA twins. This correlation is not squared because it already expresses the proportion of shared variance between relatives.

Narrow heritability. The proportion of trait variance in a population that is due to additive genetic differences among the members of that population. Like broad heritability, narrow heritability only applies to populations, not to individuals. Narrow heritability is responsible for most of the genetic resemblance between relatives other than MZ twins.

Nonadditive genetic variance. Genetic variance resulting from the interactive effects of genes; see *Dominance* and *Epistasis*.

Nonshared environment. Unique events that family members experience apart from one another that make them differ from one another in a given trait. If one child in a family took a course in contemporary politics or followed a vegetarian diet, this child could differ from his siblings in knowledge of world events and in body weight.

Pairwise concordance. A measure of twin resemblance for discrete ("either-or") traits, equal to the number of concordant pairs, divided by the number of concordant pairs plus discordant pairs. If fifteen twin pairs were concordant for schizophrenia and ten pairs were discordant, the pairwise concordance rate would be 15/25 or 60 percent.

Passive genotype-environment correlation. The association of genetically based behaviors and environments that arises because parents transmit both genes and environments to their children. Bright children are likely to have inherited their abilities from their parents, who also provide them with intellectually stimulating experiences.

Phenotype. Observable or measurable characteristics that are a function of one's genes and environments. For example, a person's height can be observed and measured, and is an outcome of the genes inherited from parents in conjunction with diet and health care.

Probandwise concordance. A measure of twin resemblance for discrete ("either-or") traits, equal to the number of affected individuals in concordant pairs divided by the total number of affected individuals. In fact, there are two types of concordant pairs, those in which pair members are independently identified (doubly ascertained) and those in which they were identified because they were twins. Doubly ascertained twin pairs are counted twice. If twenty affected twin individuals in ten twin pairs were found independently, five affected twins were found in another five pairs because their co-twins were affected, and ten discordant twin pairs were found, then the probandwise concordance rate would be $(20+5)/35$ or slightly higher than 71 percent.

Probe. A single-stranded molecule of DNA used to identify a complementary sequence of another DNA molecule.

Reactive (evocative) genotype-environment correlation. People's responses to individuals based on the expression of these individuals' genetically based behaviors. Athletically minded children are likely to be taken to ball games and related activities by their parents.

Shared environment. Events family members experience in common that make them alike in a given trait. If two siblings took piano lessons in their home or athletic training at school, they would show more similar musical ability and sports skills than if only one sibling had had these experiences.

Standard deviation (SD). A measure of the distribution of scores around a mean, equal to the square root of the variance. For example, the IQ test score population distribution follows a symmetrical bell-shaped curve in which the mean is 100 and the standard deviation is 15. Ninety-five percent of the population scores between 70 and 130 in IQ, or 2 standard deviations above and below the mean.

Standard error. The standard deviation of the sampling distribution. If the mean of a population is measured several times, it will differ, and the standard error gives an index of the spread.

Statistical control. Statistically removing the effects of one variable on another. For example, age or education might affect a person's answers to questions in an interest inventory. If a researcher wanted to study sex differences in personal interest categories, it would be wise to first statistically remove the effects of age and education on the interest scores.

Stem and leaf plot. A method for displaying the frequency with which some classes of variables occur.

Variance. The distribution or spread of scores around the mean of a sample or population.

Notes

Introduction

Epigraph: Walter Mischel, *Introduction to Personality* (New York: Holt, Rinehart & Winston, 1981), 311.

1. See, for example, Lois W. Hoffman, "The Changing Genetics/Socialization Balance," *Journal of Social Issues* 41 (1985): 127–148.
2. Laura E. Berk, *Child Development,* 8th ed. (Boston: Allyn & Bacon, 2008), 119. Berk emphasizes the limitations of heritability estimates of behavior, but she included findings from recent behavioral genetic studies in her textbook.
3. Francis Galton, "The History of Twins, as a Criterion of the Relative Powers of Nature and Nurture," *Fraser's Magazine* 12 (1875): 566–576, p. 566.
4. Richard D. Rende, Robert Plomin, and Steven G. Vandenberg, "Who Discovered the Twin Method?" *Behavior Genetics* 20 (1990): 277–285, p. 277.
5. Thomas J. Bouchard Jr. and Peter Propping, "Twins: Nature's Twice-Told Tale," in *Twins as a Tool of Behavioral Genetics,* ed. Thomas J. Bouchard Jr. and Peter Propping, 1–15 (Chichester, U.K.: John Wiley & Sons, 1993).
6. Ibid.
7. Leslie B. Arey, "Direct Proof of the Monozygotic Origin of Human Identical Twins," *Anatomical Record* 23 (1922): 245–251; Leslie B. Arey, "Chorionic Fusion and Augmented Twinning in the Human Tube," *Anatomical Record* 23 (1922): 253–261; also see Amram Scheinfeld, *Twins and Supertwins* (Baltimore: Penguin Books, 1967).
8. Horatio H. Newman, Frank N. Freeman, and Karl J. Holzinger, *Twins: A Study of Heredity and Environment* (Chicago: University of Chicago Press, 1937).
9. Gordon Allen, Letter to the Editor, March 9, 1956, *American Journal of Human Genetics* 8 (1956): 194–195, www.ncbi.nlm.nih.gov/pmc/articles/ PMC1716686.

10. Nancy L. Segal, *Entwined Lives: Twins and What They Tell Us about Human Behavior* (New York: Plume, 2000).

11. Kaare Christensen, James W. Vaupel, Niels V. Holm, and Anatoli I. Yashin, "Mortality among Twins after Age 6: Fetal Origins Hypothesis versus Twin Method," *British Medical Journal* 310 (1995): 432–436.

12. John C. Loehlin and Robert C. Nichols, *Heredity, Environment and Personality: A Study of 850 Sets of Twins* (Austin: University of Texas Press, 1976).

13. Allen Morris-Yates, G. Andrews, P. Howie, and S. Henderson, "Twins: A Test of the Equal Environments Assumption," *Acta Psychiatrica Scandinavica* 81 (1990): 322–326.

14. Adam P. Matheny, Ronald S. Wilson, and Anne B. Dolan, "Relations between Twins' Similarity of Appearance and Behavioral Similarity: Testing an Assumption," *Behavior Genetics* 6 (1976):343–352; Robert Plomin, Lee Willerman, and John C. Loehlin, "Resemblance in Appearance and the Equal Environments Assumption in Twin Studies of Personality Traits," *Behavior Genetics* 6 (1976): 43–52.

15. David C. Rowe, *The Limits of Family Influence: Genes, Experience, and Behavior* (New York: Guilford Press, 1994).

16. Paul Popenoe, "Twins Reared Apart," *Journal of Heredity* 5 (1922): 142–144.

17. A copy of this letter was provided to me by Professor Bouchard.

18. Hermann J. Muller, "Mental Traits and Heredity," *Journal of Heredity* 5 (1925):142–144. Muller's work was followed by a series of short papers on reared-together twins in the same journal; for a review, see Sheldon C. Reed, "A Short History of Human Genetics in the USA," *American Journal of Medical Genetics* 3 (1979): 282–295. Another reared-apart twin case study was published by R. Saudek, "A British Pair of Identical Twins Reared Apart," *Character and Personality* 3 (1934): 17–39.

19. Niels Juel-Nielsen, "A Psychiatric-Psychological Investigation of Monozygous Twins Reared Apart," *Acta Psychiatrica et Neurologica Scandinavica* (1965), Monograph Supplement 183. A follow-up study that included the original material was published in 1980.

20. Robert J. Lifton, *The Nazi Doctors: Medical Killing and the Psychology of Genocide* (New York: Basic Books, 1986).

21. Arthur Jensen, "How Much Can We Boost IQ and Scholastic Achievement?" *Harvard Educational Review* 39 (1969): 1–123.

22. A similar controversy erupted in 1994 following the publication of Richard Herrnstein and Charles Murray's book, *The Bell Curve: Intelligence and Class Structure in American Life* (New York: Free Press) which discussed possible genetically based group differences in general intelligence. See John C. Loehlin, "History of Behavior Genetics," in *Handbook of Behavior Genetics*, ed. Yong-Kyu Kim, 3–11 (New York: Springer, 2009) for discussion of this and other significant events in the behavioral genetics field.

23. Leon J. Kamin, *The Science and Politics of IQ* (Potomac, Md.: Lawrence Erlbaum, 1974); Ann Clarke and Michael McAskie, "Parent-Offspring Resemblances in Intelligence: Theories and Evidence," *British Journal of Psychology* 67 (1976): 243–273.

24. Kamin, *Science and Politics of IQ*. A 1958 analysis of 42 MZA twin pairs by Burt's colleague Ms. J. Conway reported an IQ correlation of 0.778.
25. Irving I. Gottsman, interview, May 7, 2011. According to Gottesman, Shields had invited Kamin to his laboratory to see additional photographs, but Shields did not publish them to preserve the privacy of his participants. Gottesman also believes that Shields was too modest to have his picture taken with the twins.
26. Stephen Davis, "Nice One, Cyril?" *BBC TV*, January 7–13, 1984, 10–11.
27. Robert B. Joynson, *The Burt Affair* (London: Routledge, 1989). Ronald Fletcher, *Science, Ideology, and the Media: The Cyril Burt Scandal* (New Brunswick, N.J.: Transaction, 1991).
28. Nicholas J. Mackintosh, *Cyril Burt: Fraud or Framed?* (Oxford: Oxford University Press, 1995).
29. James Shields, "MZA Twins: Their Use and Abuse," in *Twin Research: Part A: Psychology and Methodology*, ed. Walter E. Nance, 79–93 (New York: Alan B. Liss, 1978); David Burbridge, "Burt's Twins: A Question of Numbers," *Journal of the History of the Behavioral Science* 42: 35–52 (2006); William Tucker, "Burt's Separated Twins: The Larger Picture," *Journal of the History of the Behavioral Science* 43 (2007): 81–86.
30. Nancy L. Segal, "More Thoughts on the Child Development Center Twin Study," *Twin Research and Human Genetics* 8 (2005): 276–281. Interestingly, Neubauer authored the foreword to Niels Juel-Nielsen's, *Individual and Environment: Monozygotic Twins Reared Apart* (New York: International Universities Press, 1980).
31. Lawrence D. Perlman, "Memories of the Child Development Study Center Study of Adopted Monozygotic Twins Reared Apart: An Unfulfilled Promise," *Twin Research and Human Genetics* 8: 271–281.
32. Segal, "More Thoughts," 2005.
33. John Money and Anke Ehrhardt, *Man and Woman, Boy and Girl* (Baltimore: Johns Hopkins University Press, 1975).
34. Milton Diamond and Keith Sigmundson, "Sex Reassignment at Birth: Long-Term Review and Clinical Implications," *Archives of Pediatric and Adolescent Medicine* 151 (1997): 298–304.
35. Leo Kanner, "Autistic Disturbances of Affective Contact," *The Nervous Child* 2 (1943): 217–250.
36. Edward O. Wilson, *Naturalist* (New York: Warner Books, 1995).
37. Gordon Allen, review of Sandra Scarr's *Race, Social Class, and Individual Differences in I.Q.* (Baltimore: Lawrence Erlbaum, Associates, 1981), *Social Biology* 30 (1983): 118–119.
38. Ullica Segerstråle, *Defenders of the Truth: The Battle for Science in the Sociobiology Debate and Beyond* (Oxford: Oxford University Press, 2000).
39. John Garcia, Frank R. Ervin, and Robert A. Koelling, "Learning with Prolonged Delay of Reinforcement," *Psychonomic Science* 5 (1966): 121–122.
40. Stephen R. Coleman, "Pavlov and the Equivalence of Associability in Classical Conditioning," *Journal of Mind and Behavior* 28 (2007): 115–134.
41. Steven G. Vandenberg, "Contributions of Twin Research to Psychology," *Psychological Bulletin* 66 (1966): 326–352. Jerome Lejeune and Patricia

Jacobs discovered that Down syndrome was caused by an extra chromosome 21.

42. The cognitive deficits associated with PKU can be largely, but not completely, offset by administering a phenylalanine-free diet and monitoring the blood levels of affected individuals.

43. Steven Pinker, *The Blank Slate: The Modern Denial of Human Nature* (New York: Viking, 2002).

44. Noam Chomsky, "A Review of B. F. Skinner's *Verbal Behavior,*" *Language* 35 (1959): 26–58.

45. Herbert A. Simon, "Information Processing Models of Cognition," *Annual Review of Psychology* 30 (1979): 363–396.

46. Lee Willerman, *The Psychology of Individual and Group Differences* (San Francisco: W. H. Freeman, 1979).

47. David Rosenthal, ed., *The Genain Quadruplets: A Case Study and Theoretical Analysis of Heredity and Environment in Schizophrenia* (New York: Basic Books, 1963); Leonard L. Heston, "Psychiatric Disorders in Foster Home Reared Children of Schizophrenic Mothers," *British Journal of Psychiatry* 112 (1966): 819–825; Irving I. Gottesman and James Shields, *Schizophrenia and Genetics: A Twin Study Vantage Point* (New York: Academic Press, 1972).

48. Loehlin, "History of Behavior Genetics."

49. Dr. Matthew McGue, interview, October 13, 2009.

50. Steven G. Vandenberg, Richard E. Stafford, and A. M. Brown, "The Louisville Twin Study," in *Progress in Human Behavior Genetics: Recent Reports on Genetic Syndromes, Twin Studies, and Statistical Advances,* ed. Steven G. Vandenberg, 153–204 (Baltimore: Johns Hopkins University Press, 1968).

51. John C. DeFries, R. Plomin, S. G. Vandenberg, and A. R. Kuse, "Parent-Offspring Resemblance for Cognitive Abilities in the Colorado Adoption Project: Biological, Adoptive, and Control Parents and One-Year-Old Children," *Intelligence* 5 (1981): 245–277.

52. Shields, "MZA Twins: Their Use and Abuse."

53. Thomas J. Bouchard Jr., "The Hereditarian Research Program: Triumphs and Tribulations," in *Arthur Jensen: Consensus and Controversy,* ed. Sohan Modgil and Celia Modgil, 55–76 (London: Falmer International, 1987).

54. Irving I. Gottesman, "Heritability of Personality," *Psychological Monographs: General and Applied* 77, no. 572 (1963): 1–21; Gottesman and Shields, *Schizophrenia and Genetics.*

55. See Thomas J. Bouchard Jr., "The Drifter: A Random Walk through Psychology" (unpublished paper, November 24, 2004).

56. Irving I. Gottesman, "Introduction," in Juel-Nielsen, *Individual and Environment,* 9.

57. James L. Jenkins and Donald G. Paterson, *Studies in Individual Differences: The Search for Intelligence* (New York: Appleton-Century-Crofts, 1961).

58. Jim Lewis was remarried to a third wife named Sandy when he visited Minnesota. I sometimes wondered if that concerned Jim Springer's wife, Betty.

59. Comment by former graduate student assistant Susan Resnick.

60. Aya Ito, Yoko Honma, Emiko Inamori, Yukari Yada, Mariko Y. Momoi, and Yoshikazu Nakamura, "Developmental Outcome of Very Low Birth Weight Twins Conceived by Assisted Reproduction Techniques," *Journal of Perinatology* 26 (2006): 130–133.
61. Elizabeth F. DiLalla and Paula Y. Mullineaux, "The Effects of Classroom Environment on Problem Behaviors: A Twin Study," *Journal of School Psychology* 46 (2007): 107–128.
62. Constance Holden, "Identical Twins Reared Apart," *Science* 207 (1980): 1323–1327.
63. James Shields, *Monozygotic Twins Brought Up Apart and Brought Up Together* (London: Oxford University Press, 1962).
64. Nancy L. Segal and Yoon-Mi Hur, "Reared Apart Korean Female Twins: Genetic and Cultural Influences on Life Histories, Physical and Health-Related Measures, and Behavioral Traits," *International Journal of Behavioral Development* 32 (2008): 542–548.
65. Nancy L. Pedersen, Paul Lichtenstein, and Pia Svdberg, "The Swedish Twin Registry in the Third Millennium," *Twin Research and Human Genetics* 5 (2002): 427–432.
66. Kari Kervinen, J. Kaprio, M. Koskenvuo, J. Juntunen, and Y. A. Kesäniemi, "Serum Lipids and Apolipoprotein E Phenotypes in Identical Twins Reared Apart," *Clinical Genetics* 53 (1998): 191–199.
67. Kazuo Hayakawa and Tadahiko Shimizu, "Blood Pressure Discordance and Lifestyle: Japanese Identical Twins Reared Apart and Together," *Acta Geneticae Medicae et Gemellologiae* 36 (1987): 485–491.
68. Shields provided brief accounts of one DZA male and ten DZA female twin pairs in his 1962 study.
69. Thomas J. Bouchard Jr., "Memo to the Twin Research Team," March 5, 1979. The second pair to participate in the MISTRA were DZA female twins.
70. Tina Adler, "Seeing Double? Controversial Twins Study Widely Reported, Debated," *The APA Monitor* 22 (1991): 1, 8; Robert Karen, *Becoming Attached: First Relationships and How They Shape Our Capacity to Love* (Oxford: Oxford University Press, 1998): 307–308.
71. Barbara Gonyo, "Genetic Sexual Attraction," *Decree* 4 (1987): 1, 5. It is believed that humans evolved cues to avoid mating with close relatives, and one is associated with cohabitating as children. This is called the Westermarck Effect.

1. The Jim Twins (February–March 1979)

1. Rosemary Rawson, "Two Ohio Strangers Find They're Twins at 39—and a Dream to Psychologists," *People* magazine, May 7, 1979, 117–120.
2. Mike Lackey, "Identical Twins, Separated as Babies in 1939, Reunited," *Lima* [Ohio] *News*, February 19, 1979.
3. Barbara S. Burks and Anne Roe, "Studies of Identical Twins Reared Apart," *Psychological Monographs* 63 (1949).
4. Joy Stilley, "Never Apart Again, Twins Say," *Tuscaloosa News,* November 16, 1969, 22; Bard Lindeman, *The Twins Who Found Each Other* (New York: Morrow, 1969).

5. "Interview with Thomas J. Bouchard, Jr.," *Intelligence* Online, www.isironline.org, Distinguished Contributor Interview, 2004.

6. Lykken's account of the Jim twins is described in his book *Happiness: What Studies on Twins Show Us about Nature, Nurture, and the Happiness Set Point* (New York: Golden Books, 1999). The material in this chapter was provided by Bouchard; Lykken was deceased when my interviews occurred.

7. David Healy, *The Psychopharmacologists II: Interviews by Dr. David Healey* (London: Altman, 1998).

8. Auke Tellegen, *A Brief Manual for the Differential Personality Questionnaire* (unpublished manuscript, University of Minnesota, 1978); Auke Tellegen, "Structure of Mood and Personality and Their Relevance to Assessing Anxiety, with an Emphasis on Self-Report," in *Anxiety and the Anxiety Disorders,* ed. A. Hussain Tuma and Jack D. Maser, 681–706 (Hillsdale, N.J.: Erlbaum, 1985).

9. Jack Darley's son, John, is the Warren Professor of Psychology at Princeton University.

10. Dr. Polesky retired in about 2000 just after the MISTRA ended.

11. Edwin Chen, "Twins Reared Apart: A Living Lab," *New York Times Magazine,* December 9, 1979, 112–130.

12. Donald D. Johnson, "Reunion of Identical Twins, Raised Apart, Reveals Some Astonishing Similarities," *Smithsonian,* October 1980, 48–56, p. 53. I found notes from a Bouchard lecture, "MZAs: Are They Really Identical?" November 10, 1982, in which the first thing Bouchard said was, "The findings are hard to believe."

13. Mike Lackey, "Jim Twins Study Spurs Detailed U-Minn. Project," *Lima* [Ohio] *News,* May 14, 1979.

14. Chen, "Twins Reared Apart."

15. Katherine Kam, "His Guide to a Heart Attack: Symptoms in Men," February 14, 2007, www.webmd.com/heart-disease/features/his-guide-to-a-heart-attack.

16. James Shields, *Monozygotic Twins Brought Up Apart and Brought Up Together* (London: Oxford University Press, 1962).

17. Confidentiality regulations prevented the release of such information by the Minnesota investigators.

18. The last pair underwent initial assessment in April 1999.

19. Constance Holden, "Identical Twins Reared Apart," *Science* 207 (1980): 1323–1327.

20. Healy, *The Psychopharmacologists II.*

21. "Interview with Thomas J. Bouchard, Jr."

2. 15,000 Questions × 137 Pairs

1. Nicholas G. Martin, Lindon J. Eaves, Andrew C. Heath, R. Jardine, L. M. Feingold, and H. J. Eysenck, "Transmission of Social Attitudes," *Proceedings of the National Academy of Sciences of the United States of America* 83 (1986): 4364–4368.

2. "Separation at the Cradle 75 Years Ago for Twins," New Zealand newspaper, unidentified, from Bouchard's newspaper archive. The estimated date is 1989, the year the twins were reunited.

3. Bent Harvald, Gudrun Hauge, Kirsten Ohm Kyvik, Kaare Christensen, Axel Skytte, and Niels V. Holm, "The Danish Twin Registry: Past and Present," *Twin Research and Human Genetics* 7 (2004): 318–335.

4. He Mingguang, "Guangzhou Twin Registry and Guangzhou Eye Study," abstract, paper presented at the 13th International Congress on Twin Studies, Seoul, South Korea, June 4–7, 2010.

5. The number of DNA markers analyzed expanded with improvements in laboratory techniques (Mary Mount, personal communication, November 23, 2009). In 1979, the Jim twins were compared across eight red blood cell groups (ABO, RH, MNSs, Lewis, Kell, Duffy, Kidd, and P), seven serum proteins (Gc, Hp, A, PGM, acP, EsD, and Bf), and two other factors (Gm and Inv). In April 1999, twins in our last pair were compared across two red blood cell systems (ABO and Rh) and five DNA fragment length polymorphisms (probe SLi737, locus D12S11; probe SLi986, locus D17S79; probe SLi989, locus D7S467; probe SLi1090, locus D6S132, and probe SLi106, locus D2S44). The DNA analysis in combination with blood group analysis was introduced in July 1994.

6. David T. Lykken, "The Diagnosis of Zygosity in Twins," *Behavior Genetics* 8 (1978): 437–473.

7. Dr. Alison MacDonald is a senior lecturer at the University of East London.

8. Robert R. Race and Ruth Sanger, *Blood Groups in Man* (Oxford: Oxford University Press, 1975).

9. Nancy L. Segal, "Zygosity Diagnosis: Laboratory and Investigator's Judgment," *Acta Geneticae Medicae et Gemellologiae, Twin Research* 33 (1984): 515–520.

10. Most cases of ectodermal dysplasia are X-linked recessive, a transmission pattern that does not fit these twins.

11. "Happiness Is a Reunited Set of Twins," *U.S. News and World Report,* April 13, 1987, 63–66.

12. See Daniel Hanson, "The Gene Illusion Confusion," review of Joseph, *The Gene Illusion* (2004), PsycCRITIQUES 50, no. 52, article 14. Hanson likened Joseph to an "adrenalized boxer" when it comes to behavioral genetic research.

13. Jay Joseph, *The Gene Illusion: Genetic Research in Psychiatry and Psychology under the Microscope* (New York: Algora, 2004).

14. Matt McGue and Thomas J. Bouchard Jr., "Adjustment of Twin Data for the Effects of Age and Sex," *Behavior Genetics* 14 (1984): 325–343.

15. Nancy L. Segal, "Oskar and Jack," in *Indivisible by Two,* 50–78 (Cambridge, Mass.: Harvard University Press, 2007).

16. "Telling Them Why," obituary, *Guardian,* September 9, 1989.

17. Jill Todd, "Finding My Twin Brought Happiness Beyond Belief," *Woman,* September 1985, 40–41.

18. John Stroud, "Last Word" (estimated date 1989). Great Britain, from Bouchard's newspaper archive.

19. Nancy L. Segal, "More Thoughts on the Child Development Center Twin Study," *Twin Research and Human Genetics* 8 (2005): 276–281.
20. William H. Tucker, "Re-Reconsidering Burt: Beyond a Reasonable Doubt," *Journal of the History of the Behavioral Sciences* 33 (1997): 145–162, p. 152.
21. Rebecca L. Hegar, "Sibling Placement in Foster Care and Adoption: An Overview of International Research," *Children and Youth Services Review* 27 (2005): 717–739; Ilene Staff and Edith Fein, "Together or Separate: A Study of Siblings in Foster Care," *Child Welfare* 41 (1992): 257–270.
22. Jeffrey Kluger, *The Sibling Effect: What the Bonds among Brothers and Sisters Reveal about Us* (New York: Riverhead Books, 2011).
23. Nancy L. Segal, "Implications of Twin Research for Legal Issues Involving Young Twins," *Law and Human Behavior* 17 (1993): 43–58.
24. Nancy L. Segal, Kevin A. Chavarria, and Joanne Hoven, "Twin Research: Evolutionary Perspective on Social Relations," in *Family Relationships: An Evolutionary Perspective,* ed. Catherine A. Salmon and Todd K. Shackelford, 312–335 (New York: Oxford University Press, 2007): 312–333; Adam Brookes, "China's Unwanted Girls," BBC News Online, August 23, 2001, http://news.bbc.co.uk/2/hi/asia-pacific/1506469.stm.
25. Nancy L. Segal and Iris Blandón-Gitlin, "Twins Switched at Birth: A Case from the Canary Islands," *Twin Research and Human Genetics* 13 (2010): 115–119; Nancy L. Segal, *Someone Else's Twin: The True Story of Babies Switched at Birth* (New York: Prometheus Books, 2011).
26. Antonio Garrido-Lestache, "Identification of New-Born Babies by Fingerprints," *International Criminal Police Review* 481 (2000): 19–24.
27. James Shields, "Twins Brought Up Apart," *Eugenics Review* 50 (1958): 115–123, p. 117.
28. Charles W. Mueller and Toby L. Parcel, "Measures of Socioeconomic Status: Alternatives and Recommendations," *Child Development* 52 (1981): 13–21.
29. "Body Watch," WGBH, Boston in conjunction with *American Health Magazine,* June 31, 1987, available on video.
30. James Shields, *Monozygotic Twins Brought Up Apart and Brought Up Together* (London: Oxford University Press, 1962), 94.
31. "Epistasis: Puzzling Inheritance Patterns Explained," www.answers.com/topic/epistasis (accessed 7/6/11).
32. Robert Plomin, John C. DeFries, Gerald E. McClearn, and Peter McGuffin, *Behavioral Genetics,* 5th ed. (New York: Worth Publishers, 2008).
33. Michael C. Neale and Lon R. Cordon, *Methodology for Genetic Studies of Twins and Families* (Dordrecht, the Netherlands: Springer, 2010).
34. It is assumed that the overall variance of the trait does not differ between the two types of twins.
35. Horatio H. Newman, Frank N. Freeman, and Karl J. Holzinger, *Twins: A Study of Heredity and Environment* (Chicago: University of Chicago Press, 1937).
36. Hermine H. M. Maes, Gaston P. Beunen, Robert F. Vlietinck, et al., "Inheritance of Physical Fitness in 10-Year-Old Twins and Their Parents," *Medicine and Science in Sports and Exercise* 28 (1996): 1479–1491.
37. The statistical reliability of heritability estimates is twenty times higher if based on MZA twins rather than MZT twins. David T. Lykken, Seymour

Geisser, and Auke Tellegen, "Heritability Estimates from Twin Studies: The Efficiency of the MZA Design" (unpublished manuscript, Department of Psychology, University of Minnesota, Minneapolis, 1981).

38. Douglas S. Falconer and Trudy F. C. Mackay, *Introduction to Quantitative Genetics,* 4th ed. (New York: Longman, 1996).

39. Thomas J. Bouchard Jr. and Matthew McGue, "Familial Studies of Intelligence: A Review," *Science* 212 (1981): 1055–1059.

40. Thomas J. Bouchard Jr., Nancy L. Segal, Auke Tellegen, Matt McGue, Margaret Keyes, and Robert Krueger, "Genetic Influence on Social Attitudes: Another Challenge to Psychology from Behavior Genetics," in *Behavior Genetic Principles: Development, Personality and Psychopathology,* ed. Lisabeth F. DiLalla, 89–104 (Washington, D.C.: American Psychological Association, 2004). If a trait shows nonadditive genetic variance, then heritability is overestimated by doubling the difference in the MZT and DZT correlations. That is because MZ twins share all sources of genetic variance, both additive and nonadditive.

41. McGue and Bouchard, "Adjustment of Twin Data."

42. Plomin, *Behavioral Genetics.*

3. Early Findings (1979–1983)

Epigraph: David T. Lykken, "Research with Twins: The Concept of Emergenesis," *Psychophysiology* 19 (1981): 361–373, p. 361.

1. Thomas J. Bouchard Jr., Leonard Heston, Elke Eckert, Margaret Keyes, and Susan Resnick, "The Minnesota Study of Twins Reared Apart: Project Description and Sample Results in the Development Domain," in *Twin Research 3: Part B. Intelligence, Personality and Development,* ed. Luigi Gedda, Paolo Parisi, and Walter Nance, 227–333 (New York: Alan R. Liss, Inc., 1981).

2. The original paper lists the twins' age as twenty-four, but they were twenty-three at the time of their assessment.

3. These twins had had varying degrees of contact over the years, but had been apart for a total of fifty-four years.

4. Bouchard et al., "Minnesota Study of Twins Reared Apart," p. 223.

5. David Rosenthal, ed., *The Genain Quadruplets: Case Study and Theoretical Analysis of Heredity and Environment in Schizophrenia* (New York: Basic Books, 1963).

6. Elke D. Eckert, Leonard L. Heston, and Thomas J. Bouchard Jr. (1981), "MZ Twins Reared Apart: Preliminary Findings of Psychiatric Disturbances and Traits . . . ," in *Twin Research 3: Part B. Intelligence, Personality and Development,* ed. Luigi Gedda, Paolo Parisi, and Walter Nance, 179–188 (New York: Alan R. Liss, Inc., 1981).

7. Frank C. Verhulst and Herma J. M. Verluis-Den Bieman, "Developmental Course of Problem Behaviors in Adolescent Adoptees," *Journal of the American Academy of Child and Adolescent Psychiatry* 34 (1995): 151–158.

8. Margaret A. Keyes, Anu Sharma, Irene J. Elkins, William G. Iacono, and Matt McGue, "The Mental Health of US Adolescents Adopted in Infancy," *Archives of Pediatric and Adolescent Medicine* 162 (2008): 419–425; Anu R.

Sharma, Matthew K. McGue, Peter L. Benson, "The Psychological Adjustment of United States Adopted Adolescents and Their Nonadopted Siblings," *Child Development* 69 (1998): 791–802.

9. Thomas J. Bouchard Jr., "The Study of Mental Ability Using Twin and Adoption Designs," in *Twin Research 3: Part B. Intelligence, Personality, and Development,* ed. Luigi Gedda, Paolo Parisi, and Walter Nance, 21–23 (New York: Alan R. Liss, Inc., 1981).

10. The objectors agreed to let Bouchard turn on a tape recorder during his lecture, but they never protested again nor appeared in his class.

11. "Freedom of Expression," editorial, *Minnesota Daily,* April 4, 1974. A campus debate on academic freedom was held several weeks later.

12. Constance Holden, "Behavioral Geneticist Celebrates Twins Scorns PC Science," *Science* 325 (2009): 27. Constance Holden, who covered the MISTRA on many occasions, was killed in a car accident in 2010.

13. Tina Adler, "Seeing Double? Controversial Twins Study Widely Reported, Debated," *The APA Monitor* 22 (1991): 1, 8.

14. Sam Fulwood III, "Scholars Gather to Debate Genetics-Crime Research: Conference: Meeting in Maryland Will Explore the Implications of Study into Whether Some People are Inherently Predisposed toward Criminal Behavior," http://articles.latimes.com/1995-09-93/news/mn-49167_1_criminal-behavior, September 23, 1995.

15. David Lykken, "Statistical Significance in Psychological Research," *Psychological Bulletin* 70 (1968): 151–159.

16. Howard F. Taylor, *The IQ Game: Methodological Inquiry into the Heredity/Environment Controversy* (New Brunswick, N.J.: Rutgers University Press, 1980).

17. Taylor's book was viewed favorably by critics of twin research. See, for example, a review by Jerry Hirsch in *Social Biology* 30 (1983): 116–118.

18. Thomas J. Bouchard Jr., "Do Environmental Similarities Explain the Similarity in Intelligence of Identical Twins Reared Apart?" *Intelligence* 7 (1983): 175–184.

19. Susan L. Farber, *Twins Reared Apart: A Reanalysis* (New York: Basic Books, 1981).

20. Positive reviews: John D. Rainer, *Social Biology* 28 (1981): 163–165; J. Thomas Dalby, *Journal of School Psychology* 20 (1982): 256–258; James R. Stabenau, *Psychoanalytic Quarterly* 53 (1984): 121–129; Howard E. Gruber, "Nature vs. Nurture: A Natural Experiment," *New York Times,* March 1, 1981. Interestingly, in that same review, Gruber offered a positive appraisal of Niels Juel-Nielsen's book *Individual and Environment: Monozygotic Twins Reared Apart* (New York: International Universities Press, 1980). See also John Rosegrant, *Journal of Personality Assessment* 46 (1982): 659–660. Rosegrant asserted that the previous reared-apart twin data were "too poor to be more than impressionistic" and that the MISTRA promised "more trustworthy data."

Negative reviews: Richard J. Rose, "Separated Twins: Data and Their Limits," *Science* 215 (1982): 959–960; Irving I Gottesman, *American Journal of Psychology* 95 (1982): 350–352; Gregory Carey, *American Journal of Psychiatry* 139 (1982): 377; Peter McGuffin, *Psychiatric Annals* 12 (1982): 358. A review by Sandra Scarr, *Journal of Social and Biological Structures* 6 (1983): 89–91, applauded Farber's efforts at organizing the material but believed Farber fell into "Kamin's (1974) trap of wanting to divide and conquer the intellectual results for seemingly political reasons" (p. 90); Scarr's comment was in reference to Leon J. Kamin, *The Science and Politics of IQ* (Potomac, Md.: Lawrence Erlbaum, 1974).

21. W. Joseph Wyatt and Donna M. Midkiff, "Biological Psychiatry: A Practice in Search of a Science," *Behavior and Social Issues* 15 (2006): 132–151.

22. Jack Kaplan, "How to Inherit IQ: An Exchange," letter to the editor, *New York Review of Books,* March 15, 2007, 56.

23. Frank Sulloway, "How to Inherit IQ: An Exchange," reply to the editor, *New York Review of Books,* March 15, 2007, 56.

24. Richard E. Nisbett, *Intelligence and How to Get It: Why Schools and Cultures Count* (New York: W. W. Norton, 2009).

25. Ibid., 26.

26. Dan Agin, "How to Inherit IQ: The Fetal Question," letter to the editor, *New York Review of Books,* October 25, 2007, 82.

27. Thomas J. Bouchard Jr. and Matt McGue, "Genetic and Environmental Influences on Human Psychological Differences," *Journal of Neurobiology* 54 (2003): 4–45.

28. Greater personality similarity has been found between later-splitting MZT twins (those more likely to be subject to fetal transfusion syndrome) than earlier-splitting MZT twins, although the reasons are unclear. Deborah K. Sokol, Cynthia A. Moore, Richard J. Rose, et al., "Intrapair Differences in Personality and Cognitive Ability among Young Monozygotic Twins Distinguished by Chorion Type," *Behavior Genetics* 25 (1995): 457–466.

29. Nancy L. Segal, Shirley A. McGuire, June Havlena, Patricia Gill, and Scott L. Hershberger, "Intellectual Similarity of Virtual Twin Pairs: Developmental Trends," *Personality and Individual Differences* 42 (2007): 1209–1219.

30. Sandra Scarr, Richard A. Weinberg, and Irwin D. Waldman, "IQ Correlations in Transracial Adoptive Families," *Intelligence* 17 (1993): 541–555.

31. Matt McGue et al., "A Comparison of Identical Twins Reared Apart on a Battery of Information Processing Measures," paper presented at the 11th Annual Behavior Genetics Association, Purchase, N.Y., 1981.

32. Thomas J. Bouchard Jr. and David T. Lykken, "Similarity in Intelligence in Monozygotic Twins Reared Apart" (abstract), and Irving I. Gottesman, Gregory C. Carey, and Thomas J. Bouchard Jr., "MMPI Personality Scale Similarity in 26 Pairs of Identical Twins Reared Apart," abstract, *Behavior Genetics* 12 (1982): 578, 585–586.

33. David T. Lykken, "Research with Twins: The Concept of Emergenesis," *Psychophysiology* 19 (1981): 361–373.

34. Thomas J. Bouchard Jr., "Twins Reared Together and Apart: What They Tell Us about Human Diversity," in *Individuality and Determinism: Chemical and Biological Bases,* ed. Sidney W. Fox, 147–178 (New York: Plenum, 1984).

35. John M. Hettema, Michael C. Neale, and Kenneth S. Kendler, "Physical Similarity and the Equal-Environment Assumption in Twin Studies of Psychiatric Disorders," *Behavior Genetics* 25 (1995): 327–335.
36. Thomas J. Bouchard Jr., David T. Lykken, Nancy L. Segal, and Kimerly J. Wilcox, "Development in Twins Reared Apart: A Test of the Chronogenetic Hypothesis," in *Human Growth: A Multidisciplinary Review,* ed. Andrea Demirjian, 299–310 (London: Taylor & Francis, 1986), 301.
37. David T. Lykken, Auke Tellegen, and William G. Iacono, "EEG Spectra in Twins: Evidence for a Neglected Mechanism of Genetic Determination," *Physiological Psychology* 10 (1982): 60–65.
38. David T. Lykken, Auke Tellegen, and Karen Thorkelson, "Genetic Determination of EEG Frequency Spectra," *Biological Psychology* 1 (1974): 245–259.
39. Niels Juel-Nielsen, *Individual and Environment: Monozygotic Twins Reared Apart* (New York: International Universities Press), 68.
40. The sixth channel was the electrooculogram.
41. The Shafer event is an EEG task in which the multiple EEG epochs at about 250 msec prestimulus and 750 msec poststimulus are averaged. Noise in the EEG averages to baseline, and the remaining variation is the brain's response to the stimulus.
42. Lykken was an early advocate of using silver/silver chloride electrodes in order to obtain unbiased recordings. Don Fowles, interview, May 20, 2011.
43. The two age- and sex-corrected scores were transformed to a mean of 50 and a standard deviation of 10 before analysis.
44. The composite IQ (R + M) was calculated by converting the Raven and Mill-Hill to z-scores and adding them.
45. Gerrit J. S. Wilde, "Inheritance of Personality Traits," *Acta Psychologia* 22 (1964): 37–51.
46. Gordon Claridge, Sandra Canter, and W. I. Hume, *Personality Differences and Biological Variations: A Study of Twins* (Oxford: Pergamon Press, [1974]).
47. Daniel Hankins, Charles Drage, Noe Zambel, and Richard Kronenberg, "Pulmonary Function in Identical Twins Raised Apart," *American Review of Respiratory Disease* 125 (1982): 119–121.
48. This is called the forced expiratory flow rate (25–75 percent of the total forced vital capacity, or maximum volume of gas exhaled from full inhalation).
49. This is called the instantaneous expiratory flow rate (75 percent of the total forced vital capacity).
50. This is called the forced expiratory volume (amount of air expelled during the first second of the forced vital capacity maneuver).
51. A recent large study found that twin concordance for smoking or nonsmoking does not affect the heritability of pulmonary measures; see Truls S. Ingebrigtsen, Simon F. Thomsen, Sophie van der Sluis, et al., "Genetic Influences on Pulmonary Function: A Large Sample Twin Study," *Lung* 189 (2011): 323–330.

4. Sexual Orientation, Cognition, and Medical Traits (1984–1987)

1. Some researchers thought that this was because processing speed was a major component of general intelligence, but others thought it reflected variable associations between information processing and special mental abilities.
2. Matt McGue, Thomas J. Bouchard Jr., David T. Lykken, and Dale Feuer, "Information Processing Abilities in Twins Reared Apart," *Intelligence* 8 (1984): 239–258.
3. Michael I. Posner, Stephen J. Boies, William H. Eichelman, and Richard L. Taylor, "Retention of Visual and Name Codes of Single Letters," *Journal of Experimental Psychology* 79 (1969): 1–16.
4. Saul Sternberg, "The Discovery of Processing Stages: Extension of Donders' Method," *Acta Psychologia* 30 (1969): 276–315.
5. Roger Shepard and Jacqueline Metzler, "Mental Rotation of Three Dimensional Objects," *Science* 171 (1971): 701–703.
6. The twins' mean correct response times were regressed against the size of the memory sets.
7. The twins' median reaction time for correct ("same") responses was regressed against the angular displacement of the figures.
8. These results contradict the idea that biological differences have their greatest effect on rate of cognitive processing.
9. Rudolf Barcal, Josef Sova, Miloslava Křižanouská, J. Levy, and Jiři Matoušek, "Genetic Background of Circadian Rhythms," *Nature* 220 (1968): 1128–1131.
10. Bruce R. Hanson, Franz Halberg, Naip Tuna, et al., "Rhythmometry Reveals Heritability of Circadian Characteristics of Heart Rate of Human Twins Reared Apart," *Cardiologia (Bulletin of the Italian Society of Cardiology)* 29 (1984): 267–282, p. 268.
11. This device was an ambulatory electrocardiocorder (model 445B) manufactured by Delmar Avionics in Irvine, California.
12. Franz Halberg, Eugene A. Johnson, Walter Nelson, Walter Runge, and Robert Sothern, "Autorhythmometry Procedures for Physiologic Self-Measurements and Their Analysis," *Physiology Teacher* 1 (1972): 1–11.
13. Hanson et al., "Rhythmometry Reveals Heritability," 279.
14. Franz Halberg, Germaine Cornélissen, George Katinas, et al., "Transdisciplinary Unifying Implications of Circadian Findings in the 1950s," *Journal of Circadian Rhythms* 1 (2003), doi:10.1186/1740-3391-1-2.
15. The twins' difference in sexual activity during heart rate monitoring could be considered a nongenetic effect on their heart functioning. However, one twin's decision to have sex and to let the researchers know could reflect the sisters' genetically based differences in extraversion or risk-taking.
16. Mathea R. Allensmith, Barbara McClellan, and Michael Butterworth, "The Influence of Heredity and Environment on Human Immunoglobulin Levels," *Journal of Immunology* 102 (1969): 1504–1510.
17. Antibody titers measure the level of antibodies in the blood.
18. We assessed antibodies in response to type 14 pneumococcal capsular polysaccharides.

19. Peter F. Kohler, Victor J. Rivera, Elke D. Eckert, Thomas J. Bouchard Jr., and Leonard L. Heston, "Genetic Regulation of Immunoglobulin and Specific Antibody Levels in Twins Reared Apart," *Journal of Clinical Investigation* 75 (1985): 883–888, p. 887.

20. William H. Knobloch, Nancy M. Leavenworth, Thomas J. Bouchard Jr., and Elke D. Eckert, "Eye Findings in Twins Reared Apart," *Ophthalmic Paediatrics and Genetics* 5 (1985): 59–66.

21. Not all features of the retina, such as the pattern of blood vessels, are identical for MZ twins. "Retinal Biometrics," October 10, 2011, http://360biometrics .com/faq/Retinal-Biometrics.php.

22. Hanne Nødgaard, Helle Hansen, Helle Andreasen, and Henrik Toft Sørensen, Hanne Norggaard, "Risk Factors Associated with Retinopathy of Prematurity (ROP) in Northern Jutland, Denmark 1990–1993," *Acta Ophthmologica Scandinavica*, 74 (1996): 306–310.

23. Elke D. Eckert, Thomas J. Bouchard Jr., Joseph Bohlen, and Leonard L. Heston, "Homosexuality in Twins Reared Apart," *British Journal of Psychiatry* 148 (1986): 421–425, p. 421.

24. Leonard L. Heston and James Shields, "Homosexuality in Twins: A Family Study and a Registry Study," *Archives of General Psychiatry* 18 (1968): 149–160.

25. J. Michael Bailey, "Texas, John Loehlin, and the Genetics of Sexual Orientation," paper presented at the Festschrift Honoring John Loehlin, Newport, Rhode Island, June 6, 2011.

26. J. Michael Bailey, Michael P. Dunne, and Nicholas G. Martin, "Genetic and Environmental Influences on Sexual Orientation and Its Correlates in an Australian Twin Sample," *Journal of Personality and Social Psychology* 78 (2000): 524–536.

27. Niklas Långström, Qazi Rahman, Eva Carlström, and Paul Lichtenstein, "Genetic and Environmental Effects on Same-Sex Sexual Behavior: A Population Study of Twins in Sweden," *Archives of Sexual Behavior* 39 (2010): 75–80.

28. Scott L. Hershberger and Nancy L. Segal, "The Cognitive, Behavioral, and Personality Profiles of a Male Monozygotic Triplet Set Discordant for Sexual Orientation," *Archives of General Psychiatry* 33 (2004): 497–514; Nancy L. Segal, "Female to Male: Two Monozygotic Twin Pairs Discordant for Transsexualism," *Archives of Sexual Behavior* 35 (2006): 347–358; Ray Blanchard, Kenneth J. Zucker, Ana Cavacas, Sara Allin, Susan J. Bradley, and Debbie C. Schachter, "Birth Order and Sibling Sex Ratio in Homosexual Male Adolescents and Probably Prehomosexual Feminine Boys," *Developmental Psychology* 31 (1995): 22–30.

29. Niels Juel-Nielsen, *Individual and Environment: Monozygotic Twins Reared Apart* (New York: International Universities Press, 1980); James Shields, *Monozygotic Twins Brought Up Apart and Brought Up Together* (London: Oxford University Press, 1962).

30. Benjamin Radford, "2 Percent of Americans Identify as Gay," Discovery News, April 11, 2011, http://news.discovery.com/human/about-2-of-americans-are-gay-110411.html.

31. Elke D. Eckert, Thomas J. Bouchard Jr., Joseph Bohlen, and Leonard L. Heston, "Homosexuality in Twins Reared Apart," *British Journal of Psychiatry* 148 (1986): 421–425.

32. Ibid.

33. See Gardner Lindzey, "Some Remarks Concerning Incest, the Incest Taboo, and Psychoanalytic Theory," *American Psychologist* 22 (1967): 1051–1059, for a fascinating treatment of this topic.

34. Barbara Gonyo, "Genetic Sexual Attraction," American Adoption Congress, *Decree* 4 (Winter 1987): 1, 5.

35. Karri Silventoinen, Jaakko Kaprio, Eero Lahelma, et al., "Assortative Mating by Body Weight and BMI: Finnish Twins and Their Spouses," *American Journal of Human Biology* 15 (2003): 620–627; Robert Plomin, John C. DeFries, Gerald E. McClearn, and Peter McGuffin, *Behavioral Genetics: A Primer,* 5th ed. (New York: Worth Publishers, 2008).

36. Suma Jacob, Martha K. McClintock, Bethanne Zelano, and Carole Ober, "Paternally Inherited HLA Alleles Are Associated with Women's Choice of Male Odor," *Nature Genetics* 30 (2002): 175–179.

37. Diane Amery, "Couple Wed 20 Years Discover They're Twins," *The Sun* [London], December 17, 1985, 19.

38. Niels Juel-Nielsen, 1980.

39. Eckert et al., "Homosexuality in Twins," 424.

40. Ibid., 425.

41. Hillary Lips, *Sex and Gender: An Introduction* (New York: McGraw-Hill, 2005).

42. Thomas J. Bouchard Jr., "Twins Reared Together and Apart: What They Tell Us about Human Diversity," in *Individuality and Determinism: Chemical and Biological Bases,* ed. Sidney W. Fox, 147–184 (New York: Plenum, 1984).

43. Thomas J. Bouchard Jr., David T. Lykken, Nancy L. Segal, and Kimerly J. Wilcox, "Development in Twins Reared Apart: A Test of the Chronogenetic Hypothesis," *Human Growth: A Multidisciplinary Review,* ed. Andrea Demirjian, 299–310 (London: Taylor & Francis, 1986).

44. Linda K. Dixon and Ronald C. Johnson, *The Roots of Individuality* (Belmont, Calif.: Wadsworth, 1980), 96.

45. Carole A. Roberts and Charles B. Johansson, "The Inheritance of Cognitive Interest Styles among Twins," *Journal of Vocational Behavior* 4 (1974): 237–243. The Holland scales can be derived from subjects' responses to the Strong items, although the content is not strictly comparable between the two instruments. In addition, the 1974 intraclass correlations may be inflated because they were not age- and sex-corrected.

46. Harold D. Grotevant, Sandra Scarr, and Richard Weinberg, "Patterns of Interest Similarity in Adoptive and Biological Families," *Journal of Personality and Social Psychology* 35 (1977): 667–676.

47. JoAnn C. Boraas, Louise B. Messer, and Michael J. Till, "Dental Characteristics of Twins Reared Apart," 65th Annual Meeting of the International Society for Dental Research, Chicago, *Journal of Dental Research* 66 (1987), abstract no. 27.

48. In 2007, Stephen Rich became Director of the Center for Public Health Genomics at the University of Virginia, Charlottesville.

5. Pivotal Papers: Personality and IQ (1988 and 1990)

1. Daniel Goleman, "Major Personality Study Finds That Traits Are Mostly Inherited," *New York Times,* December 2, 1986, 17–18, p. 17.
2. Auke Tellegen, David T. Lykken, Thomas J. Bouchard Jr., Kimerly J. Wilcox, Nancy L. Segal, and Stephen Rich, "Personality Similarity in Twins Reared Apart and Together," *Journal of Personality and Social Psychology* 54 (1988): 1031–1039. This paper has had over 800 citations in Google Scholar as of June 2011 (at 100 citations, a paper is considered a "Social Science Citation Classic").
3. Lisa Lynch, "Twins' Personality Study Made Big Media Splash before Journal Approval," *Science Writer,* Winter 1990, 15–19, p. 19.
4. See, for example, Lois W. Hoffman, "The Influence of the Family Environment on Personality: Accounting for Sibling Differences," *Psychological Bulletin* 110 (1991): 187–203; John S. Lang, "How Genes Shape Personality," *U.S. News and World Report,* April 13, 1987, 58–66.
5. Horatio H. Newman, Frank N. Freeman, and Karl J. Holzinger, *Twins: A Study of Heredity and Environment* (Chicago: University of Chicago Press, 1937).
6. Incomplete data for the separated twins precluded further personality comparisons between the MZA and MZT pairs.
7. Ibid., 332 p. 332.
8. James Shields, *Monozygotic Twins Brought Up Apart and Brought Up Together* (London: Oxford University Press, 1962). Shields administered the Self-Rating Questionnaire (SRQ), which was designed for his study by Professor Hans J. Eysenck. The SRQ was the forerunner of the Eysenck Personality Questionnaire.
9. Robert Plomin, John C. DeFries, Gerald E. McClearn, and Peter McGuffin, *Behavioral Genetics: A Primer,* 5th ed. (New York: Worth Publishers, 2008).
10. Shields conducted brief assessments of eleven DZA pairs.
11. David T. Lykken, Thomas J. Bouchard Jr., Matt McGue, and Auke Tellegen, "The Minnesota Twin Family Registry: Some Initial Findings," *Acta Genetice Medicae et Gemellologiae, Twin Research* 39 (1990): 35–70.
12. Auke Tellegen, "Structure of Mood and Personality and Their Relevance to Assessing Anxiety, with an Emphasis on Self-Report," in *Anxiety and the Anxiety Disorders,* ed. A. Hussain Tuma and Jack D. Maser, 681–706 (Hillsdale, N.J.: Erlbaum, 1985).
13. A fifth inventory booklet was added toward the end of the study.
14. Quoted in Constance Holden, "The Genetics of Personality" *Science* 237 (1987): 598–599.
15. Ibid., 600.
16. John Leo and Elizabeth Taylor, "Exploring the Traits of Twins," *Time* magazine, January 12, 1987, 63.

17. Goleman, "Major Personality Study."
18. Richard J. Rose, Markku Koskenvuo, Jaakko Kaprio, Seppo Sarna, and Heimo Langinvainio, "Shared Genes, Shared Experiences, and Similarity of Personality: Data from 14,288 Adult Finnish Co-Twins," *Journal of Personality and Social Psychology* 54 (1988): 161–171.
19. David T. Lykken, Matt McGue, Thomas J. Bouchard Jr., and Auke Tellegen, "Does Contact Lead to Similarity or Similarity to Contact?" *Behavior Genetics* 20 (1990): 547–561.
20. Richard J. Rose, Jaakko Kaprio, Christopher J. Williams, Richard Viken, and Karen Obremski, "Social Contact and Sibling Similarity: Facts, Issues, and Red Herrings," *Behavior Genetics* 20 (1990): 763–778.
21. Richard J. Rose was Lykken's doctoral student at the University of Minnesota, and received his Ph.D. in 1964.
22. Dr. Richard J. Rose, personal correspondence.
23. Michael V. Ellis and Erica S. Robbins, "In Celebration of Nature: A Dialogue with Jerome Kagan," *Journal of Counseling and Development* 68 (1990): 623–627.
24. Interestingly, Aristotle (384–322 B.C.) came up with the suggestion that distributive justice consists of treating equals equally and unequals unequally (*Nicomachean Ethics*, Book V, Chapter 3, "Distributive Justice, in Accordance with Geometrical Proportion"). Of course, treating children differently (or unequally) does not imply, or condone, treating one more favorably than another.
25. This was expected based on the DZA and DZT twins' intraclass correlations being less than half as large as those of the MZA and MZT twins.
26. The higher order factor of Positive Emotionality, which includes Social Closeness, also showed within-family effects.
27. *Nightline,* ABC, October 1989.
28. Thomas J. Bouchard Jr., David T. Lykken, Matthew McGue, Nancy L. Segal, and Auke Tellegen, "Sources of Human Psychological Differences: The Minnesota Study of Twins Reared Apart," *Science* 250 (1990): 223–228, p. 228. (This paper has had over 900 citations in Google Scholar as of June 2011.)
29. This paper underwent many drafts, so the sample probably included fewer than the full number of pairs that had been assessed at the time of its submission. A young set of MZA twins was also excluded from the analysis.
30. See Thomas J. Bouchard Jr., "Twins Reared Together and Apart: What They Tell Us about Human Diversity," in *Individuality and Determinism: Chemical and Biological Bases,* ed. Sidney W. Fox, 147–184 (New York: Plenum, 1984). The conference, "The Chemical and Biological Bases for Individuality," was sponsored by the Liberty Fund and held in Key Biscayne, Florida.
31. Ibid.
32. David Wechsler, *Manual for the Wechsler Adult Intelligence Scale* (New York: Psychological Corporation, 1955).
33. John C. Raven, *Manual for Raven's Progressive Matrices and Vocabulary Scales* (London: Lewis, 1986).

34. David T. Lykken, "Research with Twins: The Concept of Emergenesis," *Psychophysiology* 19 (1982): 361–373.
35. Gerald E. McClearn, Boo Johansson, Stig Berg, et al., "Substantial Genetic Influence on Cognitive Abilities in Twins 80 or More Years Old," *Science* 276 (1997): 1560–1563.
36. Nancy L. Segal, Shirley A. McGuire, June Havlena, Patricia Gill, and Scott L. Hershberger, "Intellectual Similarity of Virtual Twin Pairs: Developmental Trends," *Personality and Individual Differences* 42 (2007): 1209–1219.
37. Christiane Capron and Michel Duyme, "Assessment of Effects of Socioeconomic Status in a Full Cross-Fostering Study," *Nature* 340 (1989): 552.
38. Newman et al., *Twins,* 1937. Newman et al.'s IQ data were recalculated to yield Stanford-Binet and Otis IQ intraclass correlations of 0.68 (originally 0.67) and 0.74 (originally 0.73). Note that upon omitting four "extreme cases" (four sets of co-twins with substantial educational differences), Newman et al. found that educational and social differences accounted for just 20 percent of the IQ variance.
39. The results were 0.06 ± 0.15 (time together before separation), 0.08 ± 0.15 (time apart to first reunion), -0.14 ± 0.15 (total contact time), and 0.17 ± 0.15 (percentage of lifetime apart).
40. A 2003 study found that heritability estimates of general intelligence were near zero among seven-year-old twin children from impoverished families, with 60 percent of the variance associated with shared environmental factors. The reverse was true for twins from affluent families. The investigators indicated that it would be inappropriate to claim that outcomes among children from poor environments are more closely tied to their environments than are outcomes among children from favorable environments. It is possible that some genetic influences on general intelligence are common to genetic influences on socioeconomic status. Eric Turkheimer, Andreana Haley, Mary Waldron, Brian D'Onofrio, and Irving I. Gottesman, "Socioeconomic Status Modifies Heritability of IQ in Young Children," *Psychological Science* 14 (2003): 623–628; Nancy L. Segal and Wendy Johnson, "Twin Studies of General Mental Ability," in *Handbook of Behavior Genetics,* ed. Yong-Kyu Kim, 81–99 (New York: Springer, 2009).
41. Hermine H. H. Maes, Gaston P. Beunen, Robert F. Vlietinck, et al. "Inheritance of Physical Fitness in 10-Year-Old Twins and Their Parents," *Medicine and Science in Sports and Exercise* 28 (1996): 1479–1491.
42. Nicholas G. Martin, Lindon J. Eaves, Andrew C. Heath, Rosemary Jardine, Lynn M. Feingold, and Hans J. Eysenck, "Transmission of Social Attitudes," *Proceedings of the National Academy of Sciences of the United States of America* 83 (1986): 4364–4368, p. 4368.
43. David M. Buss, *Evolutionary Psychology: The New Science of the Mind,* 2nd ed. (Boston: Allyn & Bacon, 2004).
44. Thomas H. Maugh, "Major Study Says Personality Mostly a Matter of Genes," *Philadelphia Inquirer,* October 12, 1990, 1A, 14A.
45. Richard M. Dudley, "IQ and Heredity," letter to the editor, *Science* 252 (1991): 191; Jonathan Beckwith, Lisa Geller, and Sahotra Sarkar, "IQ and Heredity," letter to the editor, *Science* 252 (1991): 191.

46. Thomas J. Bouchard Jr., David T. Lykken, Matthew McGue, Nancy L. Segal, and Auke Tellegen, "IQ and Heredity: Response," *Science* 252 (1991): 191–192. The phrase in the quote taken from this article was also emphasized in the original text.

47. Ibid.

48. Thomas J. Bouchard Jr., David T. Lykken, Matt McGue, Nancy L. Segal, and Auke Tellegen, "When Kin Correlations Are Not Squared," *Science* 250 (1990): 1998.

49. Arthur R. Jensen, "Note on Why Genetic Correlations Are Not Squared," *Psychological Bulletin* 75 (1971): 223–224.

50. Marij Gielen, Catharina E. M. van Beijsterveldt, Catherine Derom, et al., "Secular Trends in Gestational Age and Birthweight in Twins," *Human Reproduction* 25 (2010): 2346–2353; Geoffrey A. Machin and Louis G. Keith, *An Atlas of Multiple Pregnancy: Biology and Pathology* (New York: Parthenon, 1999).

51. Nancy L. Segal, *Entwined Lives: Twins and What They Tell Us about Human Behavior* (New York: Plume, 2000).

52. Ronald S. Wilson, "Twin Growth: Initial Deficit, Recovery and Trends in Concordance from Birth to Nine Years," *Annals of Human Biology* 6 (1979): 205–220.

53. Nancy L. Pedersen, Robert Plomin, John R. Nesselroade, and Gerald E. McClearn, "A Quantitative Genetic Analysis of Cognitive Abilities during the Second Half of the Life Span," *Psychological Sciences* 3 (1992): 346–353.

54. Matt McGue, Thomas J. Bouchard Jr., William G. Iacono, and David T. Lykken, "Behavioral Genetics of Cognitive Ability: A Life-Span Perspective," in *Nature, Nurture, and Psychology,* ed. Robert Plomin and Gerald E. McClearn, 59–76 (Washington, D.C.: American Psychological Association, 1993).

55. "Sources of Human Psychological Differences," tags: "Heredity Vs. Environment" and "Racial Differences," David Duke (Web site), November 11, 2002, www.davidduke.com/race-information-library/racial-differences/sources-of-human-psychological-differences_66.html.

56. Hans H. Stassen, David T. Lykken, Peter Propping, and Gianni Bomben, "Genetic Determination of the Human EEG: Survey of Recent Results on Twins Reared Together and Apart," *Human Genetics* 80 (1988): 165–176.

6. Job Satisfaction, Cardiac Characteristics, and More (1989–1990)

1. Richard D. Arvey, Thomas J. Bouchard Jr., Nancy L. Segal, and Lauren M. Abraham, "Job Satisfaction: Environmental and Genetic Components," *Journal of Applied Psychology* 74 (1989): 187–192.

2. "The Biology of Business: *Homo Administrans,*" *The Economist,* September 23, 2010, www.economist.com/node/17090697.

3. Barry M. Staw, Nancy E. Bell, and John A. Clausen, "The Dispositional Approach to Job Attitudes: A Lifetime Longitudinal Test," *American Science Quarterly* 31 (1986): 56–77.

4. David J. Weiss, René V. Dawis, George W. England, and Lloyd H. Lofquist, *Manual for the Minnesota Satisfaction Questionnaire,* Minnesota Studies in

Vocational Rehabilitation No. 45 (Minneapolis: Industrial Relations Center, University of Minnesota, 1967).

5. Russell Cropanzano and Keith James, "Some Methodological Considerations for the Behavioral Genetic Analysis of Work Attitudes," *Journal of Applied Psychology* 75 (1990): 433–439.

6. Thomas J. Bouchard Jr., Richard D. Arvey, Lauren M. Keller, and Nancy L. Segal, "Genetic Influences on Job Satisfaction: A Reply to Cropanzano and James," *Journal of Applied Psychology* 77 (1992): 89–93.

7. William G. Iaocono and David T. Lykken, "The Orienting Response: Importance of Instructions," *Schizophrenia Bulletin* 5 (1979): 11–14.

8. Malcolm H. Lader and Lorna Wing, *Physiological Measures, Sedative Drugs, and Morbid Anxiety* (London: Oxford University Press, 1966).

9. David T. Lykken, William G. Iacono, Keith Haroian, Matthew McGue, and Thomas J. Bouchard Jr., "Habituation of the Skin Conductance Response to Strong Stimuli: A Twin Study," *Psychophysiology* 25 (1988): 4–15. Four reared-apart same-sex sibling sets were included among the DZA twin pairs.

10. David T. Lykken, "Autobiography" (unpublished manuscript, University of Minnesota, 2006).

11. The electrodes were connected to separate Beckman Type 9844 skin conductance couplers that drove two channels of a Beckman RM Dynograph.

12. Velia Trejo, Catherine Derom, Robert Vlietinck, et al., "X Chromosome Inactivation Patterns Correlate with Fetal-Placental Anatomy in Monozygotic Twin Pairs: Implications for Immune Relatedness and Concordance for Autoimmunity," *Molecular Medicine* 1 (1994): 62–70.

13. Allen H. Kline, James B. Sidbury Jr., and Curt P. Richter, "The Occurrence of Ectodermal Dysplasia and Corneal Dysplasia in One Family," *Journal of Pediatrics* 55 (1959): 355–366.

14. Bruce Hanson, Naip Tuna, Thomas J. Bouchard Jr., et al., "Genetic Factors in the Electrocardiogram and Heart Rate of Twins Reared Apart and Together," *American Journal of Cardiology* 63 (1989): 606–609.

15. Hugh W. Simpson, Carmen Kelsey, Richard A. Gatti, et al., "Autorhythmometry in Myasthenia Gravis: Detection of Chronopathology and Assessment of Condition by Rhythm-Adjusted Level of Grip Strength," *Journal of Interdisciplinary Cycle Research* 2 (1971): 397–416.

16. Hanson et al., "Genetic Factors in the Electrocardiogram."

17. Peter Watson, *Twins: An Uncanny Relationship* (Chicago: Contemporary Books, 1981).

18. Thomas J. Bouchard Jr., Nancy L. Segal, and David T. Lykken, "Genetic and Environmental Influences on Special Mental Abilities in a Sample of Twins Reared Apart," *Acta Geneticae Medicae et Gemellologiae, Twin Studies* 39 (1990): 193–206.

19. Matt McGue and Thomas J. Bouchard Jr., "Genetic and Environmental Determinants of Information Processing and Special Mental Abilities: A Twin Analysis," in *Advances in the Psychology of Human Intelligence,* vol. 5, ed. Robert J. Sternberg, 7–45 (Hillsdale, N.J.: Lawrence Erlbaum, 1989).

20. In 1983, psychologist Earl Hunt and others hypothesized that cognitive processing measures reflect basic neurological mechanisms. Earl B. Hunt, "On the Nature of Intelligence," *Science* 219 (1983): 141–146.

21. Philip A. Vernon, "Speed of Information Processing and General Intelligence," *Intelligence* 7 (1983): 53–70.

22. Keith J. Hayes, "Genes, Drives, and Intellect," *Psychological Reports* 10 (1962): 299–342.

23. Thomas J. Bouchard Jr., David T. Lykken, Auke Tellegen, and Matthew McGue, "Genes, Drives, Environment and Experience: EPD Theory-Revised," in *Intellectual Talent: Psychometric and Social Issues,* ed. Camilla P. Benbow and David Lubinski, 5–43 (Baltimore: Johns Hopkins University Press, 1996).

24. Ibid., p. 31.

25. John C. DeFries, Geoffrey C. Ashton, Ronald C. Johnseon, et al., "Parent-Offspring Resemblance for Specific Cognitive Abilities in Two Ethnic Groups," *Nature* 261 (1986): 131–133.

26. McGue and Bouchard, "Genetic and Environmental Determinants, pp. 41–42.

27. Matt McGue, Thomas J. Bouchard Jr., David T. Lykken, and Dale Feuer, "Information Processing Abilities in Twins Reared Apart," *Intelligence* 8 (1984): 239–258; Thomas J. Bouchard Jr., David T. Lykken, Nancy L. Segal, and Kimerly J. Wilcox, "Development in Twins Reared Apart: A Test of the Chronogenetic Hypothesis," *Human Growth: A Multidisciplinary Review,* ed. Andrea Demirjian, 299–310 (London: Taylor & Francis, 1986).

28. Nancy L. Segal, "Twins: The Finest Natural Experiment," *Personality and Individual Differences* 49 (2010): 317–323.

29. Constance Holden, "Offbeat Twins," *Science* 288 (2000): 1735; Dateline NBC, *"The Ties That Bind,"* March 30, 1999.

30. Thomas J. Bouchard Jr. and Kimerly J. Wilcox, "Behavior Genetics," in *McGraw-Hill Encyclopedia of Science and Technology,* 6th ed. (New York: McGraw-Hill, 1989).

31. Thomas J. Bouchard Jr. and Nancy L. Segal, "Advanced Mathematical Reasoning Ability: A Behavioral Genetic Perspective," *Behavioral and Brain Sciences* 13 (1990): 191–192.

32. Paul M. Brinich et al., *The Adoption Bibliography* (Washington, D.C.: American Adoption Congress, 1990).

33. *Le Journal International de Médecine* 178 (1990): 27–36.

34. David T. Lykken, Thomas J. Bouchard Jr., Matt McGue, and Auke Tellegen, "The Minnesota Twin Family Registry: Some Initial Findings," *Acta Geneticae Medicae et Gemellologiae, Twin Studies,* 39 (1990): 35–70.

35. Allison Kelly, "Wedding Gift of a Long Lost Brother," unlabeled newspaper article from Bouchard's archive, September 1989.

36. Elizabeth Mullener, "Nature or Nurture? Ask Twins," *The Times-Picayune* [New Orleans], February 16, 1990, A1–A8.

37. Melvin Konner, "Under the Influence," *Omni* magazine, January 1989, 62–64, 90–91.

7. Psychopathology and Religiosity (1990)

1. Gilles de la Tourette, "Étude sur une affection nerveuse characterisée par de l'incoordination motrice accompagnée d'écholalie et de coprolalie," *Archives de Neurologie* (Paris) 9 (1884): 19–42, 158–200.
2. See Niels Juel-Nielsen, *Individual and Environment: Monozygotic Twins Reared Apart* (New York: International Universities Press, 1980); Horatio H. Newman, Frank N. Freeman, and Karl J. Holzinger, *Twins: A Study of Heredity and Environment* (Chicago: University of Chicago Press, 1937).
3. R. Arlen Price, Kenneth K. Kidd, Donald J. Cohen, David L. Pauls, and James F. Leckman, "A Twin Study of Tourette Syndrome," *Archives of General Psychiatry* 42 (1985): 815–820.
4. Peter Vieregge, Cornelia Schäfer, and Johannes Jörg, "Concordant Gilles de la Tourette's Syndrome in Monozygotic Twins: A Clinical, Neurophysiological and CT Study," *Journal of Neurology* 235 (1988): 366–367; Ann Le Couteur, Anthony Bailey, Susan Goode, et al., "A Broader Phenotype of Autism: The Clinical Spectrum in Twins," *Journal of Child Psychology and Psychiatry* 37 (1996): 785–801.
5. Jesse F. Abelson, Kenneth Y. Kwan, Brian J. O'Roak, et al., "Sequence Variants in *SLITRK1* Are Associated with Tourette's Syndrome," *Science* 310 (2005): 317–320.
6. Revised versions of the Diagnostic Statistical Manual (DSM; e.g., DSM-IV) call the condition Tourette disorder, while earlier versions and other sources call it Tourette syndrome.
7. Nancy L. Segal, Maurice W. Dysken, Thomas J. Bouchard Jr., Nancy L. Pedersen, and Leonard L. Heston, "Tourette's Disorder in a Set of Reared-Apart Triplets: Genetic and Environmental Influences," *American Journal of Psychiatry* 147 (1990): 196–199; Darlene C. Ifill-Taylor, "Diagnosis of Tourette's Disorder," letter to the editor, *American Journal of Psychiatry* 147 (1990): 1386.
8. David Rosenthal, *The Genain Quadruplets: A Case Study and Theoretical Analysis of Heredity and Environment in Schizophrenia* (New York: Basic Books, 1963).
9. A number of twins shared their life stories with the media and, with their consent, I published detailed essays on three of our separated sets in my book *Indivisible by Two: Lives of Extraordinary Twins* (Cambridge, Mass.: Harvard University Press, 2007).
10. William M. Grove, Elke D. Eckert, Leonard Heston, Thomas J. Bouchard Jr., Nancy L. Segal, and David T. Lykken, "Heritability of Substance Abuse and Antisocial Behavior: A Study of Monozygotic Twins Reared Apart," *Biological Psychiatry* 27 (1990): 1293–1304.
11. Irving I. Gottesman and James Shields, *Schizophrenia: The Epigenetic Puzzle* (Cambridge, U.K.: Cambridge University Press, 1982).
12. Susan L. Farber, *Identical Twins Reared Apart: A Reanalysis* (New York: Basic Books, 1980).
13. *The Diagnostic Statistical Manual-III* (1980) introduced a multiaxial system to recognize different aspects of behavioral disorders such as clinical and personality.

14. The Research Diagnostic Criteria (RDC) and St. Louis Criteria specify symptoms of psychiatric disorders. The RDC criteria were developed in the 1970s to increase diagnostic consistency of American and European patients.

15. Probandwise concordance is calculated as the number of affected individuals in concordant pairs divided by the total number of affected individuals. Geneticists prefer this method to pairwise concordance, or number of concordant pairs divided by the number of concordant pairs plus discordant pairs. The probandwise rate is preferred for several reasons, such as enabling direct comparison with the population prevalence and rates for other relatives. Matt McGue, "When Assessing Twin Concordance, Use the Probandwise, Not the Pairwise Rate," *Schizophrenia Bulletin* 18 (1992): 171–176.

16. Elke D. Eckert, Thomas J. Bouchard Jr., Joseph Bohlen, and Leonard L. Heston, "Homosexuality in Twins Reared Apart," *British Journal of Psychiatry* 148 (1986): 421–425.

17. Nancy L. Segal, Elke D. Eckert, William M. Grove, Thomas J. Bouchard Jr., and Leonard L. Heston, "A Summary of Psychiatric and Psychological Findings from the Minnesota Study of Twins Reared Apart," *Etiology of Mental Disorder,* ed. Einar Kringlen, Nils Johan Lavik, and Svenn Torgersen *(World Psychiatric Association, Regional Symposium, August 23–26, Oslo, Norway),* 183–200 (Vindern, Norway: University of Oslo, Department of Psychiatry, 1990).

18. Robert Plomin, John C. DeFries, Gerald E. McClearn, and Peter McGuffin, *Behavioral Genetics,* 5th ed. (New York: Worth Publishers, 2008).

19. Robert Plomin, John C. DeFries, and Gerald E. McClearn, *Behavioral Genetics: A Primer* (San Francisco: W. H. Freeman, 1980).

20. Robert Plomin, John C. DeFries, and Gerald E. McClearn, *Behavioral Genetics: A Primer,* 2nd ed. (New York: W. H. Freeman, 1990), pp. 386–387. The work referenced in this passage is John C. Loehlin and Robert C. Nichols, *Heredity, Environment, and Personality: A Study of 850 Sets of Twins* (Austin: University of Texas Press, 1976).

21. Niels G. Waller, Brian A. Kojetin, Thomas J. Bouchard Jr., David T. Lykken, and Auke Tellegen, "Genetic and Environmental Influences on Religious Interests, Attitudes, and Values: A Study of Twins Reared Apart and Together," *Psychological Science* 1 (1990): 138–142.

22. Laura B. Koenig, Matt McGue, Robert F. Krueger, and Thomas J. Bouchard Jr., "Genetic and Environmental Influences on Religiousness: Findings for Retrospective and Current Religiousness Ratings," *Journal of Personality* 73 (2005): 471–488, p. 251. The article in the special issue refers to Lyndon I. Eaves, Brian D'Onofrio, and Robert Russell, "Transmission of Religion and Attitudes," *Twin Research* 2 (1999): 59–61.

23. Nicholas G. Martin, Lindon J. Eaves, Andrew C. Heath, Rosemary Jardine, Lynn M. Feingold, and Hans J. Eysenck, "Transmission of Social Attitudes," *Proceedings of the National Academy of Sciences of the United States of America* 83 (1986): 4364–4368.

24. Waller et al., "Genetic and Environmental Influences."

25. Jerry S. Wiggins, "Substantive Dimensions of Self-Report in the MMPI Pool," *Psychological Monographs* 80, no. 630 (1966): 1–42.

26. Niels G. Waller, David T. Lykken, and Auke Tellegen, "Occupational Interests, Leisure Time Interests, and Personality: Three Domains or One? Findings from the Minnesota Twin Registry," in *Assessing Individual Differences in Human Behavior: New Concepts, Methods, and Findings,* ed. David Lubinski and René V. Dawis, chapter 9 (Palo Alto, Calif.: Davies-Black, 1995). The scale is derived from factor analysis.

27. Jo-Ida C. Hansen and Donald P. Campbell, *Manual for the SVIB-SCII* (Stanford, Calif.: Stanford University Press, 1985).

28. Waller et al., "Occupational Interests." Waller chose a different thesis topic— "Genetic Tobit Factor Analysis: Quantitative Genetic Modeling with Censored Data"—and was hired by the University of California–Davis.

29. Gordon W. Allport, Philip E. Vernon, and Gardner Lindzey, *Manual for the Study of Values: A Scale for Measuring the Dominant Interests in Personality,* 3rd ed. (Boston: Houghton-Mifflin, 1960).

30. The estimated shared environmental component for the Religious Leisure Time Interests scale of 0.11 did not differ significantly from zero.

31. Only two of the fifteen correlations were statistically significant, but they were modest in size. Wiggins—Performance IQ: $r = -0.26$; Wiggins—Full Scale IQ: $r = -0.21$.

32. Jeffrey Kluger, Jeff Chu, Boward Liston, Maggie Sieger, and Daniel Williams, "Is God in Our Genes?" *Time,* October 25, 2004, p. 67.

33. Ellen Robinson-Hayes, "Beliefs Flow Out of Genes?" *Sacramento Bee,* February 17, 1990, A-1.

34. Julie Begley, "An Impossible Christmas Surprise," *The Voice* 39, December 24, 1997.

35. The twins' November 1997 reunion was taped by local Channel 3 News.

36. Dorine Leogrande, "A Tale of Two Sisters," *Connecticut Jewish Ledger,* December 12, 1997, 1, 27. At the end of one of our evenings together, the twins laughed and crossed their eyes—they had independently discovered this trick and enjoyed entertaining (or horrifying) people with it.

37. Ibid.

38. Mary E. Holmes, *Being You* (London: Austin & Macauley, 2008), 156–157.

39. Segal, *Indivisible by Two.*

40. Thomas J. Bouchard Jr., David T. Lykken, Matt McGue, and Auke Tellegen, "Intrinsic and Extrinsic Religiousness: Genetic and Environmental Influences and Personality Correlates," *Twin Research* 2 (1999): 88–98.

41. Robert Plomin and Denise Daniels, "Why Are Children in the Same Family So Different from Each Other?" *Behavioral and Brain Sciences* 10 (1987): 1–16.

42. "Theodore Wachs," Purdue University Psychological Sciences, Developmental Faculty, n.d., www.psych.purdue.edu/index.php/faculty/12-faculty/39-wachs-theodore-.html.

43. Thomas J. Bouchard Jr. and Matthew McGue, "Genetic and Rearing Environmental Influences on Adult Personality: An Analysis of Adopted Twins Reared Apart," *Journal of Personality* 58 (1990): 263–292.

44. Harrison G. Gough, "An Interpreter's Syllabus for the California Psychological Inventory," in *Advances in Psychological Assessment,* vol. 1, ed. Paul

McReynolds, 55–79 (Palo Alto, Calif.: Consulting Psychologists Press, 1968), p. 57.

45. Rudolph H. Moos and Bernice S. Moos, *Manual: Family Environment Scale* (Palo Alto, Calif.: Consulting Psychologists Press, 1986).

46. When scores do not differ greatly across individuals, it is not possible to find meaningful relationships between these scores and other measures. If most adoptees were adopted on their day of birth, it would be impossible to detect a relationship between age at adoption and birth weight, which varies considerably across newborns.

47. Note that attenuation is expected for correlations based on difference scores.

48. Constance Holden, "Double Features," *The 1990 World Book Year Book: The Annual Supplement to the World Book Encyclopedia* (Chicago: World Book, 1990), 140–153.

49. "Zweites Ich," *Der Spiegel*, April 1990, 248–250.

50. Thomas H. Maugh II, "Major Study Says Personality Mostly a Matter of Genes," *Philadelphia Inquirer*, October 12, 1990, 1A, 14A.

8. Dental Traits, Allergies, and Vocational Interests (1991–1992)

Epigraph: JoAnn C. Boraas, Louise B. Messer, and Michael J. Till, "A Genetic Contribution to Dental Caries, Occlusion, and Morphology as Demonstrated by Twins Reared Apart," *Journal of Dental Research* 67 (1988): 1150–1155, p. 1150.

1. Sidney B. Finn and Robert C. Caldwell, "Dental Caries in Twins I: A Comparison of the Caries Experience of Monozygotic Twins, Dizygotic Twins and Unrelated Children," *Archives of Oral Biology* 8 (1963): 571–585; Robert S. Corrucini and Rosario H. Potter, "Genetic Analysis of Occlusional Variation in Twins," *American Journal of Orthodontics* 78 (1980): 140–154.

2. Susan L. Farber, *Identical Twins Reared Apart: A Reanalysis* (New York: Basic Books, 1980).

3. Malocclusion refers to a difference in size between the upper and lower jaws or jaw and tooth size, leading to overcrowding or an abnormal bite. Malocclusion is most often hereditary. Jack D. Rosenberg, "Malocclusion of Teeth," MedlinePlus Medical Encyclopedia, updated February 22, 2010, www.nlm.nih.gov/medlineplus/ency/article/001058.htm.

4. Overbite occurs when the upper teeth are slightly longer than normal; overjet occurs when the upper teeth protrude visibly (buck teeth). "Difference between Overbite and Overjet," Difference Between, updated January 23, 2011, www.differencebetween.net/science/health/difference-between-overbite-and-overjet/.

5. Douglas S. Falconer and Trudy F. C. Mackay, *Introduction to Quantitative Genetics*, 4th ed. (New York: Longman, 1996).

6. John P. Conry, Louise B. Messer, Joann C. Boraas, Dorothy P. Aeppli, and Thomas J. Bouchard Jr., "Dental Caries and Treatment Characteristics in Human Twins Reared Apart," *Archives of Oral Biology* 38 (1993): 937–943.

7. Lisa Adams, "Periodontal Disease—Gingivitis and Periodontitis," Suite101, updated September 19, 2010, www.suite101.com/content/peridontal-disease—gingivitis-and-periodontitis-a287303.

8. The National Institute of Dental Research is now the National Institute of Dental and Craniofacial Research.

9. Hans-Erich Reiser and Friedrich Vogel, "Uber die Erblichkeit der Zahnsteinbildung Beim Menschen," *Deutsche Zahuntz Zeitschrift* 13 (1958): 1355–1358.

10. Sebastian G. Ciancio, Stanley P. Hazen, and John J. Cunat, "Periodontal Observations in Twins," *Journal of Periodontal Research* 4 (1969): 42–45.

11. Bryan S. Michalowicz, Dorothy Aeppli, John G. Virag, et al., "Periodontal Findings in Adult Twins," *Journal of Periodontology* 62 (1991): 293–299.

12. Information was obtained from the mesiobuccal or mesiolingual tooth surface.

13. Ginny G. Lane, "The Beginner's Guide to the Bootstrap Method of Resampling," presented at the Annual Meeting of the Southwest Educational Research Association, Dallas, Texas, January 27–29, 2000.

14. Bryan S. Michalowicz, Scott R. Diehl, John C. Gunsolley, et al., "Evidence of a Substantial Genetic Component for Risk of Adult Periodontitis," *Journal of Periodontology* 71 (2000): 1699–1707.

15. Bryan S. Michalowicz, Dorothy P. Aeppli, Ramesh K. Kuba, et al., "A Twin Study of Genetic Variation in Proportional Radiographic Alveolar Bone Height," *Journal of Dental Research* 70 (1991): 1431–1435.

16. The device is called a cephalostat head positioner. Testers used seven anatomical measures to position co-twins similarly within the apparatus.

17. Minoru Nakata, Pao-Lo Yu, Bailey Davis, and W. E. Nance, "Genetic Determinants of Craino-Facial Morphology: A Twin Study," *Annals of Human Genetics* 37 (1974): 431–443.

18. Kenneth S. Kornman, Allison Crane, Hwa-Ying Wang, et al., "The Interleukin-1 Genotype as a Severity Factor in Adult Periodontal Disease," *Journal of Clinical Periodontology* 24 (1997): 72–77.

19. Bryan M. Michalowicz and Bruce L. Pihlstrom. "Genetic Factors Associated with Periodontal Disease," in *Carranza's Clinical Periodontology,* 10th ed., ed. Michael G Newman et al., 193–208 (Philadelphia: W. B. Saunders, 2006). This chapter first appeared in the 2002 edition.

20. Gary C. Armitage and Paul B. Robertson, "The Biology, Prevention, Diagnosis and Treatment of Periodontal Diseases: Scientific Advances in the United States," *Journal of the American Dental Association* 140 (2009): 36S–43S.

21. "Allergies," The Free Dictionary, n.d., http://medical-dictionary.thefreedictionary.com/allergies.

22. Susan L. Farber. *Identical Twins Reared Apart: A Reanalysis* (New York; Basic Books, 1981). The symptoms listed here were recorded for twins in studies conducted between 1937 and 1980. Physicians currently do not believe such symptoms necessarily represent allergic reactions. For example, allergy is only one of several causes of asthma. Malcolm Blumenthal, personal communication, February 20, 2011.

23. Ibid.

24. Malcolm N. Blumenthal and D. Bernard Amos, "Genetic and Immunologic Basis of Atopic Responses," *Chest* 9 (1987): 176S–184S.

25. Peter F. Kohler, Victor J. Rivera, Elke D. Eckert, Thomas J. Bouchard Jr., and Leonard L. Heston, "Genetic Regulation of Immunoglobulin and Specific

Antibody Levels in Twins Reared Apart," *Journal of Clinical Investigation* 75 (1985): 883–888.

26. Bruce Hanson, Matthew McGue, Beatrice Roitman-Johnson, Nancy L. Segal, Thomas J. Bouchard Jr., and Malcolm N. Blumenthal, "Atopic Disease and Immunoglobulin E in Twins Reared Apart and Together," *American Journal of Human Genetics* 48 (1991): 873–879.

27. John B. Davis, "Asthma and Wheezy Bronchitis in Children," *Clinical Allergy* 6 (1976): 329–338; Jeanne M. Smith, "Epidemiology and Natural History of Asthma, Allergic Rhinitis, and Atopic Dermatitis (Eczema)," in *Allergy: Principles and Practice,* 3rd ed., ed. Elliott Middleton Jr., Charles F. Reed, Elliot F. Ellis, N. Franklin Adkinson Jr., and Jon W. Yunginger, 891–929 (St. Louis, Mo.: Mosby, 1988).

28. Malcolm N. Blumenthal and Sergio Bonini, "Immunogenetics of Specific Immune Responses to Allergens in Twins and Families," in *Genetic and Environmental Factors in Clinical Allergy,* ed. David G. March and Malcolm N. Blumenthal, 132–142 (Minneapolis: University of Minnesota Press, 1990).

29. Correlations can be calculated in the absence of a normal distribution, but should be interpreted cautiously. In the study, high values precluded normalization even after log transformation.

30. Daniel P. Moloney, Thomas J. Bouchard Jr., and Nancy L. Segal, "A Genetic and Environmental Analysis of the Vocational Interests of Monozygotic and Dizygotic Twins Reared Apart," *Journal of Vocational Behavior* 39 (1991): 76–109.

31. See, for example, John C. Loehlin and Robert C. Nichols, *Heredity, Environment, and Personality: A Study of 850 Sets of Twins* (Austin: University of Texas Press, 1976).

32. Jo-Ida C. Hansen and Donald P. Campbell, *Manual for the SVIB-SCII* (Stanford, Calif.: Stanford University Press, 1985); Donald J. Jackson, *Jackson Vocational Interest Survey Manual* (Port Huron, Mich.: Research Psychologists Press, 1977).

33. Thomas J. Bouchard Jr. and Matthew McGue, "Genetic and Rearing Environmental Influences on Adult Personality: An Analysis of Adopted Twins Reared Apart," *Journal of Personality* 58 (1990): 263–292.

34. The correlations for Achievement Orientation were: MZA ($r_i = 0.73$) and DZA ($r_i = 0.19$). The general model assumes an absence of dominance.

35. Xi-zhi Wu and Mao-zai Tian, "A Longitudinal Study of the Effects of Family Background Factors on Mathematics Achievements Using Quantile Regression," *Acta Mathematicae Applicatae Sinica* 24 (2000): 85–98.

36. Eric Turkheimer, "Three Laws of Behavior Genetics and What They Mean," *Current Directions in Psychological Science* 9 (2000): 160–164.

9. Creativity, Work Values, and Evolution (1992–1993)

1. David T. Lykken, "Trial by Polygraph," *Behavioral Sciences and the Law* 2 (1984): 75–92.

2. David T. Lykken, "The Case for Parental Licensure," in *Psychopathology: Antisocial, Criminal, and Violent Behavior,* ed. Theodore Milton, Erik Simonsen,

Morten Birket-Smith, and Roger D. Davis, 122–143 (New York: Guilford Press, 2002).

3. David T. Lykken, *Happiness: What Studies of Twins Tell Us about Nature, Nurture, and the Happiness Set Point* (New York: Golden Books, 1999).

4. David T. Lykken et al., "Heritability Estimates from Twin Studies: The Efficiency of the MZA Design" (unpublished manuscript, University of Minnesota).

5. David T. Lykken, Matthew McGue, Auke Tellegen, and Thomas J. Bouchard Jr., "Emergenesis: Genetic Traits That May Not Run in Families," *American Psychologist* 47 (1992): 1565–1577.

6. Polymorphic genes are those having multiple allelic forms.

7. Lykken et al., "Emergenesis" (1992), 1566.

8. Twin studies might miss emergenic traits when the underlying factors mimic additive transmission and traits appear familial.

9. Lykken et al., "Emergenesis."

10. Ibid., 1571.

11. Ibid., 1572.

12. Robert Plomin, John C. DeFries, and Gerald E. McClearn, *Behavioral Genetics: A Primer,* 4th ed. (New York: Worth Publishers, 2001), 172.

13. Carrie M. Nielson, "The Power of Epistasis," *Science Translational Medicine* 3 (2011): 79.

14. Niels G. Waller, Thomas J. Bouchard Jr., David T. Lykken, Auke Tellegen, and Dawn M. Blacker, "Creativity, Heritability, Familiality: Which Word Does Not Belong?" *Psychological Inquiry* 4 (1993): 235–237.

15. Hans J. Eysenck, "Creativity and Personality: Suggestions for a Theory," *Psychological Inquiry* 4 (1993): 147–178.

16. Larry Johnson and Annette Lamb, "Critical and Creative Thinking—Bloom's Taxonomy," Teacher Tap, n.d., http://eduscapes.com/tap/topic69.htm.

17. Mihalyi Csikszentmihalyi, *Creativity: Flow and the Psychology of Discovery and Invention* (New York: HarperPerennial, 1997).

18. The dimensionality of the thirty items was assessed by nonlinear factor analysis, a procedure that assesses relations and interactions among groups of related items or factors. The Creative Personality Scale was treated as a unidimensional construct because scale scores based on the unit-weighted sum of responses reflect general factor variance; Waller et al., "Creativity, Heritability, Familiality."

19. David T. Lykken, Thomas J. Bouchard Jr., Matt McGue, and Auke Tellegen, "The Heritability of Interests: A Twin Study," *Journal of Applied Psychology* 78 (1993): 649–661.

20. Itamar Gati, "The Structure of Vocational Interests," *Psychological Bulletin* 109 (1991): 309–324.

21. Daniel P. Moloney, Thomas J. Bouchard Jr., and Nancy L. Segal, "A Genetic and Environmental Analysis of the Vocational Interests of Monozygotic and Dizygotic Twins Reared Apart," *Journal of Vocational Behavior* 39 (1991): 76–109.

22. Lykken et al., "Heritability of Interests."

23. David T. Lykken, Matt McGue, and Auke Tellegen, "Recruitment Bias in Twin Research: The Rule of Two-Thirds Reconsidered," *Behavior Genetics* 17 (1987): 343–362.

24. Ibid.
25. Inventory items were scaled to remove individual differences in the twins' use of item-response categories (see the appendix to Lykken et al., "Heritability of Interests." For example, some twins might have consistently chosen 1s or 2s in the Minnesota Leisure-Time Interest Test.).
26. The mean heritability was 0.32 for items, but it increased to 0.48 for factors and to 0.53 for superfactors.
27. Lauren M. Keller, Thomas J. Bouchard Jr., Richard D. Arvey, Nancy L. Segal, and René V. Dawis, "Work Values: Genetic and Environmental Influences," *Journal of Applied Psychology* 77 (1992): 79–88.
28. Evan G. Gay, David J. Weiss, Darwin D. Hendel, René V. Dawis, and Lloyd H. Lofquist, *Manual for the Minnesota Importance Questionnaire,* Minnesota Studies in Vocational Rehabilitation 28 (Minneapolis: Work Adjustment Project, Industrial Relations Center, University of Minnesota, 1971).
29. Matt McGue and Thomas J. Bouchard Jr., "Genetic and Environmental Determinants of Information Processing and Special Mental Abilities: A Twin Analysis," in *Advances in the Psychology of Human Intelligence,* vol. 5, ed. Robert J. Sternberg, 7–45 (Hillsdale, N.J.: Lawrence Erlbaum, 1989).
30. J. Philippe Rushton, David W. Fulker, Michael C. Neale, David K. B. Nias, and Hans J. Eysenck, "Altruism and Aggression: The Heritability of Individual Differences," *Journal of Personality and Social Psychology* 6 (1986): 1192–1198.
31. Nancy L. Segal, *Indivisible by Two: Lives of Extraordinary Twins* (Cambridge, Mass.: Harvard University Press, 2007).
32. Linda Mealey, "Kinship: The Ties That Bind (Disciplines)," in *Conceptual Challenges in Evolutionary Psychology: Innovative Research Strategies,* ed. Harmon R. Holcomb III, 19–38 (Dordrecht, the Netherlands: Kluwer, 2001).
33. Nancy L. Segal, "Twin, Adoption and Family Methods as Approaches to Evolution of Individual Differences," in *The Evolution of Personality and Individual Differences,* ed. David M. Buss, 303–337 (Oxford: Oxford University Press, 2011).
34. Steven G. Gangestad, "Evolutionary Biology Looks at Behavior Genetics," *Personality and Individual Differences* 49 (2010): 289–295.
35. Thomas J. Bouchard Jr. and John C. Loehlin, "Genes, Evolution, and Personality," *Behavior Genetics* 31 (2001): 243–273.
36. Daniel G. Freedman, *Human Sociobiology: A Holistic Approach* (New York: Free Press, 1979).
37. Edward O. Wilson, *Sociobiology: The New Synthesis* (Cambridge, Mass.: Harvard University Press, 1975).
38. William D. Hamilton, "The Genetical Evolution of Human Behaviour," *Journal of Theoretical Biology* 7 (1964): 1–52.
39. Nancy L. Segal, "Twin, Sibling and Adoption Methods: Tests of Evolutionary Hypotheses," *American Psychologist* 48 (1993): 943–956.
40. Charles B. Crawford and Judith L. Anderson, "Sociobiology: An Environmentalist Discipline?" *American Psychologist* 44 (1989): 1449–1459.
41. Bruce L. Ellis, "Timing of Pubertal Maturation in Girls: An Integrated Life History Approach," *Psychological Bulletin* 130 (2004): 920–954.
42. Mealey, "Kinship," 23.

43. Linda Mealey and Nancy L. Segal, "Heritable and Environmental Variables Affect Reproduction-Related Behaviors, but Not Ultimate Reproductive Success," *Personality and Individual Differences* 14 (1993): 783–794.

44. Peter F. Briggs, *M-B History Record: Self-Administered Form* (Brandon, Vt.: Clinical Psychology, [1969]). M-B stands for Minnesota-Briggs.

45. Joseph L. Rodgers, Hans-Peter Kohler, Kirsten Ohm Kyvik, and Kaare Christensen, "Behavior Genetic Modeling of Human Fertility: Findings from a Contemporary Danish Study," *Demography* 38 (2001): 29–42.

46. Lykken et al., "Emergenesis."

47. Thomas J. Bouchard Jr., David T. Lykken, Matthew McGue, Nancy L. Segal, and Auke Tellegen, "Sources of Human Psychological Differences: The Minnesota Study of Twins Reared Apart," *Science* 250 (1990): 223–228.

48. Thomas J. Bouchard Jr. and Peter Propping, eds., *Twins as a Tool of Behavior Genetics* (Chichester, U.K.: Wiley & Sons, 1993).

49. Thomas J. Bouchard Jr., "Genetic and Environmental Influences on Adult Personality: Evaluating the Evidence," in *Foundations of Personality*, ed. P. Joop Hettema and Ian J. Deary, 15–44 (Dordrecht: Kluwer, 1993).

50. John C. Loehlin, *Genes and Environment in Personality Development* (Newbury Park, N.J.: Sage, 1992).

51. David C. Rowe, *The Limits of Family Influence: Genes, Experience, and Behavior* (New York: Guilford Press, 1994), 44.

52. Rainer Riemann, Alois Angleitner, and Jan Strelau, "Genetic and Environmental Influences on Personality: A Study of Twins Reared Together Using the Self- and Peer Report NEO-FFI Scales," *Journal of Personality* 65 (1997): 449–475. The correlation between the twins' and peers' reports was .55; the correlation between the two peers who rated each twin was .61.

53. Robert Plomin and Gerald E. McClearn, eds., *Nature, Nurture, and Psychology* (Washington, D.C.: American Psychological Association, 1993).

54. Robert Plomin, Michael J. Owen, and Peter McGuffin, "The Genetic Basis of Complex Human Behavior," *Science* 264 (1994): 1733–1739.

55. Matt McGue, Thomas J. Bouchard Jr., William G. Iacono, and David T. Lykken, "Behavioral Genetics of Cognitive Ability: A Life-Span Perspective," in *Nature, Nurture, and Psychology*, ed. Robert Plomin and Gerald E. McClearn, chapter 3; see p. xiii. Interestingly, just two years earlier, in 1991, the *APA Monitor* published an article concerning the controversial reception of the MISTRA's IQ findings.

56. The original data from Newman et al. and Juel-Nielsen were reanalyzed to derive intraclass correlations by our procedures.

57. Nancy L. Segal, "Twins: The Finest Natural Experiment," *Personality and Individual Differences* 49 (2010): 317–323.

58. Nancy L. Segal, Shirley A. McGuire, June Havlena, Patricia Gill, and Scott L. Hershberger, "Intellectual Similarity of Virtual Twin Pairs: Developmental Trends," *Personality and Individual Differences* 42 (2007): 1209–1219.

59. John C. Loehlin, Joseph M. Horn, and Lee Willerman, "Modeling IQ Change: Evidence from the Texas Adoption Project," *Child Development* 60 (1989): 993–1004.

60. Plomin et al., *Behavioral Genetics.*

61. Thomas J. Bouchard Jr., "The Genetic Architecture of Human Intelligence," in *Biological Approaches to the Study of Human Intelligence,* ed. Philip E. Vernon, 33–93 (New York: Ablex, 1993).

62. Francis Galton, "The History of Twins as a Criterion of the Relative Powers of Nature and Nurture," *Journal of the Anthropological Institute* 5 (1885): 391–406.

63. Richard L. Doty, Paul Shaman, and Michael Dann, "Development of the University of Pennsylvania Smell Identification Test: A Standardized Micro-encapsulated Test of Olfactory Function," *Physiology and Behavior* 32 (1984): 489–502.

64. Kathryn M. Abbe and Frances M. Gill, *Twins on Twins* (New York: Clarkson N. Potter, 1980).

10. Family Environments, Happiness, Sensation Seeking, and the MMPI (1994–1997)

1. Yoon-Mi Hur and Thomas J. Bouchard Jr., "Genetic Influences on Perceptions of Childhood Family Environment: A Reared Apart Twin Study," *Child Development* 66 (1995): 330–345.

2. David C. Rowe, "Environmental and Genetic Influence on Dimensions of Perceived Parenting: A Twin Study," *Developmental Psychology* 17 (1981): 203–208; "A Biometrical Analysis of Perceptions of Family Environment: A Twin Study of Twin and Singleton Sibling Kinships," *Child Development* 54 (1983): 416–423.

3. Robert Plomin, Gerald E. McClearn, Nancy L. Pedersen, John R. Nesselroade, and Cindy S. Bergeman, "Genetic Influence on Adults' Ratings of Their Current Family Environment," *Journal of Marriage and Family* 52 (1989): 791–803.

4. Jean Block, *Lives through Time* (Berkeley, Calif.: Bancroft, 1971); Rudolf H. Moos and Bernice S. Moos, *Manual: Family Environment Scale* (Palo Alto, Calif.: Consulting Psychologists Press, 1986).

5. David T. Lykken, *Happiness: What Studies of Twins Tell Us about Nature, Nurture, and the Happiness Set Point* (New York: Golden Books, 1999).

6. David G. Myers and Edward Diener, "Who Is Happy?" *Psychological Science* 6 (1995): 10–19.

7. David T. Lykken and Auke Tellegen, "Happiness Is a Stochastic Phenomenon," *Psychological Science* 7 (1996): 186–189.

8. In an effort to find evidence compatible with the idea that natural selection favored happy people, one could compare the life history and reproductive outcomes of people who vary along given happiness dimensions.

9. Jerome H. Barkow, "Happiness in Evolutionary Perspective," in *Uniting Psychology and Biology: Integrative Perspectives on Human Development,* ed. Nancy L. Segal et al., 397–418 (Washington, D.C.: American Psychological Association, 1997).

10. Cecilia Tomassini, Knud Juel, Niels V. Holm, Axel Skytthe, and Kaare Christensen, "Risk of Suicide in Twins: 51 Year Follow Up Study," *British Medical Journal* 327 (2003): 373–374. Twins in this study were not organized by zygosity.

11. Alexander Weiss, Timothy C. Bates, and Michelle Luciano, "Happiness Is a Personal(ity) Thing: The Genetics of Personality and Well-Being in a Representative Sample," *Psychological Science* 19 (2008): 205–210; Richard E. Lucas, A. E. Clark, Y. Georgellis, and E. Diener, "Reexamining Adaptation and the Set Point Model of Happiness: Reactions to Changes in Marital Status," *Journal of Personality and Social Psychology* 84 (2003): 527–539.

12. Auke Tellegen, David T. Lykken, Thomas J. Bouchard Jr., Kimerly J. Wilcox, Nancy L. Segal, and Stephen Rich, "Personality Similarity in Twins Reared Apart and Together," *Journal of Personality and Social Psychology* 54 (1988): 1031–1039.

13. Lykken and Tellegen, "Happiness Is a Stochastic Phenomenon," 189.

14. Lykken, *Happiness,* 2. In fact, an online version of Lykken and Tellegen's article shows that the comment concerning the futility of trying to be happier is crossed out and the words "Not True" are scribbled in the margin. I wondered if Lykken did that. cogprints.org/767/3/167.pdf.

15. See David T. Lykken, "The Heritability of Happiness," *Harvard Mental Health Newsletter,* 1998.

16. Daniel Goleman, "Forget Money; Nothing Can Buy Happiness, Some Researchers Say," *New York Times,* July 16, 1996, http://www.nytimes.com/1996/07/16/science/forget-money-nothing-can-buy-happiness-some-researchers-say.html.

17. Ibid.

18. Ibid., C-9. For example, Pavarotti was described as tired and emotional at the May 2002 concert due to the recent death of his father and his having the flu. "A Tired and Emotional Pavarotti Keeps Annual Charity Date in His Hometown," Hello!, May 29, 2002, www.hellomagazine.com/music/2002/05/29/pavarotti/.

19. Lykken, "The Heritability of Happiness."

20. Ibid.

21. Ibid.

22. Ibid.

23. Malcolm Gladwell, *Outliers: The Story of Success* (Boston: Little, Brown, 2008).

24. Francis Galton, *Hereditary Genius: An Inquiry into Its Laws and Consequences* (New York: D. Appleton, 1891).

25. Quinn McNemar, "Twin Resemblances in Motor Skills and the Effect of Practice Thereon," *Journal of Genetic Psychology* 42 (1933): 70–97; Daniel Q. Marisi, "Genetic and Extragenic Variance in Motor Performance," *Acta Geneticae Medicae et Gemellologiae, Twin Studies* 26 (1977): 197–204; Nicholas G. Martin, John B. Gibson, John G. Oakeshott, et al., "A Twin Study of Psychomotor Performance during Alcohol Intoxication: Early Results," *Twin Research 3: Epidemiological and Clinical Studies,* ed. Luigi Gedda, Paolo Parisi, and Walter E. Nance, 89–96 (New York: Alan Liss, 1981).

26. Paul W. Fox, Scott L. Hershberger, and Thomas J. Bouchard Jr., "Genetic and Environmental Contributions to the Acquisition of a Motor Skill," *Nature* 384 (1996): 356–358. The other psychomotor tasks have not been analyzed.

27. "Practice Not Perfect without Genes," Reuters news service, November 27, 1996.

28. Olympic gymnasts Paul and Morgan Hamm are DZ twins with nearly matching elite talent and, thus, are exceptional.

29. Erinn R. Johnson, "Delaware Girl Learns a New Word the Hard Way at Bee," Scripps Howard Foundation Wire, June 10, 2004, www.shfwire.com/node /2711.

30. David DiLalla, Gregory Carey, Irving I. Gottesman, and Thomas J. Bouchard Jr., "Heritability of MMPI Personality Indicators of Psychopathology in Twins Reared Apart," *Journal of Abnormal Psychology* 105 (1996): 491–499.

31. Starke R. Hathaway and J. Charnley McKinley, "A Multiphasic Personality Schedule (Minnesota): I. Construction of the Schedule," *Journal of Personality* 10 (1940): 249–254.

32. Interview with the author, July 2010.

33. Hal H. Goldsmith and Irving I. Gottesman, "An Extension of Construct Validity for Personality Scales Using Twin-based Criteria," *Journal of Research in Personality* 11 (1977): 381–397.

34. T-scores are standard scores that have a mean of 50 and standard deviation of 10.

35. Nancy L. Segal and Yoon-Mi Hur, "Reared Apart Korean Female Twins: Genetic and Cultural Influences on Life Histories, Physical and Health-related Measures, and Behavioral Traits," *International Journal of Behavioral Development* 32 (2008): 542–548.

36. Yoon-Mi Hur and Thomas J. Bouchard Jr., "The Genetic Influence between Impulsivity and Sensation-Seeking," *Behavior Genetics* 27 (1997): 455–463.

37. Benjamin B. Wolman, *Dictionary of Behavioral Science,* 2nd ed. (New York: Academic Press, 1989).

38. Marvin Zuckerman, *Behavioral Expressions and Biosocial Bases of Sensation Seeking* (New York: Cambridge University Press, 1994).

39. Nancy L. Pedersen, Robert Plomin, Gerald E. McClearn, and Lars Friberg, "Neuroticism, Extraversion and Related Traits in Adult Twins Reared Apart," *Journal of Personality and Social Psychology* 55 (1988): 950–957.

40. Lindon J. Eaves, Nicholas G. Martin, and Sibyl B. G. Eysenck, "An Application of the Analysis of Covariance Structure to the Psychological Study of Impulsiveness," *British Journal of Mathematical and Statistical Psychology* 30 (1977): 185–197.

41. Daisy Schalling, Gunnar Edman, and Marie Åsberg, "Impulsive Cognitive Style and Inability to Tolerate Boredom: Psychobiological Studies of Temperamental Vulnerabilities," in *Biological Bases of Sensation Seeking: Impulsivity and Anxiety,* ed. Marvin Zuckerman, 123–145 (Hillsdale, N.J.: Lawrence Erlbaum, 1983); Daisy Schalling, Marie Åsberg, Gunnar Edman, and Lars Oreland, "Markers for Vulnerability to Psychopathology: Temperament Traits Associated with Platelet MAO Activity," *Acta Psychiatrica Scandinavica* 76 (1987): 172–182. Monoamine oxidase (MAO) is an enzyme involved in activating neurotransmitters so may affect mood.

42. Deborah G. Betsworth, "An Investigation of the Genetic and Environmental Influences on Vocational Interests," (PhD diss., University of Minnesota, 1992).

43. Daniel P. Moloney, Thomas J. Bouchard Jr., and Nancy L. Segal, "A Genetic and Environmental Analysis of the Vocational Interests of Monozygotic and Dizygotic Twins Reared Apart," *Journal of Vocational Behavior* 39 (1991): 76–109.

44. Deborah G. Betsworth, Thomas J. Bouchard Jr., Catherine R. Cooper, et al., "Genetic and Environmental Influences on Vocational Interests Assessed Using Adoptive and Biological Families and Twins Reared Apart and Together," *Journal of Vocational Behavior* 44 (1994): 263–278.

45. Richard D. Arvey, Brian P. McCall, Thomas J. Bouchard Jr., Paul Taubman, and Marcie A. Cavanaugh, "Genetic Influences on Job Satisfaction and Work Values," *Personality and Individual Differences* 17 (1994): 21–33.

46. Richard D. Arvey, Thomas J. Bouchard Jr., Nancy L. Segal, and Lauren M. Abraham, "Job Satisfaction: Environmental and Genetic Components," *Journal of Applied Psychology* 74 (1989): 187–192.

47. Arvey et al., "Genetic Influence."

48. Abraham Tesser, "On the Importance of Heritability in Psychological Research: The Case of Attitudes," *Psychological Review* 100 (1993): 129–142.

49. Jere R. Behrman, Mark R. Rosenzweig, and Paul Taubman, "College Choice and Wages: Estimates Using Data on Female Twins," *Review of Economics and Statistics* 78 (1996): 672–685.

50. Lindon Eaves, Brian D'Onofrio, and Robert Russell, "Transmission of Religion and Attitudes," *Twin Research* 2 (1999): 59–61.

51. Genomics.energy.gov, "History of the Human Genome Project," Human Genome Project Information, updated May 12, 2011, www.ornl.gov/sci/tech resources/Human_Genome/project/hgp.shtml.

52. Associated Press, "Scientists Finish First Phase in Mapping of Human Genes," *New York Times,* March 19, 1996, www.nytimes.com/1996/03/19/science /scientists-finish-first-phase-in-mapping-of-human-genes.html; Nicholas Wade, "Research Team Takes Big Stride in the Mapping of Human Genes," *New York Times,* March 15, 1997, www.nytimes.com/1997/03/15/us/research-team -takes-big-stride-in-the-mapping-of-human-genes.html.

53. Thomas J. Bouchard Jr., "Genes, Environment and Personality," *Science* 264 (1994): 1700–1701. Bouchard's paper, listed under "Perspectives," followed J. H. Thomas's "Mind of the Worm," a fascinating piece on how *Caenorhabditis elegans* could inform us about behavioral complexity and plasticity.

54. Ibid., 1701.

55. Frank J. Sulloway, *Born to Rebel: Birth Order, Family Dynamics, and Creative Lives* (New York: Pantheon, 1996).

56. Aurelio José Figueredo, Jon A. Sefcek, Geneva Vasquez, Barbara H. Brumbach, James E. King, and W. Jake Jacobs, "Evolutionary Personality Psychology," *The Handbook of Evolutionary Psychology,* ed. David M. Buss, 851–877 (New York: Wiley, 2005).

57. Richard D. Arvey and Thomas J. Bouchard Jr., "Genetics, Twins, and Organizational Behavior," in *Research in Organizational Behavior 16,* ed. Barry Staw and Larry L. Cummings, 47–82 (Greenwich, Conn.: JAI Press, 1994).

58. Thomas J. Bouchard Jr., "Longitudinal Studies of Personality and Intelligence: A Behavior Genetic and Evolutionary Psychology Perspective," in *International Handbook of Personality and Intelligence,* ed. Donald H. Saklofske and Moshe Zeidner, 81–106 (New York: Plenum, 1995).

59. Ronald S. Wilson, "The Louisville Twin Study: Developmental Synchronies in Behavior," *Child Development* 54 (1983): 298–316.

60. Robert Altemeyer, *Enemies of Freedom: Understanding Right-Wing Authoritarianism* (San Francisco: Jossey-Bass, 1988).

61. Thomas J. Bouchard Jr., "Genetics and Evolution: Implications for Psychological Theories," in *Measures of the Five Factor Model and Psychological Type: A Major Convergence of Research and Theory,* ed. James Newman, 20–42 (Gainesville, FL: Center for the Applications of Psychological Type, 1995), p. 42.

62. Thomas J. Bouchard Jr., David T. Lykken, Matthew McGue, Nancy L. Segal, and Auke Tellegen, "Sources of Human Psychological Differences: The Minnesota Study of Twins Reared Apart," *Science* 250 (1990): 223–228.

63. Thomas J. Bouchard Jr., "The Galton Lecture: Behavior Genetic Studies of Intelligence, Yesterday and Today: The Long Journey from Plausibility to Proof," *Journal of Biosocial Science* 28 (1996): 527–555, p. 529.

64. Thomas J. Bouchard Jr., "Whenever the Twain Shall Meet," *The Sciences* 37 (1997): 52–57.

65. Dolly was cloned in 1996, but the event was announced in 1997.

66. Nancy L. Segal, "Behavioral Aspects of Intergenerational Cloning: What Twins Tell Us," *Jurimetrics* 38 (1997): 57–67.

67. Donors and clones would share their parents in one sense because the donor's parents conceived the donor and the donor conceived a genetically identical child. However, in another sense they would not because the donor, and not the donor's parents, actually created and possibly gestated the child. Furthermore, mitochondrial (extracellular) DNA is transmitted intact from mothers to children. A cloned child's mitochondrial DNA would typically come from an unrelated individual who provided the enucleated egg with which the donor's cell nucleus was fused; in this case the mitochondrial DNA of the clone and the donor would differ. However, if the donor also provided the enucleated egg, then the mitochondrial DNA would be the same. See Matthew J. Evans, Cagan Gurer, John D. Loike, et al., "Mitochondrial DNA Genotypes in Nuclear Transfer-Derived Cloned Sheep," *Nature Genetics* 23 (1999): 90–93.

68. Laura E. Berk, *Child Development* (Needham Heights, Mass.: Allyn & Bacon, 1997).

69. The most recent edition is Robert Plomin, John C. DeFries, Gerald E. McClearn, and Peter McGuffin, *Behavioral Genetics,* 5th ed. (New York: Worth Publishers, 2008).

70. Thomas J. Bouchard Jr. and Matthew McGue, "Familial Studies of Intelligence: A Review," *Science* 212 (1981): 1055–1059.

71. John C. Loehlin, "Partitioning Genetic and Environmental Contributions to Behavioral Development," *American Psychologist* 44 (1989): 1285–1,292.

72. Horatio H. Newman, Frank N. Freeman, and Karl J. Holzinger, *Twins: A Study of Heredity and Environment* (Chicago: University of Chicago Press,

1937); James Shields, *Monozygotic Twins Brought Up Apart and Brought Up Together* (London: Oxford University Press, 1962); Niels Juel-Nielsen, *Individual and Environment: Monozygotic Twins Reared Apart* (New York: International Universities Press, 1980).

73. Thomas J. Bouchard Jr., David T. Lykken, Matthew McGue, Nancy L. Segal, and Auke Tellegen, "Sources of Human Psychological Difference: The Minnesota Study of Twins Reared Apart," *Science* 250 (1990): 223–228; Nancy L. Pedersen, Robert Plomin, John R. Nesselroade, and Gerald E. McClearn, "A Quantitative Genetic Analysis of Cognitive Abilities during the Second Half of the Life Span," *Psychological Science* 3 (1992): 346–353.

74. Gerald E. McClearn, Boo Johansson, Stig Berg, et al., "Substantial Genetic Influence on Cognitive Abilities in Twins 80 or More Years Old," *Science* 276 (1997): 1560–1563.

75. Denise L. Newman, Auke Tellegen, and Thomas J. Bouchard Jr., "Individual Differences in Adult Ego Development: Sources of Influence in Twins Reared Apart," *Journal of Personality and Social Psychology* 74 (1998): 985–995; Kathryn McCourt, Thomas J. Bouchard Jr., David T. Lykken, Auke Tellegen, and Margaret Keyes, "Authoritarianism Revisited: Genetic and Environmental Influences Examined in Twins Reared Apart and Together," *Personality and Individual Differences* 27 (1999): 985–1014.

76. Lawrence Wright, "Double Mystery," *The New Yorker*, August 7, 1995, 45–62.

77. Roderic Angle, "Nature's Clones," *Psychology Today*, August 1997, 38–69.

78. Lawrence Wright, *Twins: And What They Tell Us about Who We Are* (New York): John Wiley & Sons, 1997.

11. "Larks" and "Owls," Ego Development, and Authoritarianism (1998–2002)

1. Yoon-Mi Hur, Thomas J. Bouchard Jr., and David T. Lykken, "Genetic and Environmental Influences on Morningness-Eveningness," *Personality and Individual Differences* 25 (1998): 917–925.

2. M. D. Drennan, J. Selby, G. A. Kerkhof, and D. I. Boomsma, "Morningness/Eveningness Is Heritable," *Society for Neuroscience Abstracts* 18 (1992): 196.

3. J. A. Horne and O. Ostberg, "A Self-Assessment Questionnaire to Determine Morningness-Eveningness in Human Circadian Rhythms," *International Journal of Chronobiology* 4 (1976): 97–110. Our form was adapted from the published one.

4. Jane Loevinger, *Ego Development: Conceptions and Theories* (San Francisco: Jossey-Bass, 1976).

5. Jane Loevinger and Ruth Wessler, *Measuring Ego Development*, vol. 1 (San Francisco: Jossey-Bass, 1970), 8.

6. Denise L. Newman, Auke Tellegen, and Thomas J. Bouchard Jr., "Individual Differences in Adult Ego Development: Sources of Influence in Twins Reared Apart," *Journal of Personality and Social Psychology* 74 (1998): 985–995.

7. Ibid.

8. Loevinger and Wessler, *Measuring Ego Development;* Jane Loevinger and L. X. Hy Le, "Measuring Ego Development: Supplementary Manual and Sentences for Form 8 of the Washington University Sentence Completion Test" (unpublished manuscript, Washington University, 1989).

9. Jane Loevinger, "The Construct Validity of the Sentence Completion Test of Ego Development," *Applied Psychological Measures* 3 (1979): 281–311.

10. Loevinger and Wessler, *Measuring Ego Development.*

11. Ego development scores were based on a cumulative frequency or "ogive" of item-level scores. Scoring rules were provided in the test manual.

12. We found ego development heritabilities of 0.54 (without controlling for cognition), 0.56 (controlling for verbal skill), and 0.47 (controlling for IQ).

13. Newman et al., "Individual Differences," p. 993.

14. Robert R. McCrae and Paul T. Costa, "Openness to Experience and Ego Level in Loevinger's Sentence Completion Test: Dispositional Contributions to Developmental Models of Personality," *Journal of Personality and Social Psychology* 39 (1980): 1179–1190.

15. Lawrence D. Cohen and P. Michiel Westenberg, "Intelligence and Maturity: Meta-Analytic Evidence for the Incremental and Discriminative Validity of Loevinger's Measure of Ego Development," *Journal of Personality and Social Psychology* 86 (2004): 760–772. Loevinger notes that word count is correlated with complexity of expression, but not all lengthy responses are complex.

16. Dewey K. Ziegler, Yoon-Mi Hur, Thomas J. Bouchard Jr., Ruth S. Hassanein, and Ruth Barter, "Migraine in Twins Raised Together and Apart," *Headache* 38 (1998): 417–422.

17. Harvald Bent and Mogens Hauge, "A Catamnestic Investigation of Danish Twins," *Danish Medical Bulletin* 3 (1956): 150–158; Kathleen R. Merikangas, C. Tierney, Nicholas G. Martin, Andrew C. Heath, and Neil Risch, "Genetics of Migraine in the Australian Twin Registry," in *New Advances in Headache Research,* vol. 4, ed. F. Clifford Rose, 27–28 (London: Smith-Gordon, 1994).

18. Dewey K. Ziegler, Ruth S. Hassanein, David Harris, and Roberta Stewart, "Headache in a Non-clinic Twin Population," *Headache* 14 (1975): 213–218.

19. Susan L. Farber, *Identical Twins Reared Apart: A Reanalysis* (New York: Basic Books, 1980).

20. Brian S. Schwartz, Walter F. Stewart, David Simon, and Richard Lipton. "Epidemiology of Tension Type Headache," *Journal of the American Medical Association* 279 (1998): 381–383.

21. In 2003, the Swedish Twin and Adoption Study of Aging reported a 0.48 heritability for migraine headaches, based on 413 pairs of MZA, DZA, MZT, and DZT female twin pairs. See Dan A. Svensson, Bo Larsson, Elisabet Waldenlind, and Nancy L. Pedersen, "Shared Rearing Environment in Migraine: Results from Twins Reared Apart and Twins Reared Together," *Headache* 43 (2003): 235–244.

22. Yoon-Mi Hur, Thomas J. Bouchard Jr., Elke Eckert, "Genetic and Environmental Influences on Self-Reported Diet: A Reared-Apart Twin Study," *Physiology and Behavior* 64 (1998): 629–636.

23. Richard R. Fabsitz, Robert J. Garrison, Manning Feinleib, and Marthana Hjortland, "A Twin Analysis of Dietary Intake: Evidence for a Need to Control for Possible Environmental Differences in MZ and DZ Twins," *Behavior Genetics* 8 (1978): 15–25.

24. Vegemite is a yeast abstract made from leftover brewers yeast with vegetable and spice additives. Marmite is a yeast abstract, namely, a byproduct of brewing beer.

25. Claude Bouchard, Angelo Tremblay, Jean-Pierre Després, et al., "The Response to Long-Term Overfeeding in Identical Twins," *New England Journal of Medicine* 322 (1990): 1477–1482.

26. Richard Luschinger and Geoffrey E. Arnold, *Genetics of the Voice, Voice-Speech-Language* (Belmont, Calif.: Wadsworth, 1965); György Forrai and Géza Gordos, "A New Acoustical Method for the Discrimination of Monozygotic and Dizygotic Twins," *Acta Paediatrica Hungarica* 24 (1983): 315–322.

27. Farber, *Identical Twins Reared Apart.*

28. James Shields, *Monozygotic Twins Brought Up Apart and Brought Up Together* (London: Oxford University Press, 1962).

29. Robert T. Sataloff, "Genetics of the Voice," *Journal of Voice* 8 (1995): 16–19.

30. Michael J. Hammer, "Comparison of Within-Pair Similarities of Monozygotic and Dizygotic Twins for Mean F_0 and F_0 Range" (M.A. thesis, University of Kansas, 1998).

31. Grant Fairbanks, *Voice and Articulation Drillbook,* 2nd ed. (New York: Harper & Row, 1960), p. 127.

32. Farber, *Identical Twins Reared Apart.*

33. Theodor W. Adorno, Else Frenkel-Brunswik, Daniel Levinson, and Nevitt Sanford, *The Authoritarian Personality* (New York: Harper & Row, 1950).

34. Robert Altemeyer, *Enemies of Freedom: Understanding Right-Wing Authoritarianism* (San Francisco: Jossey-Bass, 1988).

35. Merrill Ring was a member of the philosophy faculty at California State University–Fullerton from 1973 until his 2010 retirement.

36. John C. Loehlin and Robert C. Nichols, *Heredity, Environment and Personality: A Study of 850 Sets of Twins* (Austin: University of Texas Press, 1976).

37. Nicholas G. Martin, Lindon J. Eaves, Andrew C. Heath, Rosemary Jardine, Lynn M. Feingold, and Hans J. Eysenck, "Transmission of Social Attitudes," *Proceedings of the National Academy of Sciences of the United States of America* 83 (1986): 4364–4368.

38. Altemeyer, *Enemies of Freedom.*

39. Glenn D. Wilson and John R. Patterson, "A New Measure of Conservatism," *British Journal of Social and Clinical Psychology* 7 (1968): 264–269.

40. Kathryn McCourt, Thomas J. Bouchard Jr., David T. Lykken, Auke Tellegen, and Margaret Keyes, "Authoritarianism Revisited: Genetic and Environmental Influences Examined in Twins Reared Apart and Together," *Personality and Individual Differences* 27 (1999): 985–1014.

41. Kathryn Corson, "A Genetic and Environmental Analysis of Right-Wing Authoritarianism in Twins Reared Apart and Together" (PhD diss., University of Minnesota, 1996).

42. An assortative mating parameter was included in this model.
43. The only significant MISTRA correlation showed that high authoritarianism was associated with lower rearing socioeconomic status (–0.19). The only significant reared-together twin correlations linked higher authoritarianism with fewer years of father's education (–0.23) and lower rearing socioeconomic status (–0.17). These relationships were too small to suggest practical importance.
44. Thomas J. Bouchard Jr., Matt McGue, David Lykken, and Auke Tellegen, "Intrinsic and Extrinsic Religiousness: Genetic and Environmental Influences and Personality Correlates," *Twin Research* 2 (1999): 88–98.
45. Lindon Eaves, Brian D'Onofrio, and Robert Russell, "Transmission of Religion and Attitudes," *Twin Research* 2 (1999): 59–61, p. 59.
46. Niels G. Waller, Brian A. Kojetin, Thomas J. Bouchard Jr., David T. Lykken, and Auke Tellegen, "Genetic and Environmental Influences on Religious Interests, Attitudes, and Values: A Study of Twins Reared Apart and Together," *Psychological Science* 1 (1990): 138–142.
47. Allen E. Bergin, "Religiosity and Mental Health: A Critical Reevaluation and Meta-Analysis," *Professional Psychology: Research and Practice* 14 (1983): 170–184.
48. Wade C. Rowatt, Jordan LaBouff, Megan Johnson, Paul Froese, and Jo-Ann Tsang, "Associations among Religiousness, Social Attitudes, and Prejudice in a National Random Sample of American Adults," *Psychology of Religion and Spirituality* 1 (2009): 14–24.
49. Gordon W. Allport and J. Michael Ross, "Personal Religious Orientation and Prejudice," *Journal of Personality and Social Psychology* 5: (1967): 432–443, p. 172.
50. Edward O. Wilson, *On Human Nature* (Cambridge, Mass.: Harvard University Press, 1978).
51. Edward O. Wilson, *Consilience: The Unity of Knowledge* (New York: Alfred A. Knopf, 1998).
52. Bouchard et al., "Intrinsic and Extrinsic Religiousness," p. 89.
53. Richard L. Gorsuch and G. Daniel Venable, "Development of an 'Age Universal' I-E Scale," *Journal of the Scientific Study of Religion* 22 (1983): 181–187.
54. The Public Opinion Inventory also used this format (–4 to +4).
55. David Cesarini, Christopher T. Dawes, James H. Fowler, Magnus Johannesson, Paul Lichtenstein, and Björn Wallace, "Heritability of Cooperative Behavior in the Trust Game," *Proceedings of the National Academy of Sciences of the United States of America* 105 (2008): 3721–3726; James H. Fowler, Laura A. Baker, and Christopher T. Dawes, "Genetic Variation in Political Participation," *American Political Science Review* 102 (2008): 233–248; Alan G. Sanfey, "Social Decision-Making: Insights from Game Theory and Neuroscience," *Science* 318 (2007): 598–602.
56. Robert Plomin, John C. DeFries, Gerald E. McClearn, and Peter McGuffin, *Behavioral Genetics,* 5th ed. (New York: Worth Publishers, 2008).
57. Thomas J. Bouchard and David T. Lykken, "Life Achievement in a Sample of Twins Reared Apart: Estimating the Role of Genetic and Environmental

Influences," in *Talent Development III. Proceedings from the 1995 Henry B. and Jocelyn Wallace National Symposium on Talent Development,* ed. Nicholas Colangelo and Susan G. Assouline, 81–97 (Scottsdale, Ariz.: Gifted Psychology Press, 1999).

58. Frank Barron, *The Psychology of Creativity* (New York: Holt, Rinehart & Winston, 1965).

59. Frank Barron and Paolo Parisi, "Twin Resemblances in Creativity and in Esthetic and Emotional Response," *Acta Geneticae Medicae et Gemellologiae* 25 (1976): 213–217.

60. Niels G. Waller, Thomas J. Bouchard Jr., David T. Lykken, Auke Tellegen, and Dawn M. Blacker, "Creativity, Heritability, Familiality: Which Word Does Not Belong?" *Psychological Inquiry* 4 (1993): 235–237.

61. Laird D. McLean, "Organizational Culture's Influence on Creativity and Innovation: A Review of the Literature and implications for Human Resources Development," *Advances in Developing Human Resources* 7 (2005): 226–246.

62. Bouchard and Lykken, "Life Achievement," p. 90.

63. Francis Galton, *Hereditary Genius: An Inquiry into Its Law and Consequences* (London: Macmillan, 1891).

64. Karl Pearson, *The Life, Letters and Labours of Francis Galton,* vol. 1 (Cambridge, U.K.: Cambridge University Press, 1924).

65. Isabel B. Myers and Mary H. McCaulley, *Manual: A Guide to the Development and Use of the Myers-Briggs Type Indicator* (Palo Alto, Calif.: Consulting Psychologists Press, 1985).

66. Thomas J. Bouchard Jr. and Yoon-Mi Hur, "Genetic and Environmental Influences on the Continuous Scales of the Myers-Briggs Type Indicator: An Analysis Based on Twins Reared Apart," *Journal of Personality* 66 (1998): 135–149.

67. Thomas J. Bouchard Jr., Matt McGue, Yoon-Mi Hur, and Joseph M. Horn, "A Genetic and Environmental Analysis of the California Psychological Inventory Using Adult Twins Reared Apart and Together," *European Journal of Personality* 12 (1998): 307–320.

68. Thomas J. Bouchard Jr. and Nancy L. Pedersen, "Twins Reared Apart: Natures Double Experiment," in *On the Way to Individuality: Current Methodological Issues in Behavioral Genetics,* ed. Michele C. LaBuda and Elena L. Grigorenko, 71–93 (Commack, N.Y.: Nova Scientific, 1999).

69. Lindon J. Eaves, Hans J. Eysenck, Nicholas G. Martin, *Genes, Culture and Personality: An Empirical Approach* (New York: Academic Press, 1989); Kerry L. Jang et al., "Heritability of the Big Five Personality Dimensions and Their Facets: A Twin Study," *Journal of Personality* 64 (1996): 577–591; John C. Loehlin, *Genes and Environment in Personality Development* (Newbury Park, Calif.: Sage, 1992).

70. David L. DiLilla, Irving I. Gottesman, Gregory J. Carey, and Thomas J. Bouchard Jr., "Heritability of MMPI Harris-Lingoes and Subtle-Obvious Subscales in Twins Reared Apart," *Assessment* 6 (1999): 353–366.

71. Daniel N. Wiener, "Subtle and Obvious Keys for the MMPI," *Journal of Consulting Psychology* 12 (1948): 164–170.

72. Alan F. Friedman, Richard Lewak, David S. Nichols, and James T. Webb, *Psychological Assessment with the MMPI-2* (Mahwah, N.J.: Lawrence Erlbaum, 2001).

73. David L. DiLalla, Irving I. Gottesman, Gregory Carey, and Thomas J. Bouchard Jr., "Heritability of MMPI Harris-Lingoes and Subtle-Obvious Subscales in Twins Reared Apart," *Assessment* 6 (1999): 353–366.

74. David L. DiLalla, Gregory Carey, Irving I. Gottesman, and Thomas J. Bouchard Jr., "Heritability of MMPI Personality Indicators of Psychopathology in Twins Reared Apart," *Journal of Abnormal Psychology* 105 (1996): 491–499.

75. Seymour S. Kety, "From Rationalization to Reason," *American Journal of Psychiatry* 131 (1974): 957–963.

76. Kristian E. Markon, Robert F. Krueger, Thomas J. Bouchard Jr., and Irving I. Gottesman, "Normal and Abnormal Personality Traits: Evidence for Genetic and Environmental Relationships in the Minnesota Study of Twins Reared Apart," *Journal of Personality* 70 (2002): 661–693.

77. Richard L. Doty, Paul Shaman, and Michael Dann, "Development of the University of Pennsylvania Smell Identification Test: Standardized Microencapsulated Test for Olfactory Function," *Physiology and Behavior* 32 (1984): 489–502.

78. Bryan S. Michalowicz, Dorothee P. Aeppli, John G. Virag, et al., "Periodontal Findings in Adult Twins," *Journal of Periodontology* 62 (1991): 293–299.

79. Bryan S. Michalowicz, Dorothee P. Aeppli, Ramesh K. Kuba, et al., "A Twin Study of Genetic Variation in Proportional Radiographic Alveolar Bone Height," *Journal of Dental Research* 70 (1991): 1431–1435.

80. Bryan S. Michalowicz, Larry F. Wolff, David Klump, et al., "Periodontal Bacteria in Adult Twins," *Journal of Periodontology* 70 (1999): 263–273.

81. Bryan S. Michalowicz, Bruce L. Pihlstrom, J. S. Hodges, and Thomas J. Bouchard Jr., "No Heritability of Temporomandibular Joint Signs and Symptoms," *Journal of Dental Research* 79 (2000): 1573–1578.

82. See, for example, Nancy L. Segal, Scott L. Hershberger, and Sara Arad, "Meeting One's Twin: Perceived Social Closeness and Familiarity," *Evolutionary Psychology* 1 (2003): 70–95; Wendy Johnson, Thomas J. Bouchard Jr., Nancy L. Segal, Margaret Keyes, and Jay Samuels, "The Stroop Color-Word Test: Genetic and Environmental Influences, Reading, Mental Ability, and Personality Correlates," *Journal of Educational Psychology* 95 (2003): 58–65.

12. Twin Relationships, Social Attitudes, and Mental Abilities (2003–2005)

1. *Nightline*, ABC News, October 29, 1989.

2. Nancy L. Segal, "Twin, Adoption and Family Methods as Approaches to the Evolution of Individual Differences," in *The Evolution of Personality and Individual Differences,* ed. David M. Buss and Patricia Hawley, 303–337 (Oxford: Oxford University Press, 2011).

3. Nancy L. Segal, "Education Issues," *Twin Research and Human Genetics* 8 (2005): 409–414.

4. Horatio H. Newman, Frank N. Freeman, and Karl J. Holzinger, *Twins: A Study of Heredity and Environment* (Chicago: University of Chicago Press, 1937), 153.

5. Ibid, 195.

6. Ibid., 239.

7. James Shields, *Monozygotic Twins Brought Up Apart and Brought Up Together* (London: Oxford University Press, 1962), 51.

8. Niels Juel-Nielsen, *Individual and Environment: Monozygotic Twins Reared Apart* (New York: International Universities Press, 1980), 16.

9. Shields, *Monozygotic Twins*, 21. The majority of Shields's twins were identified following a 1953 BBC television program, *Twin Sister, Twin Brother,* in which twins were asked to complete a questionnaire published in the then-current *Radio Times.* A special appeal was made for MZA twins, although nine of the eleven DZA twins for whom Shields obtained some behavioral data were identified via the BBC.

10. Nancy L. Segal, Scott L. Hershberger, and Sara Arad, "Meeting One's Twin: Perceived Social Closeness and Familiarity," *Evolutionary Psychology* 1 (2003): 70–95.

11. Ellen A. Stewart, *Exploring Twins: Towards a Social Analysis of Twinship* (London: Macmillan Press, 2000).

12. Maria Leek and Peter K. Smith, "Cooperation and Conflict in Three-Generation Families," in *The Psychology of Grandparenthood: An International Perspective,* ed. Peter K. Smith, 177–194 (London: Routledge, 1991).

13. Daniel G. Freedman, *Human Sociobiology: A Holistic Approach* (New York: Free Press, 1979), 129.

14. Nancy L. Segal, *Someone Else's Twin: The True Story of Babies Switched at Birth* (Amherst, N.Y.: Prometheus Books, 2011).

15. Robert F. Krueger, Kristian E. Markon, and Thomas J. Bouchard Jr., "The Extended Genotype: The Heritability of Personality Accounts for the Heritability of Recalled Family Environments in Twins Reared Apart," *Journal of Personality* 71 (2003): 809–833.

16. David C. Rowe, "Environmental and Genetic Influences on Dimensions of Perceived Parenting: A Twin Study," *Developmental Psychology* 17 (1981): 203–208.

17. David T. Lykken and Auke Tellegen, "Happiness Is a Stochastic Phenomenon," Psychological Science 7 (1996): 186–189.

18. Robert F. Krueger, Susan South, Wendy Johnson, and William Iacono, "The Heritability of Personality Is Not Always 50%: Gene-Environment Interactions and Correlations between Personality and Parenting," *Journal of Personality* 76 (2008): 1485–1521.

19. Thomas J. Bouchard Jr., Nancy L. Segal, Auke Tellegen, Matt McGue, Margaret Keyes, and Robert Krueger, "Genetic Influence on Social Attitudes: Another Challenge to Psychology from Behavior Genetics," in *Behavior Genetic Principles: Development, Personality and Psychopathology,* ed. Lisabeth F. DiLalla, 89–104 (Washington, D.C.: American Psychological Association, 2004).

20. Ibid., 95. He is referring to Nicholas G. Martin, Lindon J. Eaves, Andrew C. Heath, Rosemary Jardine, Lynn M. Feingold, and Hans J. Eysenck, "Transmission of Social Attitudes," *Proceedings of the National Academy of Sciences of the United States of America* 83 (1986): 4364–4368.

21. Auke Tellegen, David T. Lykken, Thomas J. Bouchard Jr., Kimerly J. Wilcox, Nancy L. Segal, and Stephen Rich, "Personality Similarity in Twins Reared Apart and Together," *Journal of Personality and Social Psychology* 54 (1988): 1031–1039.

22. Thomas J. Bouchard and Matt McGue, "Genetic and Environmental Influences on Human Psychological Differences" *Journal of Neurobiology* 54 (2003): 4–45; Bouchard Jr. et al., "Genetic Influence on Social Attitudes."

23. Deborah Finkel and Matt McGue, "Sex Differences and Non-Additivity in Heritability of the Multidimensional Personality Questionnaire Scales," *Journal of Personality and Social Psychology* 72 (1997): 929–938.

24. Glenn D. Wilson and John R. Patterson, "A New Measure of Conservatism," *British Journal of Social and Clinical Psychology* 7 (1968): 264–269.

25. John C. Loehlin and Robert C. Nichols, *Heredity, Environment and Personality: A Study of 850 Sets of Twins* (Austin: University of Texas Press, 1976).

26. Lindon J. Eaves, Andrew Heath, Nicholas Martin, et al., "Comparing the Biological and Cultural Inheritance of Personality and Social Attitudes in the Virginia 30,000 Study of Twins and Their Relatives," *Twin Research* 2 (1999): 62–80.

27. Thomas J. Bouchard Jr., Nancy L. Segal, Auke Tellegen, Matt McGue, Margaret Keyes, and Robert Krueger, "Evidence for the Construct Validity and Heritability of the Wilson-Patterson Conservatism Scale: A Reared-Apart Twins Study of Social Attitudes," *Personality and Individual Differences* 34 (2003): 959–969.

28. Peter Watson, *Twins: An Uncanny Relationship?* (Chicago: Contemporary Books, 1981).

29. Thomas J. Bouchard, David T. Lykken, Matt McGue, and Auke Tellegen, "Intrinsic and Extrinsic Religiousness: Genetic and Environmental Influences and Personality Correlates," *Twin Research* 2 (1999): 88–98.

30. Laura B. Koenig, Matt McGue, Robert F. Krueger, and Thomas J. Bouchard Jr., "Genetic and Environmental Influences on Religiousness: Findings for Retrospective and Current Religiousness Ratings," *Journal of Personality* 73 (2005): 471–488.

31. Attitudes vary as a function of cohort as well as age. When in vitro fertilization was introduced in 1978, people worried that it would alter family dynamics and structure in negative ways. However, in vitro fertilization has been an effective reproductive technology, helping many infertile couples have the families they desired. The longitudinal MISTRA data on both twins and non-twins should shed light on factors affecting attitudinal change, both more conservative and less conservative.

32. In 2010 e-mail correspondence, Koenig wrote, "When I went on job talks the twins reared-apart were the first thing people mentioned if they had any knowledge at all about behavior genetics." I was sure that I saw Koenig at

the 2009 Western Psychological Association meeting in Portland, Oregon, but I was wrong: it was Anne, her identical twin sister who teaches psychology at the University of San Diego. I did not know Koenig was a twin. Also see Chapter 11; religiosity-personality associations were generally not found by the MISTRA.

33. Bouchard et al., "Genetic Influence on Social Attitudes," p. 95.

34. "It's Always Better with Twins": Remembering the Life and Research of David T. Lykken," special session, International Congress on Twin Studies, Ghent, Belgium, June 7–10, 2007.

35. Jürgen R. Stroop, "Studies of Interference in Serial Verbal Reactions," *Journal of Experimental Psychology* 18 (1935): 643–662.

36. Raymond De Young, "Stroop Task: A Test of Capacity to Direct Attention," EPLab OnLine Measures—Stroop Task—Version: 4.2, updated January 5, 2010, http://snre.umich.edu/eplab/demos/st0/stroopdesc.html.

37. Charles J. Golden, *Stroop Color and Word Test* (Chicago: Stoelting, 1978).

38. Lissy F. Jarvik, "Genetic Components and Intellectual Functioning during Senescence: A 20-Year Study of Aging Twins," *Behavior Genetics* 2 (1972): 159–171.

39. Richard L. Slossen, *Slossen Intelligence Test and Oral Reading Test for Children and Adults* (East Aurora, N.Y.: Slossen Educational, 1984); Richard W. Woodcock, *Woodcock Reading Mastery Tests-Revised Forms G & H-Examiner's Manual* (Circle Pines, Minn.: American Guidance Services, 1987).

40. Wendy Johnson, Thomas J. Bouchard Jr., Nancy L. Segal, Margaret Keyes, and Jay Samuels, "The Stroop Color-Word Test: Genetic and Environmental Influences, Reading, Mental Ability, and Personality Correlates," *Journal of Educational Psychology* 95 (2003): 58–65.

41. Wendy Johnson, Thomas J. Bouchard Jr., Nancy L. Segal, and Jay Samuels, "General Intelligence and Reading Performance in Adults: Is the Genetic Factor Structure the Same as for Children?" *Personality and Individual Differences* 38 (2005): 1413–1428.

42. Fluid ability refers to individuals' genetically based abilities and are not learned. Crystallized ability is intelligence based on culture and learning.

43. John C. DeFries, David W. Fulker, and Michelle C. Labuda, "Evidence for a Genetic Aetiology in Reading Disability of Twins," letter to the editor, *Nature* 329 (1987): 537–539.

44. Wendy Johnson, Thomas J. Bouchard Jr., Robert F. Krueger, Matt McGue, and Irving I. Gottesman, "Just One *g*: Consistent Results from Three Test Batteries," *Intelligence* 32 (2004): 95–107.

45. William Kessen, *The Child* (New York: John Wiley & Sons, 1965).

46. Arthur R. Jensen, *The g Factor: The Science of Mental Ability* (Westport, Conn.: Praeger, 1998).

47. A model recognizing separate mental abilities is Howard Gardner's theory of multiple intelligences, described in *Frames of Mind* (New York: Basic Books, 2011). Gardner's model has not been subjected to the same rigorous examinations as the IQ test and other psychometric measures. A more recent evolutionary based theory of intelligence refers to mental modules or content-independent mechanisms; see Leda Cosmides and John Tooby, "The Modular Nature of Human Intelligence," in *The Origin and Evolution of Intelligence,*

ed. Arnold B. Scheibel and J. William Schopf, 71–101 (Toronto: John Barlett, 1997).

48. Some participants did not complete all tests due to time constraints. When possible, missing data were dealt with by imputation of scores according to strict guidelines.

49. Johnson et al., "Just One *g*," 104.

50. Thomas J. Bouchard Jr., "Genetic Influence on Human Intelligence (Spearman's *g*): How Much?" *Annals of Human Biology* 36 (2009): 527–544, p. 532.

51. Wendy Johnson and Thomas J. Bouchard Jr., "The Structure of Human Intelligence: It's Verbal, Perceptual, and Image Rotation (VPR) Not Fluid and Crystallized," *Intelligence* 33 (2005): 393–416.

52. Wendy Johnson and Thomas J. Bouchard Jr., "Constructive Replication of the Visual-Perceptual-Image Rotation (VPR) Model in Thurstone's (1941) Battery of 60 Tests of Mental Ability," *Intelligence* 33 (2005): 417–430.

53. Wendy Johnson, Jan te Nijenhuis, and Thomas J. Bouchard Jr., "Replication of the Hierarchical Visual-Perceptual-Image Rotation Model in de Wolff and Buiten's (1963) Battery of 46 Tests of Mental Ability," *Intelligence* 35 (2007): 69–81.

54. Wendy Johnson, Jan te Nijenhuis, and Thomas J. Bouchard Jr., "Still Just 1 *g*: Consistent Results from Five Test Batteries," *Intelligence* 36 (2008): 81–95.

55. Professor Tony Vernon, personal communication, July 8, 2010. British psychologist P. (Philip) E. Vernon is Tony Vernon's late father.

56. Edward Novitski, *Human Genetics,* 2nd ed. (New York: Macmillan, 1982).

57. Thomas J. Bouchard Jr., "Genetic Influence on Human Psychological Traits: A Survey," *Current Directions in Psychological Science* 13 (2004): 148–151.

58. Ibid., 151.

59. Ibid., 148.

13. Sexual Development, Fluctuating Asymmetry, Body Size, and the Structure of Intelligence (2006 and Beyond)

1. I hope to complete a brief assessment of this pair at a later date.

2. Nancy L. Segal and Joanne Hoven Stohs, "Resemblance for Age at Menarche in Female Twins Reared Apart and Together," *Human Biology* 79 (2007): 623–635.

3. Hanan reached menarche at thirteen years, two years later than her twin.

4. Susan L. Farber, *Identical Twins Reared Apart: A Reanalysis* (New York: Basic Books, 1980).

5. Martha K. McClintock, "Menstrual Synchrony and Suppression," *Nature* 229 (1971): 244–245. Some researchers have challenged these findings on methodological grounds; see H. Clyde Wilson, "A Critical Review of Menstrual Synchrony Research," *Psychoneuroendocrinology* 17 (1992): 565–591.

6. Mean age at menarche has remained stable for the past fifty years; see Angela Diaz, Marc Laufer, and Lesley L. Breech, "Menstruation in Girls and Adolescents: Using the Menstrual Cycle as a Vital Sign," *Pediatrics* 118 (2006): 2245–2250.

7. Jay Belsky, Laurence Steinberg, and Patricia Draper, "Childhood Experience, Interpersonal Development, and Reproductive Strategy: An Evolutionary Theory of Socialization," *Child Development* 62 (1991): 647–670.

8. Segal and Stohs, "Resemblance for Age at Menarche."

9. Federico J. Soriguer, Stella González-Romero, Isabel Esteva, et al., "Does the Intake of Nuts and Seeds Alter the Appearance of Menarche?" *Acta Obstetrica Gynecologia Scandinavica* 74 (1995): 455–461.

10. Nancy L. Segal and Joanne Hoven Stohs, "Age at First Intercourse in Twins Reared Apart: Genetic Influence and Life History Events," *Personality and Individual Differences* 47 (2009): 127–132.

11. Steven W. Gangestad and Randy Thornhill, "The Evolutionary Psychology of Extrapair Sex: The Role of Fluctuating Asymmetry," *Evolution and Human Behavior* 18 (1996): 69–88.

12. Anders P. Møller and Andrew Pomiankowski, "Fluctuating Asymmetry and Sexual Selection," *Genetica* 89 (1993): 267–279.

13. Randy Thornhill and Steven W. Gangestad, "The Scent of Symmetry: A Human Sex Pheromone That Signals Fitness?" *Evolution and Human Behavior* 20 (1999): 175–201.

14. Theresa Ann Markow and Irving I. Gottesman, "Fluctuating Dermatoglyphic Asymmetry in Psychotic Twins," *Psychiatry Research* 29 (1989): 37–43.

15. Fifty-four studies of human fluctuating asymmetry have been published in *Evolution and Human Behavior* since 1997.

16. Steven W. Gangestad, personal communication, February 20, 2011. A study linking increased fluctuating asymmetry and schizophrenia predisposition was published in the mid-1980s; see Therese A. Markow and Kevin Wandler, "Fluctuating Dermatoglyphic Asymmetry and the Genetics of Liability to Schizophrenia," *Psychiatry Research* 19 (1986): 323–328.

17. Horatio H. Newman, Frank N. Freeman, and Karl J. Holzinger, *Twins: A Study of Heredity and Environment* (Chicago: University of Chicago Press, 1937).

18. Ibid., 141.

19. Sonya J. Elder, Susan B. Roberts, Megan A. McCrory, et al., "Effect of Body Composition Methodology on Heritability Estimates of Body Fatness" (2011, under review).

20. The reliability of the anthropometric measurements was not assessed. Unreliability would, however, lead to more conservative estimates of FA heritability.

21. Anders Paper Møller, "A Review of Developmental Instability, Parasitism and Disease," *Infection, Genetics and Evolution* 6 (2006): 133–140.

22. Gregory Livshits and Eugene Kobyliansky, "Study of Genetic Variance in the Fluctuating Asymmetry of Anthropometrical Traits," *Annals of Human Biology* 16 (1989): 121–129.

23. Wendy Johnson, Steven W. Gangestad, Nancy L. Segal, and Thomas J. Bouchard Jr., "Heritability of Fluctuating Asymmetry in a Human Twin Sample: The Effect of Trait Aggregation," *American Journal of Human Biology* 20 (2008): 651–658.

24. Stefan Van Dongen, "What Do We Know about the Heritability of Developmental Stability? Answers from a Bayesian Model," *Evolution* 61 (2007): 1022–1042, p. 1041.

25. Wendy Johnson, Nancy L. Segal, and Thomas J. Bouchard Jr., "Fluctuating Asymmetry and General Intelligence: No Genetic or Phenotypic Association," *Intelligence* 36 (2008): 279–288.
26. Linda Mealey et al., "Symmetry and Perceived Facial Attractiveness: A Monozygotic Co-Twin Comparison," *Journal of Personality and Social Psychology* 76 (1999): 157–165.
27. Linda Mealey, "Do Parents Show Favoritism for Their Symmetric Children?" paper presented at the Human Behavior and Evolutionary Society, New Brunswick, N.J., June 2002.
28. Thornhill and Gangestad, "Scent of Symmetry."
29. Nancy L. Segal, *Indivisible by Two: Lives of Extraordinary Twins* (Cambridge, Mass.: Harvard University Press, 2007).
30. Elizabeth Quinn, "What Is Hydrostatic Underwater Weighing?" About.com Sports Medicine, updated March 30, 2011, http://sportsmedicine.about.com /od/fitnessevalandassessment/g/UnderwaterWeigh.htm.
31. Mary E. Holmes, *Being You* (London: Austin & Macauley, 2008), 161–162.
32. Ibid., 165.
33. Ibid., 167–168.
34. Sonya J. Elder, Alice H. Lichtenstein, Anastassios G. Pittas, et al., "Genetic and Environmental Influences on Factors Associated with Cardiovascular Disease and the Metabolic Syndrome," *Journal of Lipid Research* 50 (2009): 1917–1926.
35. Sonya J. Elder, Michael C. Neale, Paul J. Fuss, et al., "Genetic and Environmental Influences on Eating Behavior—A Study of Twin Reared Apart," *FASEB Journal* 23 (2009): abstract 545.7. The published version of this research is a conference abstract, so full details of the study are unavailable.
36. Albert J. Stunkard and Samuel Messick. "The Three-Factor Eating Questionnaire to Measure Dietary Restraint, Disinhibition and Hunger," *Journal of Psychosomatic Research* 29 (1985): 71–83.
37. Nancy L. Pedersen, Robert Plomin, Gerald E. McClearn, and Lars Friberg, "Neuroticism, Extraversion and Related Traits in Adult Twins Reared Apart," *Journal of Personality and Social Psychology* 55 (1988): 950–957.
38. A 2003 reared-together study found heritabilities of 0.45 for disinhibition, 0.08 for hunger, and 0.00 for restraint. The different results from those of the MISTRA could be due to the all-female sample and abbreviated and modified version of the Eating Questionnaire. See Benjamin M. Neale, Suzanne E. Mazzeo, and Cynthia M. Bulik, "A Twin Study of Dietary Restraint, Disinhibition and Hunger: An Examination of the Eating Inventory (Three Factor Eating Questionnaire)," *Twin Research and Human Genetics* 8 (2003): 471–478.
39. Longitudinal studies track physical and behavioral traits of the same individuals continuously over time to assess age changes. Cross-sectional studies simultaneously compare physical and behavioral traits of two or more different age groups to assess age differences.
40. Kenneth S. Kendler, Lisa J. Halberstadt, Frank Butera, John Myers, Thomas J. Bouchard Jr., and P. Ekman, "The Similarity of Facial Expressions in Response to Emotion-Inducing Films in Reared-Apart Twins," *Psychological Medicine* 38 (2008): 1475–1483.

41. Segal, *Indivisible by Two.*
42. *Oskar and Jack,* directed by Frauke Sandig (New York: First Run/Icarus Films, 1996), VHS, was originally produced in Germany. A play by Mexican author Andrés Roemer, *Oskar y Jack* (Mexico City: Miguel Ángel Porrúa, 2011), based on "Oskar and Jack" in Segal, *Indivisible by Two,* has been written.
43. Thomas J. Bouchard Jr., "Genes and Human Psychological Traits," in *The Innate Mind: Foundations for the Future,* ed. Peter Carruthers, Stephen Laurence, and Stephen Stich, vol. 3, 69–89 (Oxford: Oxford University Press, 2007). This chapter summarizes a great deal of MISTRA research on intelligence, personality, and social attitudes.
44. Wendy Johnson, Jan te Nijenhuis, and Thomas J. Bouchard Jr., "Still Just 1 *g*: Consistent Results from Five Test Batteries," *Intelligence* 36 (2008): 81–95.
45. Wendy Johnson, Jan te Nijenhuis, and Thomas J. Bouchard Jr., "Replication of the Hierarchical Visual-Perceptual-Image Rotation Model in de Wolff and Buiten's (1963) Battery of 46 Tests of Mental Ability," *Intelligence* 35 (2007): 69–81.
46. Wendy Johnson, Thomas J. Bouchard Jr., Matt McGue, et al., "Genetic and Environmental Influences on the Verbal-Perceptual-Image Rotation (VPR) Model of the Structure of Mental Abilities in the Minnesota Study of Twins Reared Apart," *Intelligence* 35 (2007): 542–562.
47. In order to have unique subject data, only two members of two MZA triplet sets and two DZA triplets were included, eliminating four MZA pairs and four DZA opposite-sex pairs.
48. Lylas G. Mogk and Marja Mogk, *Macular Degeneration: The Complete Guide to Saving and Maximizing Your Sight* (New York: Ballantine Books, 1999).
49. Wendy Johnson, Eric Turkheimer, Irving I. Gottesman, and Thomas J. Bouchard Jr., "Beyond Heritability: Twin Studies in Behavioral Research," *Current Directions in Psychological Science* 19 (2009): 217–220; Wendy Johnson, "Understanding the Genetics of Intelligence: Can Height Help? Can Corn Oil?" *Current Directions in Psychological Science* 19 (2010): 177–182; Wendy Johnson, Lars Penke, and Frank M. Spinath, "Heritability in the Era of Molecular Genetics: Some Thoughts for Understanding Genetic Influences on Behavioural Traits," *European Journal of Personality* 25 (2011): 254–266.
50. Robert Plomin and John C. DeFries, "Genetics and Intelligence: Recent Data," *Intelligence* 4 (1980): 15–24; Nancy L. Segal and Jean Russell, "IQ Similarity in Monozygotic and Dizygotic Twin Children: Effects of the Same versus Separate Examiners: A Research Note," *Journal of Child Psychology and Psychiatry* 32 (1991): 703–708.
51. Irving I. Gottesman, "Biogenetics of Race and Class," in *Social Class, Race and Psychological Development,* ed. Martin Deutsch, Irwin Katz, and Arthur R. Jensen, 11–51 (New York: Holt, Rinehart & Winston, 1968). The IQ differences from Shields's study were IQ equivalents of verbal and nonverbal test scores. The MISTRA within-pair IQ scores excluded twins from outside the United States.
52. Thomas J. Bouchard Jr., "Genetic Influence on Human Intelligence (Spearman's *g*): How Much?" *Annals of Human Biology* 36 (2009): 527–544.

53. Steven Pinker, *The Blank Slate: The Modern Denial of Human Nature* (New York: Viking, 2002).
54. Wendy Johnson and Thomas J. Bouchard Jr., "Sex Differences in Mental Abilities: *g* Masks the Dimensions on Which They Lie," *Intelligence* 35 (2007a): 23–39.
55. Wendy Johnson and Thomas J. Bouchard Jr., "Sex Differences in Mental Ability: A Proposed Means to Link Them to Brain Structure and Function," *Intelligence* 35 (2007b): 197–209.
56. Sally P. Springer and Georg Deutsh, *Left Brain, Right Brain: Perspectives from Cognitive Neuroscience* (San Francisco: W. H. Freeman, 2001).
57. Elizabeth Hampson, "Variations in Sex-Related Differences across the Menstrual Cycle," *Brain and Cognition* 14 (1990): 26–43.
58. Richard J. Haier, Rex E. Jung, Ronald A. Yeo, Kevin Head, and Michael T. Alkire, "Structural Brain Variation and General Intelligence," *Neuroimage* 23 (2004): 425–433.
59. Johnson and Bouchard, "Sex Differences in Mental Abilities" (2007b).
60. Wendy Johnson, Rex E. Jung, Roberto Colom, and Richard J. Haier, "Cognitive Abilities Independent of IQ Correlate with Regional Brain Structure," *Intelligence* 36 (2008): 18–28.
61. "Twins of Fate," *48 Hours: Mystery,* CBS Television, June 20, 2002.
62. Wendy Johnson and Thomas J. Bouchard Jr., "Linking Abilities, Interests and Gender via Latent Class Analysis," *Journal of Career Assessment* 17 (2009): 3–38.
63. These percentages refer to the subsets of individuals indicating these interests and occupations.
64. Jennifer Connellan, "Sex Differences in Human Neonatal Social Perception," *Infant and Behavior Development* 23 (2000): 113–118.
65. David S. Moore and Scott P. Johnson, "Mental Rotation in Human Infants: A Sex Difference," *Psychological Science* 19 (2008): 1063–1066.
66. Laura N. Koenig and Thomas J. Bouchard Jr., "Genetic and Environmental Influences on the Traditional Moral Values Triad—Authoritarianism, Conservatism and Religiousness—as Assessed by Quantitative Behavior Genetic Methods," in *Where God and Science Meet: How Brain and Evolutionary Studies Alter Our Understanding of Religion,* vol. 1: *Evolution, Genes, and the Religious Brain,* ed. Patrick McNamara, 31–60 (Westport, Conn.: Praeger, 2006).
67. Thomas J. Bouchard Jr., "Authoritarianism, Religiousness, and Conservatism: Is 'Obedience to Authority' the Explanation for Their Clustering, Universality and Evolution?" in *The Biological Evolution of Religious Mind and Behavior,* ed. Eckart Voland and Wulf Schiefenhövel, 165–180 (Berlin: Springer, 2009). The Traditional Moral Virtues Triad was first explicated in Koenig and Bouchard's 2006 book chapter (see previous note).
68. Michael Hout, Andrew Greeley, and Melissa J. Wilde, "The Demographic Imperative in Religious Change in the United States," *American Journal of Sociology* 107 (2001): 468–500.
69. Thomas J. Bouchard Jr., Nancy L. Segal, Auke Tellegen, Matt McGue, Margaret Keyes, and Robert Krueger, "Genetic Influence on Social Attitudes:

Another Challenge to Psychology from Behavior Genetics," in *Behavior Genetic Principles: Development, Personality and Psychopathology,* ed. Lisabeth F. DiLalla, 89–104 (Washington, D.C.: American Psychological Association, 2004).

70. Remus Ilies, Richard D. Arvey, and Thomas J. Bouchard Jr., "Darwinism, Behavioral Genetics and Organizational Behavior: A Review and Agenda for Future Research," in "Darwinian Perspectives on Behavior in Organizations," special issue, *Journal of Organizational Behavior* 27 (2006): 121–141.

71. Thomas J. Bouchard Jr., "Strong Inference: A Strategy for Advancing Psychological Science," in *Experience and Development: A Festschrift in Honor of Sandra Wood Scarr,* ed. Kathleen McCartney and Richard Weinberg, 39–59 (London: Taylor & Francis, 2009).

72. John R. Platt, "Strong Inference," *Science* 146 (1964): 347–353.

73. Nancy L. Segal, "Personality and Birth Order in Monozygotic Twins Adopted Apart: A Test of Sulloway's Theory," *Twin Research and Human Genetics* 11 (2008): 103–107.

74. Frank J. Sulloway, "Birth Order, Sibling Competition, and Human Behavior," in *Conceptual Challenges in Evolutionary Psychology: Innovative Research Strategies,* ed. Harmon R. Holcomb III, 39–84 (Dordrecht: Kluwer Academic, 2001).

75. Ibid.

76. Stanley Coren, "Twinning Is Associated with an Increased Risk of Left-Handedness and Inverted Writing Posture," *Early Human Development* 40 (1994): 23–17.

77. Nancy L. Sicotte, Roger P. Woods, and John C. Mazziota, "Handedness in Twins: A Meta-Analysis," *Laterality* 4 (1999): 265–286; Marian Annett, "Cerebral Asymmetry in Twins: Predictions of the Right Shift Theory," *Neuropsychologia* 41 (2003): 469–479; Michele Carlier, Elisabeth Spitz, Marie Cécile Vacher-Lavenu, Pierre Villéger, Benoît Martin, and François Michel, "Manual Performance and Laterality in Twins of Known Chorion Type," *Behavior Genetics* 26 (1996): 409–417; Charles E. Boklage, "Embryogenesis of Chimeras, Twins and Anterior Midline Asymmetries," *Human Reproduction* 21 (2003): 579–591.

78. Charles E. Boklage, *How New Humans Are Made* (Singapore: World Scientific, 2010).

79. Sarah E. Medland, Margaret J. Wright, Gina M. Geffen, et al., "Special Twin Environments, Genetic Influences and Their Effects on the Handedness of Twins and Their Siblings," *Twin Research* 6 (2003): 119–130.

80. R. C. Oldfield, "The Assessment and Analysis of Handedness: The Edinburgh Inventory," *Neuropsychologia* 9 (1971): 97–113.

81. Nancy L. Segal and Thomas J. Bouchard Jr., "Hand-Discordance in MZ and DZ Twins Reared Apart and Together," paper presented at the III American Psychological Society, Washington, D.C., June 13–16, 1991

82. Herbert F. Crovitz and Karl Zener, "A Group-Test for Assessing Hand- and Eye-Dominance," *American Journal of Psychology* 75 (1962): 271–276.

83. [χ^2 (df = 1) = 1.33, not statistically significant]. MZA female members in two MZA/DZA triplet sets were included in the individual twin proportions.

84. [χ^2 (df = 1) = 1.15, not statistically significant].

85. James Shields, *Monozygotic Twins Brought Up Apart and Brought Up Together* (London: Oxford University Press, 1962); Niels Juel-Nielsen, "A Psychiatric-Psychological Investigation of Monozygous Twins Reared Apart," *Acta Psychiatrica et Neurologica Scandinavica* (1965), Monograph Supplement 183. Handedness data were available for eleven of Juel-Nielsen's twelve MZA twin pairs. Twins in the two hand-discordant pairs were described as "right-handed" and "ambidextrous, probably originally left-handed" (p. 247) and "both ambidextrous", but one "predominantly left-handed" (p. 177). Both twins in a third MZA twin pair were described as "right-handed" (p. 77), although one twin's early tendency toward left-handedness was "quickly corrected" by her teacher and she always "felt naturally right-handed" (p. 74).

86. James Shields, *Monozygotic Twins* (1962). Shields administered Blau's Questionnaire for Preferred Laterality to twins who displayed left-handedness, based on their responses to items in his interview booklet.

87. David J. Merrell, "Dominance of Eye and Hand," *Human Biology* 29 (1957): 314–327, p. 325.

88. Chris McManus, "The Inheritance of Left-Handedness," in *Biological Asymmetry and Handedness,* ed. Gregory R. Bock and Joan Marsh, 251–281 (West Sussex, U.K.: CIBA Foundation, 1991).

89. Wendy Johnson and Thomas J. Bouchard Jr., "The MISTRA Data: Forty-Two Mental Ability Tests in Three Batteries," *Intelligence* 39 (2011): 82–88.

90. Ibid., 83.

91. Jason T. Major, Wendy Johnson, and Thomas J. Bouchard Jr., "The Dependability of the General Factor of Intelligence: Why Small, Single-Factor Models Do Not Adequately Represent *g,*" *Intelligence* 39 (2011): 418–433.

92. See, for example, Aja L. Murray, Hayley Dixon, Wendy Johnson, and Thomas J. Bouchard Jr., "Spearman's Law of Diminishing Returns: A Statistical Artifact?" (under review); Thomas J. Bouchard Jr., "Heritability," in *Encyclopedia of the Mind,* ed. Hal Pashler (Thousand Oaks, Calif., in press).

14. Questions, Answers, and Twin Studies of the Future

1. Brian Palmer "Double Inanity: Twin Studies Are Pretty Much Useless," *Slate Magazine,* http://www.slate.com/articles/life/twins/2011/08/double_inanity .html (8/24/2011); see the response by Nancy L. Segal, Irving I. Gottesman, Nicholas G. Martin, Eric Turkheimer, and Margaret Gatz, reprinted in Nancy L. Segal, "The Value of Twin Studies: A Response to *Slate Magazine,*" *Twin Research and Human Genetics* 14 (2011): 593–597.

2. Thomas J. Bouchard Jr., "The Hereditarian Research Program: Triumphs and Tribulations," in *Arthur Jensen: Consensus and Controversy,* ed. Sohan Modgil and Celia A. L. Modgil, 55–70 (London: Falmer International, 1987).

3. Nancy L. Segal and Jean Russell, "IQ Similarity in Monozygotic and Dizygotic Twin Children: Effects of the Same versus Separate Examiners: A Research Note," *Journal of Child Psychology and Psychiatry* 32 (1991): 703–708.

4. Thomas J. Bouchard Jr. and Matthew McGue, "Familial Studies of Intelligence: A Review," *Science* 212 (1981): 1055–1059; Thomas J. Bouchard Jr., "Genetic Influence on Human Intelligence (Spearman's *g*): How Much?" *Annals of*

Human Biology 36 (2009): 527–544; Nancy L. Segal, "Twins: The Finest Natural Experiment," *Personality and Individual Differences* 49 (2010): 317–323.

5. Matt McGue, Thomas J. Bouchard Jr., William G. Iacono, and David T. Lykken, "Behavioral Genetics of Cognitive Ability: A Life-Span Perspective," in *Nature, Nurture and Psychology*, ed. Robert Plomin and Gerald E. McClearn, 59–76 (Washington, D.C., American Psychological Association, 1993).

6. Shields's January 24, 1974, letter addressed to Dr. E. B. Hook of the New York State Birth Defects Institute was provided to me by Irving I. Gottesman.

7. Wendy Johnson and Thomas J. Bouchard Jr., "Sex Differences in Mental Abilities: *g* Masks the Dimensions on Which They Lie," *Intelligence* 35 (2007): 23–39.

8. Wendy Johnson, Thomas J. Bouchard Jr., Nancy L. Segal, and Jay Samuels, "General Intelligence and Reading Performance in Adults: Is the Genetic Factor Structure the Same as for Children?" *Personality and Individual Differences* 38 (2005): 1413–1428.

9. David T. Lykken, Seymour Geisser, and Auke Tellegen, "Heritability Estimates from Twin Studies: The Efficiency of the MZA Design" (unpublished manuscript, Department of Psychology, University of Minnesota, Minneapolis, 1981).

10. David T. Lykken, "A More Accurate Estimate of Heritability," *Twin Research and Human Genetics* 10 (2007): 168–173.

11. Horatio H. Newman, Frank N. Freeman, and Karl J. Holzinger, *Twins: A Study of Heredity and Environment* (Chicago: University of Chicago Press, 1937), 132–133.

12. Steven Rose, Richard C. Lewontin, and Leon J. Kamin, *Not in Our Genes: Biology, Ideology, and Human Nature* (New York: Pantheon, 1984); Jay Joseph, "Separated Twins and the Genetics of Personality Differences: A Critique," *American Journal of Psychology* 114 (2001): 1–30; Jay Joseph, *The Gene Illusion: Genetic Research in Psychiatry ad Psychology under the Microscope* (New York: Algora, 2004).

13. Iva C. Gardner and Horatio H. Newman, "Mental and Physical Traits of Identical Twins Reared Apart: Case XX. Twins Lois and Louise," *Journal of Heredity* 31 (1940): 119–126, p. 19.

14. Niels Juel-Nielsen, "A Psychiatric-Psychological Investigation of Monozygous Twins Reared Apart," *Acta Psychiatrica et Neurologica Scandinavica* (1965), Monograph Supplement 183.

15. James Shields, *Monozygotic Twins Brought Up Apart and Brought Up Together* (London: Oxford University Press, 1962).

16. Our twins were adults, so most were probably conceived before the availability of assisted reproduction technology. Since the early 1980s, these techniques have substantially raised the DZ twinning rate and slightly elevated the MZ twinning rate.

17. The similarities of sixteen MZA twin pairs and one DZA twin pair were detected by others, leading to their reunion. Physical resemblance reunited twins in another case, in which 64-year-old MZ female twins simply recognized each other; each had always known she had a twin. More recently,

separated 35-year-old Argentine MZ female twins met by chance in a clothing store. The twins were previously unaware of their twinship; "Argentine Twins Separated at Birth Reunite 35 Years Later," http://www.20minutos.es /noticia/460527/0/gemelas/separadas/encuentro/, April 1, 2009. These twins found each other ten years after the MISTRA ended.

18. Kenneth S. Kendler, Michael C. Neale, Ronald C. Kessler, Andrew C. Heath, and Lindon J. Eaves, "A Test of the Equal-Environment Assumption in Twin Studies of Psychiatric Illness," *Behavior Genetics* 1 (1993): 21–27; Sandra Scarr and Louise Carter-Saltzman, "Twin Method: Defense of a Critical Assumption," *Behavior* Genetics 9 (1979): 527–542.

19. Robert Plomin, John C. DeFries, Gerald E. McClearn, and Peter McGuffin, *Behavioral Genetics,* 5th ed. (New York: Worth Publishers, 2008).

20. John C. Loehlin and Robert C. Nichols, *Heredity, Environment, and Personality: A Study of 850 Sets of Twins* (Austin: University of Texas Press, 1976); Robert Plomin, Lee Willerman, and John C. Loehlin, "Resemblance in Appearance and the Equal Environments Assumption in Twin Studies of Personality Traits," *Behavior Genetics* 6 (1976): 43–52; Nikole J. Cronk, Wendy S. Slutske, Pamela A. Madden, et al., "Emotional and Behavioral Problems among Female Twins: An Evaluation of the Equal Environments Assumption," *Journal of the American Academy of Child and Adolescent Psychiatry* 41 (2002): 829–837.

21. Robert Bazell, "Sins and Twins," *New Republic,* December 21, 1987, 17–18.

22. Lisa Lynch, "Twins' Personality Study Made Big Splash before Journal Approval," *Science Writer,* Winter 1990, 15–19.

23. Thomas J. Bouchard Jr., "Intensive, Detailed, Exhaustive," *Intelligence* 26 (1998): 283–290, p. 288.

24. Bouchard has turned down media invitations since his retirement, but he forwards all of them to me.

25. Dorothy Nelkin, "An Uneasy Relationship: The Tensions between Medicine and the Media," *Lancet* 347 (1996): 160–1603, p. 1601.

26. Ibid., 1601.

27. Edwin Chen, "Twins Reared Apart: A Living Lab," *New York Times Magazine,* December 9, 1979, 112–123.

28. Constance Holden, "Twins Reunited: More Than the Faces Are Familiar," *Science 80* (1980): 55–59.

29. Lewis Cope, "Twins: Why Are They Alike?" *Minneapolis Star Tribune: Picture Magazine,* February 13, 1983, 14–18.

30. Lawrence Wright, "Double Mystery," *New Yorker,* August 7, 1995, 45–46, 48–52, 54–62.

31. Jill Neimark, "Nature's Clones," *Psychology Today,* August 1997, 37–45, 64–69.

32. Frank Rich, "Separated at Birth" *New York Times,* January 12, 1995.

33. Thomas J. Bouchard Jr., "Ideological Obstacles to Genetic Research: Tales from the Nature-Nurture Wars," paper presented to "Science and the Powers" seminar, Swedish Ministry of Education and Science, Stockholm, Sweden, March 16, 1994.

34. Matt McGue, letter to the editor, *Scientific American* 269 (1993): 8.

35. Thomas J. Bouchard Jr., "Ideological Obstacles," 1994.
36. Val Dusek, "Bewitching Science," *Science for the People* 19 (November/ December 1987), 19–22.
37. John Horgan, "Trends in Behavioral Genetics: Eugenics Revisited," *Scientific American* 268 (1993): 122–131.
38. Dusek, "Bewitching Science."
39. William H. Tucker, "Burt's Separated Twins: The Larger Picture," *Journal of the History of the Behavioral Sciences* 43 (2007): 81–86, p. 85.
40. This figure was calculated in 1990. The cost of assessing one twin pair without spouses was $4,280. Participant costs varied due to changing hotel rates, airline fees, and other factors, explaining why the figures vary across grants.
41. "About the National Science Foundation," U.S. National Science Foundation, updated August 29, 2011, www.nsf.gov/about/.
42. Leon Festinger, Henry W. Riecken, and Stanley Schachter, *When Prophecy Fails: A Social and Psychological Study of a Modern Group That Predicted the Destruction of the World* (New York: Harper-Torchbooks, 1964; first published in 1956).
43. Thomas J. Bouchard Jr., letter to Richard Atkinson, April 16, 1979.
44. Proposals are rated as excellent, very good, good, fair, or poor.
45. Richard Lynn, *The Science of Human Diversity: A History of the Pioneer Fund* (Lanham, Md.: University Press of America, 2001).
46. Leila Zenderland, *Measuring Minds: Henry Herbert Goddard and the Origins of American Intelligence Testing* (Cambridge, Mass.: Cambridge University Press, 1998).
47. Harry F. Weyher, "The Pioneer Fund, the Behavioral Sciences, and the Media's False Stories," *Intelligence* 26 (1998): 319–336.
48. Paul A. Lombardo, "'The American Breed': Nazi Eugenics and the Origins of the Pioneer Fund," *Albany Law Review* 65 (2002): 743–829; Paul A. Lombardo, "Pioneer's Big Lie," *Albany Law Review* 65 (2003): 1125–1143; J. Philippe Rushton, "The Pioneer Fund and the Scientific Study of Human Differences," *Albany Law Review* 66 (2002): 207–262.
49. Ibid. The article was Arthur R. Jensen, "How Much Can We Boost IQ and Scholastic Achievement?" *Harvard Educational Review* 39 (1969): 1–123.
50. Lynn, *Science of Human Diversity.*
51. Harry F. Weyher, "The Pioneer Fund, the Behavioral Sciences, and the Media's False Stories," *Intelligence* 26 (1999): 319–336.
52. "Pioneer Fund," The Southern Poverty Law Center, 2011, www.splcenter .org/get-informed/intelligence-files/groups/pioneer-fund.
53. Irving I. Gottesman, interview, October 15, 2009.
54. Television producers only filmed reenactments of activities twins had already completed during the study week.
55. Thomas J. Bouchard Jr., Leonard Heston, Elke Eckert, Margaret Keyes, and Susan Resnick, "The Minnesota Study of Twins Reared Apart: Project Description and Sample Results in the Development Domain," in *Twin Research,* vol. 3, *Intelligence, Personality, and Development,* ed. Luigi Gedda, Paolo Parisi, and Walter E. Nance, 227–233 (New York: Alan R. Liss, 1981).

56. See the preface to: Morton Hunt, *The New Know-Nothings: The Political Foes of the Scientific Study of Human Nature* (New Brunswick, N.J.: Transaction, 1999).

57. Koch Industries is the second-largest closely held company in the United States.

58. David H. Koch is the second wealthiest resident of New York, after Mayor Michael Bloomberg, per Wikipedia.

59. Koch donated money to New York's Lincoln Center for renovation of the opera and ballet theater that now bears his name.

60. Richard B. Call passed away on March 11, 2011. The current President of the Seaver Institute is Victoria Seaver Dean.

61. Richard Lynn, personal communication, August 4, 2010.

62. The origins of general intelligence are still debated, but many within the scientific community acknowledge significant genetic effects. See Ian J. Deary, Frank M. Spinath, and Timothy C. Bates, "Genetics of Intelligence," *European Journal of Human Genetics* 14 (2006): 690–700, and references therein.

63. Plomin et al., *Behavioral Genetics*.

64. Avshalom Caspi, Alan Taylor, Terrie E. Moffit, and Robert Plomin, "Neighborhood Deprivation Affects Children's Mental Health: Environmental Risks Identified in a Genetic Design," *Psychological Science* 11 (2000): 338–342.

65. Gardner and Newman, "Mental and Physical Traits," p. 126.

66. Ibid.

67. Wendy Johnson, Eric Turkheimer, Irving I. Gottesman, and Thomas J. Bouchard Jr., "Beyond Heritability: Twin Studies in Behavioral Research," *Current Directions in Psychological Science* 18 (2009): 217–220.

68. Robert Plomin, "Genotype-Environment Correlation and Interaction," paper presented at the Festschrift Honoring John Loehlin, Newport, Rhode Island, June 6, 2011.

69. Niels G. Waller and Phillip R. Shaver, "The Importance of Nongenetic Influences on Romantic Love Styles: A Twin-Family Study," *Psychological Science* 5 (1994): 268–274.

70. Justine L. Giddens, Julie Aitken Schermer, and Philip A. Vernon, "Material Values Are Largely in the Family: A Twin Study of Genetic and Environmental Contributions to Materialism," *Personality and Individual Differences* 46 (2009): 428–431.

71. Superfecundated twins can arise when a woman releases two eggs simultaneously and has different sexual partners within a few days of one another.

72. Carol E. Franz, Timothy P. York, Lindon J. Eaves, et al., "Adult Romantic Attachment, Negative Emotionality, and Depressive Symptoms in Middle Aged Men: A Multivariate Genetic Analysis," *Behavior Genetics* 41 (2011): 488–498; Nicola L. Barclay, Thalia C. Eley, Daniel J. Buysse, et al., "Nonshared Environmental Influences on Sleep Quality: A Study of Monozygotic Twin Differences," *Behavior Genetics* DOI: 10.1007/s10519-011-9510-1, October 15, 2011, online; Amélie Petitclerc, Michel Boivin, Ginette Dionne, Daniel Pérusse, and Richard Tremblay, "Genetic and Environmental Etiology of Disregard for Rules," *Behavior Genetics* 41 (2011): 192–200.

73. Plomin et al., *Behavioral Genetics*.
74. Sarah E. Harris, Helen Fox, Alan F. Wright, et al., "A Genetic Association Analysis of Cognitive Ability and Cognitive Ageing Using 325 Markers for 109 Genes Associated with Oxidative Stress or Cognition," *BMC Genetics* 8 (2007), doi:10.1186/1471-2156-8-43.
75. "Genome-wide Association Studies," National Human Genome Research Institute, last update August 17, 2010, www.genome.gov/20019523; International HapMap Project, http://hapmap.ncbi.nlm.nih.gov/.
76. Matt McGue, "The End of Behavioral Genetics?" *Behavior Genetics* 40 (2010): 284–296.
77. Dorret I. Boomsma, "A Twin Year in Review: Behavior and Psychiatry," paper presented at the 13th International Congress of Twin Studies, Seoul, South Korea, June 4–7, 2010.
78. Peter M. Visscher, William G. Hill, and Naomi R. Wray, "Heritability in the Genomics Era—Concepts and Misconceptions," *Nature Reviews (Genetics)* 9 (2008): 255–266.
79. "Studies of European Volunteer Twins to Identify Genes Underlying Common Diseases," GenomEUtwin, last update June 7, 2006, www.genomeutwin.org.
80. U.S. Department of Energy Genome Programs, "SNP Fact Sheet," Human Genome Project Information, last updated September 19, 2008, www.ornl.gov/sci/techresources/Human_Genome/faq/snps.shtml.
81. Ciara Curtin, "The Undiscovered Variants," Genome Web: Genome Technology, March 2011, www.genomeweb.com/arrays/undiscovered-variants?page=4.
82. Gail Davies, Albert Tenesa, Antony Payton, et al., "Genome-wide Association Studies Establish That Human Intelligence Is Highly Heritable and Polygenic," *Molecular Psychiatry* 16 (2011): 996–1005.
83. Eric Turkheimer, "Genome Wide Association Studies of Behavior Are Social Science," in *Philosophy of Behavioral Biology*, ed. Katie S. Plaisance and Thomas A. C. Reydon, chapter 3 (Dordrecht, the Netherlands: Springer, 2011).
84. Mario F. Fraga, Esteban Ballestar, Maria F. Paz, et al., "Epigenetic Differences Arise during the Lifetime of Monozygotic Twins," *Proceedings of the National Academy of Sciences of the United States of America* 102 (2005): 1413–1414.
85. F. Nipa Haque, Irving I. Gottesman, and Albert H. C. Wong, "Not Really Identical: Epigenetic Differences in Monozygotic Twins and Implications for Twin Studies in Psychiatry," *American Journal of Medical Genetics, Part C: Seminars in Medical Genetics* 151 (2009): 136–141.
86. Andrew P. Feinberg, "Phenotypic Plasticity and the Epigenetics of Human Disease," *Nature* 447 (2007): 443–440.
87. Carl E. G. Bruder, Arkadiusz Piotrowski, Antoinet A. C. J. Gijsbers, et al., "Phenotypically Concordant and Discordant Monozygotic Twins Display Different DNA Copy-Number-Variation Profiles," *American Journal of Human Genetics* 82 (2008): 763–771.
88. Yong-Kyu Kim, *Handbook of Behavior Genetics* (New York: Springer, 2009).

89. Irving I. Gottesman and Todd D. Gould, "The Endophenotype Concept in Psychiatry: Etymology and Strategic Intentions," *American Journal of Psychiatry* 160 (2003): 636–645.

90. Raymond C. K. Chan, Irving I. Gottesman, Xiaojia Ge, and Pak C. Sham, "Strategies for the Study of Neuropsychiatric Disorders Using Endophenotypes in Developing Countries: A Potential Databank from China," *Frontiers of Human Neuroscience* 4 {2010}, doi:10.3389/fnhum.2010.00207.

91. Nancy L. Segal, "New Sources of Reared Apart Twins," *Twin Research and Human Genetics* 10 (2007): 786–790; Nancy L. Segal, *Someone Else's Twin: The True Story of Babies Switched at Birth* (Amherst, N.Y.: Prometheus Books, 2011).

92. Zdravka Veleva, Sirpa Vilska, Christel Hydén-Granskog, Aila Tiitinen, Juha S. Tapanainen, and Hannu Martikainen, "Elective Single Embryo Transfer in Women Aged 36–39 Years," *Human Reproduction* 21 (2006): 2098–2102.

93. The quote from David Lykken was provided by his colleague Robert Krueger, July 8, 2010; also see Robert F. Krueger, Susan South, Wendy Johnson, et al., "The Heritability of Personality Is Not Always 50%: Gene-Environment Interactions and Correlations between Personality and Parenting," *Journal of Personality* 76 (2008): 1485–1521.

94. Michel Duyme, Annick-Camille Dumaret, and S. Stanislaw Tomkiewcz. (1999), "How Can We Boost IQs of 'Dull Children'? A Late Adoption Study," *Proceedings of the National Academy of Sciences* 96 (1999): 8790–8794.

95. Laura E. Berk, *Child Development*, 8th ed. (Boston: Allyn & Bacon, 2008).

96. Thomas J. Bouchard Jr., "Whenever the Twain Shall Meet," *The Sciences* 37 (1997): 52–57, p. 57.

Acknowledgments

The Minnesota Study of Twins Reared Apart (MISTRA) was a collaborative effort, and in many ways writing this book was, too. Nearly every former investigator contributed his or her perspectives, insights, and recollections, and many provided data, documents, and photographs. However, I take responsibility for putting it all together. A comprehensive work on such a controversial study cannot please everyone, but I have tried to present a just view.

Writing *Born Together—Reared Apart* let me reconnect with former colleagues as well as retrace my steps through the old but familiar twin assessment laboratories. Working on this book also put me in touch with many of the reared-apart twins whom I came to know so well during their weeks in Minneapolis. I never tire of hearing their life stories that, in my view, offer the best blend of scientific insight and human interest.

Writing this book was also an opportunity to assess the significance of the MISTRA in light of current themes and trends in psychology and medicine. The study withstood the controversies of the past, and, in fact, its findings have been instrumental in the widespread acceptance of genetic influences on behavior and health. Future studies of adult reared-apart twins will follow a path different from ours in view of the molecular genetic advances I discuss in the book. Many current and future researchers would not be content to disentangle genetic and environmental influences as we did with inventories, tests, and questionnaires, but would attempt to tie the MZA twins' similarities to specific genes and their differences to epigenetic events. But they would be remiss not to study the twins' behaviors because, as Bouchard once said, their similarities and differences are "so up front and personal." Regardless, the MISTRA continues to inspire research across many domains of human functioning and promises to do so in the future, as evidenced by a number of planned and ongoing analyses of our data.

Thanking the many people who provided assistance and encouragement is such an enjoyable part of writing a book. The core collaborators, Elke D. Eckert,

Irving I. Gottesman, Leonard L. Heston, and Auke Tellegen, were as generous with their time and intelligence as they always were. Each was a compelling presence in this book because his or her expertise was there from the start. Gottesman also read the manuscript in full prior to publication, offering his usual penetrating insights and brilliant suggestions. He generously forwarded important articles, personal correspondence, and other fascinating material that I incorporated into the book.

I regret that David Lykken was not around to contribute his remarks and recollections of the MISTRA. He was a commanding presence, and I sense his absence from the chapters on psychophysiology, emergenesis, and the roots of human happiness. I also regret that I never got to meet again with Bill Fox who ran the psychomotor study or Bill Knobloch who tested the twins' eyes, colleagues whose passing came too soon.

I am grateful to all the MISTRA investigators and former students, most of whom met or spoke with me to reflect on the impact of their findings and the significance of the MISTRA. At my urgings, many of them read and reread relevant passages from this book so that the text would be exactly right, and they did so with interest and patience. Some even forwarded unsolicited messages at later dates with ideas and thoughts for me to consider. Thank you Dorothy Aeppli, Richard Arvey, Deborah Betsworth, Malcolm Blumenthal, Joseph Bohlen, JoAnn Boraas, Greg Carey, John Conry, Germaine Cornélissen-Guillaume, Katie Corson, Michael Crawford, David DiLalla, Maurice Dysken, Paul Ekman, Sonya Elder, John Ficken, Wally Friesen, Paul Fuss, Francie Gabbay, Steven Gangestad, Jeff Gilger, Will Grove, Franz Halberg, Michael Hammer, Daniel Hankins, Jo-Ida Hansen, Bruce Hanson, Kevin Haroian, Scott Hershberger, Mark Herzberg, Jim Hinrichs, Yoon-Mi Hur, Bill Iacono, Jim Jenkins, Wendy Johnson, Lauren Keller, Margaret Keyes, Laura Koenig, Peter Kohler, Brian Kojetin, Robert Krueger, Scott Lilienfeld, Kristian Markon, Nick Martin, Matt McGue, Louise Messer, Bryan Michalowicz, Dan Moloney, Mary Moster, Denise Newman, Bruce Pihlstrom, Susan Resnick, Stephen Rich, Victor Rivera, Susan Roberts, Beatrice Roitman-Johnson, Jay Samuels, Margaret Sanderson, Lloyd Sines, Michael Till, Naip Tuna, Niels Waller, Kimerly Wilcox, Larry Wolff, and Dewey Ziegler. Greg Carey and Eric Turkheimer generously reviewed selected sections of the manuscript, offering wise counsel as they always do. Many colleagues contributed to one or two publications over the course of the study, and scores of graduate and undergraduate students assisted in collecting and processing data; students are credited in individual papers.

Several anonymous reviewers provided me with wonderfully comprehensive sets of suggestions following submission of my book proposal and subsequent drafts. I discovered that one of these early reviewers was John Loehlin, whose comments were invaluable. John graciously took a second look at portions of the manuscript at a later date.

Small acts of kindness are not forgotten. Both Len Heston and Tom Bouchard pared down their personal libraries just as I was beginning to write, bequeathing many of the sources and photos that I used in this book. Len's copies of the three original reared-apart twin studies and Tom's collections of some participants' pictures and tapes were, and always will be, treasured items. The University of Minnesota Alumni Association helped me locate that wonderful trick photo of Bouchard sitting simultaneously behind and in front of his desk. Professor Gail Peterson made sure that I received a CD of Bouchard's last classroom lecture.

Other individuals provided invaluable assistance from time to time. They include Don Fowles, David Lubinski, Mary Mount, Antonín Pařícek, Nancy Pedersen, Laura Pérgola, Viktória Sas, and Tony Vernon. J. Philippe Rushton verified several dates for the MISTRA's receipt of Pioneer Funds, and Richard Lynn provided information about the Whitfield Institute's support.

My editor at Harvard University Press, Elizabeth Knoll, was as smart, encouraging, and good-humored as she was during her supervision of my previous book, *Indivisible by Two*. She is the kind of editor one dreams about. The other staff members at Harvard University Press, namely, Matthew Hills, Margaux Leonard, Joy Deng, and Anne Zarrella, were unfailingly helpful and gracious. The copy editor, Vickie West, and the production editor, Barbara Goodhouse at Westchester Book Group, were helpful in every way possible. Special thanks go to my friend and colleague Lauren Gonzalez, whose literary brilliance brought polish and clarity to the text.

California State University–Fullerton granted me the time and facilities I needed for the successful completion of this book. The psychology department secretaries, Frances Sanchez and Amanda Hayes, printed many copies of the fifteen chapters and two appendices for my review. Kelly Donovan (also an identical twin) worked her usual artistic magic in preparing the photographs and figures as she has done for me in the past. Several students, namely, Ammar Altowaiji, Shiloh Betterley, Amanda Killian, and Gayle Dow, helped me obtain research articles and other materials. Jaimee Munson, Jamie Graham, and Jorge Torres proofed the many tables, charts, and references with patience and efficiency.

My parents, to whom this book is dedicated, were not here to enjoy my writing of *Born Together—Reared Apart,* the one hurtful part of this process. They were thrilled when I joined the Minnesota Study of Twins Reared Apart and, as parents of twins, were always eager to learn what we were finding. My dad, Al Segal, fully supportive of his daughters' work responsibilities, was understanding when I cut short a home visit to New York just before Father's Day to test a new reared-apart pair in Minneapolis. My mom, Esther Segal, always a proud mother of twins, read nearly every twin-related paper I wrote. My fraternal twin sister, Anne, is partly—if not solely—responsible for why I do what I do. She has always been a great supporter of my interests and goals, despite our genetically based behavioral differences.

My boyfriend, philosophy professor Craig K. Ihara, weathered some lonely times during my writing and travels. He also reminded me of the other passions in my life—being with him and being his swing dance partner—and he made sure I did not forget them. Craig is also credited for suggesting the idea for this book and its title (the subtitle was mine!), and for reviewing the penultimate version of the manuscript.

Tom Bouchard's wife, Pauline, and their two children, Mark and Elizabeth, were always enthusiastic and supportive of my efforts. They knew better than anyone how much this book needed to be written—I believe his family met more twins than I did.

And what can I say about Tom Bouchard? That he was brilliant in setting up the study and in keeping it going? That the twins adored him? That he was the best mentor a postdoc could have? That he forever changed the way people think about the roots of human behavior? I could say all these things and more, and it would not come close to capturing the scientist and person that he is. Bouchard is a steadfast reductionist, but ironically, just by being himself he has shown that sometimes you just can't be.

Index

See also Juel-Nielsen, N.; Kamin, L.;
Newman, H. H.; Sample characteristics;
Science (IQ paper); Shields, J.
Cope, L., 35, 307
Copy number variations, 324, 326
Correlation, 27, 29, 58–59, 114; intraclass
correlation, 41, 58–59, 61–62, 114; and
emergenesis, 58–59; genetic correlation,
140; phenotypic correlation, 140;
cross-twin correlation, 199
Corson (McCourt), K., 218, 231–233, 242
Creativity, 126, 173–174, 180, 201, 212,
221, 236–239, 296, 366n18
Criticisms. *See* Controversies (MISTRA)
Crystallized intelligence, 190, 262, 382n42.
See also Cattell-Horn fluid-crystallized
model

Daniels, D., 147
Darley, J., 22, 25, 310–311, 344n9
Darwin, C., 239
Dental assessment, 22–23, 96, 153–157,
243–244
Diener, E., 198, 200
Diet, 227–229; and dental assessment,
153–154; and allergies, 227
DiLalla, D., 204–206, 240–241
DiLalla, L., 253
DiLeonardi, J., 33, 50, 170
Discordance, 38–39, 41, 66, 74–75, 78, 89,
91, 93, 139–141, 164, 206, 294–295,
323–325; difficulties determining, 66
Discrete trait, 57
DNA, 18, 56, 213, 282, 322–324, 345n5,
373n67; and cardiac measures, 125; and
evolution, 173. *See also* Zygosity
diagnosis
Dominant gene, 57
Dusek, V., 308
Dysken, M. W., 25, 137

Eating behavior, 68, 279–281, 296; Food
Frequency Questionnaire, 228; and
disinhibition, 280–281; and hunger,
280–281, 385n38; and restraint,
280–281. *See also* Diet
Eaves, L. J., 233, 240
Eckert, E. D., 20–24, 67–69, 85, 93, 138,
228, 308
Ego development, 218, 221, 223–225;
and cognition, 223–224; Washington
University Sentence Completion Test,
223–224, 375n12

Ekman, P., 282–283
Elder, S., 280–281, 296
Electrocardiogram (ECG). *See* Cardiac
studies
Electroencephalogram (EEG), 74–75,
109–110, 114–115, 172, 350n41
Emergenesis, 58, 61, 73, 75–78, 171–174,
176, 186; and epistasis, 58, 61, 172–173
Emotionality, 100, 102–103, 237,
251–252, 267, 355n26. *See also*
Neuroticism
Endophenotype, 325
Epigenetics, 324, 326
Epistasis, 57–58, 61, 172–173, 187.
See also Emergenesis
Equal environments assumption, 3, 73
Erlenmeyer-Kimling, N., 7
Eveningness, 221–222
Evolutionary psychology, 15, 111–112,
181–182, 186, 247, 267; life history
theory, 182, 184. *See also* Behavior
genetics; Sociobiology
Extraversion, 32, 77, 98–99, 149–151, 172,
185, 187–188, 209–210, 239, 351n15.
See also Big Five personality traits
Extrinsic religiousness, 233–234, 236

Facial expressivity, 282–283; Facial Action
Coding System, 283
Family environment, 12, 62, 71, 100, 102,
119, 147–150, 165–169, 187, 195–197,
233, 243–244; Moos Family Environment Scale, 108–109, 148–150, 166–167,
196–197, 233, 251; Block Environmental Questionnaire, 196–197, 233, 251;
and personality, 251–254
Farber, S. L., 71, 153, 226, 230,
348–349n20, 364n22
Fine, W. 35, 317
Fingerprints, 38–39; ridge count, 38,
72–73, 82, 94. *See also* Fluctuating
asymmetry (FA)
Finnish reared-apart twin study, 12, 140;
reared-together twin study, 101, 123,
125, 164
"Fireman twins," 15, 49, 64, 111, 132,
146, 151, 181, 177–178, 181, 225, 228,
255, 272, 289
Fletcher, R., 5
Fluctuating asymmetry (FA), 270–271,
322; dermatoglyphic asymmetry, 270;
composite measure vs. single traits,
272–273; and general intelligence, 273

Ophthalmology, 82, 88–89, 221
Otis IQ, 107, 356n38

Parental characteristics. *See* Sample
 characteristics
Participant identification. *See* Sample
 characteristics
Pedersen, N. L., 189, 217, 240
Periodontal examination, 22, 24, 68, 96,
 152, 154, 157–162, 165, 243–244, 296;
 alveolar bone height, 159, 161; oral
 bacteria, 159, 162, 243–244; funding,
 219, 310, 330–331; temporomandibular
 joint symptoms, 243
Personality assessment, 11, 32, 116, 222,
 354nn2,6,8, 355n21, 360n13, 368n52,
 386n43; Differential Personality
 Questionnaire, 22, 76–77; Multidimensional Personality Questionnaire, 22,
 76–77, 97–104, 172, 176, 199–200,
 254; California Psychological Inventory,
 27, 148–150, 234–235, 239–240;
 heritability, 41, 102–103, 144, 165,
 181–182, 195, 214–215, 319, 322, 326;
 temperament, 66; and IQ, 71, 108,
 110–112; and weight, 73, 281; and twin
 relationship, 76–77, 188, 240, 250; and
 environment, 147–151, 188, 214,
 251–253; and creativity, 173–174,
 237–238; psychopathology, 205, 242;
 personality "set point," 252; and birth
 order, 292–293; prenatal effects,
 349n28. *See also* Authoritarianism; Big
 Five personality traits; Conservatism;
 Controversies (MISTRA); Ego development; Interests; Minnesota Multiphasic
 Personality Inventory (MMPI);
 Multidimensional Personality Question-
 naire (MPQ); Psychopathology;
 Religiosity; Reproduction-related
 behaviors; Sensation seeking; Stroop
 Color-Word Test; Twin method;
 Vocational interests
Peterson, G., 19
Phenotype, 57, 59, 112, 322–323. *See also*
 Endophenotype
Phenylketonuria (PKU), 7, 57, 342n42
Physical facilities, 51, 108, 109, 130,
 166, 251
Physical similarity. *See* Twin method
Pihlstrom, B., 24, 96, 157–159, 161–162,
 243–244, 310, 330
Pioneer Fund. *See* Funding

Placement (in rearing homes), 50, 71, 94,
 108–109, 149, 235, 254, 303; selective
 placement, 224, 261, 308
Platt, J. R., 292
Plomin, R., 100, 112, 147, 173, 189, 217,
 236
Polesky, H. F., 24, 344n10
Popenoe, P., 3–4
Prenatal environment, 10, 13, 41, 286,
 293, 304; and homosexuality, 90.
 See also Cloning; Twin method
Propping, P., 2, 186, 190–191
Psychomotor assessment, 23, 202–204,
 299, 370n26; practice effects, 201–204;
 Rotary pursuit test, 202–203. *See also*
 Minnesota Multiphasic Personality
 Inventory (MMPI)
Psychopathology, 116, 323–324; Tourette
 syndrome, 24, 136–138, 141; drug
 abuse/dependence, 69, 139–140; alcohol
 abuse/dependence, 69, 139–140, 144,
 320; Diagnostic Interview Schedule,
 138–141; Diagnostic Statistical Manual
 (DSM)-III, 138–139, 360n6; antisocial
 personality disorder, 139–141; MMPI
 personality correlates, 195, 204–207,
 242; and religiosity, 234; and talent,
 238. *See also* Minnesota Multiphasic
 Personality Inventory (MMPI)
Pulmonary study, 22, 78

Raven/Mill-Hill, 68, 76, 105, 107
Raven Progressive Matrices. *See* General
 mental ability
Reading, 8, 32, 77, 257–261; Oskar and
 Jack, 132; genetic factor structure,
 259–260
Recessive gene, 57
Recreational interests. *See* Interests
Recruitment (of participants), 9, 35–37,
 53–54, 90, 218–219, 302; participant
 sources, 33; pairs studied per year, 37.
 See also Controversies (MISTRA);
 Sample characteristics
Religiosity, 10–11, 13, 47, 109, 116,
 141–149, 173, 177, 181, 185, 196,
 206, 213, 218, 221, 231, 233, 255–256,
 361n22; and traditionalism, 144,
 189, 199; Age Universal Religious
 Orientation Scale, 234. *See also*
 Extrinsic religiousness; Intrinsic
 religiousness; Traditional moral
 values triad